THE SPANISH AMERICAN SHORT STORY

BOOKS PUBLISHED BY THE UNIVERSITY OF CALIFORNIA PRESS IN
COOPERATION WITH THE UCLA LATIN AMERICAN CENTER

1. Kenneth Karst and Keith S. Rosenn, *Law and Development in Latin
   America: A Case Book*, Volume 28, Latin American Studies, UCLA
   Latin American Center.

2. James W. Wilkie, Michael C. Meyer, and Edna Monzón de Wilkie, eds.,
   *Contemporary Mexico: Papers of the IV International Congress of Mexi-
   can History*, Volume 29, Latin American Studies, UCLA Latin American
   Center.

3. Arthur J. O. Anderson, Frances Berdan, and James Lockhart, *Beyond
   the Codices: The Nahua View of Colonial Mexico*, Volume 27, Latin
   American Studies, UCLA Latin American Center.

4. Stanley L. Robe, *Azuela and the Mexican Underdogs*, Volume 48, Latin
   American Studies, UCLA Latin American Center.

5. Seymour Menton, *The Spanish American Short Story: A Critical Anthology*, Volume 49, Latin American Studies, UCLA Latin American Center.

(Except for the volumes listed above, which are published and distributed
by the University of California Press, Berkeley, California 94720, all other
volumes in the Latin American Studies are published and distributed by
UCLA Latin American Center Publications, Los Angeles, California 90024.)

SEYMOUR MENTON

The  Spanish American Short Story

A Critical Anthology

Published by
UCLA LATIN AMERICAN CENTER PUBLICATIONS
University of California, Los Angeles
and
UNIVERSITY OF CALIFORNIA PRESS
Berkeley   Los Angeles   London

University of California Press
Berkeley and Los Angeles, California

University of California Press, Ltd.
London, England

Copyright © 1980 by The Regents of the University of California
Library of Congress Catalog Card Number 76–7765
First Paperback Printing 1982
ISBN: 0–520–04641–2   123456789
Printed in the United States of America

ACKNOWLEDGMENTS

I am thankful to the following individuals and publishers for authorizing the translation of the stories:

The Fondo de Cultura Económica in Mexico City for the blanket authorization to translate my anthology: Seymour Menton, *El cuento hispanoamericano, antología crítico-histórica*, D.R. © 1964 Fondo de Cultura Económica, México 12, D.F.

The Organization of American States for the translation by Dr. Esther S. Dillon of Baldomero Lillo's "Gate No. 12" in *The Devil's Pit and Other Stories by Baldomero Lillo*, Washington, D.C., Organization of American States, 1959.

Ana Teresa Arévalo A. for permission to translate "The Sign of the Sphinx" by her father Rafael Arévalo Martínez.

Martín Luis Guzmán for "The Festival of the Bullets."

Ema Barrón de Revueltas for "God on Earth" by José Revueltas.

Marlene A. Dávalos and Demetrio Aguilera Malta for the latter's "The Cholo Who Got His Revenge."

Alberto Orellana Ramírez for Salarrué's "The Treasure Jug" which appears in the original in *Obras escogidas de Salarrué*, San Salvador, Editorial Universitaria, 1969.

Juan Bosch for "The Woman."

Las Américas Publishing Company for Rosalie Torres Rioseco's translations of Manuel Rojas's "The Glass of Milk" and María Luisa Bombal's "The Tree" both published in *Short Stories of Latin America*, New York, Law Américas Publishing Company, 1963.

Donald A. Yates and New Directions for "The Garden of Forking Paths" from Jorge Luis Borges, LABYRINTHS. Translation based on that of Donald A. Yates with revisions by Seymour Menton. Copyright © 1962 by New Directions Publishing Corporation. All Rights Reserved. Published by permission of New Directions.

Ramón Ferreira for "A Date at Nine."

Rogelio Sinán for "The Red Beret."

George Schade and the University of Texas Press for Juan Rulfo's "Tell Them Not To Kill Me" from *The Burning Plain and Other Stories by Juan Rulfo*, translated by George D. Schade, Austin, University of Texas Press, Pan American Paperback Edition, 1971. SBN 0-292-70132-2. Library of Congress Catalog Card No. 67-25698. Copyright © 1967 Fondo de Cultura Económica, México 12, D.F. All rights reserved.

George Schade and the University of Texas Press for Juan José Arreola's "The Switchman" from *Confabulario and Other Inventions by Juan José Arreola*, Austin, University of Texas Press, Pan American Series. Library of Congress Catalog Card No. 64-13315. Copyright © 1964 by Juan José Arreola. All rights reserved.

Arturo Uslar Pietri for "The Rain."

Jack Percal for his brother Hugo Manning's translation of Eduardo Mallea's "Conversation." The translation was first published in *Fantasy*, Pittsburgh, Pa., vol. 26, 1942, pp. 61-65, and was reprinted in Willis Knapp Jones, editor, *Spanish American Literature in Translation*, New York, Frederick Ungar Publishers, 1963, vol. II.

Random House – Alfred A. Knopf, Inc. for a specified adaptation of "The Dark Night of Ramón Yendía" by Lino Novás Calvo, translated by Raymond Sayers, from *Spanish Stories and Tales*, edited by Harriet De Onís, pages 139-164. Copyright © 1954 by Alfred A. Knopf, Inc. Reprinted by permission of the publisher; and for "Meeting" from ALL FIRES THE FIRE AND OTHER STORIES, by Julio Cortázar, translated by Suzanne Jill Levine. Copyright © 1973 by Random House, Inc. Reprinted by permission of Pantheon Books, a division of Random House, Inc.

Augusto Roa Bastos for "The Prisoner."

Monthly Review Press for Victoria Ortiz's translation of Pedro Juan Soto's "Champs" from *Spiks*, by Pedro Juan Soto, New York, Monthly Review Press, 1973. Reprinted by permission of Monthly Review Press.

Enrique Congrains Martín for "The Boy from 'Next to Heaven'."

Alvaro Menéndez Leal for "Fire and Ice."

Editorial Joaquín Mortiz for Agustín's "What's Cool."

CONTENTS

PREFACE

When the Mexican edition of this anthology was first published in 1964, there was no other anthology of the Spanish American short story that attempted to cover analytically the historical development of the genre from its inception within the Romantic movement up to its present-day mature exuberance. There is still no other anthology like it. There are many national anthologies of varying quality and several Spanish American anthologies limited to certain historical periods, usually the twentieth century. Most of the anthologies, however, are simply collections of good stories without any rational organization and very little in the way of critical apparatus. Finally, there are some anthologies that do not distinguish between the short story and selections from novels. Recent anthologies in English suffer from similar limitations: Pat McNees Mariani, *Contemporary Latin American Short Stories* (Greenwich, Conn.: Fawcett Publications, 1974); Barbara Howes, *The Eye of the Heart* (New York: Avon Books, 1973); Hortense Carpentier and Janet Brof, *Doors and Mirrors: Fiction and Poetry from Spanish America, (1920–1970)* (New York: Grossman, 1972).

The original title of this book—*El cuento hispanoamericano: antología crítico-histórica*—accurately reflects the basis for the selection of the stories. In spite of some early manifestations in the sixteenth- and seventeenth-century chronicles of the Conquest, the Spanish American short story does not make its initial appearance until after the wars of independence, during the period dominated by Romanticism. From that time to the present, my choices stem from a four-angled focus: the story that represents certain advances in the evolution of the genre; the exemplary representative of a given literary movement or tendency; the story that indicates the gestation of a distinctly national literature; the work of art with its intrinsic universal values and appeal. It is admittedly rare that these four angles converge in any one of the stories. In fact, they are more likely to be in conflict. A story that combines the most typical traits of Romanticism, Naturalism, or Surrealism may have a significance that is only historical. On the other hand, a truly outstanding story in literary terms may belie completely the generalizations made about the literature of that particular country in that particular period. Nevertheless, in attempting to fuse the work of the literary historian with that of the literary critic, I have not tried to avoid those anomalous cases that inevitably rear their heads in this type of project.

In order to trace the evolution of a literary genre, the starting point must be a definition, arbitrary as it may be. Although all definitions of literary genres tend to be somewhat arbitrary and even simplistic, the impossibility of arriving at *the* perfect definition does not invalidate proceeding on the basis of a good working definition. Therefore, I shall assume that *the short story is a narrative, completely or partly fictitious, written by a known author, which can be read in less than an hour, and whose elements contribute to the production of a single effect.* According to this definition, the novel may be distinguished from the short story because of both its length and its greater complexity; the *artículo de costumbres* (the Costumbrista sketch or essay) is excluded because of the subordination of whatever elements of a plot there may be to the moralistic, essayistic interventions of the author-narrator; the well-known *tradiciones* of Ricardo Palma and others, delightful as some of them are, usually emphasize historical facts to the detriment of the single effect or artistic unity; fables and legends belong more to the realm of folklore because of their diffuse rather than concentrated character and because they lack the creative ingredients of the individual author.

This anthology is structured according to the different literary movements and tendencies that have marked the evolution of Spanish American literature from the 1830s to the boom of the past fifteen years: Romanticism, Realism, Naturalism, Modernism, Criollismo, Cosmopolitanism (Surrealism, Cubism, Magic Realism, Existentialism), Neorealism, and the diverse and at times unbridled structural and linguistic experimentation of the 1960s and 1970s. For each movement, I point out the general traits, the historical and artistic roots, and the Spanish American variants and their causes. These brief essays serve to introduce a series of representative, or occasionally anomalous, stories preceded by a short biographical sketch of the author and followed by a critical commentary. To sum up, the two major purposes of this anthology are: to present in an orderly, comprehensive manner the best and most representative examples of the Spanish American short story and to demonstrate an analytical method, eclectic as it may be, which will help the reader interpret and appreciate more fully other short stories. These two purposes obviously preclude equal representation for the nineteen Spanish American countries although I have chosen at least one story from each country.

The translations of the stories and the critical apparatus represent a collective effort but ultimately I accept responsibility for all the translations. As the credits indicate, ten of the translations had previously been published but most of them have been modified to a greater or lesser extent. The majority of the stories were translated at the Translation Center of the Department of Comparative Literature at the State University of New York at Binghamton under the supervision of Gustavo Pellón. Boyd G. Carter participated in the translation of Gutiérrez Nájera's "After the Races" while Richard Barrutia, Julio Rodríguez Luis, and the author José Agustín helped revise "What's Cool." All footnotes in the stories, unless otherwise indicated, are the translator's. My wife Cathy assisted in the translation of the biographical notes, and along with my sons Tim and Allen offered many suggestions for solving some of the knottiest problems. To all who have helped in this project, I am deeply grateful.

The original selection of the stories and the critical analyses were tested in three graduate courses at the University of Kansas. My debt to those students is inestimable. I am also grateful to my graduate students and colleagues at the University of California, Irvine for their perceptive comments which have contributed to the reassessment of certain aspects of the book for this edition in English. I'd also like to express my appreciation to Luisa Gan Hunter for the typing of the many rough drafts as well as the final manuscript.

I am thankful to the research committees and administrators of the University of Kansas and the University of California, Irvine for their support of this project in its original form and its present translation and to Teresa Joseph of the Latin American Center, University of California, Los Angeles, for editing and designing the text.

Romanticism

The first Spanish American short stories were published during the height of Romanticism. Imported from Europe, this widespread international movement found favorable soil in America and extended deep roots that to this day have not been completely destroyed. The movement can be defined as an attitude of nonconformity and unadaptability that manifests itself in two ways: rebellion and withdrawal. Its origins are derived from history as well as from literature. In England, Romanticism first appeared with the lake poets as a protest against the effects of the Industrial Revolution. In France, the restoration of the monarchy after Waterloo disheartened the young intellectuals inflamed with the ideals of the French Revolution and Napoleon's military glory. Besides these historical events, Romanticism constituted a literary reaction against Neoclassicism, a reaction that began to manifest itself as early as the first half of the eighteenth century. With the additional ingredient of Germanic melancholy, the movement was ready to invade America.

Although the European origins of Romanticism are undeniable, the newly independent Spanish American nations provided most propitious conditions for its growth. Inspired in part by the French Revolution, the Wars of Independence were themselves Romantic: the ·fight for liberty; the great military feats; the ups and downs in the fortunes of the wars; the participation of the common people in some countries; and the anarchical conditions in general. Once the final victory over Spain was won, the emerging political leaders adopted Romanticism as a life-style. During the ensuing fifty years of anarchy, the intellectuals and writers either sustained an impassioned opposition to the tyrants; sought to establish in literature the foundations for a national culture; or turned their backs completely on the barbarism that was devastating their countries.

In their works, the Romantics generally limited themselves to four themes. The rebels, inspired by Byron, cultivated the liberal political theme of *the fight against tyranny.* The disillusioned writers withdrew from the surrounding turmoil and preferred exotic themes. *Geographic exoticism,* inspired by Chateaubriand and James Fenimore Cooper, portrayed the American Indian as the "noble savage" that Europeans had invented in an often make-believe tropical environment; *historical exoticism* converted Scott's Middle Ages into the Spanish American colonial era featuring the dungeons of the Inquisition and rivalries among the various religious orders; *sentimental exoticism* concentrated on impossible loves which were inspired by the works of Saint-Pierre and Lamartine.

In Europe, Romanticism found its best expression in poetry, and then in theater, and lastly in the novel. The short story had not yet gained recognition as an independent genre of high literary value. This was also true in Spanish America except that the theater did not develop because of the lack of large and tranquil urban centers. Although scholars have traced the antecedents of both the Spanish American novel and the short story back to the chronicles of the Conquest, both genres actually began their trajectories together under Romanticism in the 1830s — the one notable exception being Fernández de Lizardi's picaresque novel *El Periquillo Sarniento* (1816).

Esteban Echeverría

(1805-1851)

Argentinean. One of the more important figures in Spanish American Romanticism. After absorbing the rebellious Romantic atmosphere of Paris in the waning years of the absolute monarchy under Charles X, Echeverría returned to Buenos Aires in 1830 to join the other outstanding young writers of what was to become known as "the outlawed generation": Juan Bautista Alberdi, Juan María Gutiérrez, Vicente Fidel López, Domingo F. Sarmiento, and Bartolomé Mitre. In 1838 he collaborated in the founding of the Joven Asociación, or the Asociación de Mayo, which helped disseminate Liberalism and Romanticism throughout Argentina and Spanish America in general. He drafted the Código for the Asociación, the Declaración de los Principios Que Constituyen la Creencia Social de la República Argentina, which was published in its definitive form in 1846 under the title of *Dogma socialista*. In 1840 he emigrated to Uruguay where he died eleven years later. Author of the first French-inspired Romantic work, "Elvira o la novia del Plata" (1832); of the first poem with a truly Spanish American theme and atmosphere, "La cautiva" (1837); and of one of the first Spanish American short stories, "El matadero" ("The Slaughterhouse") (1838). The 1838 date is still subject to controversy because the story was not actually published until 1871, when Juan María Gutiérrez included it in Echeverría's *Obras completas*.

THE SLAUGHTERHOUSE

Notwithstanding the historical nature of my story, I will not begin with Noah's ark and the genealogy of his forefathers as is the custom with the older Spanish historians of America who should be our models. I have many reasons for not following their example, which I do not state so as not to be long-winded. I will only say that the events of my narrative took place around the year of our Lord 183__. Furthermore, we were in Lent, a time

3

when meat becomes scarce in Buenos Aires because the Church, adopting the precept of Epictetus—*sustine abstine* (suffer, abstain) —requires the stomachs of the faithful to fast and abstain, since the flesh is weak and, as the proverb goes, seeks the flesh. And since the Church holds spiritual reign, *ab initio* and by direct order of God, over consciences and stomachs, which in no way belong to the individual, it is only reasonable and just that it forbid what is evil.

The meat suppliers, on the other hand, good Federalists[1] and therefore good Catholics, knowing that the people of Buenos Aires cherish a singular docility for submitting to any kind of command, during Lent bring to the slaughterhouse only those steers necessary to feed the children and the sick who are exempt from the fast by papal bull . . . and not with the intention of having heretics stuff themselves, for there are always some ready to violate the Church's commandments against eating meat and ready to contaminate society with their bad example.

A great rainfall occurred at that time. Roads were obliterated, the lowlands became flooded, and the streets that led in and out of the city were overflowing with muddy waters. A tremendous flashflood sprang suddenly out of the Riachuelo de Barracas and extended its murky waters majestically to the foot of the cliffs of El Alto. La Plata, itself rising furiously, repelled those waters that were searching for the riverbed making them spill over fields, embankments, arbors and hamlets, forming an immense lake over all the lowlands. The city, surrounded from the north and the east by a belt of water and mud, and to the south by a whitish sea on whose surface a few small boats floated aimlessly while the chimneys and treetops turned black, looked in amazement at the horizon from its cliffs and towers as if imploring mercy from God above. It seemed to herald the coming of another Flood. The devout wailed as they launched their novenas and prayed continuously. The preachers made the sanctuaries reverberate with their thunderous pronouncements and pounded the pulpits with their fists. "This is the day of judgment," they said. "The end of the world is upon us. Divine wrath runneth over in a flood. Woe upon thee, sinners! Woe upon thee, impious Unitarians who scoff at the Church and the saints, and refuse to

[1] Followers of Dictator Juan Manuel Rosas (1829-1852). Opposed by the Unitarians.

listen reverently to the words of those anointed by the Lord! Woe upon thee if you do not beg forgiveness at the foot of the altar! The fateful hour will arrive when you will gnash your teeth and utter your frantic imprecations in vain. Your impiety, your heresy, your blasphemy, your horrendous crimes have brought the plagues of the Lord upon our land. God and the justice of the Federation declare you damned."

The poor women left the sanctuaries overwhelmed and out of breath, casting the blame for the calamity, as was natural, upon the Unitarians.

Nonetheless, the rain continued falling in torrents and the floodwaters rose, lending credence to the preachers' prognostication. The bells began to toll for rogations by order of the Most Holy Restorer,[2] who, it seems, was in a desperate state. The freethinkers, the disbelievers, that is to say, the Unitarians, began to get frightened, seeing so many remorseful faces and hearing such a plaintive uproar. There was already talk, as if it had been decided upon, about a procession in which the entire population would go barefoot and bareheaded, accompanying the image of Jesus, which would be carried by the Bishop under a canopy to the cliffs of Balcarce, where thousands of voices would beg for divine mercy by exorcising the Unitarian devil.

Fortunately, or perhaps unfortunately, since it would have been a sight to see, the ceremony did not take place because, with the La Plata River's receding little by little, the waters slipped back to their beds without need of exorcisms or prayers.

What this has to do with the main part of my story is the fact that the slaughterhouse of Convalescencia did not see a single head of cattle for two weeks, and in just one or two days all the oxen belonging to the sharecroppers and water carriers were consumed in filling the city's needs. The unfortunate children and the sick were fed eggs and chickens, while the foreigners and heretics bellowed for steak and roast beef. The abstinence from beef was widespread among the population, which never before had proved itself so worthy of the Church's blessing; and so it was that millions and millions of plenary indulgences were showered upon it. Chickens went up to six pesos, eggs to four reales, and fish was very expensive. During those days of Lent, the eating of meat and

[2]Title given to Dictator Rosas.

excesses of gluttony were sins that did not occur. On the other hand, innumerable souls went directly to Heaven and things happened that seem unbelievable.

Of the thousands of rats that made their homes in the slaughterhouse, not one was left. All died either of hunger or were drowned in their holes by the incessant rain. A multitude of black women in search of meat scraps, like vultures after carrion, spread out over the city along with many other scavengers ready to devour anything edible which was to be found. The seagulls and dogs, their inseparable rivals in the slaughterhouse, emigrated in search of food. A number of the old and sickly fell victim to consumption for lack of a nutritious broth. But the most notable thing that happened was the almost sudden death of a few foreign heretics who disrespectfully stuffed themselves with pork sausage from Extremadura, ham, and dried codfish, and went to meet their Maker as the price for such an abominable sin.

Some doctors judged that if the lack of meat continued, half the population would fall into a faint, because their stomachs were so accustomed to the stimulation of the meat's juices. It was a study in contrasts, the difference between this dreary scientific prognostication and the anathemas launched from the pulpit by the reverend Fathers against any type of animal nourishment and against the eating of meat on those days set aside by the Church for fasting and penitence. Out of this there arose a kind of intestinal war between stomach and conscience, stoked by an inexorable appetite, and the no less inexorable vociferations of the Church ministers who, as is their duty, tolerate no vice that tends to relax Catholic custom—to which was added a state of intestinal flatulence in the inhabitants, produced by fish, dried beans, and other rather indigestible foods.

This war manifested itself in the excessive weeping and disproportionate shouting in the delivery of sermons, and in the unexpected noises and clamor in the homes and on the city streets or wherever people gathered. The Restorer's government, being as paternal as it was foresighted, became a bit alarmed, believing those rumblings to be of revolutionary origin and attributing them to the same Unitarian savages whose impieties, according to those Federalist preachers, had brought the flood of Divine wrath upon the country. The government took active measures, scattering its henchmen throughout the city and ultimately, after due consultation, promulgating a decree calculated to soothe stomachs and consciences, introduced by a series of most wise and pious whereases, so that without further delay and floods notwithstanding, cattle would be brought to the stockyards.

To be sure, the sixteenth day of the shortage, on the eve of Good Friday, a troop of fifty fat steers came swimming into the slaughterhouse of El Alto. A pittance, to be sure, for a population accustomed to consuming between 250 and 300 head a day, and at least one third of whom would enjoy the Church dispensation and eat meat. How strange it is that there are some privileged stomachs and some stomachs subject to inviolable laws, and that the Church should hold the key to all stomachs!

But it is not strange, given the fact that the Devil usually enters the body through the flesh and that the Church has the power to ward him off: the point is to reduce man to a machine whose prime mover is not *his* will, but that of the Church and the Government. Perhaps the day will come when breathing fresh air, taking a walk, and even talking to a friend will be prohibited without permission from the proper authority. This is how it was, more or less, in the happy times of our devout grandparents, which were unfortunately brought to an end by the May Revolution.[3]

Be that as it may, when news of the government proclamation spread, the stockyards of El Alto filled, in spite of the mud, with butchers, scavengers, and onlookers, who with great cheers and applause received the fifty steers destined for the slaughterhouse.

"Small, but fat!" they cried. "Long live the Federation! Long live the Restorer!" The reader should take note that at that time the Federation was everywhere, even in the filth of the slaughterhouse, and there was no celebration without the Restorer, just as there is no sermon without St. Augustine. They say that the last rats, dying of hunger in their holes, were revitalized when they heard such wild cries and began to run in every direction, realizing that the usual cheers and hurrahs heralding abundance had returned to their haunts.

The first steer killed went as a gift to the Restorer, a man who was very fond of roast beef. A commission of butchers marched

[3]The Revolution of May 1810 which initiated the fight for independence from Spain.

up to offer it to him in the name of the Federalists of the slaughter-house, manifesting *in voce* their appreciation for the wise government decree, their unlimited allegiance to the Restorer and their deep hatred of the Unitarian savages, enemies of God and man. The Restorer answered the harangue, *rinforzando* the same theme, and the ceremony ended with the corresponding cheers and outcries from spectators and participants alike. It may well be supposed that the Restorer, being such a close observer of the law, such a good Catholic, and such a staunch protector of religion, had special permission from the Bishop himself not to abstain from eating meat, because, otherwise, to accept such a gift on a holy day would have set a bad example.

The slaughter continued and in a quarter of an hour forty-nine steers were stretched out on the slaughterhouse yard, some skinned, some to be skinned. The spectacle offered was lively and pictur-esque, even though it brought together all the horrible ugliness, filth, and deformity of a small proletarian class peculiar to the Rio de la Plata region. But, in order for the reader to see it at a glance, a quick sketch of the locale must be drawn.

The slaughterhouse of Convalescencia, or El Alto, located among the vegetable farms to the south of the city, is a great open expanse in the form of a rectangle at the end of two streets, one of which ends right there, the other continuing eastward.

This open space, sloping to the south, is bisected by a ditch, which was carved out by the river waters whose banks display countless rats nests and whose bed receives all the fresh and dried blood from the slaughterhouse during the rainy season. At right angles with the western side stands what is known as the cabin, a low, three-room shack with a half-roof and front porch that faces the street and a hitching post. Behind the shack, there are several picket-fence corrals made of *ñandubay* wood with stout gates to keep in the cattle.

In the winter, these corrals are a veritable mudhole in which the animals, crowded together, sink in up to their shoulders and stand as though they were stuck together, hardly able to move. In the cabin, the corral taxes as well as fines for violating the rules are collected, and there the judge of the slaughterhouse presides, an important figure, the *caudillo* of the butchers, who in that little republic exercises maximum power delegated by the

Restorer. It is not hard to figure out what kind of man it takes to discharge such a duty. The cabin, on the other hand, is so small and dilapidated that no one would even notice it among the corrals were it not identified with the name of the terrible judge, and were it not for the following red signs which stand out against a band of white painted on the wall: "Long Live the Federation!" "Long Live the Restorer and the Heroine, Doña Encarnación Ezcuna!" "Death to the Unitarian Savages!" Highly significant signs were these, symbols of the political and religious faith of the people of the slaughterhouse. But some readers may not know that the aforementioned Heroine is the late wife of the Restorer, cherished patroness of the butchers, who venerated her in death as in life for her Christian virtues and her heroism on the Federalist side in the war against Balcarce.[4] As a matter of fact, on a certain anniversary of that memorable Mazorca[5] feat, the butchers celebrated with a splendid banquet at the cabin in honor of the Heroine, a banquet that she attended with her daughter and other Federalist society women. There, in the presence of a large crowd, she offered her Federalist patronage in a solemn toast to the butchers, by reason of which they enthusiastically proclaimed her patroness of the slaughterhouse, engraving her name on the walls of the cabin, where it will remain until erased by the hand of time.

The scene of the slaughterhouse from a distance was grotesque and full of activity. Forty-nine steers were laid out on their hides and close to two hundred people were treading that muddy ground splattered with the blood from the animals' arteries. Around every steer a group of human figures of different races and complexions sprang up. The most prominent figure in each group was the butcher with the knife in his hand, his chest and arms bare, his hair long and wild, his shirt, *chiripá*[6] and face smeared with blood. Behind him, following his every move, there milled around a group of boys and black and mulatto women scavengers, whose ugliness matched that of the fabled harpies, while interspersed among them some enormous mastiffs sniffed, growled, or snapped

---

[4]Juan Ramón Balcarce, Argentine general and enemy of Rosas.

[5]The name of Dictator Rosas's secret police. The word *mazorca* means "ear of corn" but is pronounced exactly the same way as *más horca* meaning "more gallows."

[6]A coarse blanket, worn by the gauchos over their trousers and tied between their legs.

at each other as they went for the prey. Some forty-odd wagons covered with smooth dark hides were lined up irregularly along the length of the open area and a few riders, with their ponchos thrown over their shoulders and their lassos hanging from their saddles, crisscrossed quickly among them or, leaning forward on their horses' necks, cast a lazy eye on any one of those active groups, while up in the sky a swarm of bluish-white sea gulls, having returned from exile at the smell of meat, circled around drowning out the noise and the shouting of the slaughterhouse with their dissonant squawks as they projected their shadows on that horrible field of butchery. This is what was to be seen at the beginning of the slaughter.

But as it progressed, the scene changed. The groups broke up, reformed, assuming different positions and scattered on the run, as if a stray bullet had fallen in their midst or as if threatened by the jaws of an angry mastiff. Thus it was that in each of the groups the butcher was either quartering the carcass with the blows of a cleaver, or hanging the quarters on hooks in his wagon, or skinning the steer, or cutting away the fat, while from among the rabble that was eagerly watching and awaiting a stray scrap, from time to time there emerged a filthy hand with a knife that would try to slice off a piece of fat or meat, which in turn would give rise to much shouting, the angry explosion of the butcher, and the continuous hubbub of each group with wisecracks and loud yells coming from the boys.

"That old lady's sticking the fat between her tits," someone cried out._

"That guy hid it in his pants," the black woman replied.

"G'wan, you old black witch. Get outa here before I carve a notch in you," the butcher exclaimed.

"What difference does it make to you, Ño[7] Juan? Don't be that way. All I want's the belly and the guts."

"They're goin' to that witch. Shit!"

"Get the witch! Get the witch!" repeated the boys. "She's takin' the kidneys and the liver!" They showered her head with gobs of dried blood and tremendous clumps of mud.

Meanwhile in another section, two black women were dragging away the insides of an animal; beyond them, a mulatto woman

---

[7] A popular abbreviation of "señor."

was getting away with a tangle of guts when, suddenly slipping in a puddle of blood, she fell flat, covering her coveted prize with her body; on the other side, one could see four hundred black women crouching in a line unraveling in their laps the tangle of intestines and pulling off, one by one, the little pieces of fat that the butcher's greedy blade had missed, while others emptied bellies and bladders and then filled them up by blowing air into them so that once they were dry, they could be used as containers for the offal.

Several boys, prancing around on horse and on foot, hit each other with bladders or chunks of meat, which together with their clamor scattered the cloud of sea gulls that, swaying back and forth in the air, were celebrating the slaughter by screeching. Notwithstanding the Restorer's order and the holiness of the day, filthy and obscene language could be heard, outcries that were bursting with all the bestial cynicism that characterized this rabble of our slaughterhouses, outcries with which I prefer not to regale my readers.

Suddenly a bloody lung fell on someone's head, who passed it on to someone else's, until some misshapen mastiff got a good hold on it and a whole pack of dogs, pushing and pressing against one another, let out a tremendous uproar of growls and bites. One old lady ran furiously in pursuit of a boy who had smeared her face with blood, and the youngster's friends, responding to her cries and profanities, surrounded her and leaped at her the way dogs do a bull and, with insulting laughter and frequent shouts, they showered her with chunks of meat and gobs of manure until the judge called for order to be reestablished and the field to be cleared.

On one side, two boys were practicing knife-fighting, feigning horrendous cuts and slashes; on the other side, four boys, already adolescents, argued at knife point over a fat piece of intestine and tripe they had stolen from a butcher, and not far away a pack of dogs, emaciated by the forced abstinence, were employing similar means to determine which one would carry off a mud-covered liver. It was a miniature version of the barbaric way individual and social issues and rights are aired in our country. To sum it up, the scene being acted out at the slaughterhouse was something that had to be seen to be believed.

One animal with a fierce look and a short, stocky neck had remained in the corrals, and there was some disagreement over its genitals because it seemed, at once, to be a bull and a steer. Its time came. Two lassoers entered the corral on horseback while the masses teemed around it on foot, on horseback, and straddling the knotty fence rails. At the gate, there formed on foot a most striking and grotesque group of *pialadores*[8] and lassoers armed with accurate ropes, their heads covered with bright red handkerchiefs, their arms bare, and wearing red vests and red *chiripás*. Behind them were various horsemen and spectators with eager and scrutinizing eyes.

The animal, enraged and already caught by the horns with the lasso, bellowed, spewing foam, and there was no one in the world who could make him come out of the thick mud in which he seemed to be stuck; and it was impossible to hamstring him. The boys who were hanging from the fence posts yelled at him, goaded him in vain with their ponchos and handkerchiefs, and the dissonant din of harsh, shrill whistling, clapping and high-pitched and hoarse cries which arose from that unique orchestra was something to be heard.

Vulgar remarks, funny and obscene exclamations made their rounds from mouth to mouth, and each individual, excited by the spectacle or stung by the barb of some loquacious tongue, displayed his spontaneous ingenuity and cleverness.

"Son of a bitch bull."

"Damn those old bulls from El Azul."

"The cowboy who's taken us in better beware."

"But it's a steer."

"Can't you see it's an old bull."

"How can it be a bull? Show me his balls if you think so, you bastard!"

"There they are between his legs. Can't you see'm friend, big as your fist. Or have you gone blind on the way here?"

"Your mother must be the blind one if she gave birth to a son like you. Can't you see that's a clod of mud?"

"He's as stubborn and vicious as a Unitarian."

And hearing that magic word, everyone together cried out: "Death to the Unitarian savages!"

[8]Men who throw special lassos around the animal's legs, as different from the *enlazadores* (lassoers) who throw lassos around the animal's horns or head.

"Give the balls to the one-eyed man."

"Yes, to the one-eyed man, a man with balls, when it comes to fighting the Unitarians."

"The *matahambre*[9] to Matasiete, executioner of the Unitarians. Long live Matasiete!"

"There he goes!" a hoarse voice cried out, interrupting those outbursts of ferocious cowardice. "There goes the bull!"

"Look out! Watch out by the gate. There he goes, as furious as the devil!"

And in fact, the animal, hounded by the cries and above all by two sharp goads which were being stuck in his hindquarters, sensing the slackness of the rope, charged the gate, snorting and casting a reddish, flaming glare on both sides of him. The lassoer, stationing his horse firmly, gave a strong jerk on the rope which came untied from the horn and went zipping through the air with a harsh buzz. Simultaneously, a boy's head could be seen rolling off the top of one of the corral's stakes as if the swing of a cleaver had cut it off cleanly, with the trunk of his body remaining stationary, a long stream of blood spurting from every vein.

"The rope is cut," some shouted. "There goes the bull." But others, dazed and astonished, remained speechless since everything had happened as quick as a flash of lightning. The group by the gate dispersed a bit. A few of them crowded around the head and still palpitating body of the boy who was decapitated by the rope, horror on their astonished faces, and the rest, composed of riders who did not see the catastrophe, slipped away in various directions in pursuit of the bull, yelling and screaming. "There goes the bull! Cut him off! Look out! . . . Rope him, Sietepelos! . . . He's about to get you, Botija! . . . He's going mad—don't get in front of him. . . . Cut him off, cut him off, yellow belly! . . . Spur that old horse! . . . Now he's got out into Lone Street. . . . Let the Devil cut him off!"

The confusion and uproar were infernal. Hearing the din, some black women scavengers seated in a row at the edge of the big ditch took refuge and crouched among the piles of tripe and intestines that they were unraveling and rolling up with the patience of Penelope—which without a doubt saved them, because

---

[9]*Matahambre* or *matambre* ("hunger killer") is short-plate, a strip of meat directly below the hide, near the flank steak. It is rolled, filled, cooked, and then eaten as cold cuts. The name *matahambre* reinforces the brutality of Matasiete's name, "killer of seven."

upon seeing them, the animal let out a terrifying snort, angled sharply away from them, and continued forward with the horsemen in pursuit. They say that one of the women lost control of her bowels, another said Hail Marys in two seconds flat, and two of them promised St. Benedict to give up their jobs as scavengers and never again to return to those accursed corrals. No one knows if they kept their promises.

The bull, meanwhile, headed toward the city on a long, narrow street which takes off from the sharpest corner of the rectangle previously described, a street bounded by a ditch on one side and on the other by a fence of prickly pear plants, which they call Lone Street because it has only two houses on it. In its basinlike center there was a deep river of mud which was being fed by every one of the ditches. A certain Englishman, returning from his salting house, was wading through the muddy water at that time, step-by-step on a rather skittish horse, and he undoubtedly was so absorbed in his own thoughts that he did not hear the galloping horsemen nor the shouts until the bull charged at him. The Englishman's horse became startled, leaped suddenly to one side, and began to run away leaving the poor man stuck in two feet of mud. This accident, however, neither detained nor delayed the chase by the bull's pursuers; quite the contrary, with bursts of sarcastic laughter they shouted, "The gringo's all messed up! Get up, gringo!" and sped across the stream heaping mud on to his miserable body with their horses' hoofs. The foreigner made it out of the mud as best he could, looking more like a demon toasted by the flames of Hell than a fair-haired white man. Further ahead, to the shouts of "After the bull! After the bull!" four black women scavengers who were retreating with their prey lunged into the ditch full of water, their only available refuge.

The animal, meanwhile, after running about twenty blocks in different directions and startling all living creatures with his presence, went inside the gate of a vegetable farm, which turned out to be his ruination. Though tired, he still had spirit and maintained his furious expression. But he was surrounded by a deep ditch and a dense agave fence, and there was no way out. His pursuers, who had been spread out, regrouped and decided to take him back among a group of oxer , so that he might atone for his criminal offense in the very place where he had committed it.

An hour after his escape, the bull was once again in the slaughterhouse, where the small remaining crowd spoke only of his misdeeds. The adventure of the foreigner in the mud provoked, more than anything else, laughter and sarcasm. All that remained of the boy who had been decapitated by the rope was a pool of blood. His body was in the cemetery.

A moment later they roped the animal by the horns, which caused him to buck up and down and bellow harshly. They tossed one, two, three foot lassos at him but — to no avail. With the fourth one, he was caught by one foot: his spirit and anger redoubled. His tongue, stretching out convulsively, spewed foam, his nose smoke, his eyes a fiery look. "Hamstring him!" someone shouted imperiously. Matasiete immediately threw himself from his horse, cut off the hoof with one swipe and, stepping gingerly around the bull with his enormous knife in his hand, at last plunged it into the throat up to his fist, and then showed the knife, dripping with red blood to the spectators. A torrent gushed from the wound, the proud animal exhaled a few harsh roars, staggered and fell amidst the cries of the rabble who proclaimed Matasiete the victor and awarded him the *matahambre* as prize. Matasiete for a second time proudly raised his arm and bloody knife and then crouched to skin the animal with some companions.

The question of the beast's genitals, provisionally classified as a bull because of its indomitable ferocity, was still to be resolved. But all were so tired from their long chore that they quickly forgot it. Suddenly a harsh voice exclaimed, "Here's the balls!" taking two enormous testicles, the unequivocal sign of his dignity as a bull, from the animal's groin and showing them to the spectators. Many were the laughs and the comments. All the unfortunate incidents were, thus, easily explainable. A bull at the slaughterhouse was a very rare and even forbidden thing. According to the public health laws, it should have been thrown to the dogs, but there was such a shortage of meat and so many hungry people among the populace that the judge thought it best to look the other way.

In a trice, the accursed bull was skinned, quartered, and hung in the wagon. Matasiete placed the *matahambre* under his sheepskin saddle cushion. The slaughter was over by noon and a few of the riffraff who had remained until the end retired in groups on foot and on horseback or pulling meat-laden wagons by the cinch.

All of a sudden, the hoarse voice of a butcher cried, "There goes a Unitarian!" and upon hearing so significant a word, the entire mob stood still as if stunned by a sudden impression.

"Can't you see his U-shaped sideburns? He's got no insignia on his coat and no mourning band on his hat."

"Unitarian dog."

"What a dandy."

"He rides like a gringo."

"Put him in the pillory."

"Scissors!"

"Let's rough him up."

"He's wearing holsters to show off."

"All those Unitarian dandies are the worst kind of show-offs."

"What's the matter? Don't you have the nerve, Matasiete?"

"You think he doesn't?"

"I'll bet he does."

Matasiete was a man of few words and great action. When it came to violence, agility, skill with the cleaver, knife, or horse, he was not one to waste words. They had challenged him. He dug his spurs into his horse and raced full speed to the encounter with the Unitarian.

The latter was a young man of about twenty-five, handsome and elegantly dressed, who, while the aforesaid exclamations came gushing out of those insolent mouths, was trotting toward Barracas, oblivious to any danger. However, noting the menacing glances from that pack of hounds, he automatically put his right hand on the pistol in his English saddle when Matasiete's horse, charging at an angle, threw him to the ground, where he lay motionless on his back.

"Long live Matasiete!" cried the entire mob that swooped down on the victim in a mad rush, like rapacious vultures on the skeleton of an ox devoured by a jaguar.

The young man, still stunned, cast a fiery glance at those ferocious men, then looked at his horse which stood where it was, not too far away, with the idea of seeking satisfaction and revenge through his pistol. Matasiete, jumping off his horse, leaped in front of him, and, with his powerful arm, seized him by his tie and stretched him out on the ground, while at the same time he drew his knife from his belt and held it :o his throat.

A tremendous roar of laughter and another loud cheer applauded him once again.

What nobility of spirit! What courage on the part of the Federalists! Always pouncing on their lifeless victims in packs like vultures.

"Slit his throat, Matasiete—he tried to draw his pistol. Slit his throat like you did to the bull."

"Unitarian scoundrel. Let's shear him."

"He's got a nice long neck like a violin."

"Play the violin."

"A *resbalosa*[10] would be better."

"Let's try it," said Matasiete, and he began to smile as he passed the edge of the knife across the fallen man's neck, with his knee pressing down on his chest and his left hand holding him by the hair.

"No, don't slit his throat," shouted the imposing voice of the slaughterhouse Judge from a distance as he approached on horseback.

"To the cabin with him, to the cabin. Get the pillory table ready and the scissors. Death to the Unitarian savages! Long live the Restorer of Law!"

"Long live Matasiete."

"Death! Long live!" repeated the spectators in chorus, and tying his elbows together behind his back, they dragged the miserable young man, punching and shoving him amid shouts and insults, to the torture table, much as the Roman soldiers did to Christ.

In the center of the cabin's main room was a large, heavy table from which cards and drinking glasses were cleared only when tortures or executions by the Federalist henchmen of the slaughterhouse took place. In the corner, there could be seen another smaller table with writing materials, a notebook with figures and a number of chairs, one of which, a heavy armchair, stood out as being reserved for the Judge. A man seated in one of the chairs, a soldier by appearance, was singing to the tune of the guitar

---

[10]Name of a popular song (and dance) played at the throat-slitting executions perpetrated by the Mazorca. The "violin" also refers to the throat-slitting executions with the victim(s), often a whole row of them, kneeling.

"La Resbalosa," a song immensely popular among the Federalists, when the mob, arriving in a mad rush at the porch of the cabin, shoved the young Unitarian violently to the center of the room.

"It's your turn to get the *resbalosa.*"

"Commend your soul to the Devil."

"He's as mad as a wild bull."

"The club will soon tame him."

"Let's rough him up."

"For now, the scissors and the whip."

"Or else, the candle."

"The pillory would be better."

"Sit down and be quiet," exclaimed the Judge, letting himself fall into his chair. Everyone obeyed, while the young man, standing and facing the Judge, cried out in a voice full of indignation:

"Infamous henchmen, what do you intend to do with me?"

"Calm down," said the Judge, smiling. "There's no need to get angry. You'll see." In truth, the young man was beside himself with rage. His whole body seemed as if convulsed—his pale bruised face, his voice, his trembling lips betrayed the convulsive beating of his heart, the agitation of his nerves. His fiery eyes seemed to come out of their sockets, his straight black hair stood on end. His bare neck and open shirt allowed a glimpse of the violent heartbeat within his veins and the heavy breathing of his lungs.

"Are you trembling?" the Judge asked him.

"Out of rage, because I can't strangle you with my own two hands."

"Would you have the strength and the courage to do it?"

"I've got more than enough strength and courage for you, scoundrel."

"Let's have the scissors we use for trimming my horse. Cut his hair Federalist-style."

Two men seized him, one by the bonds around his arms, the other by his head, and in a minute they had cut off the sideburns which extended to the lower part of his chin, to the noisy laughter of the spectators.

"Now," said the Judge, "a glass of water to cool him off."

"One of bile, I'd make you drink, you scoundrel."

A short black man stepped forward with a glass of water in his hand. The young man kicked his arm and the glass crashed into the ceiling, spattering the surprised faces of the spectators.

"This guy's incorrigible."

"We'll soon tame him."

"Silence," said the Judge. "He's already been shaved Federalist-style—all that you need is the mustache. See that you don't forget it. Now let's get down to business. Why aren't you wearing the Federalist insignia?"

"Because I don't want to."

"Don't you know that the Restorer commands it."

"Livery is for slaves like you, not for free men."

"Free men can be made to wear it by force."

"Yes, by force and bestial violence. Those are your weapons, scoundrels. The wolf, the jaguar and the panther are strong like you. You should walk like them, on four feet."

"Aren't you afraid the jaguar will tear you to pieces?"

"I'd prefer it to having you pick apart my insides, like crows, while I'm bound."

"Why aren't you wearing a mourning band on your hat for the Heroine?"

"Because I wear it around my heart for the country, the country that you've murdered, scoundrels!"

"Don't you know that it's the Restorer's order?"

"You ordered it, slaves, to flatter your master's pride and offer him your infamous subservience."

"Insolent pup, you're getting too riled up. I'll have your tongue cut out if you say another word. Take the dandy's pants off. Tie him to the table and put the whip to his bare bottom."

No sooner had the Judge said this than four blood-splattered henchmen lifted the young man and stretched him lengthwise across the table, holding down his arms and legs.

"I would rather have my throat slit than be stripped naked, infamous villain."

They tied a handkerchief around his mouth and began to tear off his clothes. He squirmed, kicked, and gnashed his teeth. His limbs now took on the flexibility of cane, the strength of iron, and his back was the axis of a movement something like that of a snake. Drops of perspiration as big as pearls ran down his face. His eyes shot fire, his mouth foam, and the veins in his neck and forehead became black as if replete with blood, standing out against his white skin.

"Tie him down first," said the Judge.

"He's growling like a mad dog," said one of the henchmen.

In a moment they had tied his legs at an angle to the four legs of the table, turning his body face down. In order to perform the same operation with his hands, they loosened the bonds which held them behind his back. Sensing them free, with a brusk movement in which he seemed to exhaust the last of his strength, the young man got up on his arms, then on his knees and in a single movement collapsed murmuring, "I'd rather you slit my throat than strip me."

His strength was gone—he was immediately tied down in the form of a cross and the job of stripping him began. Suddenly a torrent of bubbling blood gushed from the young man's mouth and nose and began falling in streams down both sides of the table. The henchmen stopped what they were doing while the onlookers stood dumbfounded.

"He burst from rage, the Unitarian savage," someone said.

"He had a river of blood in his veins," said another.

"Poor devil. We only wanted to have some fun with him and he took the whole thing too seriously," exclaimed the Judge, wrinkling his jaguar's brow. "We'll have to report this. Untie him and let's get out of here."

The order was carried out. They locked the door and in a moment the mob slipped away behind the horse of the Judge who rode away taciturn with his head down.

Another of the Federalists' countless feats had come to an end.

At that time the throat-slitting butchers of the slaughterhouse were the apostles who spread the gospel of Rosas' Federation by the whip and the dagger, and it is not hard to imagine what kind of federation came out of their knives and heads. In keeping with the jargon invented by the Restorer, patron of their guild, "Unitarian savage" was the name they gave to anyone who was not a cutthroat, butcher, savage, or thief—that is to say, to all decent men of stout heart, to all highly educated patriots, friends of liberty and enlightenment. And, by the preceding episode, it can clearly be seen that the focal point of the Federation was the slaughterhouse.

— Translated by John Incledon

COMMENTARY

"The Slaughterhouse," considering that it is one of the first Spanish American short stories, reveals a high degree of artistry. Although it was written at the peak of the Romantic era, by the "official importer" of Romanticism from France, about the typical Romantic theme of the struggle against tyranny, and in a predominantly exalted Romantic tone, "The Slaughterhouse" transcends Romanticism and reveals characteristics of a surprising number of previous as well as subsequent literary movements. While its pungent wit and its anti-clericalism link it to the Encyclopedists of the eighteenth century, its minute descriptions, its obscene details, its multisensory tableaux, and its anonymous dialogues with a bold use of dialect herald respectively Realism, Naturalism, Modernism, and Criollismo.

Although the representation of a bloody dictatorship by a slaughterhouse does not require great imagination, the story surpasses the many other anti-Rosas works by its superb execution enhanced by the unimpassioned introduction. In the first paragraph, Echeverría adopts a Voltaire-like attitude to introduce the theme of meat in Lent and in order to indicate the complicity of the Church in the sufferings of the Argentine people. Immediately thereafter, he establishes the connection among the Church, the slaughterhouse, and the government. The description of the heavy rains, which at first appears to be a digression, actually echoes the reference to Noah in the first sentence and serves as a transition to the description of the hunger that was devastating the city.

Once the reader is projected into the slaughterhouse, the narrative becomes more vivid because of the concentration on the action in one specific place. The sketch of the slaughterhouse places the reader within the "Roman circus." He witnesses the slaughter of the animals, taking note of every detail. The Federalists are represented by the rabble which acts as a single character. Two hundred or four hundred human beasts are cornering forty-nine steers. Although the narrator distinguishes individuals—"two black women," "two boys," "one child"—he insists on the anonymity of his characters in order not to break the image of the mob's unity. Except for one allusion to Ño Juan, the only character with a name—probably a nickname at that—is Matasiete, the throat-cutting executioner of bulls and Unitarians. The name of Rosas's dead wife, Doña Encarnación, although historical, reinforces the emphasis on the carnal, the carnage, and the carnivorous Argentineans. The spectacle is repulsive to every one of the five senses: the blood and the fat of the quartered steers, the hounds' growls, the sea gulls' squawks, the decapitated boy, and the cries of the animalistic mob.

The dynamic nature of the scene is captured stylistically by the use of many verbal adjectives and a series of long but intense compound sentences. In the original Spanish, the author's insistence on the imperfect tense (used for customary or repetitive actions) creates the effect of a prolonged nightmare until he focuses on the pursuit of the bull when he switches to the preterit. This episode, in which Matasiete distinguishes himself, represents the transition from the "Roman circus" with its epic proportions to the torture of the anonymous Unitarian, in which Matasiete is also one of the principal actors.

The episode of the Unitarian dragged through the street, stripped and tied to the four legs of the table, seems at first sight to be anti-climactic to the slaughterhouse scene. Nevertheless, it is justified structurally by its parallelism with the death of the bull and by the fact that everything takes place on the day before Good Friday. The violent death of the Unitarian obviously evokes the image of the passion of Christ and makes the anomalous alliance between the Church and the Federalist government even more poignant.

Given the absence of a prose fiction tradition in Argentina and Spanish America in general at the time this story was written, the author's talent is truly amazing both in his conception of the story's structural unity and in his relatively rich vocabulary. For the taste of the sophisticated contemporary reader, the symbolism may be too obvious and the occasional moralizing interventions of the narrator superfluous, but those defects are more than outbalanced by the vivid, brilliant, and moving nature of the story.

Beyond its intrinsic literary values, "The Slaughterhouse" reflects the strong antipathy held by the upper class Unitarian intellectuals for the riffraff, the rabble, the mob . . . the common man who supported the Rosas dictatorship. Over a hundred years later, a very similar situation occurred during the government of Juan Perón. Many of the more famous Argentine authors from Echeverría to Borges, unlike their Mexican colleagues, do not identify at all with the masses. They consider themselves an intellectual elite and treat the rabble (*la chusma* rather than *el pueblo*) with contempt.

Manuel Payno

(1810–1894)

Mexican. Throughout his long life, he was actively engaged in national politics. He was minister of finance on several occasions, a diplomat, senator, and a prolific journalist. He fought in the Mexican War of 1845 and was later a political enemy of Dictator Santa Ana. A Conservative, he participated in the 1857 coup d'etat against the Reform government of Juárez and subsequently allied himself with the forces behind Emperor Maximilian. His published stories and novels extend over a period of fifty years. His first short stories were written at the height of Romanticism between 1839 and 1845. His first novel *El fistol del diablo* (1845–1846), overly long, is a blend of Costumbrismo and the fantastic. *El hombre de la situación* (1861), on the other hand, is a delightful, short picaresque novel about the adventures of a Spanish immigrant and his descendants. "Secret Love" and Payno's other stories were published individually in the literary journal *El Museo Mexicano* in 1843 and 1844 and were republished in 1871 in book form under the title *Tardes nubladas*. His masterpiece is *Los bandidos de Río Frío* (1889–1891), a two-thousand-page novel which, in spite of its length, still makes for enjoyable reading.

SECRET LOVE

Alfred had not visited me for a long time when, at the least expected moment, he appeared in my room. His pallor, his long, disheveled hair falling over his sunken cheeks, his sad languid eyes, and, above all, the marked symptoms of serious illness which he displayed, alarmed me so that I couldn't help asking him the cause of his illness, or, rather, just what was wrong with him.

"It's crazy, a whim, a fancy which has put me into this state; in a word, a secret love."

"Really?"

"It's a story," he went on, "that would mean nothing to most people, but perhaps you will understand; a story, I repeat, of the

23

sort that leaves such deep scars on a man's soul that not even time has the power to erase them."

Alfred's sentimental, and at the same time solemn and gloomy tone moved me so profoundly that I begged him to tell me this story of his secret love, and he continued:

"Did you ever meet Caroline?"

"Caroline! Do you mean that young girl with the sensitive, expressive face, the slim waist, and the dainty feet?"

"That's the one."

"Well, to tell the truth, I did meet her once, and I was very much interested in her . . . but. . . ."

"That young girl," continued Alfred, "I loved with the kind of tender, sublime love that one devotes to a mother, to an angel; but it seems as if fate stepped into my path to prevent me from ever revealing to her my ardent, pure, and holy passion, which would have brought happiness to her and to me.

"The first night I saw her was a ball; as light, airy and unreal as a sylph, with her beautiful white face full of happiness and joie de vivre. I instantly fell in love with her and tried to make my way through the crowd to get close to this celestial being, whose existence from that moment seemed to me not to belong to this world but to some higher region. I approached trembling, with labored breath, my forehead bathed in a cold sweat . . . oh, love! True love is indeed a cruel sickness. Well, as I was saying, I approached and tried to speak a few words, and I don't know what I said, but the fact is that she, with indescribable charm, invited me to sit by her side; I did, and she, parting her delicate lips, made a few inconsequential remarks about the heat, the breeze, et cetera. But to me her voice seemed like music, and those insignificant words sounded in my ears in such a magical way that I can still hear them at this moment. If that woman had said right then and there: *I love you, Alfred;* if she had taken my icy hand in her delicate alabaster fingers and pressed it, if she had allowed me to place a kiss upon her white forehead. . . . Oh! I'd have wept with gratitude, I'd have gone mad, I might have died of happiness.

"A moment later, a stylish gentleman asked Caroline to dance. Cruelly he wrenched my beloved, my treasure, my angel, from my side. The rest of the evening Caroline danced, chatted with her friends, smiled at the shameless libertines; and for me, who worshiped her, she had never a smile, not a glance, not a word. I left, humiliated, jealous, cursing the ball. As soon as I got home I threw myself on my bed and burst into tears of rage.

"The next morning the first thing I did was set about trying to find out where Caroline lived; but my efforts were in vain for some time. One night I saw her at the theater, as beautiful and as gorgeously dressed as ever, with that angelic smile on her lips and her black eyes sparkling with happiness. At times Caroline laughed at the jokes of the actors; at other times her face softened at the pathetic scenes. Between acts her eyes traveled all over the orchestra and the boxes, studying the stylish coats, the shimmering watch chains and tiepins of the men-about-town. She waved charmingly to female acquaintances with her fan, she smiled, she chatted . . . but, for me, nothing . . . not once did she turn her gaze toward my humble seat, despite the fact that my eyes, burning and flooded with tears, followed her slightest movements. That night, too, was one of insomnia and delirium, one of those nights when the bed burns, when fever causes the blood vessels to throb, when a fantastic image sits, fixed and motionless, on the edge of the bed.

"It was imperative that I come to a decision. In fact, I finally found out where Caroline lived, who the members of her family were, and what kind of life she led. But how was I to make an entrance into those sumptuous homes of the wealthy? How was I to insinuate myself into the heart of a girl of such high station, who spent half her time resting on soft silken ottomans and the other half dressing up to meet her friends for outings and for going to the theater in her splendid carriage? Oh! If these rich and proud women only knew the value of the pure, ardent love which they ignite in our hearts; if they would only look into the interior of our beings, which are totally filled, so to speak, with loving; if they would but reflect that for us poor men, upon whom fortune has not bestowed riches but whom nature has endowed with honest and loyal hearts, women are a priceless treasure and we cherish them with the same delicate, painstaking care that they use when keeping their fragrant Madonna lilies in a vase of mother-of-pearl; then there's no doubt that they would love us a great deal; but . . . women are never capable of loving our souls. Their frivolous natures cause them to pay more attention to a fancy waistcoat than to an honorable heart; to a gold chain or a necktie than to a well-tuned mind.

"Thus my torment. To follow, gloomy, sad, and humiliated, devoured by my hidden passion, a woman who ran madly and carelessly through the magic, continual social whirl that the upper class of Mexico enjoys. Caroline went to the theaters, I followed her there; Caroline wound her way breezily and brilliantly through the luxuriant, tree-lined lanes of Alameda Park, and there I was again, seated in the dark corner of a bench. Wherever she went she was brimming with happiness and good fortune, while I dragged myself around depressed, with my soul filled with bitterness and my heart oozing blood.

"I resolved to write her. I gave a letter to the footman, and that night I went to the theater with high hopes. Perhaps tonight Caroline would look at me, perhaps she would fix her attention on my pale face and take pity on me . . . that was a lot to ask for: after pity would come love, and then I would be the happiest of men. Vain hope! During the entire evening I never succeeded in getting Caroline to turn her attention to me. At the end of a week I was convinced that the footman had never given her my letter. I redoubled my efforts and finally succeeded in getting a girl friend of hers to place in her hands a note written with all the feeling and candor of a man who is truly in love; but, my God, every day Caroline received so many similar notes; she heard so many declarations of love; she had so much flattery lavished upon her by everyone from her parents to the servants that she didn't even bother to open my letter and gave it back without even asking out of curiosity who had written it.

"Have you ever felt the hideous torment of being scorned by a woman whom you love with all the power of your soul? Do you understand the terrible martyrdom of running day and night, insanely delirious with love, after a woman who laughs, who doesn't feel, who doesn't love, who doesn't even know the man who loves her?

"Five months this misery lasted, and I, faithful and resigned, never ceased to dog her steps and observe her actions. The contrast was always the same: she, rash, full of joy, laughing and watching the drama of life through rose-colored glasses, while I, sad, driven mad by a secret love that no one could comprehend, looked at everyone through the dim light of an infernal veil.

"A thousand women passed before my eyes—some with pale, interesting faces, others full of vitality, their round cheeks shining like mother-of-pearl. I saw a few with lithe bodies, narrow waists, and small feet; others were robust, with athletic builds; some looked somber and romantic, others had laughing faces of classic happiness. But none of them, not one of these flowers that glided before my eyes, whose aroma I detected, whose beauty I could feel, made my heart so much as skip a beat or caused my mind to entertain the slightest feeling of happiness. They were all meaningless to me; I loved only Caroline, and Caroline . . . oh! Women's hearts soften, as Anthony says, when they see a beggar or someone who is hurt, but they are insensitive when a man says to them: 'I love you, I adore you, and your love is as vital to me as the sun to the flowers, as the wind to the birds, as the water to the fish.' What madness! Caroline was unaware of my love, as I have told you, and this fact was worse for me than if she had loathed me.

"The last night I saw her was at a masked ball. She was disguised in a black silk cloak, but the instinct of love made me recognize her. I followed her in the lobby of the theater, in the boxes, in the bar, wherever the entertainment led her. The pure angel of my love, that chaste virgin with whom I had dreamed of an entire lifetime of domestic bliss—to see her surrounded by the hubbub of a carnival, eager to dance, full of enthusiasm, intoxicated by the flatteries and expressions of love being lavished upon her. Oh! If only I had any rights to her heart, I would have called her, and in a tender, persuasive voice said to her: 'Caroline, my dearest, you are following the road to perdition; prudent men never choose for their wives the women they meet in an environment of debauchery and voluptuousness; for heaven's sake, come away from this party whose atmosphere clouds your beauty, whose pleasures wither the white flower of your innocence; love me alone, Caroline, and you will discover a sincere heart into which you can pour all your own feelings; love me, for I will not lose you or allow you to die amid the tears and torments of tragic passion.' I'd have told her a thousand more things, but Caroline refused to hear me; she ran away from me and laughingly gave her arm to those who regaled her with frivolous, deceitful words which society calls gallantry. Poor Caroline! I loved her so much that I wished I had the power of a god to snatch her away from the dangerous road on which she found herself.

"I noticed that one of those syrupy, vacuous dandies lacking in both morals and talent, who because of one of life's many anomalies is appreciated and even respected by society—was chatting most intently with Caroline. At the first opportunity I took him outside the ballroom, I insulted him, I challenged him, and I would have fought him to the death; but he just laughed and said: 'What rights do you have over this woman?' I paused a moment and in a voice choking with sadness answered, 'None.' 'Well, then,' my antagonist went on, laughing, 'I do have some, and you're going to see them.' The scoundrel took out of his pocket a garter, a lock of hair, a portrait, some letters in which Caroline called him her treasure, her only master. 'Now you see, my poor man,' he said as he walked away, 'Caroline loves me, but nevertheless I'm going to leave her this very night, because other amorous mementoes such as those which you have just seen are laid out on my dresser and claim my attention; they are from simple, innocent women, and Caroline has already changed lovers eight times.'

"Upon hearing these words I felt that my soul was taking leave of my body, that my heart was shrinking, that I was strangling with the tears in my throat. I fell onto a chair in a faint, and in a little while I saw no one at my side but a friend who was trying to moisten my lips with a little wine.

"Three days later I found out that Caroline had been stricken with a violent fever and that the doctors despaired of her life. At that point nothing could stop me; I went to her home, determined to declare my love to her, to let her know that even if she had wasted her youth on frivolous and transient pleasures, that if her heart was dying of the desolation and terrible emptiness of never having found a man who truly loved her, I was there to assure her that I would weep at her grave, that the holy love I had borne her would always be kept alive in my heart. Oh! Such promises would have soothed the poor child who was dying at the dawn of her life, and she would have turned her thoughts to God and died as peacefully as a saint.

"But it was madness to speak of love to a woman in the last moments of her life, while the priests were reciting psalms at her bedside, while her family, in tears, were lighting Caroline's gaunt, withered features with holy tapers. Oh, I was insane; I, too, stood at death's door, with fever raging in my soul. What idiots and madmen we men are!"

"So what finally happened?"

"In the end Caroline died," he replied, "and I, ever faithful, followed her to the grave, just as I followed her to the theater and to the balls. As the cold earth covered the last remains of a creature who such a short time before had been so beautiful, so joyous, and so happy, my fondest dreams also disappeared, the last remaining illusions of my life."

Alfred walked out of my room without a word of farewell.

— Translated by Marcia Cobourn Wellwarth

COMMENTARY

"Secret Love," in spite of all the Romantic ingredients, is somewhat redeemed by its sincerity and by its literary devices. Nowadays the plot certainly seems ridiculous: the love is impossible because Alfred is poor and Caroline is rich; fate prevents him from declaring his love; he idealizes her so much that he continues to love her even after discovering that she has had eight lovers; he follows her to the cemetery and buries himself alive in the greatest despair over a love that he never dared to declare. The sentimental plot is accompanied by the typically Romantic descriptions, the exaltations, exclamations, and faints. Nonetheless, the story is not without interest. Although the present-day reader may find it difficult to identify with Alfred, the latter's attitude is totally sincere. The discovery of Caroline's frivolity might have been the denouement but the persistence of Alfred's love converts what would have been a trick-ending short story into a truer emotional one. Unlike many sentimental novels, the action moves rather rapidly because of the relatively few descriptions, the frequent use of the preterit tense, and the short dialogues with which the narrator frames the story.

For a story written in the primitive stages of the genre, "Secret Love" has a well-planned structure. The initial paragraph is narrated in first person. Alfred enters and in the ensuing dialogue, little by little he dominates the scene to the point of replacing the original narrator. During the unfolding of Alfred's tale of woe, the original narrator's presence is felt in only two moments ("Have you ever felt the hideous torment . . ."; "as I have told you . . ."), but those two moments are necessary to justify the original narrator's final question and the last sentence of the story.

Within the somewhat artificial frame of the dialogues between Alfred and the original narrator, Alfred's story has a tight unity based on the first and last night he saw Caroline and on the one-sentence summary of his love on the last page: "I . . . followed her to the grave, just as I had followed her to the theater and to the balls." The mention of the title words in Alfred's first sentence and once again a little past the middle of the story also serves to reinforce the structure. A stylistic trait that not only lends unity to the story but also a degree of artistic rhythm is the use of series of three parallel words or phrases: "my ardent, pure and holy passion"; Caroline danced, chatted . . ., smiled"; "who doesn't feel, who doesn't love, who doesn't even know . . ."; "so beautiful, so joyous, and so happy."

Bearing in mind that Jorge Isaacs's Romantic masterpiece *María* and all its imitations were not written and published for at least twenty-five years after "Secret Love," Payno's story must be considered as one of the most important examples of the sentimental phase of Latin American Romanticism. Furthermore, the predominance of emotion over reason in the protagonist and the sincere expression of those emotions are traits that subsequently developed into a national characteristic of Mexico's prose fiction.

José Victorino Lastarria

(1817-1888)

Chilean. He is considered the father of his country's literature. A disciple of José Joaquín de Mora and Andrés Bello, Lastarria has been called the "Chilean Sarmiento." Like the latter, he argued against Bello's moderate, conservative position with regard to Spain but sided with him, against Sarmiento, in his position that one Spanish language based on Castilian should be maintained in all of Spanish America. He founded the Sociedad Literaria in 1842 and stressed the necessity of breaking with tradition in order to create a national literature. He tried to encourage his contemporaries and his followers by writing the first Chilean short stories. In addition to his literary interests, he was a lawyer, professor, congressman, and cabinet member. In Congress, he spoke out against the recognition of Emperor Maximilian in Mexico and was the spokesman for anticlerical Liberalism through the middle years of the century. He later wrote *Lecciones de política positiva* (1875), based on Comte, which argued in favor of Federalism. His *Recuerdos literarios* (1878) is one of the best nineteenth-century works of literary criticism in all of Latin America. "Rosa" was first published in the newspaper *El Progreso* on June 21, 1847, and it then reappeared in Lastarria's journal *El Aguinaldo* in 1848, in his *Miscelánea literaria* in 1855, and in volume two of his *Miscelánea histórica e literaria* in 1858.

ROSA

HISTORICAL EPISODE

On February 11, 1817, the populace of Santiago was gripped by paralyzing fear. Anguish and hope, which for so many days had aroused their spirits, were now changing to a kind of fatal depression reflected in every face. The Army of Independence had just made its way down from the snowcapped Andes and was threatening to put an end to the ominous Spanish power;

31

hanging in the balance were liberty, the fortunes of many, and the ruin of those who for so long had ruled the country. Yet neither group dared reveal its fears, since even the slightest indication might prove fatal.

The night was somber. A stifling heat made the atmosphere oppressive. The sky was hidden by thick, heavy clouds which here and there revealed a star dimmed by the night mist moving through the air. A profound silence, broken from time to time by a distant, forlorn barking, heralded the widespread consternation that struck fear in every heart. In short, the night was one of those when people feel oppressed without knowing why; they need a sign, a hope. All illusions fade; there are no friends, there are no loves because skepticism comes to wither all such feelings with its cruel doubt; there are no memories, there are no images because the entire soul is absorbed with the present, with this unbearable reality with which an angry nature silences and saddens us. We tremble without realizing it; the buzz of an insect, the flight of a nocturnal bird freeze us with terror and seem to forecast some sinister, horrible unknown.

I

It was ten o'clock, the streets were dark and deserted except for one man wrapped in a large cape, alone under the balconies of an ugly building. Alternately leaning against the wall and moving about slowly, he seemed to be ever on the alert.

Suddenly the melodious prelude of a guitar cuts the air, trembling as if afraid, and then a man's voice, soft and hushed, speaks these lines:

> What of your vow, what has become
> Of the love you promised to me,
> Pretty Rosa?
> Could it be that another love
> Has taken your heart and made you
> Forget my plea?
>
> Don't you recall, pretty Rosa,
> That when I was leaving, you swore,
> Weeping, sobbing,
> To love me forever; gently
> With a tender kiss you then sealed
> Our sweet good-bye?

I love you now as I did then
Because during all my exile
Along with me
I carried a sweet dream of you
To ease and soften the harshness
Of my cruel fate.

Return, Rosa, now to your love.
My passion, do not deny.
Well might I die
If you should scoff at my real pain,
If my weeping you should disdain,
Fair Enchantress!

At the end of the stanzas, a muffled sound came from the balcony and a soft murmur seemed to be saying: "Carlos, Carlos! Is that you?"

"Yes, Rosa mine, I have come back to see you, to be with you forever."

"Forever? Isn't that a dream?"

"No, my dear, for today when I return bringing liberty for my country and my heart for you, your father will take pity on us. I will plead his cause before the independent government and he will consider me a husband worthy of his daughter."

"Oh, Carlos, don't deceive me for your deception is cruel. My father is determined; he detests you because you fight for independence. Your victories only enrage him."

"I shall prevail, if you love me. Promise to be faithful to me and I shall overcome his opposition."

"Wait a moment! You are in danger out there!"

The dialogue ceased. After a short silence, the man in the cape could be seen entering the building through a concealed door which closed behind him.

But the street does not remain without movement. Shortly thereafter, a cloaked figure is spied cautiously leaving the house. He quickly disappears, then returns with armed men who secure the entries to the building; confused cries of alarm, of supplication, the sound of arms, several pistol shots from inside shatter for a few moments the silence of the city.

A fresh breeze from the south had cleared the atmosphere, the stars shone in all their splendor, and the moon seemed to be crowning the towering peaks of the Andes; its soft, reddish glow contrasted with the dark shadows cast by the mountains and lent them an overpowering and sinister appearance.

The creaking bolts and the iron doors of the prison sounded in the plaza. A prisoner is being taken into its cells.

II

At one o'clock on the twelfth, the Marqués de Avilés was seated at the table with his entire family. An official of the royal government has just arrived.

"What news do you bring us, Mr. Counselor?" asks the Marqués.

"Nothing good. The insurgents began mounting Chacabuco slope at seven this morning; our army is waiting for them on this side and at this very moment the fate of the colony is being decided, Marqués. By the way, hasn't your grace read the *King's Gazette?*"

"No, read it and we shall listen."

"It carries the news Your Grace has just heard along with this important paragraph."

The Counselor reads: "Last night in a respectable house of this city, the insurgent colonel Carlos Del Río was apprehended. It is known beyond a doubt that this criminal was the victor against our outposts in the Cordillera and that the insolent San Martín, thinking to gain great advantage from the colonel's audacity and cleverness, sent him to Santiago for the purpose of contacting the traitors hiding in this city. But Divine Providence, which protects the cause of the King, our Lord, delivered the plot of this evil drama into the hands of the government and last night one of His Majesty's best servants captured the insurgent who had dared to violate the sanctuary of this gentleman's home with an unholy purpose. His Majesty will reward this important service and the traitor will today view his crime from a scaffold to which he will soon be followed by his accomplices."

When the Counselor reached this point in his reading, Rosa, who was at the side of her father, the Marqués, falls faint with a cry of grief. Everyone becomes alarmed, the Marquesa cries out, the Counselor is disturbed, some run out, others come in, only the Marqués remains calm, telling the Counselor: "Pay no attention to this crazy girl. It was I who offered this service to our King. I had this insurgent arrested here in my house for he has had my Rosa nervous and upset for some time now. What could you expect? They almost grew up together. The close contact,

eh? . . . the boy became involved with the insurgents and I refused to see him and today he has returned, up to his old tricks
again."

After a few moments, thanks to the Marquesa's help, Rosa regains consciousness; her beautiful moist eyes, her heightened color,
her trembling lips, her disheveled hair, her rumpled clothing,
all reveal the sharp pain tearing at her heart. She is an angel
asking for compassion who obtains in reply only a cóld, satanical
smile.

"Father, dear," she says, kneeling at the Marqués's feet, "I
promise never to see Carlos again but let him live. . . ." A sob
drowns her voice.

"Let him die," replies the old man coldly, "because he is a
traitor to his King."

"Have I not tried to please you, Father? Have I not sacrificed
myself up until now in order to respect your wishes? I shall sacrifice myself even more, if that is possible, but let him live."

"He shall live and be your husband, if he gives up this blas-
phemous, ungodly cause he has embraced, if he returns to the
service of his King." With these words the old man becomes emotional.

Rosa rises with grave majesty and, as if doubting what she has
heard, gives her father a long look of grief and dismay, finally
stating in a firm voice: "No, Sire! I prefer to die of grief and to
have Carlos also die with honor for his country, for his cause.
I could not love him if he were dishonored."

She left. A movement of shock, like that produced by lightning,
agitated all those present.

The darkness of night was already conquering the twilight that
makes all visible things appear hazy and vague.

There was great activity in the town, fear and happiness alternate on every face. No one knows what is happening, all ask, all
become nervous, running, fleeing; the horses' hoofbeats and the
uproar of soldiers arriving from the garrison create a state of
alarm. The people crowd around the palace, the President is going
to leave for no one knows where. All are present: the Marqués,
the Marquesa, the Counselor and many other important officials.

Rosa takes advantage of the general confusion, leaves her house,
disguised in a heavy shawl. She hears cheering for the homeland,
realizes immediately that the Independents have triumphed in

Chacabuco, and runs to the prison to rescue her lover. She arrives, sees all the doors open, finds no guards. All is silence, the cells deserted. Terrified, she runs calling "Carlos," but only the echo of the darkened vaults answers her. Finally she enters a patio: there is Carlos, his chest cruelly torn open, his head bowed, his arms tied to a pillar in the corridor. The cowardly followers of the King had killed him one hour earlier.

Rosa takes in her hands the gallant colonel's head which still maintains the beautiful expression of his noble, intelligent spirit. She tries to revive him with her breath . . . freezes with horror . . . trembles and falls to her knees . . . an iron hand lifts her, it is the Marqués who with a tremulous voice and tear-filled eyes tells her: "Accept the will of God."

III

It was the twelfth of February, 1818. The sound of bells, the artillery salvos, the military music, the cheering of the populace who fill the streets and plazas, everything indicates that the declaration of Chilean independence is being proclaimed.

The country is free, praise to the heroes who in a hundred battles victoriously waved the tricolor flag. Praise and eternal honor to those who shed their blood for the liberty and good fortune of Chile.

At this very instant, in the Capuchin temple, a very different scene was taking place: the doors were open, some priests were celebrating the mass at the illuminated altars; a pious woman or two were praying. The nuns were chanting the funeral service, its mournful bell pierced the air with plaintive sounds. Through the lattices at the center of the choir, one could see a coffin.

The coffin contained the body of the Marqués de Avilés's daughter, as beautiful and as pure as ever, her brow encircled with a garland of roses.

— Translated by Betty Becker

COMMENTARY

"Rosa," in addition to its typically Romantic defects, suffers from artificiality. The various ingredients of the story seem to come straight out of the pages of a Romantic "recipe book": (1) historical period: national war of independence; (2) historical conflict: the Insurgents versus the Royalists; (3) personal conflict: the impossible love between a dashing rebel hero and the daughter of a staunch Royalist; (4) setting: the city of Santiago with the nearby gigantic snowcapped peaks of the Andes; (5) Romantic atmosphere: the dark sinister night, the mysterious, cloaked men, the prison cell, the heroine's fainting, and the coffin. Even the final phrase, "garland of roses," emphasizes the story's artificiality with its too obvious allusion to the heroine's name.

Although the literary quality of this story is relatively low, it is included in this anthology for historical reasons. Because of its brevity, it must be considered a short story although it would really be more accurate to call it a rough outline for a novel. The historical novel, which was extremely popular in Spanish America during the Romantic period, could not be successfully compressed by Lastarria into five or six pages. Everything in "Rosa" happens so quickly that there is hardly time for the protagonists to be sufficiently developed. A somewhat broader treatment of the ideological conflict between Carlos and the Marqués would have perhaps justified the latter's total disregard for his daughter's emotions.

In the original Spanish, "Rosa" is written with a special orthography that was introduced by Sarmiento, Lastarria, and others in order to affirm the New World's linguistic (as well as political) independence from Spain. Nevertheless, Lastarria was indebted to the Spanish Golden Age theater for the division of the story into three "acts," the form of Carlos's poetic serenade, and the melodramatic elements of the plot. Only occasionally does Lastarria hit upon a particularly felicitous phrase that reflects his genius, which was to be revealed in his later nonfiction works.

Although "Rosa" contains all the typical traits of the historic aspect of Romanticism, the story did not prove to be the model for subsequent Chilean literary efforts, as Lastarria had hoped. Its rapid rhythm and its interest in the past were the antithesis of the slow-moving realistic narratives that were to characterize Chilean literature from the following generation on, up through Manuel Rojas and José Donoso in the mid-twentieth century.

Realism

In Europe by the middle of the nineteenth century, Realism had replaced Romanticism. In Spanish America, although Realism made its debut in the early 1860s with Chilean Alberto Blest Gana (1830-1920), it did not reach its peak until the end of the century. The three short story writers that have been chosen as representatives of the movement were born at least twenty years after Blest Gana: José López Portillo y Rojas (1850-1923), Tomás Carrasquilla (1858-1940), and Manuel González Zeledón (1864-1936). Because of their relatively late preeminence and because of the prolonged and anachronistic influence of Romanticism through the end of the nineteenth century, critics Joaquín Casalduero and Fernando Alegría refer to the movement, respectively, as "sentimental Realism" and "Romantic Realism."

Reacting against the exalted tone of Romanticism, Realism was characterized by a commonsense verisimilitude. Instead of seeking exotic themes, the Realist examined the world around him. He was interested in the daily problems of his neighbors, who usually belonged to the middle class. The most outstanding international champion of Realism was Honoré de Balzac (1799-1850), who, like his confreres Dickens (1812-1870) in England and Pérez Galdós (1843-1920) in Spain, proposed to sketch panoramically the new society that was emerging from the Industrial Revolution and the French Revolution. Rejecting the heroic protagonists of Romanticism, the Realistic author chose interesting middle class types and usually caricatured them in a somewhat patronizing way. Observing society through prisms similar to those of their contemporary caricaturists Cruikshank (1792-1878) and Daumier (1808-1879), the authors saw their characters as prototypes of certain human traits: miserliness, generosity, naïveté, envy, and ingratitude. The predilection for caricature among the Spanish American Realists was so strong that it formed the basis of a widely cultivated independent genre, the *artículo de costumbres,* related to the English essays of *The Spectator* (1711-1712) of Addison and Steele but more directly inspired by the sketches of the Spaniards Larra (1809-1837) and Mesonero Romanos (1803-1882). The Realistic protagonist rarely has psychological complexity. He almost never evolves within the work, and all his actions tend to reinforce the type that the author wishes to create. The conflict usually occurs between representative types rather than within any one character.

One of the favorite themes of the Spanish American Realists was the opposition between rural virtue and urban evil. Even though there might be an occasional unhappy ending, the detailed descriptions of the environment, rural or urban, were presented in a nonconflictive, at times idyllic, manner. In this period, most of the national capitals still retained their picturesque charm and provided appropriate settings for the Realists, as did the provincial capitals.

In spite of the extensive production of Realistic short stories in Spanish America, the genre had still not been clearly defined. Some Realistic short stories border dangerously on the short novel, while others greatly resemble the Costumbrista sketch. Be that as it may, Realism, more than Romanticism, Naturalism, and Modernism, fulfilled the very important function of stimulating interest in contemporary Spanish American themes which was to constitute the basis of the mature literature of the twentieth century.

José López Portillo y Rojas

(1850-1923)

Mexican. Born in Guadalajara of an old, wealthy family, he became a lawyer, journalist, and professor, and occupied important positions in the regime of Dictator Porfirio Díaz: governor of Jalisco and minister of foreign affairs. He, Emilio Rabasa, and Rafael Delgado were the three Mexican novelists who at the end of the nineteenth century reflected the influence of Spanish Realists Galdós and Pereda. His best novel, *La parcela* (1898), is one of the first in Mexican literature to have a completely rural setting, although its viewpoint is that of the hacienda owner. He also wrote two other novels: *Los precursores* (1909) and *Fuertes y débiles* (1919); four collections of stories of varying length: *Seis leyendas* (1883), *Novelas cortas* (1900), *Sucesos y novelas cortas* (1903), and *Historias, historietas y cuentecillos* (1918). In spite of its nineteenth-century Realism, "Unclaimed Watch" first appeared in the 1918 volume. López Portillo also wrote poetry, plays, travel books, literary criticism, and history. His grandson and namesake was elected president of Mexico in 1976.

UNCLAIMED WATCH

I

"The insolence of these reporters is positively unbearable!" exclaimed Judge Felix Zendejas, as he angrily struck the table with the newspaper he had just finished reading.

Don Felix was a middle-aged man, in his thirties or forties; he was overweight, had a round face with a ruddy complexion, a full beard, sparkling eyes, a long nose, bushy eyebrows, and a character that was as vigorous as his facial features. He always spoke at the top of his lungs, and when he discussed something he never discussed it, he preached it dogmatically. He would not tolerate objections; he was always right, or pretended to be so, and if somebody disagreed with him, he'd fly off the handle, the discussion would degenerate into an argument, and soon the argument would wind up in a quarrel. It could be said that the material he was made of was melinite or roburite, since with the slightest amount of friction or jarring he'd become inflamed, would roar like thunder, and then burst into a terrifying conflagration; a dangerous blasting cap disguised as a man.

During the meal, he exchanged few words with his wife Otilia because he had been so absorbed in reading the newspaper, which he had found quite interesting, all the more so because it had hurt his gall bladder; he had such an excitable temper that he was purposely and constantly looking for excuses to blow up.

From his reading, Zendejas came to the conclusion that "these scribbling dogs," as he irreverently called reporters, were continuing every day to denounce robberies, and more robberies, committed in various ways in different parts of the city—all of them alarming in nature because they revealed so precarious a state of affairs in the metropolis which seemed to have been converted into the crossroads of the *camino real*. Assaults on homes were becoming daily occurrences; in plain daylight, in the middle of the street, the bandits performed their escapades, and their audacity had reached such heights that even the center of the city had turned into a stage for their scandalous acts. The paper said they had snatched purses from two or three women and taken bracelets right off other women's arms, and rings right off their fingers; and had ripped a pair of diamond earrings from the blushing lobes of one distinguished woman's precious ears, leaving them split in two, or rather, in four. The repeated perpetrations of these atrocities indicated the existence in Mexico City of a band of ruffians, or rather a tribe of Apaches, and this tribe was thriving in comfort, as though it were operating in the open and unprotected countryside.

After reading through what the paper had to say, Zendejas flew into such a rage that you could have roasted beans on his skin, and with a little more fuel he would have been pawing and snorting like an untamed bull bedecked with *banderillas*.

"We absolutely *must* find some way to put an end to this outrage!" he repeated, pounding the paper with his fist.

His wife, who was used to his perpetual raging, as a salamander is used to living in fire (no doubt by virtue of the law of adaptation to one's surroundings), did not in any way become discouraged when she felt the air around her filled with rumbling and bellowing. She even dared to observe, with perfect calm:

"But, Felix, don't you think that the bandits' insolence is worse than that of the reporters?"

She was about twenty-eight years old, had a dark complexion, graceful movements, dark eyes, and straight hair, with the distinguishing characteristic that she would comb it in a Greek or Roman style, or whatever style occurred to her, but always over her ears in soft waves.

At this remark, her husband cast a look at her that any painter would have represented as flames darting from his pupils; but she didn't worry or get upset over that hot shower with which Zendejas enveloped her, and she calmly continued to sip a cup of tea.

"You, too, Otilia?" shouted the judge in his deep bass voice. "As if these mercenary pens weren't enough to make me rage! The same old tune, every day! Robbery everywhere, all the time. At that rate, there wouldn't be a single person living in the capital who hadn't been held up. . . . Why, not even if there were a hundred thousand thieves packed into this city! If you ask me, it's all a pack of lies that these sensationalist reporters dream up just to boost sales."

"Excuse me, dear, but I don't think it's such a bad idea for reporters to deal with such matters; I find it appropriate and even necessary."

"The fact is, it's a lot of fuss about nothing."

"You don't know that for certain."

"I do know it, and you don't. If things were as bad as these papers claim, there'd be many more arrests of thieves and pickpockets. . . . In my district there have been very few."

"But the number will go up once the police become more active, don't you think so?"

"No, I don't think so."

"Time will tell."

Otilia's calm disposition had the virtue of neutralizing the hurricanes and earthquakes raging within Zendejas; which should come as no surprise, since it is a well-known fact that passivity is the

best antidote for violence, just as woolen mattresses are for cannon-
balls.

"Besides," debated her husband, "do you think it's right for
those dogs (the reporters) to make the judges responsible for
everything that goes on? Let them skin the policemen alive and
eat the police chiefs! But the judges! What have we got to do
with all this nonsense? And yet, they won't leave us alone."

"Delayed or twisted justice gives very bad results, Felix."

"I never delay or twist it. Was that comment directed at me?"

"Heaven forbid! I'd never say, or even think, such a thing. I
know you are honest and hard-working; but your colleagues. . . .
What about your colleagues?"

"My colleagues are . . . the way they are. Some good, some
bad."

"So you see, they could use a little prodding."

"Well then, let them prod the others; but why me? Tell me,
wife, why is it my fault that in front of the Cathedral after the
twelve o'clock Mass they snatched a gaudy pearl necklace from
that silly hick mentioned here (pointing to the paper) who had
the bad taste to walk around half-choking herself?"

"It's obviously not your fault; but they weren't talking about
you in the paper."

"Not me personally, but I feel they're alluding to me when they
talk about the corps to which I belong."

"What corps is that? You don't belong to the militia."

"The honorable judicial corps."

"Only in that sense; but that's another matter."

"No, my dear lady, it is not, because when they say such things,
when they keep shouting, 'It's the judges' fault. Things are the way
they are because they're pardoning dozens of bandits each day!'
Or when they shout, 'They're a bunch of good-for-nothings! Criminal cases are sleeping as soundly as the just.' When they start
saying things like that, everyone who's a judge must take up the
cudgel. Furthermore, all you need is a little common sense to
realize that these attacks are absurd. We're pardoning dozens of
bandits each day, are we? Let's just suppose it's the truth. Well
then, how can you say criminal cases are sleeping soundly? If
there are daily pardons, obviously the criminal cases are not
sleeping soundly. On the other hand, if the criminal cases are

sleeping soundly, that's unjust, so how can you say they are sleeping soundly as the just? These reporters are a bunch of idiots
who don't know what they're talking about."

Don Felix reached the depths of resorting to the minutiae of
dialectic in order to give vent to his anger; he moved from one
point to another; he complicated and confused matters; but that
didn't bother him at all; what was important for him was to cut,
to split, to chop, and to smash, just like a stampeding buffalo in
the jungle.

"You are right about that," answered his wife. "The paragraph
is very badly written."

"You admit I'm right?"

"Indirectly; but don't get upset over such a small matter. Do
your duty; don't pardon the guilty, work diligently, and just let
the world go on spinning."

"I already do all that, woman, without your telling me. I don't
need anyone to prod me. But what I'll never do will be to let the
world just go on spinning."

It occurred to Otilia to reply, "Well then, stop it!" But fearing
that Zendejas wouldn't know how to take her little joke, she just
smiled and said aloud:

"What are you planning to do then?"

"Send the editor of this paper a very harsh letter telling those
awful reporters what's what."

"I wouldn't do that if I were you, Felix."

"Why not, wife?"

"Because I think it would be like stirring up a hornets' nest."

"Well, I could handle it. I'd beat the nest and the hornets too!"

"I'm sure you would, but you couldn't get away without being
stung."

"A few stings wouldn't bother me."

"In that case, then, don't worry about what the papers say or
how they exaggerate."

Her observation precluded any reply; Zendejas felt trapped and
he couldn't come up with a good response. Therefore, changing
his tactics, he shouted:

"What makes me most indignant is knowing that not just
women but also full-grown men are claiming to be victims of the
criminals. How can that be! Don't they have any guts? Why don't

they defend themselves? It's understandable that timid females get things snatched from them and end up complaining; but men, big strong men! . . . That's really grotesque."

"But what can you do to stop some quick hand from pulling your watch or your wallet out of your pocket!"

"For strong hands, there is no such thing as quick hands. Nobody has stuck his hands in my pocket, and I pity the man who dares to try it! He'd pay dearly for it. My clothing is as sensitive as my skin, and if anything so much as brushes against me, I throw out my hand, and it's caught, held, then crushed to smithereens."

"But what if you were surprised in a deserted street by armed thieves?"

"Nobody surprises me. I'm always on my guard, keeping an eye out for anything and everything. I'm fully aware of who's in front of me, who's at my side, and who's behind me; where he's got his hands and what moves he's making. . . ."

"But what if you're coming around a corner?"

"I never do that haphazardly the way most people do. Instead, before I turn the corner, I step down off the sidewalk so I've got a good view of both sides of the street corner. . . . Plus I never forget my revolver, and if necessary, I keep my hand on the handle in plain view, or inside my pocket."

"I pray you won't find yourself put to the test."

"Oh, quite the contrary. I wish I had the chance to teach those troublemakers a good lesson. I'm sure they'd never want to try anything again! If every man would defend himself and fight back against these criminals, this 'plague,' which the press says is devastating the city today, would already be over and done with."

Otilia said nothing, but she did say a few prayers to herself, in hopes that her husband would never be attacked, because she didn't want him to get hurt, and she didn't want him to hurt anyone else either.

That's how the after-dinner conversation ended.

Next on the agenda: Zendejas got up and went to his room to take his usual little afternoon nap, because he couldn't do without it if he wanted to keep a clear head on his shoulders. You see, he had the unfortunate habit of eating well and digesting badly.

Actually it is quite common in the human species for appetite and indigestion to rule on equal terms.

Meanwhile Otilia got busy putting the food away in the icebox and giving some orders to the servants.

II

As soon as Zendejas found himself in his bedroom, he closed the door and the window, to keep the light and noise from bothering him; next he took off his jacket and vest; then he put his watch on the nightstand, where he could consult it from time to time, so as not to oversleep; he unbuttoned his pants to give his ample stomach plenty of room to expand, for it grew abruptly after the intake of food. After that, he stretched himself out lazily, half dizzy from the pleasant feeling of drowsiness creeping over his encephalic mass.

The animal mechanism of that respectable official was well disciplined. Of course, since the person who controlled it was endowed with extraordinary *energy!* Don Felix always did exactly what he demanded of himself, and no more, and he expected the same from everyone else, by golly! Even his sleep was subject to his will, and when he said he would *sleep for twelve hours,* he snored away for half the day; but when he decided to rest for five minutes, he'd open his eyes after a twelfth of an hour, or at the most, one or two seconds later. Naturally! Everything is subject to a man's will; it's just that men lack *energy.* He was one of the few *energetic* men around. He never let himself be led by the tide nor did he let himself be caught with his guard down and everyone who had to deal with him soon realized that, because as far as he was concerned there were no valid excuses, compromises, or halfway measures: everything was strictly business, straightforward and to the point. By golly!

As proof of all this, he leaped out of bed half an hour later than he had intended; which nobody suspected, and which will be consigned to the archives of history until the end of time. Nevertheless, knowing within himself that he had slept beyond what he had planned put him in such a dreadful mood that he got up as though possessed, threw on the clothes he had taken off, and quickly (but carefully) buttoned up the ones he had left undone so as to facilitate the expansion of his abdominal organs. Then he grabbed his revolver and hat and left the room, with the angry face typical of a man of strong character who wouldn't put up with anyone's looking askance at him or even slightly touching his coat.

Otilia, who had gone up to the adjoining room to make sure the children didn't make any noise and was waiting there so she could say good-bye when her husband left, couldn't help remarking:

"You've slept a little more than usual today."

"Exactly what I intended," answered Zendejas. "No more, no less."

"I am glad that you were able to rest, you were tired."

"Who told you I was tired? I could work twenty-four hours a day without feeling the least bit tired."

"Yes, you're a very strong man."

"Whenever I see those spoiled brats of the new generation, they just make me laugh: they're all so feeble and depraved. Not like me. There's real muscle here. . . ."

And flexing his right arm, he used his left hand to point to the sinuous mountain of his well-developed biceps. After that he pinched his thighs, which he thought were like bronze, and he ended up by striking a few strong blows on his chest, which protruded like that of a wet nurse. That tangible display of his physique filled him with vanity and helped calm his bad mood; so by the time he and his young wife had walked slowly to the front hallway, he had already forgotten the delay incurred thanks to the god Morpheus.

"Well, see you later, Otilia," he said to his wife, as he lovingly squeezed her hand.

"See you later, Felix," she answered lovingly. "Don't come home late . . . you know we live on the outskirts and times are bad."

"Don't worry about me," replied the judge confidently.

"Try not to walk by yourself."

The judge responded to her advice with a kind of snort, because it wounded him that his wife didn't think he was brave enough to handle even the giant enemies of Don Quixote. Aloud, all he said was:

"Take care of the children."

He set out down the street immediately, while Otilia stayed by the door, watching him with loving eyes until he turned the corner. Then the young woman went in and continued with the usual daily chores which took up most of her time; for she was an extremely meticulous housekeeper. Her only worry was what time Zendejas would be coming home because the street where they lived was so isolated, and there had been so many assaults that she just couldn't relax.

Meanwhile, propelled by his contrary nature which continually buoyed his spirits, and also by the belligerent pride that filled his conceited person, Don Felix went along saying to himself: "That was some advice Otilia gave me! Don't come home late, and make sure not to walk by myself. . . . As if I were a timid, scared little boy! It looks like she doesn't know me very well. . . . I'm not afraid of either shadows or ghosts, and as for men, I'm as much a man as any of them. . . . Well now, so my wife won't offend me like that again, I'm going to teach her a lesson by returning home late, alone, and by the most deserted streets . . . and if anyone dares to get in my way, I swear I'll strangle him, or slap his face, or kick him in the pants, or I'll kill him. . . ."

He was so engrossed in visualizing a possible attack and the different degrees of effectiveness of his own various defense tactics, that, without realizing it, he was acting out with energetic and unconscious gestures the exploits he planned to perform; he'd cup his right hand, stretch it out in front of him, and then shake it vigorously, as though he'd caught the culprit by the scruff of his neck; or he'd throw punches in the air, as though there were faces all around him just asking for it; or, raising his legs up high, one after the other, he'd kick furiously at parts (which may not and should not be mentioned) of the human anatomy belonging to the figures who paraded through the limbo of his feverish imagination.

Anyone who saw him acting in that wild fashion without any bugles announcing the imminent arrival of the enemy would have declared him a raving lunatic and not what he really was: a fairly sane, though high-strung, judge. Fortunately, however, the street was deserted, and there was nobody to witness his unbridled mime; so he was able to arrive at the courthouse with his usual dignity and be greeted by the employees as respectfully as ever.

Seated at his desk, he set to work with great determination and gave his attention to studying several cases that were at the sentencing stage, in order to polish them off by means of brilliant decisions through which both his incomparable acumen and his never sufficiently appreciated *energy* would shine. And he became so absorbed in his task that time passed without his noticing it; the sun went down and night fell, but even then he went on, showing no signs of fatigue or boredom; rather, he continued to work with the same persistence, in spite of the dim, red light which the supreme government had put at his disposal since there were only two incandescent light bulbs in the main office, and they were so old that they had lost their brightness and looked like dying cigarette butts inserted in glass globes hanging from the ceiling. Fortunately, the judge had eyes like a cat.

Another judge, equally industrious, who had also stayed late reading tedious briefs and scribbling notes, came to distract the judge from his work at about eight o'clock:

"You sure are hard at it, partner!" he said.

"That's what you have to do to keep up with the work," answered Zendejas.

"I'm the same way, partner."

"We have to silence those who slander us. They say we're lazy, and we've got to prove we're not by our actions."

"I agree. . . . But listen, old pal, don't you think we've worked enough for now and that we're entitled to a little amusement, as a reward for all our hard work?"

"You're right, partner," answered Don Felix, stretching and yawning. "It's time to put this aside."

"And go to The Principal to see the first show."

"Excellent idea," agreed Zendejas.

The invitation struck him just right. With his mind made up to go home late, alone, and by the most deserted streets (to prove to his better half that he wasn't afraid, that he didn't even know what *that* was, and that he was hardly aware of *such a thing* from hearsay), he took advantage of this opportunity to kill time and show up at home sometime after midnight. Therefore, within a few minutes he had put away the cases and the lawbooks in their respective places, washed his face, put on his hat, gone outside with his colleague, and headed for the old theater.

Both judges argued at the box office over who should pay; but Zendejas, who wouldn't tolerate anyone's disagreeing with him or placing obstacles in his way, got to buy the tickets. And so, the two dignified magistrates pompously entered the temple of happiness and took seats down front, where they could have a better view of the actresses. They also provided themselves with good pairs of opera glasses, which throughout the show never left their eyes, so that they were able to enjoy looking at the vaudeville stars and chorus girls at such close range, it almost seemed they could reach out and pinch them.

The show consisted of clever repartee, laughter and cavorting, lively singing and dancing, off-color jokes, and clapping and shouting as if there were no tomorrow. Those two good gentlemen, who were not really as good as they seemed, enjoyed the suggestive pranks on stage until they could barely stand it. They roared at the most risqué scenes of the zarzuelas with such uncontrollable laughter that it sounded like the crashing of two heavily flowing waterfalls side by side; totally uninhibited, they communicated to each other their delight in all they saw; they applauded gleefully, stamped on the wooden floor with their feet, and called for encores of the raciest songs and the most alluring dances like a couple of schoolboys on vacation who find everything new and fun and full of excitement.

It was after nine-thirty when they left the theater, and they went straight to the Bach Restaurant where they dined slowly and sumptuously until well after eleven when they left to go to their respective homes. After walking together for a few blocks, they cordially took leave of each other:

"See you tomorrow, partner. Sleep well!"

"Good night, partner. I hope the meal won't upset your stomach!"

Zendejas stationed himself on the corner of 16th of September Street to wait for the trolley that would take him to his destination, which was the Colonia Roma; but his luck was so bad that, one after another, he watched all the trolleys from the Plaza de la Constitución go by—all, that is, except the one he needed. We said he had bad luck, be we ought to correct ourselves, because the truth is, he felt just the opposite, that things were turning out

just the way he wanted because now he would get home even
later, which was exactly what he had intended all along, owing
to his own pride and petty sense of honor as a brave and daring
man.

It was shortly before midnight when he got aboard a Tacubaya
trolley, having finally decided that, according to his plans and
intentions, it was time to go home. When he got off at the Insurgentes stop, it had already struck twelve; he crossed Chapultepec
Avenue and turned down one of the wide streets into the new
neighborhood; on purpose he walked along choosing the newest
and most deserted streets, where there were few houses and absolutely no pedestrians. He had a vehement desire to meet up with
some nocturnal thief so he could teach him a lesson, but not a
living soul appeared in that deserted place. Nevertheless, true to
his habits, and so as not to be taken by surprise by whoever
might come along, he continued to take all the precautions that
prudence advised; and in addition to never letting his hand leave
his pistol, not for even a second, he would step down off the
sidewalk before reaching each corner, look in all directions, and
listen intently to every noise.

He'd been walking quite a distance when, as he crossed one of
the most isolated avenues, he caught the sound of heavy, uneven
footsteps coming from the opposite direction, and soon he saw the
dark silhouette of a suspicious-looking man appear at the next
intersection. When the man moved into the circle of light projected
by the street lamp, Zendejas noticed that he was elegantly dressed
and, furthermore, that he was lit to the gills. So drunk was he
that he wasn't only staggering, he was reeling; but when Don Felix
saw him approaching, he said to himself: "I don't like the looks
of this ostentatious display of drunkenness. Not at all! Who knows
. . . he might be pretending so he can catch me off guard. Keep
an eye on him, Zendejas!"

And he didn't take his eyes off him, as the saying goes, even
though, it seemed that, broad as the street was, it wasn't broad
enough for the wild gyrations executed by that off-balance body.
Plus the fact that in his mad joy, he was singing in a mournful,
off-key voice:

> Grace! Grace!
> My, what a face!

or else:

> Sal! Sal!
> My, what a gal!

or else:

> Fay! Fay!
> Oh, how gay!

It almost made you think that that priest of Bacchus had just come from celebrating some of the mysteries of the cult — in the company of one or more priestesses — and for this and other reasons, as he went on his way, he seemed to be recalling some of their names, the charm of the flames ("the sparks of the dames"). Surely that was another reason why he was taking so many steps in the wrong direction now, in addition to all the others that he must have taken previously!

Don Felix formulated his plan as soon as he analyzed that fellow's irregular pattern. . . . Not so irregular! . . . Taking into account geometry as well as morals and public safety! If he really *was* drunk, he had to avoid being surprised. He watched, and each time the man strayed from a straight path, he'd say to himself:

"Now he's going to the right? Well then, I have to go right! . . . Now he's going in a straight line? Well, I guess I have to be ready to go either way! . . . Oh, hell! He sure does change direction quickly! . . . No, the important thing is not to let him run into me! . . . He's going to run into me! . . . No, he's not going to run into me! Great Scott!"

As Don Felix spouted out this last exclamation, the drunk, or whatever he was, had already run into him, like an erratic asteroid colliding with a well-behaved planet in a fixed orbit. How could the accident have occurred, in spite of Zendejas's precautions? Neither the judge nor the drunkard ever managed to find out.

The fact was that at the least expected moment, Don Felix found himself face to face, or rather, stomach to stomach, with the living pendulum who had seemed to be everywhere at once in his stubborn efforts to escape the perpendicular line.

"Idiot!" screamed Zendejas, full of anger.

"What? What?" muttered the fellow slurring his words. "Why don't people watch where they're going? . . . They're always getting in the way! . . . They won't let a man pass! . . .

"Go to hell!" shouted Don Felix again, trying to disentangle himself from that inert body that prevented him from moving.

With some effort, by pulling his foot back and poking with his elbow at the mass on top of him, Zendejas finally freed himself of the weight and left the drunkard a short distance away, half standing and half falling. Then the judge grabbed him by the lapels of his jacket, and as punishment shook him furiously several times, finally letting him go so he could follow the laws of his dangerous instability. The poor man spun around on the heel of one shoe, threw one foot into the air, almost fell, then raised his other foot, went through a few more strange contortions like a doll bending over and straightening up, and then finally managed to recover some semblance of balance. As he continued on his way, it seemed his slow, laborious, zigzagging walk had never been interrupted.

No sooner did he find himself free of Zendejas's grasp than he recovered his good humor, and he continued droning in his off-key voice, which was occasionally interrupted by a hiccup:

> Don't kill me, don't kill me
> With pistol or dagger!

Don Felix also continued on his way, enraged like a wild bull, as much from the bumping as from that miserable wretch's making fun of his terrible, unleashed anger. But suddenly a strange thought occurred to him. What if that drunk was really a thief? And what if that stumble had been planned, just a strategy used to rob him without his noticing it? No sooner had he thought this than he found himself checking his watch pocket. . . . And, in fact, he found . . . that he did not find his silver pocket watch or the gold-plated watch chain from which it hung.

Having discovered this, he turned around quick as a flash and, let's not say he ran, but rather he flew, after the enigmatic person, who was moving away as best he could with his stumbling feet and noisy steps punishing the asphalt of the public streets.

As soon as he was within reach, the judge grabbed him fiercely by the scruff of his neck with his left hand, just as he had gone over it in his mind as he was leaving his house, while, with his right hand, he took out and started to flaunt his relucent, redoubtable revolver.

"Halt, villain!" he shouted.

"Again? . . . Don't yank so hard!" mumbled the man.

"You're no drunk, you're faking it!" shouted Zendejas.

"Oh! Oh! Police! Police!" roared the drunk.

"If only they *would* come," yelled Don Felix, "so they could lock you up down at headquarters, assign a judge, and put you on trial."

"Put me on what?"

"Trial."

"Well then, in that case, my friend, I'll try. What can I do for you?"

"Hand over the watch."

"What watch do I owe you?"

"The one you took from me, you thief."

"This watch is mine, all mine . . . with an automatic winder and it chimes the hours."

"Chimes? What kind of humbug is that! You're a member of the band."

"I'm not a musician. . . . I'm a property owner."

"Sure, someone else's property."

As this conversation took place, the drunk was trying to defend himself, but he didn't have enough strength; at the same time, Don Felix didn't know what to do with him, because with each step the drunk would fall on top of him or slip out of his hands, to one side or the other, on the verge of collapsing. Exasperated, the judge dropped him violently and without mercy, and when he had him on the ground, he pointed his weapon at the drunk's chest, and again demanded:

"The watch and the chain, or I'll blow your brains out!"

All the drunk could exclaim was:

"Holy smoke! . . . Holy smoke! . . . Holy smoke!"

He wouldn't, or couldn't, move either hand or foot. Zendejas took the only option left to him: with his own hand he transferred the watch and chain he found on the drunkard's person into his own coat pocket. After that, he stood up and gave the man on the ground a few more kicks, and he was about to set out for home again when he heard the man muttering through his clenched teeth:

"Holy smoke! . . . This guy must be one of the members of the band!"

"So you still haven't had enough? . . . Well, take that! . . . And that! . . . Thief! . . . Villain! . . . Scoundrel!"

Each one of these exclamations was punctuated with furious kicks, which the judge showered on the stranger, who did nothing but mutter at each blow:

"Holy smoke! . . . Holy smoke! . . . Holy smoke! . . .

Tired at last of administering a beating without glory, Zendejas left the drunk (fake or real, he couldn't figure out which) and resolutely resumed his walk home, while the stranger staggered to his feet, after several unsuccessful attempts, and gradually moved away with a mixture of long and short steps, forward and backward, and leaning alarmingly like the Tower of Pisa, now toward right, now toward the left.

III

Otilia didn't know how to interpret her husband's not arriving on time, and she was extremely upset. Rarely did ten o'clock find Zendejas away from home, so that when the young woman realized it was past midnight and her husband had not yet returned, she imagined the worst, as always occurs in cases like this.

"Surely something has happened to him," she was saying to herself. "There's no other way to explain why he's out so late. . . . Could it have been the robbers? . . . And if they recognized him and he defended himself, as he most certainly would, they might have wounded him, or maybe even killed him. . . . Heaven forbid! . . . May the Mother of God be with him!"

With thoughts like these in her head, she went on crocheting the never-ending quilt which she meant to use as a bedspread in the master bedroom, but every now and then she'd stop moving her agile, feverish fingers, either to wipe away a tear as it slipped down from her eyelashes, or else to make the sign of the cross in the direction of the street from which the absent man was supposed to come. . . . What would she do if she were left a widow? There was no other man in the whole world like Felix. . . . And her poor children? There were three of them, and they were still so young. Savings? They had none; his salary was small, and they struggled to make ends meet. They lacked many of the necessities of life and they had learned to do without them. There's no use; they'd be forced out into the street; she'd have to give up the

house, which, though it was on the outskirts, was comfortable and
gave them privacy; she'd end up renting a flat in some apartment
house. How dark and dingy those flats are! The children would all
get sick there.

Her imagination continued working ceaselessly. She'd have to
take in sewing jobs to support herself and the children. What a
miserable life! The children would be running around dirty and
barefoot; they wouldn't be able to attend a private school; they'd
have to go to the public ones, with all the riffraff; and they'd
learn bad habits; they'd get mixed up with the wrong kind of
people; it would be their undoing. . . .

She went so far along that road of speculative adversities that
she saw herself in total poverty, a widow, and all alone in the
world. Black clothing covered her attractive body, and the black
veil of widowhood draped over her shoulders. How well the outfit
looked on her! It gave her an exceptionally intriguing appearance.
Would she have suitors again? . . . If her charm and youth were
taken into account, perhaps she would, but then again, considering her poverty, perhaps not. . . . Many men might be attracted
to her, but only ones with bad intentions. . . . And would she give
in? Or wouldn't she? . . . Human nature is so frail! Women are so
sentimental! And men are so evil! Let nobody say, "Never shall I
taste of this water." Oh, Lord!

And Otilia burst into tears without really knowing whether
she was crying so hard because of the tenderness she felt over Don
Felix's unfortunate and premature death, or whether it was because she'd been left a widow or because of her orphaned children
and their wretched clothing or because they were being ruined
in the public schools; or maybe it was seeing herself, so young
and attractive dressed in black, or because she had no admirers,
or because she saw herself being seduced by perverted men who
would take advantage of her inexperience, her sensitivity, and her
helplessness . . . but especially her sensitivity! . . . Because she
knew herself well: she was extremely sensitive. That was her weakness; that was the slit in the plate of armor that was her virtue.
. . . If anyone were sharp enough to notice it, that's where he'd
plunge his dagger, and she would be a lost woman. . . . Oh, how
horrible! How wretched is the fate of a young beautiful, unprotected woman with a sensitive heart. . . . Why couldn't she have

been born with a piece of stone for a heart? . . . That organ
would be her downfall; she knew it, but there was nothing she
could do about it.

Fortunately the doorbell rang several times just as the young
woman's wild imagination pushed her over this precipice and
engulfed her in the depths of those calamities, passions, and
adventures from which it was not possible, no, to emerge with
dry eyes. . . . Fortunately, the ringing of that little electric bell
came just in time to save her, pulling her out of that abyss of
gloom and tragic events into which she had thrown herself headlong. The young woman's dangerously sensitive heart jumped for
joy repeatedly when it discovered it was free from all those risks:
widowhood, black clothing, the death of her children, the feeling
of being stalked, slipping, and falling into disgrace. In contrast,
the doorbell sounded joyous and triumphant. It chimed in that
special way, which said Zendejas was returning victorious and
happy, for having put the morning star in its place, or for having
taken a swipe at some insolent bum, or for having given some
busybody a good kick in the pants. Otilia sensed all that as she
ran to open the door, rejoicing that she was free from all the
misfortunes, snares, and traps that the terrifying future seemed to
hold in store for her.

Don Felix, in fact, did come in beaming over the results of the
battle he had just won against the clever thief who had accosted
him on a public street, and over the recovery of his watch and
chain.

"Felix!" exclaimed Otilia in a faint voice, as she threw herself
into his arms. "What have you been doing? Why are you so late?
You've had me terribly worried."

"Don't be upset, wife," answered Zendejas. "Nothing happened
to me, and nothing ever could. I could go for a walk alone anywhere in the Republic, and no one would dare touch me."

"Where have you been?"

"At work, at the theater, at the restaurant. . . ."

"It never dawned on me that that's where you'd be. Meanwhile
I've been sitting here alone, unable to sleep, and imagining the
most horrible things. . . . I've been so upset thinking about you. . . ."

The young woman was careful not to tell Don Felix about the

mourning clothes, the sensitivity of her heart, and the seduction which she had seen looming on the horizon.

Holding hands, they went into the living room.

"Wait a minute! You've been crying!" exclaimed Don Felix, drying the tears running down her face with his handkerchief.

"Of course, because I love you so much and I was so afraid for you!" she answered, leaning her head on the judge's shoulder.

"You silly little girl," Zendejas went on lovingly. "There's no reason to be alarmed."

"Felix, can I ask you a favor?"

"Whatever you want."

"Don't come home late anymore."

"I promise, dear. There's no reason to now, since I've accomplished what I set out to do."

"What do you mean, Felix?"

"I had a good scuffle with a robber . . . one of those guys the press talks about so much."

"Really? How did that happen? . . . Tell me, Felix," asked the young woman, extremely interested.

Zendejas, complying with his wife's request, told her about his recent adventure, not exactly the way it happened, but embellished with minor incidents and details which, though not really factual, helped a great deal to bring out the fierceness of the battle, the strength of the champion, and the brilliance of the victory. The young woman, fascinated, listened to his story and felt proud that her husband was such a strong, brave man; but, like all loving and delicately sentimental wives, she couldn't help worrying about the injuries that her husband's robust body might have suffered in such a terrible encounter, so she asked the judge in her sweetest voice:

"Let me see your hand: it's not swollen, is it? . . . You didn't twist your ankle, did you?"

"Both are still firm and strong," replied Don Felix with obvious satisfaction, waving his clenched fist and shaking his right foot in the air.

"Thank Goodness!" exclaimed his wife, heaving a sigh of relief.

"It just goes to prove what I've been trying to tell you all along," Don Felix went on. "If all the men around here with hair on their chests would do what I did when attacked by those thieves, if they'd beat them up and get back the stolen goods, this plague of robberies would soon be over. . . ."

"Maybe you're right. . . . So . . .that thief took your watch and chain away from you?"

"Yes, by pretending to be drunk. He fell on top of me like a dead man, and while I was trying to get him off me, he swiped them without my feeling a thing."

"Those pickpockets certainly are quick. . . ."

"Yes, they are, but fortunately I soon realized what must have happened. . . . If it weren't for that, I'd have lost a couple of my most prized possessions."

As he said this, Zendejas took them out of his pocket to look at them gloatingly. Otilia stared at them too, curious and interested, as is always the case when one looks at things that have been lost and are now found; but upon seeing them, instead of rejoicing, both husband and wife found themselves confused. Why?

"But, Felix. . . . What have you done?" asked the frightened Otilia.

"Why do you ask, woman?" replied the judge, hardly knowing what he was saying.

"Because this watch and chain are not yours."

"How can that be?" responded Zendejas in a feeble voice when he realized that his wife was right.

"You can see for yourself," she went on, taking both objects in her hands to examine them closely. "This is a gold watch, and yours is made of silver. . . . It looks like a repeating one."

The young woman pushed a spring on the side, and a clear, silvery little bell gave the time in quarter-hours and even minutes.

"And look, it has initials on the lid: A.B.C.; they must stand for the owner's name. . . . It's a very good watch, quite valuable."

Zendejas was left in a daze, and he felt drops of sweat covering his forehead.

"And the chain," his wife went on, continuing her analysis, "is wide and expensive looking, made out of fourteen-carat gold mesh, and look at this charm at the end of it: made of the same metal and shaped like a little elephant, with ruby eyes and fine enameled feet and ears."

With that painful evidence in front of him, Zendejas lost almost all the cold as well as the hot blood in his veins, turned white as a sheet, and murmured with supreme anxiety:

"That makes me a thief, one of the band!"

"That's crazy! . . . Don't say such things."

"Yes, I am a half-wit, a stupid ass," repeated Don Felix, feeling desperate.

And, in keeping with his impetuous nature, he started to beat himself soundly on the head with his fists, until his wife stopped the savage attack by grabbing his wrists.

"Let me go," he said indignantly. "I deserve this, and more. Let them throw me in jail. I'm a criminal . . . an impostor of a judge."

"No, Felix, it's just that you made a mistake. It was night time, the man was drunk, and he fell on top of you. Anybody would have thought the same thing."

"Plus, I've lost my watch," added Zendejas.

"That's right," said his wife. "How do you explain that?"

The judge perceived a ray of hope. In the course of passing judgments and handing down sentences, he had grown accustomed to deducing, inferring, or subtilizing.

"I've got it!" he exclaimed, cheerful and calm once again. "The drunk was a fake, and he'd robbed that watch and chain from somebody else, before he ever ran into me. . . . Then he robbed me of mine, and in trying to get back the one that belonged to me, I hit on the pocket where he'd put the other's possessions; but he got away with mine."

The explanation seemed unlikely; Otilia stood and thought a moment.

"Could be," she murmured at last. "Are you sure you were wearing your watch?"

"I never forget it," replied the judge firmly.

"Well, even so, let's go check your room."

"There's no point in it."

"But there's nothing to lose. . . ."

"As you wish."

And the couple adjourned to Zendejas's bedroom, where they found the judge's silver watch, with his inexpensive plated watch chain, lying peacefully on the nightstand, exactly where their owner had left them when he climbed into bed to take his nap.

Felix felt terrified, as if he had seen Medusa's head.

"It's here," he murmured painfully. "So that gentleman (he no longer called him a drunk or a thief) has been robbed by this hand. Not the slightest doubt remains."

Otilia, grieved, made no reply, and her husband went on:

"What happened can be easily explained now: that man, who must be rich and carefree was out on a binge in that neighborhood. . . . He had more than a few too many, and he was really drunk. I mistook him for a thief and carried off his property. . . . I stole at night, on a public street, and while armed. . . . I'm ruined. . . . First thing tomorrow I'm turning myself in to the authorities: a good judge begins his work at home."

"There's no way," objected Otilia, horrified at the thought. "It would make you look ridiculous, a regular Don Quixote."

"Why would it be ridiculous?" asked Zendejas, angrily.

"Because we'd never hear the end of it: how you had it out with some old man in a drunken stupor who couldn't even defend himself, and what a great hero you are!"

"No, that's not fair because on numerous occasions I have demonstrated that the weak and the strong are all alike to me, and that I fear no one, no, not even Lucifer himself."

"But people are mean, especially the envious ones."

"You're right about that: the envious ones, the envious ones! repeated Zendejas. "All my brave friends envy me," he went on, thinking to himself. "And how they'd love to take advantage of the quid pro quo, to make me the laughingstock of the city!" Then he continued aloud: "But what should I do then? I certainly can't keep someone else's property!"

"Let me think a minute," replied Otilia, concerned. ". . . Let me see those initials again. . . , A.B.C. What was the man like? Describe him to me, Felix."

"Let me see. . . . Kind of on the old side, heavy, almost as heavy as I am, clean-shaven."

"With glasses?"

"I think so, but he lost them in the scuffle."

"Listen," the young woman continued thoughtfully. "Couldn't it be Antonio Bravo Caicedo? . . . A.B.C.: the initials fit."

"You mean the rich and famous one? Why, his name is known all over this city!"

"That's the one."

"There's no way, dear."

"Why not?"

"Because he's such a serious person; his conduct is beyond reproach; wherever he goes, he's always accompanied by his daughters, who are very beautiful; and, wait a minute, if I'm not mistaken, he's. . . ."

"He's what, Felix?"

"An active member of the Temperance Society."

"That doesn't matter," answered his wife. "Men are so contradictory, and so evil. . . ." (She was thinking, at that point, about the dangers of her widowhood.)

"You're right about that; they certainly are evil." Out of instinct the judge refrained from saying *we* certainly are evil, no doubt because he remembered the mental and visual excesses he had just committed at The Principal.

Anyway, there followed a long discussion between husband and wife, in which they examined the situation in detail and analyzed all suppositions from every possible angle; and the more they dug into the matter, the more they suspected that the watch and chain belonged to that elderly, rich, and hypocritical Antonio Bravo Caicedo; a thousand indications proved it, a thousand small details made it undeniable. Who would have thought it!. . . That such a respectable man would really be so unrespectable! How true is the saying "The flesh is weak. . . ." But Bravo Caicedo was fat. . . . What a complicated affair! . . . From the looks of things one might conclude that the fatter the flesh, the weaker it is. . . .

Having solved for the unknown quantity, or rather, for the unknown man, they still needed to find a way to return the stolen goods. Should they send the objects to the owner's house? No, that would mean compromising him, exposing him, embarrassing him. . . . And then, even though the most likely explanation was that that august person was the clumsy drunkard of the encounter, nevertheless, there was still the possibility that some other individual was the true owner of the jewelry. Antonio Bravo Caicedo (A.B.C.), it's true, had a monopoly on the production of pulque, but not on the first three letters of the alphabet.

IV

In short, after looking at it, considering it, and wracking their brains over it, the honorable couple resolved that the property in question should be deposited at the courthouse with Zendejas, and that he should place an announcement about it in the newspapers, one written so cleverly that it would neither denounce the judge himself, nor bring the rich old man's disgraceful behavior into public view.

Having decided upon this course of action, Don Felix, being an honorable man, refused to lay his head on his pillow before relieving his conscience of its heavy burden. The document had to be sketched out and written in its final form so that the next day it would be ready to send to two or three of the evening papers when their doors opened. The judge worked feverishly, made several rough drafts, consulted Otilia, crossed out, made changes, added, erased, and scribbled away on several sheets of paper, until, finally, when it was almost dawn, he finished the arduous task of giving shape to the little paragraph, whose definitive version was conceived in the following words:

NOTICE

This morning shortly after the office opened, a gold watch was left at this courthouse. Self-winding, with a chain, also of gold, and topped by a small elephant charm with ruby eyes and black enameled ears and feet. The watch contains the initials A.B.C. inside its cover. The serial number is 40180, and it is a Longines. All this is being made known to the public so that the objects can be claimed by their owner. They were placed in the hands of the undersigned judge, along with a paper containing an exact and specific description of the person from whom the jewelry was removed by mistake. There is mention of the street, the hour, and other pertinent details.

But the repeated publication of those lines proved useless. To this very day, as this story is being written, nobody has shown up to claim the watch and chain; perhaps because Antonio Bravo Caicedo is not the owner of the jewelry, or, maybe because he is, but wishes to remain anonymous at all costs. So that, if any reader's initials are A.B.C., if he was walking through the Colonia Roma that night and had had a bit too much to drink, if he had something to do with Grace, Fay, or Sal, and, finally, if he lost these objects in a street scuffle, he knows that he can go to claim them at the courthouse where they are on deposit.

— Translated by Roberta H. Kimble

COMMENTARY

"Unclaimed Watch" successfully combines the caricature of Judge Zendejas and a rather well-developed plot. A disciplined, hardworking, brave, short-tempered, and supremely egotistical man, Don Felix is clearly a close relative to some of Charles Dickens's picturesque characters. Nonetheless, López Portillo y Rojas, by using a well-measured quantity of ridicule, succeeds in humanizing the monster and does not let him degenerate into a clown. A very important role in this process is played by the apparently naïve young wife who has learned to handle her difficult husband with the utmost discretion.

The principal instrument in the creation of Judge Zendejas is the narrator's picturesque language. The detailed description of the irascible "blasting cap" in the first paragraph belies his "happy" name, Felix. From time to time throughout the story, the narrator, in keeping with the Realistic style, seems to address the reader directly with parenthetical remarks: "when he discussed something, he never discussed it, he preached it dogmatically"; "Zendejas lost almost all the cold as well as the hot blood in his veins"; "out of instinct the judge refrained from saying *we* certainly are evil." The Realistic author, at the same time that he enjoys poking fun at his protagonist, also enjoys playing with words, that is, punning: "member of the band," "the fatter the flesh, the weaker it is," and one or two others lost in translation.

The story's burlesque tone combines with all the ominous antecedents to produce an ending that is both unexpected and logical. The news items about crime in the city, the judge's bravado, and the wife's sincere concern prepare us for a tragic ending, but the tone of the whole story will not permit it and therefore the judge's egregious mistake and his consequent embarrassment and attempt to excuse himself are completely justifiable.

The judge's victim, A.B.C., also comes in for his share of criticism. A member of the Temperance Society, he obviously allows himself to accept more than an occasional drink. Furthermore, his wealth has been accumulated through the monopolistic production of pulque.

In addition to describing his characters physically and morally before setting them in motion, López Portillo y Rojas, in typically Realistic fashion, also mentions some very specific local details which lend verisimilitude to the story in spite of its caricaturesque features: the trolley cars, the Plaza de la Constitución, the Colonia Roma, and 16th of September Street, Insurgentes and Chapultepec Avenues, and the Tacubaya district.

Besides being a representative Realistic story, "Unclaimed Watch" is also typically Mexican: the quick pace, the picaresque humor, the popular flavor, the emphasis on action, and the portrait of the self-effacing and understanding wife. Although the following story is equally representative of Realism, many of the differences may be ascribed to the different countries of origin.

Tomás Carrasquilla

(1858-1940)

Colombian. He was born in a small town in the province of Antioquia to a wealthy, aristocratic family. His law studies were interrupted by the Revolution of 1874. With the exception of two visits to Bogotá (1896 and 1915-16), he spent his entire life in Antioquia where he served as secretary of his local court and later judge. He began writing relatively late in life. Classified for many years along with the other Spanish American Costumbristas who followed in the footsteps of the Spaniard Pereda, Carrasquilla has recently been "discovered" as one of the first truly artistic novelists and short story writers of Spanish America. Although his characters and settings are those of his region, his works transcend those of the other Costumbristas because of his linguistic artistry and the greater subtlety of his character portrayal. His complete works include the historical novel, *La marquesa de Yolombó* (1928); three regional novels, *Frutos de mi tierra* (1896), *Grandeza* (1910), and *Hace tiempos* (1935-1936); and several long short stories. "Little Saint Anthony," although written in 1899, was not published until 1914, in Spain in a collection of six stories by Carrasquilla entitled *El padre Casafús*.

LITTLE SAINT ANTHONY

Aguedita Paz was one of those members of the human race devoted to God and his holy service. Slightly past the age of becoming a nun when the religious passion came over her, she tried to turn her house into a simulated convent, in the decorative sense of the word, her life into that of an apostle, and all, all of herself she gave to the affairs of the church and the sacristy, to the conquest of souls, for the greater honor and glory of God, offering advice to people whether they needed it or not and spending less time on things like aiding the poor and visiting the sick.

Back and forth, from her little house to the church and from the church to her little house, she would spend her time, day

67

after day, what with appeals and the usual saintly petty intrigues over church repair funds, altar arrangements, the mending and patching of ecclesiastic garments, the caring for the images, sweeping clean, and adorning every spot related to the divine service.

In such idle pursuits and campaigns, she became intimately enmeshed in friendly relations with Damiancito Rada, a very poor, young snot-nose, very devout and the chief altar boy in processions and ceremonies, upon whom the good lady bestowed an affection that was both tender and extravagant, something quite rare, to be sure, among unmarried and devout people. Damiancito provided her with both a trusty right arm and a shoulder she could cry on, he helped her in sweeping and dusting, in the cleaning and polishing of candelabra and censers; all by himself he handled the albs and folded the corporal cloths and other trappings used during Mass; he was in charge of getting the flowers, moss, and forage for the altar, and he was the chief helper and adviser on high holy days when the bells pealed loud, when much wax and tallow melted on those altars, when so many floral wreaths, so many bright-colored ornaments were hanging on the various walls.

On top of all this, Damiancito prayed constantly and set a fine example, receiving communion faithfully, studying diligently in and out of school, with an obedient, sweet, and modest character; rejecting the noisy games of the mobs of kids, and very prone to burying himself in *The Saintly Nun, Love of Christ in Practice,* and other books no less pious and uplifting.

Such unusual as well as edifying qualities were the reason why Aguedita, thanks to her clairvoyance and intuition, came to see in him not a mere Mass-saying priest, but a doctor of the church, at least a bishop who in the not so distant future would shine like a star of wisdom and saintliness for the honor and consecration of God.

The bad part of it was the poverty and ill-fortune of the predestined one's parents and the nonaffluence of his patroness. But she wasn't one to give up such lofty ideals: this misery was the net with which Old Nick wanted to thwart the flight of that soul meant to soar serenely, serenely, like a dove, to its God; but no, Old Nick would not succeed. And deliberating constantly on how to break out of this diabolical net, she began to train Damiancito in weaving and crocheting; and the disciple turned out to be so intelligent, that at the end of a few months he raffled off a night-gown with branch patterns and arabesques which were a delight to the eye, all wrought by Damián's delicate hands. No less than fourteen one peso bills neatly stacked resulted from that creation.

After this came another, and then a third, which brought the sum of three condores. Such profits aroused Aguedita's ambition and boldness. She went to the priest and asked permission to hold a bazaar in Damián's benefit. The priest agreed and Aguedita, armed with his consent and an abundance of eloquence and seductive charm, found support among the town's upper class. Her success was a dream come true that almost drove the good woman crazy in spite of her usually being very level-headed; but sixty-three pesos!

The prestige that came with all that money; the fame of Damián's virtues that by now spread throughout the parish, the almost ascetic and decidedly ecclesiastic ugliness of the beneficiary formed a halo around him, especially among the women and the pious in general. "Aguedita's little priest" everyone called him, and for a long time they spoke of nothing but his virtues, his austerity, and his penances. The little priest fasted on Ember Days and Lent before the Mother Church ordered him to because he had barely turned fifteen; and not stuffing himself at noon and snacking every once in a while as is the practice nowadays, but rather with an eminently Franciscan frugality, and there were times when his fasting was so extreme that it became a transgression. Aguedita's little priest would wander through the pastures in search of solitude, to talk with his God and spout a few paragraphs from *The Imitation of Christ*, a work that in these lonely walks he always took along with him. Some women woodcutters said that they had seen him at the bottom of a ravine, kneeling, looking mournful and striking his chest with a grinding stone. There were some who maintained that in a very remote and wooded site, he had made a cross from a willow tree and on it he would crucify himself naked for hours on end, and no one doubted it since Damián would return haggard and emaciated from the trances and crucifixions. In short, Damiancito became the parish saint, the lightning rod capable of saving so many sinners from divine fury. For the beggar women, it became necessary for their small contributions to pass through Damián's hands and one and all asked to be included, at least partly, in his saintly prayers.

And since virtue's perfume and the odor of saintliness have always held so much magic, Damián, in spite of being a weakling of a brat, shriveled and skinny, with a pale aged face, with a shrunken chest and hunchbacked, with a physique that made him seem more like a fetus than a young boy, appeared good-looking and interesting. He was no longer just the little priest: he became "Little Saint Anthony." They called him Little Saint Anthony and that was the name he answered to. "He's so adorable!" —the older women would say when they saw him leaving the church, with his tiny steps, with patches on the elbows of his jacket and patches on the seat of his pants, but oh, so neat and proper, "So beautiful, his way of praying, with his eyes closed! The religious fervor of this child is positively edifying! That humble and gentle smile. Even in the way he walks you can see his saintliness!"

Once the money was collected, Aguedita didn't rest on her laurels. She met with the boy's parents, arranged his clothes, received communion with him in a Mass which they had devoted to the Holy Trinity for the success of their enterprise; she put the finishing touches on him and gave her final bit of advice, and one very cold January morning, Little Saint Anthony was seen leaving in a new outfit, astride Señor Arciniegas's little old mule, almost lost in the factory foreman's heavy blankets, escorted by a peddler who carried his suitcase and to whom he was entrusted. Aguedita, closely related to several very wealthy women in Medellín, had taken the necessary steps beforehand to see that her protégé was well recommended; therefore, when he arrived at the Del Pino sisters' boardinghouse, he found everything set for him.

The saint's seductive power manifested itself immediately and the Del Pino sisters, Doña Pacha and Fulgencita, just couldn't do enough for their ward. Master Arenas, the tailor of the seminary, was called in immediately to take the would-be seminarian's measurements, to make him a cassock and cloak with great precision and economy, and a Carmelite brown flannel suit for important occasions and street processions. They got him the sash, a three-cornered hat, and shoes; and Doña Pacha presented herself in the Seminary to recommend Damián to the Rector. But, oh misfortune! he couldn't get a scholarship: they were all committed and there was a superabundance of candidates. But this did not discourage Doña Pacha; upon returning from the Seminary, she went to the Cathedral and implored the Holy Spirit to help illuminate her in this predicament. And she was illuminated. What happened was that it occurred to her to meet with Doña Rebeca Hinestrosa de Gardeazábal, a very rich and pious widow to whom she painted the little saint's indigence so convincingly that she obtained lunches and dinners for him. Radiant with joy, Doña Pacha flew home, and in the twinkling of an eye she converted a small storage room near the false door into a little cell for the seminarian; and although they were poor, she offered to do his wash, give him free lighting, afternoon snacks, and breakfast.

Juan de Dios Barco, one of the boarders, the one most spoiled by the ladies for his exemplary Christian devotion, whom no one could beat when it came to the Apostle's Creed or matters relating to Saint Vincent, made the boy a gift of some of his clothes that were in very good shape and a pair of boots, which were a bit too big and loose around the heels and a bit worn out. Juan got him the textbooks and other school supplies at a great discount at the Catholic Bookstore, and lo and behold our Little Saint Anthony all decked out as a friar.

Three months had not gone by, and already little Damián was lord and master of his landladies' hearts as well as those student boarders and each and every other guest who sought shelter in that all so popular boarding house in Medellín. It was contagious.

What most charmed the women was that even temper; that smile, that angelical look that didn't even fade while he was asleep; there was something there, something indefinable, something resembling a stunted and sickly angel, which made even his rotted and uneven teeth gleam like ivory or mother-of-pearl; that spiritual light that filtered through his eyes, through the pores of this so ugly boy who was at the same time so beautiful. It got to the point that he became a necessary part of the women's life. Gradually, thanks to the pleas which emerged from the most tender

fibers of his landladies' little souls, Damián began staying sometimes for lunch sometimes for dinner; and finally the day arrived
when a message was sent to Señora de Gardeazábal informing her
that they would take complete care of their marvel.

"What is most appealing to me about this young fellow," Doña
Pacha said, "is his reserve, his discretion with us and with other
adults. Haven't you noticed, Fulgencia, that if we don't speak to
him, he won't speak to us on his own?"

"You can't say too much, Pacha, that boy's diligence! Why he
has the good sense of an old man! And his vocation for the priest-
hood! And his shyness: not even out of curiosity has he raised his
eyes to look at Candelaria."

The latter was a young girl raised by the ladies with much
prudence, manners, and the fear of God. Without elevating her
above her social station in life, they nevertheless spoiled her as
though she were their own daughter; and since she wasn't bad
looking and in such a house there are always dangers lurking, the
ladies, even if they regarded her as a closed flower garden, they
didn't let her out of their sight for an instant.

As soon as Doña Pacha found out about her student boarder's
talent as a fringemaker and weaver, she put him to work, and soon
several wealthy and socially prominent women had him making
antimacassars and slipcovers. Once the news spread through
Fulgencia's réclames, he was commissioned to make a bedspread
for a bride. . . . Oh! There the ladies did indeed see the fingers
of an angel! On that delicate and immaculate netting, similar to
a heavenly spider's web, there appeared bunches of white lilies
with petals and unusually serious and dignified, coquettishly so,
butterflies flew like the souls of virgins. The washwoman's services
were not needed; from those miraculous fingers came that dazzling
purity to watch over the nuptial bed.

From the price of the bedspread Juancho was able to get him
a suit of very good cloth, custom-made shoes, and a Tyrolean hat
with a deeply creased crown and an elegant brim. Enthused over
his finery, Doña Fulgencia made him a bow tie from the remnant
of a woman's blouse that she happened to have around. On it she
stamped, perhaps subconsciously, the enchanting design of the
aforesaid butterflies. In this attire, little Damián looked ethereal,
like a revelation from the celestial worlds; and as though this attire

could influence the flights of his priestly mind, he grew, not only in gaudiness and elegance, but also in his knowledge of the intricacies of the Latin tongue. Crouched over a small crooked-legged table, he translated from Latin to the vernacular and from the vernacular to Latin, at times Cornelius Nepote and a bit of Cicero, other times Saint John of the Cross, whose Hispanic serenity flowed in some beautiful hyperbatons worthy of Horace. Perhaps little Damián would be a second Caro in time.

The head of his chaste little bed was a hodgepodge of lithographs and medallions, of certificates and holy pictures, each one more religious than the next. In one spot, Our Lady of Perpetual Help, with her skinny face that so resembled Damián's; in another Martín de Porres, who armed with his broom represented Heaven's blacks; in another, Bernadette, kneeling before the white apparition; and in still another, ciboria amidst the clouds, bunches of grapes and sheaves of wheat, and the Scapulary of the Sacred Heart, in high relief with its large spurts of blood standing out against the circle of white flannel.

Doña Pacha, by dint of her enthusiasm over the virtues and saintliness of her little priest, perhaps due to her own religious devotion, was on the verge of falling into a schism: she greatly admired the priests and especially the Rector of the Seminary, but she couldn't accept the idea, not even if it were wrapped in the holy wafer, that they wouldn't give a scholarship to someone like Damián, that poor little boy with no earthly, material wealth; but so rich in spiritual values. The Rector might know a lot, as much if not more than the Bishop; but neither he nor his Grace examined him nor much less understood him. Surely if they had done so, they would have desubsidized the most brilliant student and replaced him with Damiancito. The Church of Antioquia was going to have its own little Saint Thomas Aquinas, that is if Damián didn't die, because the boy did not seem to belong to this world.

While Doña Pacha fantasized about the moral superiority of Damián, Fulgencita began spoiling the weak body that held that soul, a body hardly comparable to the aforementioned bedspread. Hot chocolate without flour, concentrated and foamy, that hot chocolate in which the sisters took delight in their hours of sybaritism, was served to him in a cup as large as a cowbell. The best of

victuals, the Sunday delicacies with which they regaled their
boarders, made their way in friarly rations, to the seminarian's
tummy which gradually began to expand. And as for that bed
which was formerly a sewing room bench, there were now delicately soft pillows and mattresses, and starched white sheets and
pillowcases changed weekly, and tender loving innocent designs
on the quilt, and fringes made of yarn soft to the touch. The
most loving mother wouldn't go through and examine the under-
garments of her only son as did Fulgencia with his shirts, his socks,
and that other article of clothing that maiden ladies may not
name. And although the señora was somewhat squeamish and not
fond of getting involved with anyone else's clothing, clean or dirty,
the seminarian's little wardrobe never even remotely caused her
any bit of repugnance. But how could it when, quite the contrary, handling his clothes made her imagine that she smelled the
fragrance of purity that must be given off by the smooth wings of
angels. Famous as a cigar maker, she fashioned for Damiancito
some long, aristocratic ones, which were for him to smoke while
alone in his brief moments of leisure.

Doña Pacha, with the same degree of devotion to the little saint,
would often get alarmed at Fulgencia's treats and indulgences,
which seemed to her somewhat sensual and anti-ascetic, such as
the aforesaid delicacies and the cigars. But her sister would reply,
arguing that a young boy as studious and dedicated as he needed
very good food; that without good health there wouldn't be any
priests, and that they could not begrudge such a healthy soul a
few insignificant choice morsels and much less the aroma of a
cigar; and just as that soul was itself nourished on celestial sweetness, so the poor body that enveloped it could taste something
sweet and flavorsome, especially since Damiancito offered up all of
his pure and innocent pleasures to God.

After the rosary with the holy mysteries in which Damián served
as the chorus, with his eyes completely closed, in deep concentration, ecstatic, kneeling on the rough Antioquian mat that covered
the floor, after this long dialogue with the Lord and his Holy
Mother, when the landladies had finished their early evening
chores, Damián would read to them from some mystic book,
generally by Father Faber. And that nasal voice, breaking its way
through those chipped teeth, created the tone, the accent, the

mystic character of a sacred oratory. Reading *Bethlehem,* the poem of the Lord's infancy, a book in which Faber put his whole heart, Damián made such faces, such looks, that to poor Fulgencia he seemed to be transformed or something like that. More than a few tears came to the good woman's eyes during these readings.

And that's how the first year passed, and, as was to be expected, the results of the exams were stupendous; and so great was the ladies' affliction when they thought that Damiancito would leave them during the vacation, that he himself decided not to return to his town but rather to remain in the city, in order to review the courses already completed and to prepare for the next ones. This he accomplished to a T; between texts and lace, between nets and notebooks, praying at times, frequently meditating, he spent the school vacation; and he went outside only on necessary errands and to do the shopping whenever it occurred to the ladies and perhaps to go on evening walks to the more solitary outskirts of the city, but only because the ladies made him.

The next year passed; but not before that precocious saint's prestige, knowledge, and sublime virtue had increased considerably. But Doña Pacha's holy hatred for the Rector of the Seminary did not pass: not a day went by without her roasting him for the injustice and favoritism which was running rampant and was prevailing even in the seminaries.

At the end of that year, about the time that the exams were ending, since it occurred to Damián's parents to visit Medellín, and since Aguedita was going to attend the December spiritual exercises, the landladies concluded, with parental permission anticipated, that Damián would not spend this year's vacation in his home town either. The ladies came to that conclusion not so much because they would miss him, but because of the extreme poverty and wretched life of his parents, simple and innocent peasants, for whom feeding their son, even for a few days, would surely constitute a severe hardship. Damián, this obedient and submissive boy, agreed to everything with the meekness of a lamb. And his parents, after blessing him, left, with tears of gratitude for the kindness of Damián's landladies and for God who had given them such a son.

They! poor countryfolk, a pair of starving nobodies, parents of a little priest! They couldn't believe it. If the Almighty would only let them live long enough to watch him chant Mass or raise the host with his hands, the body and blood of our Lord Jesus Christ. Very poor, they were very fortunate; but whatever they had, a little land, the cow, the four plants in the little vegetable patch, they would give it all up, if it were necessary, to see Damiancito ordained. Well, and how about Aguedita? She swelled up with celestial joy, the glorification of God stirred within her whenever she thought of that priest, who was practically of her own making. Even the local parish, considering itself Damián's home town, was beginning to feel the winds of glory, the holy breeze: it was the little Padua.

Doña Pacha was unyielding in her idea about the scholarship. With the tenacity typical of charitable, zealous souls, she looked and looked for the right opportunity: and she finally found it. It so happened that one day, around the month of July, Doña Débora Cordobés, a kindly and religious woman from the same town as the Rector of the Seminary and his close relative, appeared in the house, as if fallen from the sky, and as a boarder. No sooner did Doña Pacha find out about the relationship than she entrusted Doña Débora with the scheme. The latter offered herself enthusiastically, promising to obtain from the Rector whatever she wanted. The very same day she requested, by phone, an interview with her illustrious relative and to the Seminary she went the next morning.

Doña Pacha stayed behind gargling her Te Deums and Magnificats, converted into a thanksgiving machine; Fulgencita ran to pack his suitcase and arranged all the little priest's belongings; not without getting a little depressed over their separation from this child who was the object of veneration and respect in the house. The hours went by and there was no sign of Doña Débora. Who did come was Damián with his books under his arm, as neat and smiling as always.

Doña Pacha wanted to surprise him with the news, holding it back until everything was definitely arranged, but Fulgencita couldn't wait and gave him some hints. Such was the tenderness of that kind soul, so grateful, so indebted was he to his landladies, that in the midst of his happiness Fulgencita noted a certain anguish, perhaps sadness at the thought of leaving them. As he was going out, Fulgencita tried to stop him; but the poor lad couldn't stay, he had to go to the Plaza de Mercado to take a letter to the muleteer, a very interesting letter for Aguedita.

No sooner does he leave than in walks Doña Débora. She arrives red in the face from hurrying in the heat. As soon as they hear her, the Del Pino sisters pounce on her, they question her, they try to pull the great news out of her with a jerk. Doña Débora sits down on a divan exclaiming:

"Let me rest a minute and I'll tell you."

They get closer, they surround her, they besiege her. They don't breathe. Somewhat recovered, the messenger says:

"My dears, the little saint has taken you in! I spoke with Ulpianito. He hasn't been to the Seminary for over two years. . . . Ulpianito didn't even remember him!"

"Impossible! Impossible!" the two ladies shouted in unison.

"He hasn't returned. . . . Not even once. Ulpiancito inquired with the associate Rector, with the assistants, with the professors, with everyone at the Seminary. No one has seen him. The porter, when he heard about the inquiries, said that that boy was given to bad habits. Some say they've seen him following evil ways. Some stories have it that he has even been seen with Protestants. . . ."

"It's a mistake, Miss Débora," Fulgencita interrupts furiously.

"They just don't want to give him the scholarship," Doña Pacha exclaims angrily. "Who knows what kind of mix-up they've gotten that poor little angel into!"

"You're right, Pacha," Fulgencita declares. "They've fooled Miss Débora. We're witnesses of that boy's progress; he himself has shown us his monthly certificates and his examination grades."

"But then, ladies, I don't understand, either Ulpiano has deceived me," Doña Débora says, bewildered, almost hesitating.

Juan de Dios Barco appears.

"Listen, Juancho, for the love of God," Fulgencita exclaims as soon as she spies him. "Come over and listen to these wild inventions. Tell him, Miss Débora."

She sums it up in three words; Juancho protests; the ladies stand firm; Doña Débora gives in.

"They can't do this to me," Doña Pacha screams, running to the telephone.

Tilin . . . tilin. . . .

"Operator. . . . The Rector of the Seminary! . . ."

Tilin . . . tilin. . . .

And they start in. She doesn't hear, she doesn't understand; she gets mixed up, she disagrees, she chokes up; she gives the phone to Juancho and listens trembling. The serpent that coils around Nuñez de Arce slithers by her. Juancho says good-bye, hangs up the receiver, and becomes lost in thought.

And that dull Germanic face, like that of a Zouave soldier of Christ, turns to the ladies; and with that unalterably simple voice, says:

"That lit-tle ras-cal sure had the wool pulled over our eyes!"

Fulgencia collapses into a chair. She feels that she is crumbling apart, that she is melting morally. She doesn't suffocate because the boiler bursts out sobbing.

"Don't cry, Fulgencita," Doña Pacha shouts, her voice hoarse and quivering. "Leave him to me!"

Fulgencia gets up and grabs her sister by the arms.

"Don't say anything to him, dear. Poor boy!"

Doña Pacha sends her reeling with a tremendous blow.

"Don't say anything to him! Don't say anything to him! Just let that little brat come here now! Jesuit! Hypocrite!"

"Don't, Pacha, for God's sake. . . ."

"No one can make a fool of me, not even the Bishop! Bum! Rake! Deceiving poor old ladies; stealing from them the bread that they could have given to a poor deserving person. Oh, wicked man, sacrilegious communion taker! Inventor of tests and certificates! He might even be a Protestant!"

"Look, dear, don't go and say anything to that poor boy. At least let him have lunch."

And each tear fell like a drop of ice down her wrinkled cheek.

Doña Débora and Juancho intervene. They beseech her.

"All right!" Doña Pacha finally decides, raising her finger. "Fill him up with lunch till he bursts. However, don't give that shameless rascal any of our hot chocolate. Let him drink sugar water or he can leave without any dessert."

Straightening up, swelling with indignation, she runs to serve lunch.

Fulgencita looks up at Saint Joseph, her favorite saint, appearing to ask him for help.

A few moments later, the little saint arrives, very humble, with his faint angelical smile a bit more accentuated.

"Go eat lunch, Damiancito," her trembling voice showing both tenderness and bitterness.

The young fellow sat down and ate of everything, chewing nervously, not looking up at Fulgencita, not even when she served him the unusual cup of sugar water.

When he finished the last gulp, Doña Fulgencia offers him a handful of cigars as she often did. Little Saint Anthony accepts them, lights up, and goes to his room.

Once the lunch was over, Doña Pacha went to look for the Protestant. She enters his room and doesn't find him there; not his suitcase, nor even his bedcovers.

That night they call Candelaria to prayer and she doesn't answer; they look for her and she doesn't appear: they run to her room, they find it open, her trunk empty. . . . They understand everything.

The next morning, when Fulgencita was straightening up the scoundrel's room, she found a filthy slipper of the kind he used to wear; and as she picked it up, there fell from her eyes, a tear like the divine forgiveness of the crime, a tear that was clear, bright, and from deep down within her.

— *Translated by Antonia García*

COMMENTARY

Carrasquilla clearly reveals a greater artistic consciousness than his predecessors. What is important about this story is not so much the plot with its unexpected ending but the creation of the small town, and later the provincial city atmosphere at the end of the nineteenth century. The author succeeds in capturing the religious air and the slow rhythm of life in Colombia at that time by using just the right style. His sentences tend to be long owing to the use of series of parallel adjectives or phrases; compound phrases and even compound words (some of which are lost in translation: "rodillijunto y patiabierto" and "ojicerrado"); repetition of the same word; and alliteration.

Besides the soporific rhythm, Carrasquilla's prose is noted for its popular flavor based on picturesque and archaic expressions and a variety of diminutives and other suffixes.

Carrasquilla creates the ultrareligious aspect of provincial life in order to mock it. Although the ending is unexpected, there are previous hints for readers already familiar with Carrasquilla's writings. The title of the story, referring to Saint Anthony of Padua, indicates that the protagonist is going to be the patron saint of unmarried women, that is, adored by them. No matter how much Damián's passive attitude may justify his nickname, there are some occasional words and phrases that make the reader suspect that there is something more than religious love involved. The most direct insinuation — which is also ironic — of the ending occurs in Fulgencia's statement to the fact that Damián has not even looked at Candelaria. The following paragraph then goes on to explain how the ladies watched over the good-looking Candelaria in order to protect her against the potential "wolves". Actually, interplay between Damián's ascetic ugliness and vocation and sensuous love continues up to the end of the story: the bedspread for the bride, the somewhat sensual and anti-ascetic indulgences lavished by Fulgencia; Damián's concern about the possibility of leaving the ladies' house for the Seminary; and the very interesting letter he sends to Aguedita.

In order to capture the violent impression produced by the discovery of Damián's crime, Carrasquilla abandons the descriptive narrative and presents the action through a combination of short sentences and paragraphs with very realistic and picturesque dialogue. Another example of dualism may be found in the many references to both saints and classical writers from the Romans Cicero and Horace to the Colombian Miguel Antonio Caro and the Spaniard Núñez de Arce.

Although the plot is not extraordinary, the way it is developed and written places it in artistic terms above the other realistic stories. The pleasant tone, the more-or-less middle class characters, the fondness for the picturesque, the detailed descriptions, and the Regionalism in general correspond to nineteenth-century Realism. Carrasquilla's artistic consciousness, which distinguishes him from his contemporaries in other countries, may be attributed to his own genius but it may also be due in part to the Colombian tradition of having the greatest number of writers adept at handling the niceties of the language. It is in this respect, and not in the matter of pronunciation, that Colombians are said to speak the best Spanish in all Spanish America.

Manuel González Zeledón (Magón)

(1864-1936)

Costa Rican. He was born in San José and studied at the National Institute. At an early age he entered government service and went to Bogotá in 1890 as vice-consul. After a few years in the National Congress, he was named head of the Bureau of Statistics. In 1906, disillusioned with politics, he moved with his family to the United States where he continued to reside for the next thirty years. President Ricardo Jiménez named him consul general in New York in 1910 and in 1932, at the beginning of his third non-consecutive presidential term, he appointed him ambassador in Washington.

Magón's literary works are limited essentially to Costumbrista sketches. Along with his cousin Aquileo J. Echeverría (1866-1909), the author of the volume of Costumbrista poetry entitled *Concherías*[1] (1905), Magón, whose early prose sketches first appeared in print in 1895, is considered one of the founders of his country's literature. "The 'Clipse" was published in the newspaper *La República* in San José on August 29, 1897. It was included in the collection of Magón's stories and sketches *La Propia y otros tipos y escenas costarricenses* (1912).

THE 'CLIPSE

This isn't just a tale. It's a true story that flows from my pen just as it came bursting from the lips of Mr. Cornelio Cacheda, who is a good friend of mine, like the many I have on God's good earth. He told it to me about five months ago, and the wonder of it so surprised me that I thought it a crime not to pass it on so that scholars and observers can study the case with the care it deserves.

Perhaps I could go into a serious analysis of the matter, but I'll reserve that for after I've heard my readers' opinions. Anyway, as for the wonder mentioned above, here goes, plain and simple.

[1]*Concho* in Costa Rica is the word for the typical small farmer.

Cornelio came to see me and brought with him a couple of two-and-a-half-year-old girls, born in the same "litter," as he put it, called María de los Dolores and María del Pilar—both as blond as a stalk of wheat, white and rosy like a ripe peach, and pretty as "pictures"—that's one of Cornelio's expressions. There was a marked contrast between the childlike beauty of the twins and the truly irregular features of Cornelio—ugly as can be with dark brown skin and coarse, down to his dirty fingernails and the cracks in his heels. Naturally it occurred to me right away to ask him who was the happy father of that fair pair. The old man cackled with pride, twisted his prune face, wiped away the saliva with the back of his hairy hand, and answered:

"Well, I'm their daddy, believe it or not! They don't look much like me, but their mama really ain't so bad lookin', and fer the pow'r of ar great God, nothin's impossible."

"But tell me, Cornelio. Is your wife a blonde or do they look like their grandparents?"

"Nope. In the whole family there's not a one that's been like them Siamese cats or fair-haired pups. We've all been half-breeds."

"Well, then, how do you explain that the girls were born with that hair and coloring?"

The old man let loose with a loud guffaw, set his arms akimbo, and gave me a look of supreme disdain.

"What are you laughing about, Cornelio?"

"Well, didn't I hafta laugh, Mr. Magón, when I see a poor, ignorant feller like me, a hick farmhand, knows more 'n a man like you, one that everyone says is so edgeecated and well read, so's ta even write laws fer the Presydent and his ministers?"

"O.K. then, explain it to me."

"Now you'll see how it was."

Cornelio took a good-sized lump of molasses out of his saddle-bags, gave a piece to each little girl, and drew up a stool, on which he eased himself down, gloating over his impending triumph; he blew his nose noisily, covering each opening with the respective forefinger while blowing violently through the other; he rubbed with the sole of his right paw, cleaning the floor; he wiped off his hands on the inside of his jacket, and began his explanation with these words:

"Ya know that 'bout this time in March, three years ago, there was a 'clipse, where the whole middle of the sun turned black; O.K., well 'bout twenty days before, Lina, my wife, turned up pregnant with those little girls. From then on, there was this real uneasiness got hold of her; it was amazin'. There was no stoppin' 'er. She'd leave the house day 'n night, always lookin' up at the sky; she'd go ta the empty lot, the brook, the thicket fence, 'n always accordin' to her fancy 'n that illness, so there weren't nothin' ta do but let 'er have 'er way. She'd always been full of cravin's, every time she's pregnant. Ya see, when the oldest was born, it was just the same; like one night she woke me up late at night 'n made me go look fer male plumtree shoots for her. Guess it was better ta go than have the poor little thing born with its mouth open. I brung her the shoots. After that there were other cravin's, but I'd never seen her so full of 'em as with these little girls. Well, now ya see, like I's sayin', spyin' at the sky, day 'n night, it got a hold of her, 'n the day of the 'clipse I'd been out in the brambles by the fence since the crack of dawn.

"So's not ta wear ya out with the story, things went on like that till these little girls was born. I don't deny that seein' 'em so blond and fair wasn't an uphill struggle fer me, but ever since it seems like they've brung God's blessing. The schoolmarm likes 'em 'n sews all their clothes for 'em; the politician gives 'em the loose change in his pockets; the priest asks me for 'em so's ta put 'em by the altar with pure linen petticoats 'n sequins fer Corpus Christi 'n the days of Holy Week; they take 'em out in the procession, puttin' 'em next ta the Nazarene 'n the Holy Sepulcher; fer Christmas Eve, they change 'em inta real purty dresses 'n put 'em by the manger, next ta the Holy Family. 'n all the expenses come outta the organizers' pockets, 'n they always give 'em a big coin, or even paper money, or some other good present. Blessed be ar God, who brought 'em ta serve Him from out of an ugly daddy like me! . . . Lina's even so stuck up 'bout 'er little girls that she just can't stand it when people don't praise 'em. She's already had some good fights with the old bags of the neighborhood over these orn'ry little kittens."

I interrupted Cornelio, afraid that his panegyric would never end and I put him back on the track.

"O.K., but what about it?"

"What about it? Well, don'cha see that it's 'cause their mama saw the 'clipse that they're blondies? Din'cha know that?"

"No, I didn't, and I'm surprised you figured it out without having any education."

"Why try 'n fool ya, Mr. Magón; I wasn't the one as figured out the riddle. Ya know that Italian builder that made the church steeple in town? A big guy, with reddish hair 'n real white skin, who's been eatin' at ar house fer four years?"

"No, Cornelio."

"Well, he's the one as explained the 'clipse thing ta me."

— *Translated by Roberta H. Kimble*

COMMENTARY

Manuel González Zeledón (Magón) was the founder of Costa Rican Costumbrismo, the most dominant characteristic of that country's literature from its inception to the present day.

Magón's Costumbrismo may be attributed to several national factors, but it is also closely linked to Spanish American Costumbrismo in general, which was particularly fashionable throughout the second half of the nineteenth century. Its great popularity in Costa Rica stems from the homogeneous character of the country. For Magón, as well as for today's writers, the tremendous differences that exist in the social hierarchy of other Latin American countries are not found in Costa Rica. Because of the absence of a long university tradition and the emphasis placed on primary and secondary education, the cultural hierarchy is also less extreme. Geographically, the barriers between metropolitan writers and small farmers are easily surmounted. Therefore, when Magón wrote his Costumbrista sketches, he was basing them on his own experiences. Magón and those who have followed in his footsteps can associate and identify with the common man without any difficulty. Nevertheless, Magón himself admitted that he became inspired to write through his contact with Colombian literature: "In 1889 I went to Bogotá and while there the Costa Rican government named me vice-consul. There I began to write mainly about Costa Rica, and I published in several newspapers under different pseudonyms. During the two and a half years I spent in Bogotá, I made close friends with several outstanding Colombian poets and prose writers: Jorge Isaacs, Jorge Pombo, Santiago Pérez Triana, Roberto McDouall, José Asunción Silva, Julio Flórez, Samuel Velázquez, Rivas Frade and Rivas

Groot and others whose names have faded from my memory. This contact was very useful as a literary education and helped me form my own style."[1]

Of all of Magón's sketches, "The 'Clipse" is the one that is closest to being a true short story. The well-known "La propia" is basically a skeleton of a novel while his other pieces are really more Costumbrista sketches in which the author has such a good time describing the setting, the Costa Rican people and their peculiar customs and speech at the end of the nineteenth century that the plot is often neglected to the point of disappearing. Even in "The 'Clipse," the story's humor springs to a great extent from Cornelio's picturesque speech, but it does not quite predominate over the climax. Upon reading the final sentence, the reader becomes aware of the story's tight unity. Only at that time does the significance of the protagonist's name become clear. Both "Cornelio" and "Cacheda" suggest Spanish words for "horns," the symbol of the cuckolded husband. The author's active participation in the story helps make it more credible. Magón's erudition and his picaresque sense of humor act as foils for the protagonist's simpleness, but the author consistently treats him as a friend, albeit somewhat condescendingly. The eagerness to preserve for posterity the picturesque language of his protagonist demonstrates a bond of national identification between the two. For Magón and his followers, the roots of Costa Rican nationalism are not to be found in pre-Columbian archaeology nor in the heroic exploits of the conquest and the War of Independence, but rather in the daily lives of their less educated neighbors.

The brevity of "The 'Clipse," in tremendous contrast with the preceding stories by Carrasquilla and López Portillo y Rojas, established a tradition that the majority of Costa Rican short story writers are still following, the most notable examples being Joaquín García Monge (1881–1958), Carlos Salazar Herrera (1906), and Alfonso Chase (1945).

[1]Letter from Magón to José María Arce dated March 21, 1933, and printed in José María Arce, *Cuentos por Manuel González Zeledón* (San José: Universidad de Costa Rica, 1947), p. 232.

Naturalism

Naturalism, which in Europe replaced Realism, coincided with it in Spanish America without losing its own identity. Because of the improved intercontinental communications at the end of the nineteenth century, Spanish American authors were able to read Zola's works almost at the same time as they were being published in France. Although the hegemony of Naturalism in France lasted only seventeen years (1870–1887), in America it did not decline until after 1910. It began first and most strongly in Argentina, in the 1880s, with the publication of Eugenio Cambaceres's novels *Música sentimental* (1882), *Sin rumbo* (1883), and *En la sangre* (1887). Since Buenos Aires was the largest Spanish American city with a very European atmosphere, it is not unusual that Naturalism should have had its greatest impact there and that it should have lasted forty years: *La gran aldea* (1884) by Lucio V. López, *Irresponsable* (1889) by Manuel Podestá, *La bolsa* (1890) by Julián Martel, *Libro extraño* (1904) by Francisco A. Sicardi, and *Historia de arrabal* (1922) by Manuel Gálvez. In other countries, Naturalism left its mark on only a few works by individual authors: Magariños Solsona and Carlos Reyles in Uruguay; Augusto D'Halmar in Chile; Carlos Loveira in Cuba, and Manual Zeno Gandía in Puerto Rico. Even in Mexico, with a novelistic tradition dating back to the beginning of the nineteenth century, Federico Gamboa was the only outstanding adherent of Naturalism.

Because it tends to be held in contempt by current critics, Naturalism in Spanish America has still not been properly studied. Through a lack of understanding, many critics have not clearly separated it from Realism. Both in its world view and in its method, Naturalism, far from resembling Realism, respresents its negation. Rooted in the positivistic philosophy of Comte, the evolutionary theories of Darwin, and the experimental medicine of Claude Bernard, the Naturalist author looked upon man as an aggregate of atoms whose actions were determined exclusively by animalistic needs. The protagonist did not stand out as a caricature; rather he was overwhelmed by the weight of heredity and environment. The Naturalist rejected picturesque themes located in pleasant settings; he was determined to probe into the festered sores of society with a merciless scalpel. The protagonist, transformed into a *bête humaine*, lived in the worst conditions. The favorite themes were alcoholism, prostitution, adultery, and the misery of the masses. If it is true that the Naturalists chose sordid themes to prove their theory, it is no less true that all of them, by exposing human degradation, were advocating a greater understanding of the problems and of the conditions responsible for this degradation.

Firm believers in determinism, the Naturalists constructed their works according to a pseudoscientific method. The descriptions were detailed to the point of copying every minutia of reality. Since the protagonists' actions were governed by their antecedents, the authors felt obliged to present complete panoramas of their family backgrounds, as well as of their environments before making them actually come to life. Preoccupied with these "clinical studies," the Naturalists were less interested in dialogue than the Realists.

Because of the foregoing traits, the small number of Naturalistic short stories is not surprising. The scientific pretensions of the authors prevented them from fitting all their raw data within the confines of a short story. Guy de Maupassant, of course, is the exception, but the majority of the Naturalists preferred to conduct their "experiments" in long novels, and in many cases, in series of novels.

Nevertheless, as one of many anomalies in Spanish American literature, two of the authors represented in this section have the distinction of being among the first Spanish American authors to be known principally and almost exclusively as short story writers: Javier de Viana and Baldomero Lillo.

Javier de Viana

(1868-1926)

Uruguayan. He was one of the first professional short story writers in Latin America. After spending his childhood on a ranch, he went to Montevideo to study medicine and applied for a scholarship to study psychiatry in Paris. Failing to receive it, he turned to journalism: "I have been a ranch owner, a cattle and sheep breeder, a cowboy and even smuggler; a revolutionary many times, a candidate for Congress on several occasions, always an unsuccessful one. . . . I have been, above all, a journalist. . . ."[1]

After losing his modest holdings in the Revolution of 1904, he went to Buenos Aires with the hope of supporting himself by writing short stories. Pressured by editorial deadlines, the quality of his work deteriorated. He died poor and alone on the outskirts of Montevideo. Author of two novels, *Gaucha* (1899) and *Gurí* (1901), and more than a dozen volumes of short stories, among them *Campo* (1896), *Macachines* (1910), *Leña seca* (1911), and *Yuyos* (1912). "The Loves of Bentos Sagrera" appeared in Viana's first and best volume of stories, *Campo*.

THE LOVES OF BENTOS SAGRERA

When Bentos Sagrera heard the dogs barking, he put the *mate* down leaning the *bombilla*[2] against the handle of the kettle, got up and left the dining room hurriedly to see who was coming so as to decide quickly on whatever measures might be necessary.

It was late afternoon, and it was growing dark. A strong wind was blowing from the east dragging along huge threatening storm clouds, heavy and black. At this hour and with this weather whoever was arriving at the ranch was undoubtedly intending to spend

---

[1] Javier de Viana, "Autobiography" in *Pago de deuda, Campo amarillo y otros escritos* (Montevideo: Claudio García, Inc., 1934), p. 20.

[2] A metal strawlike tube with a strainer at the end used for drinking the *mate* tea. The *mate* is also the small gourd in which the *mate* tea is served.

the night, something which Bentos Sagrera did not permit except for certain people who were close to him. That's why he was hurrying in order to reach the sheds before the stranger could loosen his horse's saddle strap and take off the saddle. His ranch was not an inn, damn it!—he had said that many times, and whoever it was could go and look for an inn, or sleep out in the open, after all, his animals slept out in the open and they were worth more than most of those ragged bums who came by asking for lodging.

On many occasions he had found himself in such straits, because his hired hands, who were more good-natured than he—sure, it was no skin off their backs if the leather harness straps disappeared!—allowed some guys to unsaddle; and then it was much harder to get them to continue on their way.

Sagrera's ranch was one of those old establishments of Brazilian origin, which abound at the border and resemble prisons or fortresses. A long building with stone walls and a flat roof; a few sheds, also of stone, in front; and on both sides a high wall with only one small door leading out to the open fields. The kitchen, the ladder, the stove, and hired hands' quarters were all enclosed within the wall.

The owner, who was short and stocky almost like a square block, crossed the patio crunching the gravel under his thick feet, encased in heavy red calfskin boots. He opened the little door cautiously and stuck out his bushy-haired head to observe how the man who had just arrived was fighting off a pack of dogs, which were barking furiously and jumping at the horse's stirrup, snout, and tail, causing it to rear up on its hind legs and back up snorting all the while.

"Down, dogs!" their master repeated several times, until he got the dogs to withdraw, one by one, to the shed, although some still sniffed suspiciously at the rider who, not completely reassured, hesitated to dismount.

"You've got your house well guarded, Bentos, my friend," said the visitor.

"Just a few dogs raised for the fun of it," answered the owner of the ranch with a marked Portuguese accent.

The two men shook hands like old pals; and while Sagrera ordered his men to unsaddle the horse and take it to the small corral, they wondered at their master's strange and unusual friendliness.

Once they were in the spacious room which served as a dining room the rancher called to one of his hands and had him bring a fresh kettle of water; and the interrupted bitter *mate* sipping continued.

The visitor, Don Brígido Sosa, was an old comrade of Sagrera, and, like him, a wealthy rancher. They were united, not so much by friendship, but by circumstances, business matters, and the mutual respect that prominent men in a given area have for one another.

Sosa owned five tracts of land in Mangrullo, while Sagrera was the owner of seven in Guasunambí, and they were both known as important personalities and were respected, albeit not loved, in the entire district and even beyond its borders. Sosa was tall and thin, with a rather dull nondescript expressionless face: one of those rural types who are born to tend cattle, hoard gold coins, and eat meat with *fariña*.[3]

Sagrera, on the other hand, was short and stocky, almost square, with hams like a hog, a neck like a bull, short arms, fat and tough like the wood of a *coronilla* tree; hands broad and hairy, feet like two irons or two huge chunks of wood. His small head was covered with thick black hair, with just a few gray strands; a low, receding forehead, large eyes, set wide apart, giving him the appearance of a beast; a long nose shaped like an eagle's beak; a large mouth, with a fleshy sensual upper lip appearing through the tangled hair of his unshaven face.

He was proud and arrogant, miserly and selfish, and he lived like most of his fellow landowners, secluded in his ranch, without any fun or affection. His wife had died more than five years ago, and since then, he alone occupied the huge house, against whose walls his shouts and curses reverberated at all hours. When somebody suggested that he should marry, he would smile and answer that as far as women were concerned, he had more than his share out in the country, and that he had not yet forgotten the bad times his "devil of a mate" had put him through.

[3] Like Brazilian *farofa*, *fariña* is fried manioc meal.

Any hired hand who heard him would shake his head and go off muttering that that "devil of a mate" had been a saint and had died exhausted from being beaten by her husband, to whom she had contributed most of what was now his fortune.

But since these things were not common knowledge and perhaps were nothing more than kitchen gossip, the rancher retained his reputation as a respectable man, most worthy of esteem, very wealthy, and although very coarse and extremely selfish, still capable of giving out one hundred percent for some unfortunate neighbor.

Sosa had come to see him about a business deal, and, anticipating great profits, the rancher from Guasunambí gave him a royal welcome. For dinner he offered him a stew with noodles, cooked giblets and *fariña,* and a lamb, plump like a fattened turkey, roasted on a spit and served with dry crackers and *fariña*. In that region *fariña* was eaten with everything and was the indispensable complement of every dish. And as a special treat, in honor of the guest, a *canjica com leite*[4] was served, which, according to the Brazilian expression, "was as unforgettable as a good dish of pork and beans."

Outside, the wind, which had traveled a great distance leaping wildly over the bald hills, furiously attacked the compact villages, and went after the fruit trees of the nearby orchard, making them bend, shaking them back and forth until it finally tore off their few remaining leaves, and moved on at full speed, propelled by new blasts that came from the east. Overhead, the clouds collided with a clamor and the rain lashed the walls of the big house and pounded furiously on the zinc roofs of the sheds.

In the dining room, Sosa and Pancho Castro—the latter was Sagrera's foreman—had finished dinner and were chatting and sipping bitter *mate* and chasing it with drinks of brandy that the foreman poured continuously.

Pancho Castro was an old Indian, with a smooth, angular face, and small, shifty eyes which were half-hidden by his wrinkled eyelids. He was a big talker who was fond of spinning yarns, although he had a limited repertoire, which he nevertheless repeated but always with different details.

[4]Grated corn, sugar, cinnamon, and coconut milk.

"It sure is rainin'!" he said. Makes me recall the time on the ranch of the late Don Felisberto Martínez, on the banks of the Tacuarí. . . ."

"Here comes a story!" exclaimed Sagrera, and the old man, without getting offended by the rancher's scornful tone, continued very seriously: "Had it ever rained! Holy Mary! The whole countryside was under water; all the ditches were full, all the arroyos were runnin' wild, and the Tacuarí was a great big lake. . . ."

He interrupted himself to brew a *mate* and gulp down a shot of brandy; then he proceeded: "It was a night jus' like this one; but much colder and much darker, really dark: ya couldn't hardly see what ya were sayin'. We had worked the whole night roundin' up the herd that was drownin' all over the place and even so, everythin' was a mess. We were soaked to the bone when we got to the kitchen, where they had a fire goin', which was a godsend. After eatin' we put the *mate* on to brew and started to tell stories. Ole Tiburcio . . . you mus' remember ole Tiburcio, Tumpamba's Indian, big as a ranch and ferocious enough to scare the livin' daylights out of ya. . . ! One heck of a man who could tame a horse like nobody else. Only once did I see him with his back on the ground, and that was with a wild, black and white horse of the late Manduca, when he got the crazy idea of gallopin' one mornin' when it had been rainin' cats and dogs, and in spite of his. . . ."

"All right, Oldtimer," Sosa interrupted with marked impatience, "leave the wild horse bucking and get on with your story."

"I'll bet he's going to come up with one we've heard a thousand times," added Don Bentos.

"Awright, if you're awready laughin' at me, I won't tell nothin'," said the old man, offended.

"Hell, let the old geezer get angry!" exclaimed his boss, and then, swallowing half a glass of brandy, leaned back in his chair and added: "Since he's acting stubborn and won't talk, I'll tell you a different story."

"Let's hear it," replied Sosa; and Don Pacho muttered at the same time that he refilled the glasses: "Yeh, let's hear it!"

The rancher coughed, rested his big hairy, apelike hand on the table, and began as follows: "This is something that actually happened to me. It was at least some fourteen or fifteen years ago. I had gotten married to my late wife, and I moved from Chuy to settle down here, because these fields belonged to her, almost all of them. During the first year I continued riding over to Chuy to look after business and also to. . . ."

Don Bentos interrupted himself, drank a little brandy, and after sipping the *mate* that the foreman handed him, he continued: "To visit a little gal I had at a ranch on the coast."

"I've heard you talk about that," said Sosa. "She was a blonde, a Brazilian."

"Exactly. She was the daughter of a ranch hand from Yaguarón. I had had my eyes on her for a long time; but her old man Don Juca, he watched over her as though she were a prize race horse and didn't give me the least little chance. But the girl had really grown fond of me, with good reason, cause I was a handsome devil who drove the girls wild, and when I stepped out on that dance floor, no one dared to compete with me.

"The old man wanted to marry her off to some blockhead policeman, and since I figured that despite having the edge on him in every respect, I was in danger of losing the race, and I didn't want to use force — not 'cause I didn't know how, but 'cause I didn't want to get into trouble — so I started to plot. Hell! I was famous for being crafty and this was the time to prove it. One day when I had gone to visit my friend Monteiro Cardoso, the scheme came to me. Monteiro was furious because someone had just slaughtered one of his cows. 'It couldn't 've been anyone else but old man Juca!' he told me.

"Old man Juca was working on Colonel Fortunato's ranch, which was next to Monteiro's, and the latter was convinced that the old man was stealing from him. I said to myself: 'She's mine!' and answered at once: 'Listen, pardner, I think that old man is a sneaky thief, and it would be good to make an example of him.'

"That's all that Monteiro was waiting to hear, and he was beside himself with delight when I promised that I myself would spy on the old ranch hand and would nab him with the goods. Here's the way it happened: one night, together with the mulatto Anselmo, we killed one of Monteiro Cardoso's sheep and buried it in old man Juca's cornfield. The next day I notified the police: they went to the patch and discovered the carcass. The old man yelled, denying everything and threatening; but it was no use:

they simply tied him up and took him off to the clink after having tanned his hide a bit with those curved whip handles."

Bentos Sagrera smiled, crossed his right leg while holding his foot with both hands, coughed loudly, and continued: "A few days later I went to Juca's house and found poor Nemensia in a pool of tears, furious at that no-good Monteiro Cardoso, who had done that just to get her poor father in trouble. I told her I had come to console her and guaranteed her that I would set him free . . . provided she treated me right. Since the blonde was kind of eager herself. . . ."

"Jus' like in the story I was gonna tell, when the late Tiburcio, the horse-breaker . . . ," said the foreman.

"It didn't take her long to open her mouth and say yes," continued Don Bentos, interrupting the Indian. "I took her to the ranch I had set up on the coast, and we talked, and. . . ."

The rancher paused to take another drink, and then, winking and arching his eyebrows, he continued narrating with the loquaciousness of a drunk, all the details of that night of pleasure secured with his infamous treachery. Next, he let out a heavy sonorous, continuous roar of laughter, like the bellowing of a wild bull.

A tremendous gust of wind entered the patio, whipped against the granite walls of the house, ran the length of the outside wall lifting every dry leaf, scrap of paper or rubbish it found on the gravel, and, after whirling about wildly and howling furiously in search of an exit, it struck several times, with rage, with deep anger—as if it were trying to protest against the rancher's lewd cynicism—the solid dining room door, behind which the three drunken men listened indifferently to the roaring storm.

After a few moments rest, the host continued: "For three months all went well, even though the blonde'd get mad, and accuse me of puttin' off the ole man's release from jail; but afterward, when they did let him go an' he found his nest empty, he set out to catch his little bird at all cost and to take revenge for my dirty trick. I found out about it, took Nemensia to another cage, and waited. One night he caught me unawares, appearing at the ranch when I least expected him. The old man was a persistent devil, and since I natcherly didn't want to get into trouble, I had one of my ranch hands keep talkin' to him while I had a race horse brought from the stable, a pinto. . . ."

"I knew that horse," interrupted the foreman. "He was a lazy good-for-nuttin'."

"What!" exclaimed the rancher, offended.

"A lazy good-for-nuttin!; I saw'm when he entered a race at the Cerro; he ran against four washed-up nags, and ate their tails for the 300 yards."

"'Cause he wasn't feeling good."

"'Cause he was a lazy good-for-nuttin'," the foreman insisted. "He was true to his color . . . he was a pinto!"

"Go on, pardner, with the story, it promises to be a good one," said Sosa, to end the dispute. And Don Bentos, looking at the old Indian with scorn, carried on:

"Well, I saddled the pinto, mounted, gave him free rein, and went off to Cerro-Largo, leaving old Juca at the ranch, as enraged as a lassoed bull. Then I headed for Montevideo, where I hung around for a few months, and that's why I never found out how they did away with the poor devil. The talk around the district was that it'd been my boys, under my orders; but that ain't true. . . ."

Don Bentos grimaced cynically, as if to have it understood that he really was responsible for the murder of the old ranch hand, and he calmly continued his story: "After these events, everythin' was peaceful once again. Nemensia forgot about the old man; I made her believe that I had some Masses said for the dead man's soul, and she was convinced that I wasn't guilty of anythin'. But, I'll tell you, pardner, no one yet has seen a short-legged horse that ain't full of tricks or a woman that ain't got her flaws! The blonde turned out to be jealous like a female jaguar with newborn cubs, and she made my life mis'rable naggin' me every day for one thing or another."

"'Xacly like that mulatta Gabriela in the story I was goin' to tell," blabbered the Indian, letting his head fall on his arm that was resting on the table.

Don Bentos used the interruption to drain the glass of liquor, and, after wiping off his mouth, continued, looking at his friend: "Damn, was she ever jealous! And course, since I let her have'r way in the beginnin', she was unbearably spoiled and out of sheer

love for me, she began to bother me worse than a new boot.
Course, there were other hen houses around where I could play the
rooster—in the countryside, close by, Don Gumersindo Rivero's
daughter, and the daughter of the tenant farmer Soria, Soria from
the Canary Islands, and Rumualda, mulatto Medina's wife. . . ."

"Quite a pretty flock!" exclaimed the visitor, flatteringly; to
which Sagrera answered with a grunt of deep satisfaction.

And he resumed the thread of his story.

"I almost couldn't bear goin' to the ranch; she was always in
tears and always throwin' up to me what I'd done and what I
hadn't done, and blah, blah, blah, as if she weren't better off with
me than she would've been with the cop who was gonna get hitched
to her, and as if she weren't well paid with the house I gave'r and
the meat I sent'r from the ranch every day, and with the milk
cows I'd lent'r and the horses I'd given'r! . . . No, sir, as if all
that were nothin'! It was always 'Any day I'm goin' to run away
with the first guy who comes along' or 'The day you least expect
it you'll find me drowned in the lagoon . . . ' and I'd hear this
tune without a letup, from the moment I arrived until I put my
foot in the stirrup the next day to leave. The worst thing was
that that damn woman had discovered my weakness, and whenever I'd get sick and tired of it all, and whacked her bottom,
instead of gettin' angry, she'd cry and crawl and hug my knees
and caress me, just like my pale yellow dog Itacuaitiá when I whip
him. The more I'd hit'r the more humble she'd become; until
finally I'd feel sorry for her and pick'r up and caress'r, and then
she'd be as happy as could be. Just like Itacuaitiá 'xactly! . . . And
so it went, the woman had a child, and then another, and then
still another, as though she were expectin' me to love'r the rest
of my life. And since my bones weren't gettin' any younger, I said
to myself: 'The best way to get out of this trap would be to find
a woman and get married, then everythin' would be settled and
that'd put an end to these scenes.' When Nemensia found out
about my plan, you should've seen the fuss she raised! There was
no way to console'r, and I only got'r to calm down a bit by prom-
isin' to spend most of my time with'r. A short time later I married
my late wife and we came to live in these parts. At first all went
well and I was very happy with my new life. Busy with the construction of this house—which at first was only a few shacks;

enthused with the new little woman, and finally, since I was always at home, I forgot about everythin' else. Even the blonde, Nemensia, was driven clear out of my mind and she had been careful not to send me any messages. But after a while, my little honeylamb couldn't resist and she sent a ranch hand over here to remind me to keep my word. I played dumb and didn't answer; and four days later when I'd already kinda forgotten about the blonde, I got a note threatenin' to come and cause a scandal if I didn't go see'r. I realized that she just might do it, and if she came and the missus found out, there'd be a free-for-all! There was nothin' I could do but shrug my shoulders and sneak away to Chuy, where I spent a few days. After that I went on livin' a little here, a little there, until — I don't know if it's because some blabbermouth told'r (you can always count on that) or because my frequent trips gave me away — the missus found out about my affair with Nemensia and she started a row, like a stampede of wild steers at midnight, on a moonless night. If Nemensia was jealous, this one, God help us! . . . Between bawlin' me out and spoutin' sermons, she had me wetter than a marshland in the rainy season, and more distressed than an animal with worms. It was useless for me to try to make'r understand that if it wasn't Nemensia it'd be someone else, and that she had no choice but to accept the bit and reconcile herself to'r fate, 'cause I was that kind of man and that's how it had to be. No siree! . . . That Brazilian gal was a tough one to ride and when I crossed'r, she bucked and chased me with whatever she could find. One time she almost stuck a knife in my belly cause I slapped'r. Lucky for me, I dodged in time, 'cause if I hadn't, that ungrateful bitch would've had me on the skewer ready for the barbecue. Fortunately this didn't last long, 'cause my late wife wasn't like Nemensia, who was content to cry and threaten me with throwin' herself in the lagoon: the missus was a woman who said and did things without askin' anyone's opinion. If she said it was straight, straight it was; an' if she said it was crooked, crooked it was: once she made up'r mind, watch out, you had to give'r room like a steer that's just been gelded. Some time passed without'r sayin' nothin' to me; she went around broodin' and serious, but acted much nicer to me than before, but since it's hard to put one over on me, 'cause I see things comin' a long way off, I said to myself: 'The missus is getting ready to rope me; but when it comes to dodgin' the lassoes, not even the wild horses bred in the brambles of the Rincón de Ramírez can beat me, and I knew I'd leave'r holdin' the rope, with the rolled up slack around'r neck.' I began to observe'r carefully but always playin' possum as if I didn't 'spect'r of plannin' nothin'. It didn't take too long for me to catch on to her game, and . . . Sosa, my boy, the devil sure is funny! . . . Do you know I was happier than if I had won a big race! . . . Can you imagine the scheme consisted of making the blonde Nemensia disappear! . . ."

"Make her disappear, or do away with her?" asked Sosa, winking and contracting his mouth into a dirty grin.

And Bentos Sagrera, with a very similar look, immediately replied:

"Make'r disappear or do away with'r; you'll see soon enough."

Then he continued: "As I was sayin', I already had it up to here with Don Juca's daughter, and I saw a way to have my path cleared and at the same time patch things up with my wife; I welcomed that idea as though it were a new branded calf. It's true that I felt a little sorry, 'cause it was kind of nasty to do such a thing to the poor blonde; but, pardner, what could I do! You don't look a gift horse in the mouth, and since after all I wasn't gonna get my hands dirty, nor was I a party to the deed, I jus' sat back and calmly awaited the results. The missus was spending more and more time chattin' with the nigger Caracú,[5] a poor, stupid nigger who had been my father-in-law's slave, and who obeyed my late wife like a dog. 'Well,' I said to myself, 'the best thing for me would be to· go to Montevideo, and give them a free hand, and besides, if somethin' dirty should happen I won't be caught in the mess.' And so I left at once.

"The missus and Caracú couldn't have hoped for anythin' better," continued the rancher, after pausing to refill the glasses and empty the contents of his own. "That very night that I went off to the capital, the nigger headed for the ranch in Chuy with his script memorized and ready to act it out word for word because these niggers are like dumb mutts, you can't imagine how dumb they are! Caracú was only twenty years old, but 'customed as he was to the whippin's of my late father-in-law, he never realized

---

[5]"Caracú," a nickname meaning "Bony."

what it was to be free, and so it was that he continued bein' a slave and obeyin' my wife in everythin' she would order'm to do, without stoppin' to think if it was good or bad, or even if it was gonna hurt'm or help'm; in short: he was like an old worn-out nag that puts up with everythin' and never kicks back. He must've had the idea that he wasn't responsible for nothin', or that since the missus ordered'm to do somethin', this somethin' had to be good and permitted by the authorities. God damn, that poor nigger Caracú was stupid. . . . The truth of the matter is that only a savage would have done what that nigger did. I swear to God I didn't think he was capable of doin' that kind of thing . . . because, hell, that was just too damn much, Sosa my pal, it was too much! . . ."

The rancher, who had been stalling for a few moments, as if overcome by a scruple which kept him from revealing once and for all the secret of a great infamy, was suddenly interrupted by a long, horrendous thunderclap which exploded, like a charge from a powerful battery.

The house trembled as if a powder magazine had blown up in the huge patio; the Indian Pancho Castro awoke startled; the visitor, who certainly didn't have a very clear conscience, turned intensely pale; Bentos Sagrera remained pensive, a certain fear marking his hairy face; and for several moments the three men sat still and silent, with their eyes wide open and their ears following attentively the decreasing reverberation of the thunder. The foreman was the first to break the silence: "I'll tell ya, friends!" he said, "that was one hell of a blast! It sure must've hit somethin'! Who knows if tomorrow I won't find my white horse blown to bits. 'Cause, I'll tell ya, my friends, those white animals are chased by lightnin' like hens by a fox! . . ."

And as he noted that the two ranchers continued absorbed in thought, the old Indian added sneeringly: "Yep, nothin' like brandy ta give a man courage!"

And with difficulty, because his head was woozy and his arms weak, he filled his glass and gave the bottle to his boss, who didn't pass up the opportunity to serve himself and his guest. For most men out in the country, brandy is a marvelous liquor: besides serving as a cure for all illnesses, it has the quality of restoring happiness each and every time it's swallowed.

And so it was that the three men engaged in this "party" re-gained their good mood: the Indian struggling to keep his eyes open; Sosa anxious to know the outcome of the story; and Bentos Sagrera undecided whether to proceed or not with the crudest part of his tale.

Finally, ceding to the urging of his friends and to the communi-cative influence of alcohol, which makes even the most reserved men vomit up their most intimate secrets—their bad deeds as a mysterious punishment, and their good ones as if they were asphyx-iating in a terrible combustion chamber and dying to escape—he resolved to continue, not without first having asked by way of an apology: "Ain't it true that it wasn't my fault, that I'm not re-sponsible for what happened?"

Sosa said: "How could anybody say it was your fault, pardner!"

And the foreman added, as he nodded: "Course not! . . . Course not! . . . Hell, no! . . . Hell, no! . . ."

With such assurances, Sagrera considered himself free of all remorse and continued his story: "Caracú the nigger, as I was sayin', who I didn't think capable of such an awful crime, went to Chuy ready to carry out my wife's scheme. . . . Terrifyin'! . . . It chills me just to tell it! . . . I don't know what my poor late wife was thinkin' of! . . . Anyway, the nigger arrived at the ranch and there he stayed for a few days, waitin' for the right moment to strike. I should tell you that it was one of the coldest and rainiest winters we've ever had. One storm today, another tomorrow, and it never stopped rainin', and every night darker than a bat's cave. You couldn't hardly go outside and you had to let the herds drown or die of cold, 'cause the men were stiff and numb, crippled by that damn weather. Pardner, there wasn't even anythin' to eat! Stringy beef, scummy octopus, dog meat, from the very dogs we skinned alive 'cause they were dyin' of starvation. What luck that I was in Montevideo where there's always good food mixed with greens. Well, Caracú kept on waitin', and when the real dark night that he was waitin' for came along, he saddled his horse, sayin' he was returnin' here, and he left. At the ranch everyone thought that the nigger had a secret girl friend nearby and they let him go without suspectin' anythin'. How could they suspect poor Caracú who was good as bread and tame as a milk cow! They kidded'm a bit tellin'm to 'barbecue the meat' just the way he liked it, and not to be afraid of the scarecrows 'cause since the night and he were the same color, they would help each other. Nonetheless, you could tell that the young fellow was an experienced camper and was well prepared because he had put one lasso on his horse's neck, and another below his saddle blanket, as if he were goin' to tie'm most securely with a rope in case he had to sleep outdoors. And they let'm leave without havin' gotten anythin' out of the darkie. Caracú was like an animal when it came to findin' his way, and so it was that he took off in the direction of blonde Nemensia's ranch, and trottin' and gallopin', he made a beeline for her place. A couple of hundred yards before arrivin', he dis-mounted in a little hollow and tied the horse. There—the nigger himself later told every little detail—he cut up some tobacco, got a light from his tinderbox, lit the cigarette, and began to smoke as calmly as if right then and there he was goin' into a hall to dance, or to ask permission of the guard at the corral gate to rope a steer. That rascal had a wicked soul! Then, after smokin' a while in a squattin' position, he put out the butt, stuck it behind his ear, removed the lasso that was on his horse's neck, and the one he had under the saddle blankets, and started off on foot, very slowly, toward the ranch houses. In those houses there were no dogs except for a spotted puppy that the nigger himself had given'r; so that when he got close, the dog only barked a little and then calmed down immediately recognizin' his old master. Caracú felt around for the door of the shack, the only door it had which opened out onto the patio. When he found it, he began to listen; not a sound came from inside: poor folks go to bed early, and Nemensia was surely snorin' by that time. Then with one rope he tied the door good an' tight to the corner pole, so that no one could open it from inside. I don't know how he tied it, but he himself said it would've withstood a charging steer. He then went around to the other side where there was a little window and repeated the operation. Meanwhile, inside, the poor blonde and her three pups were sleepin' like logs, secure in their knowledge that rustlers never bother with a poor man's ranch. And Nemensia, who liked to sleep as much as a lizard and whose sleep was sounder than a rock . . . ! After this whole operation and quite sure that they couldn't get out, the heartless nigger—it's hard to believe that there could exist men capable of committin' such a crime!—well, the heartless nigger, as I was saying, Sosa my friend, set the house on fire on all four sides. As soon as he saw that everythin' was burnin' and that with the help of a strong wind that was blowin' it was goin' to be like a brushfire in summer, he took the butt from behind his ear, lit it with a piece of straw and slowly walked away back to the hollow where he had left his horse. In a little while he began to hear tremendous screams from the poor devils who were roastin' inside; but even with that the nigger had the nerve to stay right there without tryin' to flee! What a beast, pardner, what a beast. . . ! Well, there are all kinds of men! Let's have a drink. . . . Eh! Don Pancho! . . . Helluva weakling when it comes to drinkin'! . . . Well, as I was sayin', the nigger didn't budge from that place until he saw everythin' burned and turned into embers. The next day my buddy Manuel Felipe went out ridin' through the countryside early in the mornin' lookin' for a horse that had gone astray. He went off toward the coast and stopped dead in his tracks when he saw the shack reduced to rubble. He looked around, dismounted, stirred among the ashes and found a boy completely charred, and then Nemensia's body in the same condition and he couldn't take anymore of it and rode off to the police station to report what had happened. The commissary went to the ranch to see if he could find any clue, and as soon as he opened his mouth, the nigger Caracú said: 'Ah did it!'

"At first they didn't want to believe him at all.

"'What do you mean "you did it"?' the commissary answered him. 'Are you trying to make fun of the law, darkie?'

"'No suh; ah did it!'

"'Why?'

"''Cause de boss lady tol' me to.'

"'To burn the shack?'

"'Yassuh.'

"'With the people inside?'

"'Yassuh! . . . Causs!'

"'And don't you realize what a terrible crime this is?'

"'De boss lady tol' me to do it.'

"And there was no one who could convince'm otherwise.

"'De boss lady tol' me,' he answered to every observation of the commissary or of the hired hands. And so they tied'm up and took'm away. When I found out about it, I shivered, Sosa my friend! . . . But later I was pleased, 'cause I was finally free of Nemensia and of the naggin' of my late wife, without having had to do anythin' at all myself. 'Cause I didn't have anythin' to do with it, God's truth, nothin'!"

That's how Bentos Sagrera wound up the tale of his loves; and then, slapping his thighs with the palms of his hands: "So! What do you think of that?" he asked.

Don Brígido Sosa remained silent for a moment, looking at the foreman, who was snoring with his head on the table. Then, suddenly: "And the nigger?" he said, "what happened to him?"

"The nigger, they shot'm in Montevideo," the rancher answered calmly.

"And the missus? . . ."

"The missus was dragged into the investigations, but we managed to get things fixed up."

"That was lucky!"

"It sure was. But it also cost me a bundle of pesos."

Don Brígido smiled and said flatteringly: "That's like plucking a hair from a rabbit."

"Not really, not really!" answered Bentos Sagrera, feigning modesty.

And he slapped his thighs and laughed again with such noise that he drowned out Castro's snoring, the whistling of the wind, and the steady beating of the rain on the corrugated tin roof of the large shed where the hired hands were quartered.

— Translated by Flaurie Imberman

COMMENTARY

Although this story appears to be one of those endless yarns spun by a rural oldtimer, actually it has a tight unobtrusive artistic unity based on the unmasking of the protagonist. Bentos Sagrera is no longer the heroic barbarian gaucho immortalized by Sarmiento in *Facundo* (1845); nor the persecuted folk hero of José Hernández's *Martín Fierro* (1872, 1879); nor the picturesque country bumpkin of Estanislao del Campo's *Fausto* (1866); nor the incarnation of the Argentine soul as depicted in the poems of Rafael Obligado (1885, 1906) and so many other earlier as well as later poets. Bentos Sagrera is the degenerate, animalistic gaucho: the man who, as a result of living in the lonely expanses of the pampas facing a hostile nature, has become the classic example of Zola's human beast. Crafty and cruel, Bentos Sagrera is totally devoid of any sense of morals. He feels absolutely no compunctions about his crimes, despite what he says.

The protagonist's bestiality is created not only by his deeds. The narrator sets the stage by dehumanizing the rancher with an abundance of similes and metaphors. Bentos Sagrera had "hams like a hog, a neck like a bull . . . feet like two irons or two huge chunks of wood . . . large eyes, set wide apart, giving him the appearance of a beast; a long nose shaped like an eagle's beak." The other characters are also dehumanized: "he watched over her as though she were a prize racehorse"; "the blonde turned out to be jealous like a female jaguar with newly born cubs." The abundance of these animalistic comparisons, although they support the author's naturalistic view of human beings, do not appear in the least contrived since they are in keeping with the rural environment.

Although the protagonist's own narrative style is not exactly concise, suspense as well as unity are maintained through the repetition of several motifs: the rain, the *mate* tea, and the unfinished story of the old Indian foreman. What makes the story so effective is that Bentos Sagrera reveals his own character as he himself cynically delights in telling the story of his crimes.

Like his Uruguayan contemporaries Horacio Quiroga and dramatist Florencio Sánchez, Javier de Viana lived for many years in Buenos Aires and published his works there. His Naturalistic vision of the decadence of the gaucho as the heroic prototype of both Uruguay and Argentina set the stage for the portrayal of the gaucho's vain struggle against the inroads of modern civilization in Florencio Sánchez's play *La gringa* (1904), Roberto Payró's play *Sobre las ruinas* (1904), and Benito Lynch's novel *Los caranchos de la Florida* (1916), and ultimately for the poetic, nostalgic, idealized vision of Ricardo Güiraldes's *Don Segundo Sombra* (1926) which more or less closes out the cycle of gaucho literature.

Baldomero Lillo

(1867–1923)

Chilean. He was born and raised in the southern coal mining town of Lota. Although he completed only a year or two of high school, his interest in literature, fostered by his father, led him to read *Don Quijote* and *Gil Blas de Santillane* as well as Chilean Blest Gana's Realistic novels of the 1860s. He later read Zola and Dostoyevsky voraciously. For several years, Lillo worked as a clerk in general stores where he came into close contact with the wretched conditions under which the miners lived. In 1898, he moved to Santiago where his brother Samuel, a well-known author in his own right, helped him find a job in the printing office of the University of Chile. Like some of the miners in his stories, Baldomero Lillo died of tuberculosis.

Of Lillo's total literary production of forty-five short stories, he is best known for "Gate No. 12" and the seven other mining stories published under the Latin title *Sub terra* (1904). A second collection, *Sub sole* (1907), also contains some strong social protest but there is greater thematic variety and not all the stories are as sombre and tragic as those of *Sub terra*. Other stories published in newspapers and journals were posthumously collected and printed under the titles *Relatos populares* (1942) and *El hallazgo y otros cuentos del mar* (1956).

GATE NO. 12

Pablo clung instinctively to his father's legs. His ears buzzed and the floor sped downward beneath his feet giving him a strange sensation of anguish. He felt as though he were being hurled into that black hole he had glimpsed as he entered the cage. His large, round eyes looked fearfully at the dark walls of the shaft down which they were dropping with dizzying speed. In that silent descent, without a sound save the dripping of water on the iron ceiling, the lamplights seemed on the verge of going out, and in their feeble rays of light a long interminable series of black

shadows that shot upward like arrows could be vaguely distinguished on the uneven shaft wall.

A minute later, the speed diminished abruptly; his feet felt
more solidly planted on that sinking floor and the heavy iron cage,
with a harsh rasping of chains and hinges, came to a halt at the
entrance to the gallery.

The old man took the little boy's hand and together they entered
the dark tunnel. They were among the first arrivals. Work in the
mine had not yet begun. Of the gallery, which was high enough
to allow a miner to stand erect, only a part of the ceiling, crossed
by great thick beams, could be seen. The side walls were invisible
in the profound darkness that filled the vast, gloomy excavation.

Forty yards from the digging area, they stopped before a kind
of grotto hollowed out of the rock. From the cracked, sooty ceiling
hung a tin lantern whose weak beam of light gave the room the
appearance of a crypt, draped in black and full of shadows. In
the rear, a little old man sat behind a table writing in an enormous
ledger. His black suit contrasted sharply with his pale, deeply
wrinkled face. At the sound of footsteps he raised his head and
fixed a questioning glance on the old miner who, advancing timidly,
in a submissive and respectful voice said:

"Sir, I've brought the boy."

With one sweeping glance, the foreman's penetrating eyes took
in the weak little body of the boy. His delicate limbs and the childish innocence of the dark face with its wide-open shining eyes, like
those of a frightened little animal, made an unfavorable impression
on the foreman. Although hardened by the daily contemplation
of so much misery, he felt a twang of pity at the sight of that little
fellow, yanked from his childish games and condemned, like so
many others, to languish miserably in damp galleries, next to the
ventilation doors. The hard lines of his face softened and with
assumed severity he addressed the old man who, concerned over
the foreman's scrutiny of his son, stared anxiously awaiting a reply:

"Heavens, man, this child is still too weak to work. Is he your
son?"

"Yes, sir."

"He's so young. You should have pity on him and rather than
bury him in here, you should be sending him to school for a
while."

"But, sir," stammered the shaky, supplicating voice of the miner, "there are six of us at home and only one working. Pablo is eight already and he should earn the bread he eats. As a miner's son, he'll have to follow in the footsteps of his elders whose only school was the mine."

A sudden fit of coughing drowned out his trembling voice, but his moist eyes implored with such insistence that the foreman, won over by that silent appeal, raised a whistle to his lips. Its piercing sound echoed down the deserted passageway. Hurried steps were heard and a dark silhouette appeared in the doorway.

"Juan," exclaimed the little man, pointing to the miner's son, "take this boy to Gate No. 12. He will replace José, the hauler's son, who was run over yesterday."

Then turning to the old miner, who was about to murmur his thanks, he said severely, "I've noticed that in the last week you haven't reached the five-car minimum for every driller. Don't forget that if it happens again you'll have to be laid off and a more active man put in your place," and with an energetic gesture of his right hand, he dismissed him.

The three walked along silently and the sound of their footsteps gradually grew faint in the dark tunnel. They walked between the two rails whose ties, sunken into the muddy floor, they tried to avoid by lengthening and shortening their steps. They guided themselves by the spikes which held the ties to the rails. The guide, still a young man, went on ahead, while the old miner, deeply concerned, his head sunken on his chest, followed dragging Pablo by the hand. The foreman's warning had filled the old man's heart with despair. For some time it had been apparent to all that he was losing ground. Each day he drew nearer to that fatal borderline which, once passed, turns an old worker into a worthless piece of junk in the mine.

Hopelessly from dawn to dark, for fourteen long hours, twisting and turning like a serpent in a narrow gallery, he would furiously attack the coal, picking at the unending lode that so many generations of miserable men like himself had scratched at ceaselessly in the bowels of the earth.

But that tenacious, ceaseless unyielding struggle soon turned even the most vigorous of the young into decrepit old men. There in that dark, damp, narrow hole, their backs became hunched and their muscles grew weak. Like the recalcitrant colt who trembles at the sight of the whip, these old miners felt their tired flesh quiver as they returned to their digging each day. But hunger is a more effective stimulus than the whip or the spur. So they silently went on with their exhausting task. The whole vein, eaten away in a thousand places by that human worm, vibrated slightly and crumbled piece by piece, bitten by the square tootĥ of the pick, just as the sandy shore gives way to the onrushing sea.

The guide stopped, suddenly tearing the old man away from his sad meditations. A gate blocked their path in that direction, and on the floor, leaning against the wall, barely discernible in the flickering light of the lamps was a small, vaguely outlined, huddled shape; it was a ten-year-old boy crouched in the hollow of the wall.

With his elbows on his knees and his pale face between his emaciated hand, silent and motionless, he seemed not even to see the workers who crossed the threshold and then left him again swallowed up by the darkness. His open, expressionless eyes were fixed stubbornly on high, absorbed, perhaps, in the contemplation of some imaginary scene which, like a desert mirage, attracted his pupils, thirsty for light, moist with nostalgia for the distant day's bright light. In charge of handling that gate, he spent the interminable hours of his interment submerged in a sad stupor, weighted down by that enormous sepulchral stone that crushed in him forever all the restless and graceful mobility of childhood. It is the suffering of these children that leaves, in the souls of those who understand them, an infinite bitterness and a feeling of sharp condemnation of human selfishness and cowardice.

After walking along a narrow passage, the two men and the boy finally came out into the high open haulage gallery, from whose ceiling heavy drops of water fell continuously. From time to time there could be heard a muted distant noise as though a gigantic hammer were pounding the earth's crust above their heads. Although Pablo was unable to figure it out, that sound was made by the crashing of the waves on the rocky shore. They walked on still a little further and finally found themselves in front of Gate No. 12.

"This is it," said the guide, stopping before a gate that swung from a wooden frame fitted into the rock. So thick were the shadows that the reddish glow of their lamps scarcely revealed the obstacle before them.

Pablo, who failed to understand the reason for their stopping, looked silently at his companions, who, after a quick, brief exchange of words, began cheerfully and eagerly to show him how to operate the gate. Following their directions, the boy opened and shut it several times, dispelling all his father's fears that he would lack the necessary strength for such a task.

The old man showed his approval by caressing with his calloused hand the tousled head of his firstborn who still showed no fatigue or fear. His youthful imagination, impressed by that new and strange spectacle, was bewildered, disoriented. It seemed from time to time as though he were in a dark room and he expected at any moment that a window would be opened to let in the bright rays of the sun. Although his inexperienced little heart no longer suffered the fright that the descent in the shaft had produced, his suspicions were now aroused by the unusual displays of affection from his father. A light went on at the far end of the gallery and then the squeaking of wheels on the tracks and a heavy and fast pounding of hooves resounded on the floor.

"It's the car!" both men exclaimed. "Quick, Pablo," said his father, "let's see if you can do your job."

Fists clenched, Pablo pushed his tiny body against the gate until it touched the wall. No sooner had he done it than a dark, sweating, panting horse rushed by pulling a heavy carload of coal.

The miners exchanged an approving glance. Pablo was now an experienced gate boy. The old man bent over him, and in flattering tones told him that now he was a big boy, not like those crybabies up above that clung to their mother's skirts. He was a brave man now, a real worker, a fellow comrade who would be treated as such. And in a few words he made him understand that they would have to leave him alone. He mustn't be afraid. There were lots of boys like him in the mine doing the same work. He was near and would come to see him from time to time. When the day's work was done, they would return home together.

Pablo listened with increasing fear. His only answer was to clutch his father's overalls with both hands. Up to then, he had not fully comprehended what they wanted of him. The unexpected turn that this innocent little excursion had taken filled him with a deerlike fright. He must get out of this place. He wanted to see his mother and his brothers and sisters, to be out in the daylight again. All his father's kind persuasion brought forth only the cry:

"Let's go home!"

Promises, menaces, nothing availed. He could only wail in mounting and unbearable fear:

"Let's go home, Daddy!"

At first, the old miner's face showed violent annoyance, but when he saw those desolate, supplicating, tear-filled eyes turned up to him, his rising anger changed to infinite pity—he was so small and weak! The paternal love so long suppressed in him suddenly flooded his whole being.

The memory of his own life—forty years of work and suffering—suddenly stood out clearly before him. He had to admit with regret that all that was left of that immense labor was an exhausted body that would soon be thrown out of the mine and relegated to the waste pile. That this child awaited a similar fate in the mine made him want desperately to deny a victim to this insatiable monster that dragged scarcely grown children from their mothers' laps to convert them into pariahs whose backs received with equal stoicism the brutal lash of the master and the scraping caresses of the rock in the narrow, sloping tunnels.

But the spark of rebellion in him was quickly extinguished by the memory of his poor home and the hungry, unclad beings for whom he was the only provider. His own experience taught him that his dream was foolish. The mine never freed those whom it had caught. Like new links that substituted for the old broken down ones in the endless chain down there, sons succeeded fathers and in the deep pit the rising and descending of the human tide never ceased. The young ones, breathing the poisoned air of the mine, grew up with rickets, weak and pale, but they had to resign themselves, for to this they had been born.

So, with a determined gesture, the old man untied from his waist a strong, thin cord and in spite of the child's struggles and protests, he fastened it about Pablo's waist and attached the other end to a thick bolt in the wall. Old pieces of cord hanging on that iron rod indicated that this was not the first time it had served such a purpose.

The child, frightened to death, let out penetrating shrieks of awful anguish and they had to drag him forcibly from between his father's legs, which he grasped with all his strength. His pleas and cries filled the tunnel. The tender victim, even more unfortunate than the biblical Isaac, heard not a single friendly voice that would deter the paternal hand turned against his own flesh because of the crime and the iniquity of men.

His cries to the departing old man were so heartrending, piercing, and vibrant that the poor father felt his resolve weakening again. But that lasted only a minute, and, covering his ears so as not to hear the shrieks that tore his heart, he quickened his pace in order to get away from the place. Before leaving the gallery, he stopped a moment and heard a weak voice, crying in the distance, "Mama! Mama!"

The father then ran desperately away pursued by the wailing cry and he never stopped until he reached the vein. At the sight of it, his grief turned to fury and, grabbing the handle of his pick, he attacked it madly. His blows hit the rock like heavy hail on resounding glass. The steel pick buried itself in that shiny black mass knocking out enormous pieces that fell in a pile at the miner's feet, while a thick cloud of dust covered the flickering light of his lamp like a veil. The sharp fragments flew swiftly all about him, cutting his face, neck, and bare chest. Trickles of blood mixed with the copious sweat ran down his wet body that was like a wedge in the opened breach. He pushed against it with the frenzy of a prisoner who bores through the wall that locks him in, but without the hope that gives strength to the prisoner who looks forward to a new life full of sunlight, air, and freedom once his digging is completed.

> —*Based on a translation by Esther S. Dillon in* The Devil's Pit and Other Stories by Baldomero Lillo, *Washington, D.C.: Organization of American States, 1959.*

COMMENTARY

Although the stories of *Sub terra* may have been influenced by Zola's *Germinal,* they are so directly inspired by conditions
in the Chilean coal mines of the period that it would be fruitless to
pursue Lillo's indebtedness to his French mentor. Unlike all the previous
stories in this anthology, with the exception of "The Slaughterhouse,"
the social group is more important than the individual. The author
insists on the fact that the protagonists represent the thousands whose
lives are chained to the mines without any hope of freedom. In keeping
with the Naturalist doctrine, Lillo alludes to the generations of miners
who have been sacrificed and to the miner's son who, in the most de-
terministic way, is condemned to inherit his father's occupation.

The force of this story does not lie in an unexpected ending. Quite
the contrary, the ending is only the culmination of a long series of
details about the miner's tragic life. One of the most successful features
of the story is the fine balance maintained between the two protagonists.
Linked by a feeling of anguish, Pablo and his father take turns in
eliciting the reader's compassion. Their physical attachment — Pablo
clings to his father's feet at the beginning and end of the story — makes
their separation even more heartrending. The author prepares us for
this cruel moment with the foreman's words about the death of José's
son and with the view of the other gate boy. Nevertheless, Pablo's
sudden terror has a profound impact upon the reader who realizes that
until the awful moment of truth, the child was unaware of the purpose
of his descent into the mine.

With the same subtlety that Lillo uses in shifting the reader's sympathy
back and forth between father and son, he transforms his very realistic
scene into a poetic vision of hell. Although the comparison of a mine
with Hell is nothing extraordinary, Lillo carries it off rather discreetly.
He never mentions Hell or the Devil; he prefers to-leave to the reader
the pleasure of creating the image on the basis of a few hints. He
insists throughout on the darkness of the mine: "dark walls," "profound
darkness," "dark tunnel," "black shadows," "lamplights seemed on the
verge of going out," "the flickering light of the lamp"; the "reddish
glow of their lamps" is suggestive of the Devil; the foreman is transformed into a grotesque figure by his black suit and a diminutive size;
the allusion to the Biblical sacrifice of Isaac suggests the possibility that
Pablo is being sacrificed to the Devil.

Lillo's typically Chilean slow-moving prose is not rich in imagery. The
few similes and metaphors are rather commonplace comparisons with
animals: "twisting and turning like a serpent," "that human worm,"
"deer-like fright." Nevertheless, this story has lasting literary value
derived from both its being a powerful example of Naturalism and of
social protest, and its conveying the sincere emotions of the protagonists
in a tightly structured episode which serves as a microcosm of the lives
of many generations of miners.

Augusto D'Halmar

(1882-1950)

Chilean. Augusto Geomine Thomson, who is better known by his pseudonym, was born in Valparaíso. He revealed an interest in the humanities in high school where at the age of fourteen he founded a literary magazine. In 1904, imbued with the humanitarian principles of Tolstoy, he and some friends organized a short-lived "monastic" colony. After serving as consul to India (1907-1908), he covered World War I as a frontline reporter. He traveled extensively before returning to Chile in 1934 to become the director of Valparaíso's Municipal Museum of Fine Arts. Although he made his literary debut as a Naturalist with the novel *Juana Lucero* (1902), he soon became the Chilean master of fantastic literature.

A very prolific writer—his complete works were published in 1934 in twenty-five volumes—his best novel is considered to be *Pasión y muerte del cura Deusto* (1924) and his best stories are to be found in the collections *La lámpara en el molino* (1914) and *Capitanes sin barcos* (1934). "In the Provinces" is from the former.

IN THE PROVINCES

La vie est vaine;   *La vie est brève;*
un peu d'amour,   *un peu d'espoir,*
un peu de haine,   *un peu de rêve,*
et puis "bonjour."   *et puis "bonsoir".*[1]

Maurier

I am fifty-six years old, and for forty years I've had a pen stuck behind my ear. It's just that I never thought a pen would be good for anything besides keeping records in the daily ledger or transcribing letters with set openings: "In reply to your request of. . . , it is my pleasure to inform you. . . ."

[1]Life is vain; a little love, a little hate, and then "good-bye." Life is short; a little hope, a little dream, and then "good night."

What happened was that I left my hometown when I was sixteen, after my mother died. I had no ties left there, and I've been living in this provincial environment ever since. Here we all understand each other verbally, so I haven't had any reason to write.

Sometimes I would have wanted to; I would have liked for someone, somewhere on this earth, to receive my most intimate secrets. But who? Pouring out my heart to just anyone would be ridiculous. After people get an idea about you, it's hard for them to change it. I am, first of all, a bald, overweight man, a store clerk: Borja Guzmán, bookkeeper for the Delfín Emporium. A fine thing it would be for me to proceed now to reveal all kinds of sentimental secrets! Everyone is assigned, or chooses, his own role in this farce, but you have to sustain it till the very end.

I should have gotten married, and I didn't. Why? Not for lack of desire, because even though I wouldn't have had a house all to myself, that actually made me dream of forming a home. Well then, why? Life! Ah, life! The salary that old man Delfín kept me at was raised by his son, but it was reduced as soon as the business changed hands. The store has had three owners, but my situation hasn't changed nor has my luck gotten any better. Under these conditions it's hard to save any money, especially if you don't sacrifice your stomach. Your brain, your arms, your heart, they all work for it: but you disregard Smiles[2] and then when you'd like to set yourself up in business, you can't find the way to do it.

Is that what made me stay single? Yes, until I was thirty-one; because from that time on nothing counts. Something happened that year to put an end to my past, my present, and my future. I stopped living. Now I'm nothing but a dead man leafing through the pages of his life.

Aside from this, I haven't had much time to be bored. We open the store at nine in the morning, take a break for lunch and dinner, and close up at the first sound of the evening band concert.

From then until this time of night, I stay on my revolving stool, with my feet resting on the top rung, and my padded elbows on the desk. After I put the books away and put out my lamplight, I cross the small town square, and, with the turn of a key, a door opens up: I am home. I grope my way toward the bureau and give myself some light; there, to the right, there's always a candle. The

[2] The author of a series of popular books on how to succeed in life.

first thing I see is a photograph, against the sky-blue wallpaper of the room; then the white spot of the bed, my poor bed, which Veronica never knows how to make up, so I remake it every night. A cretonne curtain covers the window, which looks out on the town square. If it's not too cold, I pull it back and open the shutters, and if I'm not too sleepy, I get my flute out of its case and fit the pieces together with bandages and string. It's old, almost as old as I am; the tube is bad, and the keys are so loose they don't control the air any more, and they may even let a note escape with a disappointing boldness. Standing before the window sill, I warm up my lip with a series of scales and variations and then I start on the elegy dedicated to my departed ones. . . . Is there anyone who doesn't have his dead hopes or memories?

The small city sleeps under the firmament. If the moon is out, one can clearly make out the belfry of the parish church, the cross of the cemetery, or the silhouette of a couple hidden behind the oak trees of the square, although the young lovers prefer the countryside where they can hear the chorus of the frogs supported by a blend of other noises and perfumes. The wind disseminates the moans of my flute and carries them up to the stars, the same stars that for years and centuries were loved by those who now sleep in their dust. When a star crosses through space, I formulate a constant wish. In so many years, many stars have detached themselves while my desire goes unfulfilled.

I play and play. Two or three sad motifs. Maybe I used to know more, and I might have learned others; but these were the ones she liked best, a quarter of a century ago, and these are the ones I've kept.

I play and play. There's a cricket outside the window who, stimulated by my music, keeps trying to get in tune. The dogs bark at the noises and the shadows. The clock in some church strikes the hour. In the more affluent homes, they are stoking their fires, while the wind that sweeps through the deserted streets tries to blow out the gaslights.

Then, a moth gets into my room, I set aside my music and attempt to keep it from charging into the flame. Isn't that what someone with experience should do? Besides, I was beginning to get tired. You have to blow hard to get a response out of that crippled flute, and my excessive weight causes me to lose my breath.

Next I close the window and get undressed; with my nightcap and slippers on, and the candlestick in my hand, I take one last look at the picture, and then I go to bed. Pedro's face is tender and caressable, but her eyes have such a haughty look that they make me turn away. Two decades have passed, and in my imagination I can still see her like that: that's just the way she used to look at me.

That's been my existence for twenty years: a picture and a few old tunes; but it's a well-known fact that as we get older, we become more demanding. I'm no longer willing to settle for so little, and I'm now resorting to my pen.

If only somebody knew my story! If someone would only discover my memoirs, the sad novel of a happy man, *Don Borja, the Man from the Delfín Emporium*. If someone would only read them. . . ! But no, manuscripts like this one, that are written because we have nobody to confide in, disappear with their authors. We destroy them before embarking on our final voyage and something must warn us when the time draws near. Otherwise there's no accounting for the fact that at a given moment — one that is really no different from any other, maybe even less special than many previous moments — we do away with that compromising but beloved *something* that we all keep hidden, and when we do, it is without suffering or fear of any regret. It's like passage which, once it is booked, makes it impossible to postpone the trip. Or maybe we depart simply because there's nothing left to detain us. Our last bonds have slipped off . . . the ship is weighing anchor!

As I said, it happened twenty years ago, or rather, twenty-five, since it all began five years earlier. At that point I couldn't exactly say I was a young man, and I was already bald and fairly heavy; I've always been overweight: hard times just make my fatty tissue grow thicker. My first boss had passed away, and the Emporium was taken over by his nephew, who lived in the capital; I knew nothing about him. I'd never even seen him before, but it didn't take long for me to get to know him through and through; tough and ill-tempered with his employees, with his wife he behaved like a perfect lover, and remember that he had been married for ten years. My God, how they seemed to love each other! I also became familiar with their grief, though at first glance, they seemed to be quite happy. The desire to have a son was gnawing at him, and though he tried to hide it, she had begun to suspect something. From time to time, she would ask him: "What are you longing for?" and he'd cover her mouth with kisses. But that wasn't really an answer. Was it?

They allowed me to become a close friend of theirs after they discovered my love for music. "We should have guessed, you have the lungs for it." That was the compliment he paid me before his wife on our first soirée together.

Our first soirée! How did I manage to do so well in the presence of this couple from the capital—I, who played by ear and whose only teacher was a band musician. I remember I performed *The Fantasy*, which I have just gone over tonight, *A Young Girl's Laments*, and *The Swallow and the Prisoner;* and yet all I could think about was the hostess's beauty as she stepped down to congratulate me.

From that day on, as soon as the store closed, we would get together in the little living room downstairs—you can still see a light in that same room, but other people live there now. We would spend several hours immersed in our small repertoire of songs, which she had never allowed me to vary in the least, and which she came to know so well that one wrong note would irritate her.

At other times she hummed along with me, and though she did it softly, you could tell that her voice had a wide range, of which she herself was probably unaware. Why, in spite of my insisting, wouldn't she consent to sing? Oh! I didn't have the slightest influence over her. On the other hand, she had such an imposing effect on me that although I wanted on many occasions to sit down and chat with her, I never dared to. Didn't she let me share her company so she could listen to me play? Well then, play was what I had to do.

The first few times, her husband sat in on the concerts, and, lulled by the music, he'd doze off; but he finally decided not to stand on ceremony, and whenever he was tired he would leave us and go to bed. Sometimes one or more of their neighbors would join us, but they must not have found the whole thing very entertaining, since more often we were alone. It was on such a night, as I was preparing to shift from one motif to the next, that Clara (her name was Clara) stopped me with a point-blank question, "Borja, have you noticed how sad he is?"

"Who? The boss?" I asked, also lowering my voice. "He seems preoccupied, but. . . ."

"Then, it is so, isn't it?" she said, fixing her feverish eyes on me. And as though she were talking to herself, "He is eating his heart out, and he can't help it. Oh, may God have mercy on us!"

I just sat there puzzled, and I must have stayed like that for a long time, until her commanding voice shook me out of it:

"What's the matter with you? Go on, play!"

After that, she seemed more concerned and acted as though she was annoyed at me. She would sit down further away, in the shadows, as if I were the cause of some deep displeasure in her; she would make me stop playing so she could follow her train of thought better, and upon returning to reality and finding in my eyes that silent submission as I awaited her next command, she would become irritable for no reason at all.

"What's the matter with you? Go on, play!"

At other times she would accuse me of being timid, trying to get me to confess my past and my "gallant" exploits; according to her, I couldn't possibly have been so rational all my life, and she'd ironically praise me for being so reserved, or she'd twist up her face in a fit of uncontrollable laughter and say, "Saint Borja, the timid and discreet."

I would feel myself turning redder by the moment, under the glare of her fiery eyes, simply because I could never help but be aware of how ridiculous I looked. Through every moment of my life, my being bald and overweight has deprived me of the self-confidence that I needed. Who knows? Maybe that's why I'm a failure!

Things went on like this for a year, and during that time I lived only for the evenings. When I recall it, it seems that one evening was fused with the next one, so that the intervening hours were hardly perceptible in spite of the fact that back in those days they must have seemed an eternity to me. . . . One whole year compressed into one long night.

I'm coming to the high point of my life. How can I describe it so that I myself will be able to believe it? It's so inexplicable, so absurd, so unexpected!

One night, while we were alone, and after I had stopped playing in response to one of her gestures, I was staring at her adoringly.

I thought that she was absorbed in thought, when suddenly I saw her jump up and turn out the light. Instinctively I stood up, but in the darkness I felt two arms encircling my neck and a mouth breathing excitedly, searching for mine.

I staggered out. Once back in my room, I opened the window and spent the night sitting by it. I couldn't get enough air. My heart was pounding as though it would jump out of my chest; I could feel it in my throat, choking me. What a night!

I waited for the next one with fear. I felt I was the plaything of some dream. The boss scolded me for making an error, and even though he did it in front of everyone, I didn't feel angry or ashamed. That night he attended our little concert. She seemed to be terribly depressed.

And another day went by without our being able to get off by ourselves. The third day came and I threw myself at her feet covering her hands with kisses and tears of gratitude, but haughty and disdainful, she rejected me, and in her coldest voice asked me to play.

No, I must have dreamed that moment of bliss! Would you believe that I never, never again touched my lips to even the tips of her fingers? On one occasion when wild with passion, I tried to claim my rights as her lover, she ordered me to leave in such a loud voice that I was afraid she'd wake up the boss, who was sleeping upstairs.

What a martyrdom! The months went by and Clara's sadness seemed to dissipate, but not her anger. How could I have offended her?

Until finally one night I was crossing the town square with my case under my arm, and her husband, in person, blocked my path. He seemed extremely excited, and he kept his hand on my shoulder with a disturbing familiarity while he spoke.

"None of that music," he told me. "My wife's nerves are on edge, and we have to start having a little respect for whims like this."

I didn't understand.

"Yes, sir. Come to the bar with me, and we'll drink a toast to the future boss."

He was born. From my desk, amidst her screams while giving birth I heard the first feeble cry of a newborn child. How my heart did beat! My son! Because he was mine. She didn't have to tell me! Mine! Mine! I, the lonely bachelor, the man who had never had a family, to whom no woman had ever bestowed her favors unless there was money involved! I now had a son, the son of the woman I loved!

Why didn't I die when he was born? On my desk's green blotter, I broke into such violent sobs that the lampshade shook, and someone who came to ask me something left on tiptoes.

It wasn't until a whole month had passed that I was taken into the heir's presence. His convalescing mother had him on her lap, and was rocking him lovingly. I bent down, moved to the point of anguish, and trembling, with my fingertips I raised the netting that covered him and I was finally able to see him. I felt like shouting, "Son!" But when I looked up, I found Clara staring at me, quietly, almost ironically.

"Careful!" she warned me. And then, out loud, "Don't go and wake him up."

Her husband, who was with me, kissed her delicately behind the ear.

"You must have suffered so much, my poor dear!"

"You can't begin to imagine," she answered, "but, who cares, as long as I've made you happy!"

And then, without respite, I was forced to endure the horrible penance of hearing that man call the baby *his* son, when he was mine, when he was *my* son.

Idiot! I was tempted a thousand times to shout the truth in his face, to make this proud and self-confident man see how superior I was to him. But, what would the consequences be, especially for the innocent little boy? I held my peace, and silently, with all my soul, I worshiped and loved that little creature, my flesh and blood, who would learn to call a stranger "father."

Meanwhile, it got harder and harder to figure out Clara's behavior. Our musical sessions, needless to say, were never resumed, and with the slightest pretext, she would refuse to receive me in her house whenever I called.

She seemed to be following an irrevocable decision, and I had to be content with seeing my son whenever his nursemaid took him for a walk in the town square. Then both of us, the husband and I, would follow him from the office window, and our moist eyes, filled with pleasure at the sight, would meet with a look of understanding.

But during those next three memorable years, as the child grew, it became easier for me to see him since the boss, every day more and more doting, brought him to the store and kept him at his side until they came after him.

One morning when I had him in my arms, Clara came to get him. Never have I seen such a fierce rage! She was like a lioness rescuing her cub! Her words were not pronounced; they were spit in my face, "Why are you kissing him like that? What are you trying to do, you scoundrel?"

It seemed to me that she was living in constant fear of the boy's getting to love me or of my talking. At times, the latter fear gained the ascendancy over the other and, so as not to exasperate me too much, she'd let him come close to me; but at other times, she'd keep him completely to herself, as though I could somehow hurt him.

What a strange woman! I've never understood what I meant to her. A whim, a plaything, an instrument!

That's how things stood, when suddenly a foreigner arrived, and we spent half the day looking over the books and the invoices. At lunch time the boss informed me that he had just signed a deed transferring ownership of the store, that he was sick and tired of the business world and small-town life, and that he'd probably be going back to the capital with his family.

But why describe the horribly painful pressures of those last days of my life? In January, it will be twenty years and it still upsets me when I recall them.

Dear God! Everything I had loved was leaving! A stranger was taking everything away so he could enjoy it in peace! He was depriving me of all that was mine! With that in mind, I was sorely tempted to break my silence. Oh! How I would have loved to destroy the happy ignorance in which that thief would live and die! May God forgive me!

They left. The night before, as a final whim, the woman who destroyed my life, but who also gave it a momentary intensity I didn't deserve, had me play her three favorite pieces and when I was finished, she rewarded me by letting me kiss my son. If the

power of suggestion exists, the imprint of that kiss must be preserved in his soul.

They left! When we were already at the little station, where I
had gone to say good-bye, he handed me a small package, saying
that he had forgotten it the night before.

"Something to remember us by," he repeated to me.

"Where shall I write to you?" I screamed when the train was
already starting to pull away, and from the train platform he
called, "I don't know. We'll send you our address!"

It seemed like an order for me to keep my distance. Through
the train window I saw my son, with his nose pressed up against
the pane. Behind him stood his mother, serious, with a blank
look on her face.

I went back to the store, which would continue to carry out its
role in society with no apparent change, and I hid the package.
I didn't open it until I was alone in my room that night.

It was a photograph. The same one I have with me today; a
portrait of Clara with her son on her lap, clasped to her bosom
as though to hide or defend him.

And she has held him prisoner, cut off from my affection so
effectively that I've had no news of him for twenty years, not even
once; and I'll probably never see him again on God's good earth!
If he's alive, he must be a full-grown man by now. Is he happy?
Maybe his future would have been too restricted at my side. His
name is Pedro . . . Pedro and the other man's last name.

Every night I take the photograph, kiss it, and read the inscrip-
tion on the back that they wrote down for the child: "From Pedro,
to his friend Borja." "His friend Borja! . . ." Pedro will go to his
grave never knowing that such a friend ever existed!

—Translated by Roberta H. Kimble

COMMENTARY

D'Halmar presents adultery not as a crime of passion
nor as an immoral act but simply as a logical necessity. Clara, whose
name reflects her clear thinking, loves her husband and sins in a very

cool and calculated manner in order to satisfy her husband's desire to have a child. Once her purpose is accomplished, Clara rejects forever the man who was her lover for only one night.

Although the epigraph in French indicates the Naturalist author's objective and matter-of-fact attitude toward life, the story's value rests on the character development of the protagonist-narrator. A middle-class bachelor, he seems to be leading a totally uneventful life. And yet, what a tragedy to devote the past twenty-five years to the recollection of so ephemeral an event! Although he suspects the truth, his masculine vanity forces him to think that Clara did love him, even if only for one night.

The story of this bachelor is made even more tragic by the fact that he himself is the narrator. Unlike the majority of the Naturalists as well as the majority of Chilean novelists and short story writers, D'Halmar rejects the long, minute descriptions in favor of a more unrhetorical, elliptical style which puts him decades ahead of his colleagues. In keeping with the conversational tone, paragraphs and sentences are usually short, there are relatively few adjectives, and similes and metaphors appear infrequently.

This relatively simple style and the pragmatic spirit of the plot notwithstanding, the story is embellished with a kind of poetic, oneiric tone that stems from the flute leitmotiv, from the conjuring up of distant memories, and from the strangeness of the episode.

The initial impression that the narrator is rambling on without a fixed plan disappears with the recognition of the story's structural unity. The photograph of Clara and Pedro, in addition to framing the story, gives it a note of suspense owing to the fact that Pedro's identity is not revealed until the very end. Although this suspense is somewhat contrived, it does not weaken at all the sincerity with which the protagonist unfolds his undramatic tragedy.

D'Halmar's analysis of an individual's complex psychological feelings, presented in a poetic, oneiric tone helped start an important Chilean trend to which some of the better twentieth-century writers belong: María Luisa Bombal, Manuel Rojas, and Fernando Alegría.

Modernism

In the development of the Spanish American short story, the Modernists made a significant contribution. Whereas relatively few Modernist novels were written, the short story was assiduously cultivated by the Modernists for forty years, 1880-1920, with some truly excellent results.

Although Modernism was artistically a reaction against Romanticism, Realism, and Naturalism, in Spanish America all four of these movements coincided. Some anachronistic Romantics continued writing until the end of the nineteenth century, while the Realists and the Naturalists reached their peaks in the same decade of the 1890s that witnessed the triumph of Modernism.

The fundamental trait of this movement was the supremacy attached to artistic sensibility. In their eagerness to create art for art's sake, the Modernists rejected the sentimental stories and the melodramatic episodes of the Romantics, the overly localized scenes of the Realists, and the excessively "scientific" and "ugly" case studies of the Naturalists. The Modernist hero was the sensitive artist (or simply the sensitive man) incapacitated by the bourgeois society surrounding him. The Modernists were sickened by the political, social, and cultural barbarism of their compatriots and they sought refuge in an exotic world. Many abandoned their countries, while others searched for escape in the ivory towers on their own roofs. Their ideal was France, symbolized by eighteenth-century palace life at Versailles through which they became enthusiasts of the Greek ideal and extended to Renaissance Italy, Medieval Byzantium, or the Germany of the Wagnerian gods.

The core of Modernist style was synesthesia or the correspondence of the senses. Ruben Darío wrote a poem entitled "Symphony in Gray Major," which was later parodied by fellow Modernist José Asunción Silva in "Strawberry-with-Milk-Colored-Symphony." Prose became for the first time more than an instrument for communication. It had to be beautiful: its palette of soft shades had to please the eye; its alliteration, assonance, onomatopoeic effects, and rhythm composed a symphony that delighted the ear; its marbles and exotic fabrics tempted the reader to extend his fingers and touch them; while the aromatic perfumes, the sparkling wine, and the succulent delicacies aroused the senses of smell and taste. In order to achieve these effects, the Modernists had to expand the literary language through foreign words, new forms of Spanish roots, and new similes and metaphors.

The foreign influence was not limited, however, to new words. The Modernists, in contrast with the Realists, were cosmopolitans, who identified with their fellow artists around the world. They felt equally at home in the cafés of Buenos Aires or Paris. Their literary magazines, which played a basic role in the movement, published works by French, Italian, Spanish, Portuguese, German, English, and American authors. Besides their debt to the French Parnassians and Symbolists, the Modernists also felt a great admiration for artists as diverse as Walt Whitman, Edgar Allen Poe, Oscar Wilde, Richard Wagner, and D'Annunzio.

The war of 1898 between Spain and the United States had a profound effect on Modernism. The interest in the exotic gave way to a self-analysis that was both personal and continental — but not national — and to a discovery of the American landscape. By 1896, the initiators of the movement (José Martí, Manuel Gutiérrez Nájera, Julián del Casal, and José Asunción Silva), with the exception of Rubén Darío (1876-1916), had died and a second generation of Modernists gave new vigor to the movement with greater thematic and stylistic variety: Ricardo Jaimes Freyre (1868-1933), Amado Nervo (1870-1919), Leopoldo Lugones (1874-1938), Julio Herrera y Reissig (1875-1910), José Santos Chocano (1875-1934), and Rafael Arévalo Martínez (1884-1975). The artistically written philosophical essays of José Enrique Rodó (1871-1917) belie the nonintellectual, hedonist image of the Modernists.

Although the majority of the Modernists expressed themselves principally in verse, the following short stories exemplify the evolution of the movement from art for art's sake to social protest.

Manuel Gutiérrez Nájera

(1859–1895)

Mexican. The most famous of his several pseudonyms was the Duque Job. Although he imitated French style in both dress and writing, he never traveled outside of Mexico. His parents were well educated and from childhood on, he read French as well as Spanish authors. He spent his life writing for the newspapers: poetry, feature articles, travel notes, literary criticism, and short stories. The stories were published in two volumes: *Cuentos frágiles* (1883), which contains "After the Races," and *Cuentos color de humo* (1890–1894). Along with José Martí, he is credited with initiating Modernism in Latin America in the early 1880s. In 1894, with Carlos Díaz Dufoo, he founded the *Revista Azul* which introduced Mexican and Spanish American Modernists and their European precursors to Mexican literary circles. The journal ceased publication shortly after his premature death.

AFTER THE RACES

When Berta put her silver hairpins and her ruby earrings on the marble tabletop, the bronze clock surmounted by the figure of Galatea asleep among roses chimed twelve in its high pitch. Berta let her trembling Venetian blond braids kiss her waist and blew out the wax candle so that she wouldn't see herself undressed in the mirror. Then, stepping with her bare feet on the forget-me-nots of the carpet, she felt her way to her narrow bed of rose-colored wood, and, after a very brief prayer, she lay down on the white quilt which had the fragrance of new Dutch linen and violets. In the cozy bedroom the only sounds were the silent steps of the elves who wanted to see Berta asleep and the tic-toc of the tireless pendulum, eternally in love with the hours. Berta closed her eyes, but didn't sleep. The horses of the Hippodrome raced through her imagination at full speed. How beautiful life is! A house covered with tapestries and surrounded by a belt of white camellias on the porches; below, the carriages, their lacquer brilliantly reflecting the sun's rays, their cushioned and warm interior, smelling of Russian leather and kidskin; the horses pawing in the spacious stables, and the beautiful leaves of the banana plants standing erect in Japanese vases; above, a resplendent blue sky of new satin with the notes of songbirds rising, like crystal souls, through the fluid amber of the atmosphere; inside, a white-haired father who can never find enough pearls or enough golden lace for his daughter's wardrobe; a mother who keeps vigil at her bedside when she's sick, and who would like to surround her with cotton balls as if she were made of fragile porcelain; the children who crawl about naked in their cradles, and the untarnished and cheerful mirror hanging above the marble-topped dressing table. Outside, in the street, the movement of life, the coming and going of the carriages, the hustle-bustle; and in the evening, after the ball or the theater, the disconsolate figure of a young man in love who waits for her and who departs satisfied only after he has seen her step down from her coach or close the shutters of her balcony. Much splendor, many flowers, and a new silk dress: that's living!

Berta thinks about the races. Caracole should have won. In Chantilly, not long ago, he won a prize. Pablo Escandón would not have paid eleven thousand pesos for a bad mare and a bad stallion. Furthermore, the man who purchased the mare in Paris was Manuel Villamil, the greatest Mexican expert in the sport of kings. Berta, next Sunday, is going to make a formal wager with her daddy: she'll bet on Aigle; if she loses, she will have to embroider some slippers; and if she wins, they will buy her the mirror that Madame Drouot has in her shop window. The frame is trimmed with blue velvet obliquely outlining the glass, below a garland of flowers. How pretty it is! Her face reflected in that mirror will look like that of a houri, who, peeping through the roses of paradise, looks at the world.

Berta half opens her eyes, but closes them again at once, because the bedroom is dark.

The elves, anxious to see her asleep in order to kiss her on the mouth, without her feeling it, begin to encircle her with sleep-inducing poppies and to burn grains of opium in little pipe bowls. The images begin fading and slowly vanish from Berta's imagination. Her thoughts flicker. She no longer sees the Hippodrome bathed in resplendent sunlight, nor the red-clad judges officiating in the pretorium, nor does she hear the crack of the whips. Only two figures remain in the mirror of her memory blurred by the mist of her dreams: Caracole and her boyfriend.

> *Now all is at rest in unprotected slumber;*
> *The blue lily dozes in the window;*
> *Do you hear? From its tower the bell*
> *Peals midnight; sleep, sleep.*

The playful little genie that opened Berta's bedroom for me, as though he were opening a box of candy on New Year's Day, placed a finger on my lips and, taking me by the hand, led me through the rooms. I was afraid of stumbling on a piece of furniture, waking up the servants and the owners. I moved, therefore, with caution, holding my breath and almost gliding over the carpet. After a few steps I bumped against the piano, which complained in B-flat; but my companion gave a puff, as if he were blowing out the light of a candle, and the notes fell silently on the carpet: the breath of the genie had broken those soap bubbles. In this manner we passed through several rooms: the dining room from whose walnut-paneled walls protruded immense candelabra with their spermaceti candles extinguished; the porches, full of flowerpots and filigreed birdcages; a corridor, long and narrow, like a hollow reed, which led to the sleeping quarters of the servants; the twisted spiral staircase used to climb up to the roof, and a labyrinth of little rooms, full of furniture and useless junk.

At last, we arrived at a little door through whose keyhole a faint ray of light filtered. The door was barred on the inside, but since nothing resists the touch of the genies, my companion entered through the keyhole and removed the andiron which was being used as a bolt. We entered: there was Manon, the seamstress. On the floor barely covered with tattered matting, lay a book displaying its white pages, while a dying candle was licking the edges of the candlestick with its salamander tongue. Manon must have been reading when sleep surprised her, as indicated by that imprudent light which could have started a fire, by the worn-out volume that lay next to the iron cot, by the bare arm drooping from the mattress with the cold immodesty of marble, and by the crumpled blankets. Manon is beautiful, like a wilted lily. She is twenty years and would like to read life, just as when she was a girl she liked to browse through the volume of engravings which her father kept under lock and key on a shelf of the library. But Manon is an orphan and is poor: she will never again see obedient maids and submissive servants around her as before; they have departed leaving her alone, poor, and sick in the midst of life. Of that former existence, which on occasions she imagines was only a dream, nothing remains but a complexion that still has a scent of almonds, and a head of hair that hunger, misery, and work have not yet made coarse. Her thoughts are like those enchanted little children who appear in stories; in the daytime they go about barefoot and dressed in plain smocks; but let night arrive, and you will see how those poor little beggars don jackets of rustling silk and adorn themselves with pheasant feathers.

That afternoon, Manon had attended the races. In Berta's house everybody loves her and indulges her, as one loves and indulges a little lapdog, dressing it in wool in the winter and placing in its mouth sponge cake soaked in milk. There are some showers of affection that feel like hailstorms. Everybody was aware of the former social position of the humble seamstress, and for this reason they treated her with more than average consideration. Berta gave her her old dresses, and she would take her along when she went for a ride or shopping. The orphan received those displays of affection, as the poor beggar receives the coins that a pious hand tosses from a balcony. Sometimes those coins can crack a man's skull.

That afternoon, Manon had attended the races. They left her in the carriage, because it doesn't look right for an aristocratic family to be accompanied on outings by the maids; they left her there, in case Berta's dress or the ribbons on her bonnet should tear. Manon, glued to the windows of the carriage, looked at the track and the stands, in the way a poor little sick girl gazes, through her balcony window at life and the movement of the passersby. The horses dashed across the arid track like lightning with their manes fluttering in the wind. Horses! She too had experienced that pleasure, half spiritual and half physical, of galloping along a sandy road. The blood runs faster, and the air lashes as if it were angry. The body feels young, and the soul thinks that it has regained its wings.

And the stands, glimpsed from afar, seemed like enormous bouquets made of satin leaves and flesh carnations. Silk caresses like a lover's hand and she felt an infinite desire to experience once again that touch. When a woman walks, her skirt moves along singing a hymn in her praise. When would she hear those stanzas again? And she looked at her hands, and the tips of her fingers mistreated by the needle, and she peered obstinately at that picture of splendor and gaiety, as on St. Sylvester's Eve when the poor children see the cakes, the sweets, the caramel pyramids which they will not taste and which adorn the display windows of the confectioners' shops. Why was she banished from that paradise? Her mirror told her: "You are beautiful and you are young." Why did she suffer so much? Then, a secret voice arose inside her, saying: "Don't envy those things. Silk will tear, velvet gets creased, skin gets wrinkled with the years. Under the blue surface of the lake there is much mud. Everything has its bright side and its gloomy side. Remember your friend Rosa Thé? Well she lives in that music hall heaven, so full of powder, and of glitter, and of painted flats. And the husband she chose deceives her and flees from her side in order to run after women who are worth less than she. There are shrouds made of silk and coffins of lignum vitae, but in all of them the worms swarm and chew."

Manon, nevertheless, yearned for those triumphs and that finery. Therefore, as she slept, she dreamed of celebrations and parties. A gallant suitor, resembling those knights-errant who figure in the German legends, stopped under her window and, climbing up a ladder of blue silk, arrived at her side, wrapped his arms strongly around her and climbed down, swaying in the air, into the shadows of the olive grove below. There, a horse as nimble, as nervous as Caracole, waited. And the knight, carrying her in his arms, as you would carry a sleeping child, mounted the spirited horse which ran at full speed through the forest. The mastiffs of the village barked and even the windows flew open, revealing many a timorous face; the trees fled and fled in the opposite direction, like an army in rout, and the knight pressed her against his chest and with his burning breath curled the fine hairs on the back of her neck.

At that moment dawn emerged, fresh and perfumed, from its marble bathtub filled with dew. Don't enter—oh cold light!—don't

enter the small room where Manon dreams of love and riches!
Let her sleep, with her white arm drooping from the mattress like
a virgin who has become intoxicated with rosewater! Let the stars
come down from the blue sky, and fasten on to her tiny ears of
transparent porcelain!

— *Translated by Dennis Seager*

COMMENTARY

"After the Races" is a magnificent example of the first
phase of Modernist literature which is enhanced as a short story by its
Romantic traces. What instills life into the tableau is the compassion
for Manon expressed by the narrator. In opposition to the absolute
objectivity of the Parnassian aesthetics followed by the triumphant
Modernists of 1896 (date of Rubén Darío's *Prosas profanas*), Gutiérrez
Nájera (or the narrator) intervenes directly in the story. The elves allow
him to enter both bedrooms and he himself ends the story with an ex-
hortation to the dawn's early light. The contrast between the rich señorita
and the poor seamstress is also more in keeping with Romanticism than
with Modernism.

As a work of art, "After the Races" displays a structural unity that
attests to the maturity of the short story genre in Mexico and Spanish
America. The two scenes that comprise the story are tightly linked.
The most obvious line that connects them is the author's "trip" guided
by the elf, but there are also a series of details in Manon's scene which
match those of the preceding one: the dying candle, the memory of
the races, the windows in the carriage, the gallant suitor, the blue sky,
and the porcelain. Whereas the Naturalists dehumanize their characters by converting them into beasts, the Modernists dehumanize them
by transforming them into art objects. Berta's mother takes care of her
daughter "as if she were made of fragile porcelain"; Manon has "tiny
ears of transparent porcelain"; Bertha has "Venetian blond braids"
and "Manon is beautiful, like a wilted lily."

Besides the unity between scenes, each one has its own structure.
Berta's is divided in three: the descriptions of her bedroom, her thoughts,
and her dream. The description of the bedroom itself has a structure
that clearly distinguishes it from the detailed descriptions of the Naturalists. The exclamations "How beautiful life is!" and "That's living!"
reinforce Berta's world view and also form a frame around the inventory
of the "Modernist museum." Other structural reinforcements are the
"marble tabletop" and the "marble-topped dressing table"; "the bronze
clock" and "the tic-toc of the tireless pendulum"; and the phrase "many

flowers" that encompasses the roses on the clock where Galatea sleeps, the forget-me-nots on the carpet, the rose-colored wood of the bed, the fragrance of violet from the quilt, and the white camellias on the porches. The second part of Berta's scene is based primarily on her thoughts about the races, a theme introduced in the middle of the first paragraph: "the horses of the Hippodrome raced through her imagination at full speed." The realistic moment is captured with a somewhat less ornate style in which verbs, some in the preterit tense, predominate. The second part ends with a description of Madame Drouot's mirror which recalls the previous description of the bedroom and introduces the dream of part three. The description of the mirror frame places us within the bedroom while its glass helps produce the Impressionist "painting" of the dream: "the mirror of her memory blurred by the mist of her dreams." The end of Berta's scene is marked by two allusions to the first part: "her thoughts flicker" and the extinguished candle; the bell in the tower (from the poem) and the bronze clock.

The transitional scene, that is, the one that links the two bedrooms, also reinforces the total structure of the story with the phrase "as if he were blowing out the light of a candle."

Paralleling Berta's scene, Manon's scene is also divided into three parts. The description of her bedroom is notable for its lack of furniture and decorative elements. All that is seen is the iron cot but the multisensory luxury of Berta's bedroom is balanced by a series of images that the author uses to describe Manon. Her bare arm has "the cold immodesty of marble"; she is "beautiful, like a wilted lily"; her complexion "has a scent of almonds"; and her thoughts at night "don jackets of rustling silk and adorn themselves with pheasant feathers." The unity of this first part is based on a progression toward the fantastic and the two allusions to books. The second part, like that of Berta's scene, is an interpretation of the day at the races. In order to emphasize Manon's plight, the initial sentence is repeated word for word. In each paragraph allusions are made to Manon's tragic situation while little by little reality transforms itself into fantasy. The poor children on St. Sylvester's Eve echo the enchanted little children of part one and reinforce the compassion expressed for Manon. Manon's dream, which parallels Berta's, comes to an end with elements that put the finishing touches on both Manon's tripartite scene and the whole story. The allusion to the "white arm drooping from the mattress" echoes the initial introduction of Manon while the mention of light, rosewater, porcelain, and blue sky evokes the first part of Berta's scene. The importance of the leitmotiv of the clocks is perceived when the story ends at dawn, thus completing the chronological frame of the story which began at midnight.

Several examples of the multisensorial appeal (colors, the tic-toc, the perfumed flowers, the different fabrics and metals, marble, and sweets) which contribute to the beauty of this story have already been pointed out. This multisensorial appeal, however, which in the majority of the

French Parnassians and the Spanish American Modernists is often cold and artificial, in Gutiérrez Nájera is distinguished by its *gracia* or delicate charm. There are examples of alliteration and diminutives, but what most creates the sensation of *gracia* are the images where the inanimate object is delicately humanized. Berta's braids tremble as they kiss her waist; the pendulum is in love with the hours; the notes of the songbirds rise like crystal souls; "the notes fell silently on the carpet"; "the breath of the genie had broken those soap bubbles."

In keeping with the Mexican tradition, Gutiérrez Nájera, even in his most Parnassian moments, cannot completely put aside social problems. In the midst of compiling the Modernist inventory, there is a sincere compassion for the poor which prevents the story from becoming sickeningly sweet. True, the poor seamstress in this story is hardly a representative of the Mexican proletariat, but in other stories Gutiérrez Nájera expresses the same compassion for the more typically Mexican street urchins.

Rubén Darío

(1867-1916)

Nicaraguan. The Modernist par excellence, Darío is also one of the most famous poets of the Spanish language. At age thirteen, he was already writing poetry and at fifteen he undertook the first of his many trips, which were to characterize his entire life. In 1882, in El Salvador, he met the poet Francisco Gavidia who introduced him to French literature. In 1886, he went to Chile where he worked as a newspaperman and published *Azul* (1888), the first of his four key volumes. A second enlarged edition appeared in 1890 in Guatemala where Darío was then living. He married while in Costa Rica and then went to Spain in 1892. He returned to Latin America through Cuba and became Colombian consul in Argentina. The years of 1893-1898 spent in Buenos Aires mark the high point of Modernism, represented by Darío's publication of *Prosas profanas* and *Los raros* in 1896 and his surrounding himself with an entourage of other brilliant young poets including Argentinean Leopoldo Lugones and Bolivian Ricardo Jaimes Freyre. After 1898, Darío lived almost entirely in Europe, especially in Paris. His next two important books of verse, *Cantos de vida y esperanza* (1905) and *El canto errante* (1907), indicate a partial rejection of the Parnassian and Symbolist *préciosité* usually associated with his name in favor of a more personal expression and a concern for the destiny of Latin America in a hemisphere increasingly dominated by the United States. "The Ruby" appeared in the first edition of *Azul.*

THE RUBY

"Ah! So it's true! So that Parisian scholar has succeeded in extracting from the depths of his retorts, from his matrasses, the purple crystal with which the walls of my palace are inlaid."

And upon saying that, the little gnome scurried back and forth, from one place to another, with short hops, through the deep cave that served as his dwelling, causing his long beard and the bell on his pointed blue cap to shake.

It *was* true, a friend of the centenarian Chevreul — a would-be Althotas — the chemist Frémy, had just discovered the method of making rubies and sapphires.

Excited and deeply moved, the gnome, who was erudite and had a rather lively temperament, continued his monologue.

"Oh, sages of the Middle Ages! Oh, Albertus Magnus, Averroes, Raimundus Lullus! All of you failed to see the shining wonder of the Philosopher's Stone, and lo and behold, without studying the Aristotelian formulas, without knowing the cabala and necromancy, here comes a man of the nineteenth century to invent in broad daylight what we produce in our subterranean world. The magic formula! For twenty days fuse a mixture of silica and lead aluminate; colored with potassium dichromate or with cobalt oxide. Words that truly resemble a diabolical language."

Laughter.

Then he stood still.

The corpus delecti was there, in the center of the grotto, on a large golden rock: a small ruby, round, gently sparkling, resembling a pomegranate seed in the sunlight.

The gnome blew a horn which he carried at his waist, and the echo resounded throughout the vast cavern. Within a few moments, an uproar, a mad rush, a clamor. All the gnomes had arrived.

The cave was spacious, and in it there was a strange white glow. It was the splendor of the carbuncles that sparkled in the stone roof, inlaid, sunken, bunched together, in a multitude of groups; with a soft light illuminating everything.

In that radiance, one could see the marvelous abode in all its splendor. On the walls, on top of pieces of silver and gold, among veins of lapis lazuli, a great array of precious stones created fanciful designs similar to the arabesques of a mosque. Rainbows emerged from the crystals of the diamonds, clear and pure like drops of water; near the hanging stalactites of chalcedony, the emeralds radiated their resplendent green; and the sapphires, in bouquets that dangled from the walls, resembled large trembling blue flowers. Rows of gilded topazes and amethysts encircled the area; and from the pavement thickly set with opals, from on top of the polished chrysoprase and the agate, a thin stream of water gushed forth from time to time and fell with musical sweetness, in harmonious drops like the notes of a metal flute blown very softly.

There was Puck, that rascal Puck who had meddled in the matter. He had brought the corpus delecti, the false ruby, the one that lay there upon the golden rock like a sacrilege amongst all that sparkling wonder.

When the gnomes got together, some with their hammers and small hatchets in their hands, others dressed up in their bright red pointed hoods embroidered with jewels, all of them curious, Puck said: "You have asked me to bring you the latest example of human counterfeiting and I have satisfied your desires."

The gnomes, seated with their legs crossed Turkish style, pulled on their mustaches, gave thanks to Puck by slowly bowing their heads, while those closest to him examined with amazement his pretty wings, similar to those of a dragonfly.

He continued: "Oh Earth! Oh, Woman! From the time I saw Titania I've been nothing but a slave of the one; an almost mystical admirer of the other."

And then, as if he were speaking in a blissful dream state: "Those rubies! In the great city of Paris, while flying invisibly, I saw them everywhere. They sparkled on the necklaces of courtesans, on the bizarre ornaments of the parvenus, on the rings of Italian princes, and on the bracelets of the prima donnas."

And with a mischievous smile he continued: "I stole into a certain very fashionable crimson colored boudoir. . . . There was a beautiful woman asleep. From her neck I plucked the medallion and from the medallion the ruby. There you have it."

Everyone burst out laughing. What a jingling of bells!

"Wow, that Puck sure is a devil!"

And then they gave their opinions about that fake, man-made, or what's worse, sage-made stone!

"Glass!"

"Witchcraft!"

"Poison and cabala!"

"Chemistry!"

"It pretends to imitate a section of the rainbow!"

"The rubicund treasure from the depths of the globe!"

"Made from the solidified rays of the setting sun."

The oldest gnome, walking with gnarled legs and a long snow-white beard, looked like a patriarch with his face covered with wrinkles. "Gentlemen!" he said. "You don't know what you're saying."

Everyone listened.

"I, I am older than all of you, since I'm now barely fit to hammer the facets of the diamonds; I, who witnessed the building of these deep fortresses; I, who chiseled the bones of the earth, who molded the gold, who one day gave a punch to a stone wall, and fell into a lake where I raped a nymph; I, the elder, I shall tell you how the ruby was made. Listen."

Puck smiled, inquisitively. All the gnomes surrounded the ancient fellow whose gray hairs appeared pale in the brilliance of the jewels and whose hands cast moving shadows on the walls covered with precious stones, like a canvas covered with honey where grains of rice were flung.

"One day, our squadrons that were in charge of the diamond mines went on strike, a strike that shook the whole earth, and we fled through the craters of the volcanoes.

"The world was happy, everything was full of vigor and youth; and the roses, and the fresh green leaves, and the birds in whose beaks the seeds enter and the chirping bursts out, and the whole countryside greeted the sun and the fragrant springtime.

"The hills in bloom were full of harmony produced by the warbling of birds and the buzzing of bees; it was a great and sacred wedding orchestrated by light: on the trees the sap glistened profoundly, and among the animals everything was stirring either in the form of bleating or chanting, and in the gnomes there was laughter and happiness.

"I had gone out through an extinct crater. Before my eyes there was an enormous field. With one leap I put myself on a large tree, an old evergreen oak. Then I climbed down the trunk, and I found myself near a stream, a small clear river where the waters babbled crystalline jokes to one another. I was thirsty. I tried to drink there. . . . Now, listen more closely."

"Arms, backs, naked breasts, white lilies, roses, small ivory rolls topped with cherries; echoes of golden festive laughter: and there amongst the foam, amongst the choppy waters, beneath the green branches. . . ."

"Nymphs?"

"No, women. I knew which of the caves was mine. By banging on the ground, I made the black sand open up and arrived at my palace. You poor little young gnomes, you have much to learn!

"I scurried along beneath the shoots of some new ferns, over some stones which had been polished by the foamy murmuring current; and she, the beautiful one, the woman, I seized her by the waist, with this arm which was once so muscular; she shouted, I banged on the ground; we descended. Above, all was fear and wonderment; below, the arrogant and victorious gnome.

"One day I was hammering a chunk of an immense diamond which shone like a star and which broke into small particles with the stroke of my mallet.

"The floor of my workshop resembled the remains of a shattered sun. The beloved woman was resting on one side, a human rose amongst sapphire flower pots, a golden empress on a bed of rock crystal, completely naked and magnificent like a goddess.

"But in the midst of my palace, my queen, my beloved, my beauty, was deceiving me. When a man is truly in love, his passion penetrates everything, and he is capable of transcending the earth.

"She was in love with a man, and from her prison, she would transmit her sighs to him. They would pass through the pores of the terrestrial crust and reach him; and he, equally in love with her, would kiss the roses of a certain garden; and she, his beloved, I noticed, would experience—sudden convulsions in which she extended her lips, pink and fresh like the petals of a centifolia rose. How could they feel each other's presence? With all my magical powers, I do not know.

"I had just finished my work: a huge pile of diamonds all made in one day; the earth opened up its granite crevices like thirsty lips, awaiting the brilliant breaking up of the rich crystal. At the end of the task, tired, I broke one last rock with my hammer and fell asleep.

"I awoke a little while later, upon hearing something like a moan.

"From her bed, from her quarters which were richer and more dazzling than those of all the queens in the Orient, my beloved, my abducted woman, had fled in desperation. Oh! And trying to escape through the hole opened by my granite mallet, naked and beautiful, she destroyed her body, once as white and smooth as orange blossoms, marble and roses, on the edges of the broken diamonds. With her wounded sides dripping blood, her groans were so touching they brought me to tears. Oh what grief!

"I got up, took her in my arms, and gave her my most ardent kisses; but the blood continued to flow inundating the room, and the huge diamond mass became tinged with scarlet.

"As I kissed her, I seemed to detect a perfume escaping from her burning lips: her soul; her body remained inert.

"When our grand patriarch, the godlike centenarian from the bowels of the earth, passed through, he found that multitude of red diamonds. . . .

A pause.

"Do you understand?"

The gnomes, very gravely rose.

They examined more closely the false stone, the work of the sage.

"Look, it doesn't have facets."

"It has a dull gleam."

"Impostor!"

"It's round like the shell of a scarab."

And in turn, one by one, they went to pull out of the walls pieces of the arabesque, rubies as large as an orange, red and sparkling like a blood-tinged diamond; and they said:

"This is ours, oh Mother Earth!"

It was an orgy of brilliance and color.

And laughing, they began to throw into the air giant luminous stones.

Suddenly, with all the dignity of a gnome:

"Well then, we condemn it."

Everyone understood. They took the false ruby, broke it into many pieces and flung the fragments—with terrible disdain—into a pit below which led into a very ancient carbonized jungle.

Then, with joined hands they began dancing a wild sonorous

dance on their rubies, on their opals, within the confines of those gleaming walls.

And they celebrated with laughter seeing themselves enlarged in the form of their shadows. By this time Puck was flying outside, in the buzzing of the new dawn, on his way to a flowering meadow. And he murmured — with his usual blushing smile,

"Earth. . . . Woman. . . . Because you, oh Mother Earth! You are great and fertile, your breast is inexhaustible and sacred; and from your dark womb flows the sap of the sturdy trees, and the gold and the diamond-like water, and the chaste lily. Everything that is pure and strong and that may not be falsified! And you, Woman, you are spirit and flesh, all love!"

— Translated by Jill Gibian

COMMENTARY

If Gutiérrez Nájera envelops his human scenes in a veil of fantasy, Rubén Darío goes one step further in "The Ruby." He invents a fantastic situation with fantastic characters in a fantastic environment and treats it all as though it were human. Actually, the chemist Frémy, the sequestered woman and her beloved appear to be more fantastic than the gnomes themselves. Like human beings, the gnomes talk, shout, laugh, and exaggerate their own importance by sitting Turkish-style, pulling on their mustaches, and casting enlarged shadows as they dance. In contrast, the chemical mixture is described with "words that truly resemble a diabolical language."

Darío, more than any of his Modernist colleagues, was the great "artisan." His wide variety of stylistic techniques enriched the language and laid the groundwork for the mature flourishing of Spanish American literature in the twentieth century. A close look at "The Ruby" will reveal some of the typical "Rubendarian" characteristics.

The structure of Darío's stories reveals a complete mastery of the genre. In "The Ruby," the jewel, around which the whole story revolves, is really only a pretext for the expression of man's vanity, also expressed through the gnomes, as opposed to the mysterious power of nature. The division of the story in six scenes gives it an unexpected degree of dramatic movement: the denunciation of the false ruby; the description of the cave; the story of how Puck obtained the false ruby; the myth of the ruby's origin; the destruction of the false ruby; and Puck's summary. The dynamic quality of the story also stems from the short, abrupt sentences with which some of the scenes begin, end, or are interrupted. The unity of the six scenes is achieved through the concentration on the theme of the ruby, the presence of Puck and his smile, the rhetorical exclamations, and the parallelism between Puck's theft of the false ruby and the gnome's kidnapping of the woman.

Darío's talent is revealed not only in the story's structure but also in its poetic prose. Musical effects are achieved in the original through internal rhyme, alliteration, and various forms of repetition. The richness of the vocabulary is revealed in the series of parallel phrases and in the abundant use of adjectives. Multisensory similes are also used frequently to enhance the story's artistry: a ruby "resembling a pomegranate seed in the sunlight"; "a great array of precious stones created fanciful designs similar to the arabesques of a mosque"; "a thin stream of water gushed forth from time to time and fell with musical sweetness, in harmonious drops like the notes of a metal flute blown very softly."

The mere presence of all these poetic elements in a short story would not suffice to explain a great writer's artistry. What distinguishes Rubén Darío from those who imitated him with less success is that he was able to adapt these elements with subtlety to the theme of each story producing a perfect fusion. His work represents the high point of the Parnassian phase of Modernism.

Rafael Arévalo Martínez

(1884–1975)

Guatemalan. A poet, novelist, short story writer, and essayist, he met Rubén Darío in Guatemala before World War I and his first book of poetry dates back to 1911. Fifty years later he was still actively writing: *El embajador de Torlania* was published in 1960. More widely known for his poetry and for his psychozoological short stories: "The Man Who Resembled a Horse," "The Colombian Troubador," "Mr. Monitot" and others, Arévalo Martínez is also the author of an anti-imperialist novel that satirizes the Organization of American States, *The Office of Peace of Orolandia* (1925); of two Utopian novels, *El mundo de los maharachías* (1938) and *Viaje a Ipanda* (1939); of a penetrating biography of Guatemalan dictator Manuel Estrada Cabrera entitled *Ecce Pericles* (1945), and of a philosophical treatise, *Concepción del Cosmos* (1954). He was director of the National Library from 1926 until the 1944 Revolution when he was named ambassador to Washington. His later years were spent in relative seclusion with his family in Guatemala City. His daughter Teresa, also a writer, is publishing a personal biography of her father. "The Sign of the Sphinx" (1933) was inspired by the Nobel prize-winning Chilean poetess Gabriela Mistral, who in 1931 wrote a poem entitled "Carta Lírica a Rafael Arévalo Martínez."

THE SIGN OF THE SPHINX

(Narrated by J. M. Cendal, university professor)

Hic sunt leones
(From the ancient maps)

As soon as I finished my morning ablutions, I wrote the letter to Elena and sent it by messenger. While writing to her, I found myself trembling from my discovery and the desire to communicate it to the strange and beautiful woman. The letter said:

> Guatemala City, January 22, 19 . . .
>
> *My fearful friend:*
>   *I have just discovered what your sign is. There is no doubt. I now know the key to your tragic life, which explains everything. Your hieroglyph is that of the lioness. I am rushing over to visit you as soon as I can.*
>
> J. M. Cendal

A little while later I was with Elena. I found my friend in her bed with her beautiful lioness's body covered by a dressing gown, and her lioness's head, with its shining tangled hair, crestfallen on the sheets. Her magnificent eyes glowed in the dim light of the bedroom. She seemed mournful and ill. I explained my letter to her.

"Sweet friend," I said, "I was preparing to seek relief for my weariness in a cold shower when I received the clear vision of your sign, which explains your life. I became so disturbed that I couldn't tell you what I did immediately afterward."

"First of all: what is a sign?"

"The basic division of the human race into four principal groups is called a sign. The first sign is that of the ox: people who follow their instincts and who are predominantly passive; the second is that of the lion: violent people, predatory, in whom passion predominates; the third type is that of the eagle: intellectual, artistic people, in whom the mind predominates; the fourth and last is man: the superior people, amongst whom the will is the predominant characteristic. You are a pure and beautiful example of the lioness type. I'll not give you more details now because it would take too long to explain them."

"I accept."

And I saw my friend's beautiful eyes shine with understanding and majesty.

"And now, would you like us to study how I arrived at this marvelous vision? The road that led to the discovery may be divided into five sections. The first one: which begins with the initial intuition of when I clearly became aware of your strong magnetic force, in the Palace Theater, while we were both watching a film; a force that, when I was near you, filled me with vitality and energy. The second: when, while we were playing chess, you took one of my pieces with such a rapid, such a feline movement, that it appeared to be the act of a wild beast falling upon its prey. The third: when I conceived of you as a sphinx. The fourth: when you showed me your painting "The Lion." The fifth and definitive one: the dazzling light — when tearful and wild with grief, you were lying on the rug in your room, then I received the clear vision of your tragic nature as a lioness. There are other less visible markers on this enchanted shadowy path, in search of the unknown, some that I have just pointed out and others that will gradually make their appearance; although they don't have the same importance as those already enumerated.

"And in order to manifest them to you now, I will dispense with chronological order, and will resort immediately to order of importance, in which there are only two: when you appeared to me as a sphinx, and when tearful and wild with grief, your true nature as a lioness clearly appeared.

"If you had continued subordinate to your husband; if you had not obtained, with the divorce, your freedom of action, I probably never would have been able to arrive at the realization of your lioness's nature; but, once emancipated, *you were able to reconstruct* your *woodland cave.* You were able to rent a beautiful house, and furnish it elegantly. You yourself told me that you preferred to eat little and to skimp on your urgent needs provided that you had comfortable living quarters, that would lend the appropriate setting for your spirit. Naturally, a spacious living room would form part of the house you selected. Against the middle of one of the walls, you constructed a large type of canapé, so low that it scarcely rose ten centimeters from the ground, and you covered it with luxurious fabrics and with pillows and cushions, each one singularly beautiful and soft. Large pillows that were true works of art, with strange and disturbing shades of color. On this soft layer, you then developed the habit of lying down in order to read and relax. This spacious bed that your fancy designed was actually the instinctive work of your subconscious. You were searching for a way to adopt your habitual position of rest, the only one in which you can rest: *the bed of the grotto in which the lioness rests.*

"You will remember, however, that it was not on this low bed where I had the first vague notion of your sign but rather on a sumptuous sofa which was a great deal higher. I was resting on it, and when you were getting ready to read a famous work, whose title escapes me, with your magnificent warm voice that I love so much, I begged you to sit by my side so that I could enter into the radius that contains your aura and receive your warm flow of animal life; but you refused and *stretched yourself out on the rug by my feet.* In that position, you read. And then I had the perturbing vision that you were a sphinx, a vision that filled me with anxiety and confused me, because properly speaking, there is no *sign of the sphinx.* It's a symbol far too superior for humans."

"And then?"

"The fact of the matter is that what I saw clearly then was your body, definitely animal-like, stretched out on the floor; *your large quadruped body; the beautiful, robust body of a wild beast;* and that bestial form was so clear to me, that I accepted it without hesitation; and I declared: 'what a powerful and beautiful animal body'; but from it — you were lying down — there emerged — *you made it emerge* — a beautiful feminine head, classic, that resembled a beautiful Greek or Roman medallion. You are very beautiful and have a most beautiful feminine face. Your large Greek nose, so straight and noble; your wide forehead; your modest chin; such a beautiful woman's face set upon the powerful form of a beast, stretched out at my feet. The disturbing perception could not be ignored; so I said to you: 'You puzzle me and you worry me, *because you look too much like the sphinx.*' Do you understand my reasoning process? The face of a woman, large and well defined, on the powerful body of a lion, recumbent. What else is the sphinx? Remember: the sphinx has the face and breasts of a woman, and the body and paws of a lion. And here I have to tell you, by way of digression, something else that is strange: *I don't know why, but I have fixed in my mind, the feminine face of the sphinx, an image that appears frequently.* Do you understand? And this frequent vision made it possible for me to identify you so quickly. I saw the body of the lion and the head of the woman and I gasped: 'sphinx.' Except that if my perception of the woman's face was clear, that of the lion's body was not precise enough for me to affirm: that is the body of a lion. Nevertheless, the vague sensation sufficed for the fettered god within my tired soul to murmur: sphinx.

"Several days passed. I continued under that mysterious, that terrifying captivation of yours. I was drawn to you like a compass needle is drawn toward the north — don't laugh: in *this* situation, it's not a cliché; I turned toward you as the heliotrope turns toward the light. I would have searched for you even though to approach you might mean walking into an indescribable torture. You were for me something more precious than life itself; my greatest love; blood of my blood; the marrow of my bones. I looked for you, I mean, every night until one day when I discovered that I was so tired because of you, so worn out, that I decided not to continue looking for you. I knew that to see you was to run the risk of dying from lassitude. The spirit tires, the god within becomes weary. 'I feel the fatigue of the *god* who harasses me,' said the poet. Then I composed those cruel verses which I will read to you again later and which begin: 'I suffered from her as from a fever/ as one suffers from an obsession./ If I had continued to bear her presence/ I would have died.' Do you remember? As I said, I was very tired that night, and I decided to take a rest from you and to refrain from seeing you; but while in bed my thoughts continued to torment me, and I needed to escape from myself as well. How? By sleeping? I couldn't. 'When one is so tired that he can no longer rest. . . .' Was I searching for artificial paradises? I flung the key that opens your door into the sea. What was I to do? I decided that a good book is also a narcotic, a nepenthe, as Rubén[1] would say; and I remembered that you had repeatedly offered me and given me the book *She*, by Rider Haggard; and that I always left it behind in your living room, because you filled me in such a way that I didn't have time to read. I finally decided to stop by your house, but only for a moment, for two reasons: in order to borrow the aforementioned book and to notify you that I would not keep our date for that night.

[1] An allusion to Modernist poet and short story writer Rubén Darío (see p. 135).

"But I was not reckoning with that unknown and mysterious guest, that inner demon that sometimes possesses me. I had scarcely entered your home and had barely spoken to you, when I fell victim once again to your bewitching, your enchanting presence, and I was no longer able to leave. You fascinate me. As usual, your simple command: 'Don't leave' chained me to you.

"I was so tired that I lay down next to you, on the bed, the bed where you were crying, in the throes of great sorrow, with your magnificent lioness's body convulsing, while a tragic sign marked your face. Do you remember? And then, finally—I hadn't seen it sooner because man's weak spirit stumbles along—*I saw you as a beautiful reclined lioness.* If, in spite of being dead tired, I had not gone to your house that night—had my spirit not led me by the hand—I perhaps would never have discovered your terrible hieroglyph. But the fact is that I did arrive. And I did see it. Your face was distorted with grief. The powerful hand of grief had erased the fragile visage of the woman, and only the expression of the lioness remained on the previously human face. I repeat to you that it was the result of grief. I clearly saw the lionine snout. There was the blood of innumerable victims in your half-opened jaws. And I understood that you were not—never could be—*the sphinx, but rather the lioness.*"

"Is there blood, then, on my mouth now?"

"Yes: there is blood. Perhaps you don't know the *equivalencies:* what on the earthly plane are bleeding victims, on the plane of the soul are spiritual victims.

"I've always told you: you have a tragic sign."

II

"And again I affirm that if I hadn't arrived at your house that night, the strange revelation of the sign of the beast would not have occurred, because everyone has a cloak that hides his hieroglyph, a fabric that clothes the animal, making it difficult for the spectator to penetrate with the eyes of his soul to see the hidden beast; but grief tore at your flesh that night among the ambiguously shaped shadows; grief had created circles under your eyes; grief accentuated the squareness of your chin; grief made your whole face swollen. Oh what a skillful sculptor is grief! Sorrow was acting upon your astral body and was making your passionate body emerge: your *kamarupa*.[2] It was shaping the malleable matter and was delivering to me your live and radiant form. And thus I saw the lioness, the beautiful lioness that exists within you. For a moment, I still hesitated. That vision of your sign was too disturbing, it explained too many things, making it hard for my distrustful mind to accept its marvelous discovery. I trembled like an explorer of subterranean treasures who finally spies a large ring among the layers of earth that have been moved about; and who suspects that there is a chest, or actually sees the chest itself, and dies of expectation and of desire. What will the mysterious chest contain? Will it be gold or a corpse? Was I going to find the gold of recognition or the corpse of mistake? I left disconcerted and trembling with hope. But before I did, do you remember? I dared to take your right hand in mine *because I was so hurt by your sorrow and I wanted to console you* — an ineffectual desire because your grief was the grief of a lioness. I, who am always so respectful, dared to take your hand, to move it slightly away from your body and let it rest gently on the silky rug, with the palm facing downward; then I caressed it tenderly. And then a new idea sprang to my mind as a hare springs in the presence of the hunter. 'Oh, the rare bewitchment of moonlight shadows! Oh, the strange nocturnal hunter of the unknown!' And it was that pure, that most beautiful feminine hand, resting on the rug, that was at the same time a wonderful and terrible lioness's paw, in spite of its beauty. Twice you withdrew it, contracting it; and you tucked it in your breast as do cats with their soft felt paws; or as do lions — and in general all felines — when they are going to sleep. I wish that you could see a cat resting. You'd observe how she hides her paw in her breast, and how, happy to hide it, she folds it gracefully over the joint of her leg before bringing it against her breast. I used to observe those feline movements so intensely that you felt obliged to tell me: 'I always rest in this position; that's why my arms fall asleep on me every night, to the point of causing me real torture.'

"I unconsciously looked for your retractile nails hidden by your soft silky fingertips.

---

[2]The astral body, in theosophy, is the supersensible substance belonging to each individual, a second body, that accompanies him through life and survives him in death. Kama, in Hindu mythology, is the god of erotic desire and death.

"And around that most beloved white feminine hand, which was also the paw of a wild beast, there reposed on the floor, as she did, the *maya*[3] bodies of two of my hallucinatory sensations: my corporal respect for the lioness and my incapacity to console her tumultuous affliction.

"And because of this inherent respect of mine and the respect that other men have for you, I don't need to give you many explanations. A lioness always commands respect. As I was saying before, I took your hand with the hesitation of an inexperienced lion tamer approaching a lioness in heat.

"Still feeling unsure of myself, I left. Once at home, I sought out my bed immediately. Sleep rounded out my awareness. As I've already told you, I got up the next day to take my morning bath; and was getting ready to let the cold water run over my body, when all of a sudden, in a flash, the understanding of your true sign came to me; there was no longer any doubt: the understanding that explained your life: the clear recognition of your lioness sign.

"And now I shall attempt to explain to you, even though only in broad terms, some of the excruciating enigmas that fill you with fear. Let us proceed in order.

"Do you recall, Elena, your deepest sorrow? The one that you felt time and time again, when men would complain that you weren't sufficiently feminine? Do you remember the harsh, unjust accusation by that girl friend who called you by an infamous name? And do you remember how often this doubt about your femininity tormented you and made you bleed? Today I understand it and I can now explain it to you. Before I say anything, I have to tell you that I don't know of any woman's soul as pure and beautiful as yours: you are a treasure of femininity; you are rich in femininity; you are female, magnificent and radiant; but don't forget that you are the female of the lion, the lioness, and that the lower species are afraid of you. They are terrified. I repeat, you are female but the female of the lion. *What they called masculinity was really strength.* Your femininity cannot manifest itself, however, without a lion. For the rest, you will be the ruler, the señora, the queen. You cannot have lovers, only

[3]In Hinduism, *maya* is the production of an illusion.

serfs or tamers. You need a lion to bring out in you all your amazing femininity; but lions are not plentiful. Hence your continuous torment.

"And now you see what a bright torchlight illuminates from top to bottom your tragic life! Now you will be able to understand why your marriage failed. You married a strong digitigrade, a quadruped also of the feline genus. I could not determine to which species he belongs; but he is undoubtedly another feline. A terrible feline, with sharp claws, noble and strong within his species, feline, like yourself; but less powerful than a lioness. How could you commit this error, my beautiful lioness? Did the famous and handsome movie actor seduce you onstage? Were you a victim of the power of enchantment of the screen, of that magic art recently born, which combines and integrates its five other sister arts? Didn't you realize that you were heading for disaster! Don't you see how there will always be hateful and antagonistic feelings between the lion and other felines, because they express two distinct and opposing principles? Your husband continually felt the lion's spiritually snapping and awful swiping at him; and he ended up leaving you, undoubtedly still loving and admiring you at the same time; since I've already told you that he has a fine and generous soul. One does not stand up to a lioness or any other great feline with impunity. Your soul is very heavy, it is the soul of a lioness.

"With regard to that other great sorrow in your life, I'm referring to that childhood friend of yours, Romelia, the one who insulted you with that dreadful word, the one who betrayed you after many years of receiving your kindness, it too can be easily explained. Romelia is a kitten. A friendship between a kitten and a lioness! What a tragedy! You can say the awful phrase: *I am a lion: the others are cats.* Romelia constantly felt defenseless in your presence. Finally, and naturally, she blurted out that terrible accusation of masculinity. That kitten equated strength with masculinity; power with lack of femininity; potency for cruelty. She had always been jealous of you, and she wound up envying you; hating you. Then, in spite of her small size, feline-like, she inflicted upon you that terrible wound, so devastating that it almost reached your heart, so deeply did it penetrate; that wound which afterward with their steel-like little claws, other lesser ignoble little beasts, the voracious mustelids, opened wider, with their little claws and their canine teeth; that very wound in which a serpent would later deposit the deadly venom of its fangs: that wound that I am now curing for you—the charge of masculinity. You told me that one day Romelia, jealous over the love of someone who was courting both of you, dared to threaten you with a whip. You also related to me the terrible psychological reaction you felt upon seeing yourself offended; and while you were speaking, I saw in you such majesty, such wounded majesty, that I understood everything that followed afterward: how your friend—reacting rapidly in response to her constant affection and against her momentary violence—fell at your feet, begging your forgiveness, repentant, sorrowful and afraid; and how she desperately kissed the hem of your dress. That day her friendship was in danger of falling into the abyss. She pleaded so much, sincerely repentant of her momentary blindness, that the young, the magnanimous, the generous lioness forgave her; but, in part, she forgave her because she was not aware of her true nature as a lioness; and because society had shackled her with its thousands of prejudices.

"And now that we've clarified those two terrible tragedies of your life, the tragedies of your departed first friend and your first love, that ended in disappointment, let us continue with the minor and daily tragedy that torments you: let us pass on to that other complaint that you have expressed to me so many times, that subsequent friendships didn't last very long either. I am fascinating, you told me, fascinating to a point that is difficult to express; I am dazzling, perturbing, domineering, I see my friends at my feet, running like servants to satisfy my every whim. They adore me, they humble themselves before me in order to please me; but that fascination lasts for only a short time; I then lose them. Now you understand, don't you? It's the swipe of the lioness's paw *that wounds when it wants to caress* beings of other species.

III

"After this interpretation would you like for me, the intuitive one, to continue explaining your terrible sign? Is there anything you would like me to clarify for you? Perhaps we should discuss that admirable painting of yours 'The Lion on the Verge of

Devouring Its Tamer?' Or those suitors who wanted to kiss you? Or your tremendous magnetism?"

"For the sake of order, let me remind you that you first told me that there were five stages in my coming to know myself; and then afterward you went on to explain to me only the third and the fifth points, the most important ones. The first one concerning that magnetism which they say I possess, the second regarding the game of chess, and the fourth point pertaining to the painting of 'The Lion' have not yet been described."

"That is true; and your precision is but further evidence of that lucid, powerful and far-reaching intelligence that is characteristic of a lioness. My bewitchment at the Palace Theater will occupy only a little time since later I will need to deal with it at length. Right now I wish to say that I accompanied you to the two seats in the orchestra at the Palace completely free of your magnetic force. I was escorting Miss Nobody. You were nothing more than an old friend of mine, not very intimate, whom I liked somewhat but for whom I had little respect. But that night, while I was at your side, your terrible force began to work upon me. When you touched me, it was as if the flames of life had been ignited, flames that up to then lay half-extinguished owing to a twofold disease of the body and the spirit which frequently attacks intuitive beings who fall prey to those forces which they imprudently dare to unleash and confront. Suddenly I found myself laughing; I experienced a wonderful mental agility to which I was not accustomed, which rejuvenated me, making me feel twenty years younger. My thoughts acquired sharpness and clarity. A great serenity calmed my fearful impassioned body. I have advanced sufficiently on the road of recognition to know that I owed that intensification of life to you: to the very nearness and warmth of your personality. I then realized that you were an inexhaustible fountain of energy; a noble and strong spirit; and I began to appreciate you: that is to say, to love you."

"And what about the chess game?"

"That is very easy to explain. We played chess one afternoon. The chessboard that you own is a very fine one, and those white and violet pieces are a delight. Suddenly, your long, thin, white hand swooped down so rapidly upon my queen, in order to take

her away from me, that I saw in your movement the incontro-
vertible explanation of who you really were: the beast of prey, the
beast of prey in the air, on the land, or in the sea. Eagle, carni-
vore, or shark. I became disturbed: I gazed with true fear upon
the beautiful woman who sat before me. *Only the large carnivores
move like that.* Although for a moment I refused to accept the
cruel truth, I nonetheless already felt myself captive of a strange
fear. My entire unconscious told me that *that* was the truth: that
I was seated before a powerful destructive force.

"You play chess very well, Elena; and you also provide with me
incomparable delights behind those ivory pieces. Your hands are
so delicate, so white, so well proportioned! Your magnificent hands
capable of moving with such tragic consequences. You thus give
vent, oh great battler, to your need for violence, in this game that
so resembles a fight."

"And now explain to me about the painting, 'The Lion.'"

"I will be brief because I have to explain a world of things to
you in only a few words. You are a marvelous painter. That painting was a true revelation for me. In it there appears an imprisoned lion that one day, disregarding the punishment of the whip
and the red-hot iron, inflamed, and *because the fixed look had
lost all its strength for quite a while now,* turns against his tamer,
stands up to him, and turns him into a coward, and finally makes
him flee, leaving the door ajar in his fearful flight through which
his prisoner will also go out, to recover his native freedom. . . .

"What more can I tell you about this work? That it is a terrible
symbol in which the lion not only turns against his tamer, but also
against society? That the bars that held you prisoner are bars of
prejudice, the whip, a whip of ignorance, the red-hot iron, an
iron of superstition."

"Yes. It's true. No need to say more."

"And now that we have begun discussing your paintings, permit
me to digress, even though we shall momentarily leave the road
that we are traveling together. Let me speak to you about something that has very little to do with your sign; but is something
that moves me greatly. Allow me to speak to you of that other
wonderful painting of yours, 'The Net.'"

"The Net?"

"In every woman there is a sorceress. In the simplest charcoal vendor's wife there is a sorceress. Women guard the sacred treasure of their species and possess magic arts with which they enslave men. The thread from which they form their nets is habit. Every woman studies man, unconsciously, without realizing it, and nature has endowed her with the power to recognize him intuitively. Every woman is familiar with the same signs as the man who is privy to the secret knowledge, only with greater refinement than he; she is familiar with the instinctive type, whose sloth and gluttony must be catered to; she knows the emotional type, the human beast, who can be lulled and dominated only by feeding his vanity with flattery or with an obstacle to be overcome; she knows the intellectual type, whose idiosyncrasies she must discover in order to satisfy them, and whose physical laziness she has to make up for by doing things for him. With regard to the man of determination, which is the fourth sign, the woman has fewer weapons against him; but nonetheless she does have some.

"In every woman there is a perpetual deceiver. She was born to deceive. It's part of the craft. She deceives as naturally as animals breathe. Man thinks, woman seduces. She seduces the clerk in the grocery store who gives her a special price; she seduces the lawyer who doesn't charge her for his services; she smiles and seduces the fellow bus rider who gives up his seat for her; her smile is her means of seduction, and the day that she fails to seduce is the day she is condemned to perish causing in turn the death of mankind. Woman seduces as naturally as a tree's leaves turn green from chlorophyll, as a blotter absorbs ink; as an animal breathes. Her nature is seduction.

"Thus every woman weaves a net around her lover, fettering him with the manifold threads of habit. Habit persists and maintains the beloved man at her side even after his passion has disappeared. You, with a truly feminine sagacity, making use of your innate knowledge of magic and aided by your artistic intuition, painted this marvelous picture of the net woven around the beloved man; woven with sorrow; a net whose threads are tinged with the blood of your heart; a net intended to make life a little easier for him, to gently envelop him, tenderly, and to retain him; a net that was draining its divine weaver gradually leading her to

death. How could you express such profound things in a plastic
work? That is one of the secrets of your divine art, which has
made you famous."

When I reached this point, Elena lowered her head in sorrow.

Suddenly she raised it and cried out with a voice amazingly
hoarse, filled with despair.

"I've already broken the threads of that net. When I destroyed
them, I felt it was my own heart that I was breaking. . . .

"And not satisfied with that, do you understand? . . . I broke
the only distaff that a woman has to weave her net."

"Beware of saying such things because this symbolic breaking
of the distaff is a rejection of your femininity and of love. And
if you really broke it, you must find yourself another one, any
way that you can, although it may cost you your life.

IV

"Let us look now at the problem of your suitors.

"You spoke to me of that patron who holds a high position in
the bank with its accompanying social power. He performed
wonders for you. One day, in your house, he tried to kiss you.
You stopped him with a look. Poor devil! How he must have run
with his tail between his legs when he saw the lioness in you
appear."

"What is his sign?"

"Although I know him by sight, I can't envision his sign at this
moment; I would need to study him, but I can certainly tell you
that he is an evil type; a carnivorous beast, a leopard or something
like that. With regard to the man who one day wanted to rest
his head against your breast, that one's a gray bear. A dangerous
beast. I distrust him. You can never tell when the savage side of
him will appear. Do you remember him? He was also a friend of
yours who showered you with gifts. Another poor devil who never
knew your true nature as a lioness. What else do you want me to
tell you?"

"I don't need to ask you anything else. I understand."

"In that case, allow me to speak to you of another strange
episode in our strange relations. It's somewhat more extensive
than the previous ones; and, oh! so precious for me. . . .

"Have you by chance forgotten that time when at the beginning of our friendship I suddenly saw you while I was walking along a busy thoroughfare? You saw me too. You stopped your car, and invited me to get in and to accompany you on an outing to Amatitlán. Why did I accept? I can't say. I am a man of modest habits and lead a very ordered life: I live in a pension, nice but somewhat homey, away from the noise and suitable for my studies and my artwork; I eat very little and at regular hours; I rarely drink, and rarely do I go out to a show; I have few male friends, only one female friend; limited social contact. . . . So why did I accept? Perhaps, it was the artist within me, the Bohemian and impulsive side that one finds in all artists, who didn't offer much resistance to your strange invitation to go away on the spur of the moment, for one or two weeks, vacationing in Amatitlán, without telling my landlady, without meeting other social obligations. As far as my artwork is concerned, I will not complain because I had no commitments. But the part of me that is a university professor should have protested. Instead, I simply replied: 'But how do you expect me, Señora, to just pick up and leave with what I have on, without any extra clothing, without a toothbrush?'

"Your only reply was: 'Let's go. All of that can be bought in Amatitlán.'

"'Suits also?'

"'If we are going to be there for several days, we will send to the capital for them.'

"And away we went. You were dressed with rare elegance in a beautiful tailored suit. You drove very well; but were extremely daring. You brought your car up to dangerous speeds. You and the car seemed to form a single animal, fast and ferocious, that terrified the few pedestrians on the road and left a dog dying, crushed pitilessly by the dreadful monster.

"Today, in a new light, I understand perfectly what happened. I'm a man with a disciplined will: I don't like anyone to make me deviate from the road that I am following, or from the daily routine that I lay out for myself each morning in the solitude of my room. I don't want to be like those women who go shopping for gloves and return with thousands of expensive trinkets. . . . Thousands, amongst which the gloves that were needed are not to be found. But you picked me up like a lioness takes a defenseless lamb in her mouth. You were stronger than me. . . .

"We arrived at the marvelous lakeside town. You brought me to a chalet that had been graciously offered to you for a short period of time. Your secretary and a young servant girl awaited us there. Little Alice, the only child of your frustrated marriage, had remained in a boarding school. They brought us food from the hotel. It was then that I began to feel that sweet attraction through which you exerted your mysterious influence over all my faculties and senses. From that experience I returned dominated by a great love, your prisoner forever.

"What a divine vacation! Later on, I will speak to you of the sorcery of that immense blue gem fallen from the skies that is called Lake Amatitlán. And of those dawns, when we would wake up, jump out of bed, and find ourselves living a life of magic inside an immense sapphire, so transparent and pale blue was the sky, so deep blue was the lake, and so tinted with different shades of blue were all the surroundings. All matter seemed translucent and would take on a blue hue; and gentle mountains with feminine curves enclosed the landscape, like a chorus of maidens who with joined hands spanned the horizon. The chalet was set upon a hill; a stairway descended, gently, to the lake that murmured at our feet; and you would frequently go down to the lake to bathe, truly resembling an undine. But let us return to our mornings. Upon waking, I would leave my room, half-dressed, and head straight for the balcony which looked out on the lake, like one who peeks out at a supernatural arcadia. And the fascination of the marvelous painting would begin. Seated on a bench contemplating the splendor of the water, I was able to detect the distant fishing boats, those tiny brush strokes, and I would doze off waiting for you to return. When you came out on that same balcony, I would call you to my side, and together we would lose ourselves in the marvelous view. And it was so sweet, that I abandoned myself to the sweet illusion that you were mine, and that nobody could take you away from me. Because by then, you'll understand I was already feeling for you an irresistible attraction. You made me the prey of your mysterious spell.

"Oh, who could give me the power to express what I felt during the long walk that we took one morning along the enchanted road that borders the lake! Suddenly, you stopped in front of a shrub with long hollow thorns, among which there entered and exited an agitated colony of ants. Well-versed in botany — well-versed in plants, as in many other branches of human and divine knowledge — the shrub absorbed your attention. I *shared your delight.* For the first time, the plant kingdom was revealing itself to my dazzled eyes. You were smiling maternally and you were initiating me into your occult science. And thus you were enriching my life. Do you understand? That is the word. *You were enriching my life.* The surge of life accentuated its inebriating rhythm.

"Afterward we continued along the flowery path. When we got tired, we looked for an appropriate tree trunk in order to rest. We both smiled like children when you found one. It seemed to have awaited our visit since the world was made. It had been created especially for us, from the beginning of time, to the exclusion of every other purpose except that of providing us with a place to rest for an hour. Take note, Elena, that this is a real enchantment and that woman is truly an enchantress. She wears a maya, the fabric of illusion; a maya, the fabric of life."

"Oh, what a sweet and beautiful episode you have just told me. So sweet as even to surprise me who lived it . . . no: that's a lie — I passed through it then and only now am I living it. . . . It has touched me even in this hour of despair . . . in this hour of desolation."

"I have gone on for too long. If we continued on the trail of the lion, we would never finish. The trail bifurcates endlessly. However, in order not to tire you, it behooves me to follow the dictates of art in telling this story and to avoid overloading it with details. I still think I've dwelt too long upon it; but your rare sign interests me so greatly. . . ."

"Don't leave out anything for my sake, I am as interested as you are."

"For example, I could talk to you of your stride, long and rapid, so resembling that of the lion; of your manner of eating and caressing; of your magnificent eyes, phosphorescent in the darkness; of your love for this darkness that makes you go around turning off the electric lights, which I turn on instinctively; I could speak to you of a hundred more details. Above all, I could speak to you of your artwork. You must have preserved in your memory, precise and cruel as it is, how I met you, when you exhibited your paintings in a modest hall in a distant city.

"There were not many people. The gallery, although nice, was modest. The paintings were few. Just enough to appear discreetly in an exhibition. In some of the exhibited works there was true mastery; unmistakable mastery. The artist's skill was too apparent. Above all, what was striking about them was the self-confidence, the precise execution, the clarity of vision, and a strange constancy. In what lofty spot had the painter situated herself in order to obtain those incomparable views of sunsets, of the moonlight, shimmering upon the waters of the lakes, of the tall grasses? They were tropical landscapes, captured with singular vigor and a certain touch to which men are not accustomed. At times, the painting suffered from carelessness, from violence in its execution; but always the claw of the lioness that was your trademark remained clear. And in spite of this skill, in rare contrast with it, in the compositions there was something wild and primitive. It seemed that a savage, an intuitive being, had suddenly acquired the mastery of a plastic art and painted his visions of the jungle. I was especially impressed by a small masterpiece that was barely an unfinished sketch; but with a supernatural kind of light, it had captured an African jungle. The sky, the mountains, the earth seemed to burn, in a flood of raging fire; it was the apotheosis of red. I tried to buy it, and so I made your acquaintance."

"A bitter acquaintance. . . ."

"Allow me, now in order to conclude, to speak to you of Alicia. Do you recall that one day, after I had earned a certain degree of familiarity, you invited me to step into your dining room at the time of the noon meal? Oh, and how I did then enjoy your noble figure, so majestic and sovereign, stooping to pour such tenderness on your little child! I'm not sure if it was precisely the contrast between your majestic bearing and the display of such tenderness that moved me so much. You were a queen feeding her daughter. You bewitched me."

"Continue."

"Do you fully understand now your sign of a lioness? When I felt that singular delight in seeing you help little Alicia, in the dining room of your home, it was, without my realizing it, because I was moved by the contrast between your majestic stature as a lioness and the defenseless quality of childhood. It was as if Grace were being carried in the arms of Might. That was the strange delight that I experienced when I saw you caress Alicia and over which I lavished in vain such pointless epithets as *lordly, majestic.* Because Alicia, fruit of a hybrid union, is not a lion cub."

"What is she?"

"Only a girl, delightfully fragile. . . .

"But now it is time for me to take my leave and allow you to rest."

And having concluded my story, I stopped talking.

Elena, who until then had listened attentively to me, but with the increasing anger and dismay of a patient who sees the doctor leading toward a fatal diagnosis, suddenly abdicated her goddess-like majesty. She threw herself upon the bed and began to sob in anguish.

"Then, there is no cure for my condition?"

"A lion."

"But: are there any lions still left on the face of the earth?"

— Translated by Jill Gibian

COMMENTARY

A second-generation Modernist, Rafael Arévalo Martínez (1884) shares with his predecessors a great artistic sensitivity, but he no longer feels impelled to beautify the language. His psycho-zoological stories made a valuable contribution to the development of Spanish American prose fiction. For the first time, exterior reality is almost completely excluded. What constitutes the heart of the story is the true essence of the characters, their inner reality. Plot and suspense are practically eliminated and the short story in the hands of Arévalo Martínez becomes a psychoanalytical case study inspired by the writings of Freud.

"The Sign of the Sphinx" presents the case of a masculine woman who resembles a lioness. Although the almost scientific style of the university professor narrator tends to convert the story into an essay, the final words reveal the protagonist's inner drama, her despair at the dim possibility of finding a lion strong enough to make her feel feminine.

The identification of the protagonist with the lioness should in no way be confused with the bestialization technique of the Naturalists. Arévalo Martínez does not degrade his characters by comparing them to animals. On the contrary, he makes them stand out more, searching for the keys to the understanding of their characters in the zoological world. Like the lioness, Elena is beautiful and haughty; energetic and silent. The narrator, who participates directly in the story, informs Elena at the beginning that he arrived at the discovery of her lioness sign through five distinct moments which he briefly describes. However, a slight degree of suspense is achieved by his expanding on the five moments in a different order: 3, 5, 1, 2, 4.

In addition to her present status as a lioness, other aspects of Elena's life are revealed to us in a nonchronological order. First we find out that she is divorced after having suffered through a tragic marriage. Then we learn that her husband was a famous actor who left her. Little by little, Elena's past is filled in with her suitors, her "kitten" friend and the "lamb professor-narrator." Only toward the end is her daughter Alicia mentioned. The narrator recounts the Amatitlán episode before telling of his first meeting with Elena. The description of Lake Amatitlán is one of the few poetic passages in all of Arévalo Martínez's stories.

The style of this story in general is clear, logical, and rapid. Verbs predominate in order to give movement to a story devoid of action in the traditional sense. A few rhetorical questions and exclamations maintain our awareness of the narrator's role whose own fascination with the lioness leads the reader to speculate about his hidden psychological problems.

Arévalo Martínez's characters do not participate, for the most part, in their country's problems or even social milieu; they live intensely in their own inner worlds. Paradoxically, this introspective trait is one of the earmarks of Guatemalan literature in general.

Ricardo Jaimes Freyre

(1868-1933)

Bolivian. He lived for many years in Argentina where he published his first book of poetry, *Castalia bárbara* (1897). Along with Darío's *Prosas profanas* (1896) and Lugones's *Montañas del oro* (1897) it is considered to represent the high point of Modernism. He introduced Nordic themes, free verse, and other metric innovations, and in 1912 wrote *Leyes de la versificación castellana*. He also authored several books on the history of Tucumán where he taught literature, history, and philosophy in high school and at the university for twenty years. In 1921 he returned to Bolivia to become minister of Public Education and a year later was appointed minister of Foreign Affairs. After serving as his country's diplomatic representative in Chile, the United States, and Brazil, he spent his last years in Argentina. "Indian Justice" was first published in 1906 under the title "En las montañas" in the *Revista de Letras y Ciencias Sociales* (V, 29) of Tucumán. The story appeared with the title "Justicia india" for the first time in José Sanz y Díaz's *Antología de cuentistas hispanoamericanos* (Madrid: Aguilar, 1945).

INDIAN JUSTICE

The two travelers were drinking the last of their wine, standing by the open fire. The cold morning breeze caused the brims of their wide felt hats to tremble lightly. The fire was already turning pale under the hesitant gray light of dawn; the corners of the large yard were vaguely visible, and the heavy crude clay pillars which supported the roof of straw and reeds were beginning to stand out against the shadows in the background.

Tied to an iron ring attached to one of the pillars, two horses were waiting completely harnessed, with their heads down, chewing long blades of grass with difficulty. Squatting by the wall, a young Indian, with a bag full of corn in one hand, was tossing the yellowish grains into his mouth.

163

When the travelers were ready to leave, two other Indians appeared at the huge rough gate. They lifted one of the thick beams which, anchored in the heavy walls, barred the door and they entered the vast yard.

They looked poor and wretched, and they were made to look even more wretched and poor by their torn jackets, their coarse open shirts, and the many knots in the leather laces of their sandals.

They slowly approached the travelers who were already jumping on their horses, while the Indian guide was tying the bag of corn to his waist and fastening tightly the laces of his sandals around his legs.

The travelers were still young; one was tall, very white, with a cold, hard look; the other was small and dark with a happy air.

"Señor . . . " muttered one of the Indians. The white traveler turned toward him.

"Hi, what's the matter, Tomás?"

"Señor . . . give me my horse. . . ."

"Again, you imbecile! Do you want me to travel on foot? I've given you mine in exchange, that's enough."

"But your horse is dead."

"Of course it's dead; but only because I rode it for fifteen hours straight. It was a great horse! Yours isn't worth a thing. Do you think it'll last many hours?"

"I sold my llamas to buy this horse for the feast of Saint John. . . . Besides, señor, you've burned down my hut."

"Of course, because you came to bother me with your constant whining. I threw a firebrand at your head to chase you, and, since you turned your face away, it fell on a heap of straw. It isn't my fault. You should've received my firebrand with respect. And you, Pedro, what do you want?" he asked, addressing the other Indian.

"I'm coming to beg you, señor, not to take my land away. It's mine. I've sown it."

"That's your business, Córdova," the gentleman said, addressing his companion.

"No, indeed, that's not my business. I've done what I've been ordered to do. You, Pedro Quispe, you're not the owner of this land. Where are your legal titles? Where are your papers?"

"I don't have any papers, señor. My father didn't have any papers, either, and neither did my father's father. And nobody has wanted to take the land away from us. You want to give it to someone else. I haven't done you any harm."

"Do you have a bag full of coins stored somewhere? Give me the bag and you can keep the land."

Pedro looked at Córdova in anguish.

"I don't have any coins, nor could I obtain so much money either."

"In that case, there's nothing else to be said. Leave me alone."

"At least, pay me what you owe me."

"But are we never going to finish? Do you think me stupid enough to pay you for a sheep and a few chickens you've given me? Did you imagine we were going to die of hunger?"

The white traveler, who was beginning to become impatient, exclaimed:

"If we keep on listening to these two imbeciles, we'll be here forever."

The top of the mountain, on whose slope stood this large rustic lodging, was beginning to shine struck by the first rays of the sun. The narrow strip of barren land was slowly becoming light, and the desolate barren landscape, hemmed in by the blackish mountain ranges, stood out under a blue sky, broken up here and there by the fleeing gray clouds.

Córdova made a sign to the guide, who moved toward the gate. The two men on horseback followed after him.

Pedro Quispe rushed toward them and seized the reins of one of the horses. A crack of the whip on his face made him draw back. Then, the two Indians ran out of the yard, swiftly toward a nearby hill, climbed it with the speed and confidence of vicuñas, and upon reaching the summit, looked around.

Pedro Quispe brought to his lips a horn he was carrying slung on his back and drew from it a long deep sound. He stopped for a second and then continued with quick shrill notes.

The travelers were beginning to move up the side of the mountain; the guide, with sure and firm steps, was walking unconcerned, devouring his grains of corn. When the sound of the horn echoed, the Indian stopped, looked at the two men on horseback with alarm and started to run very swiftly along a path that led into the mountains. A few moments later, he disappeared in the distance.

Córdova, addressing his companion, exclaimed:

"Alvarez, those rascals have taken our guide away."

Alvarez stopped his horse and looked uneasily in every direction. "The guide. . . . And what do we need him for? I fear something worse."

The horn kept echoing, and on top of the mountain Pedro Quispe's body was outlined against the blue background and the reddish bareness of the peaks.

It was as if a magic spell were being cast over the ridges and in the mountain passes. From behind the huge heaps of hay, out of the fields of tall wild grass and rough thickets, from under the wide canvas huts in the Indian camps, out of the doorways of the shacks, and on the peaks of faraway mountains human shapes could be seen emerging and disappearing rapidly. They would stop for a moment, look toward the mountain upon which Pedro Quispe continued to draw sounds from his horn, and afterward creep over the hills, climbing cautiously.

Alvarez and Córdova continued going up the mountain; their horses were panting as they moved along the very narrow path and the rough, rocky terrain; the two men, now deeply worried, let themselves be carried on in silence.

Suddenly, a huge boulder, torn loose from the mountaintop, passed by them, with a loud roar; then another . . . and another. . . .

Alvarez spurred his horse forward at full speed, making it flank the mountain. Córdova immediately did the same; but the heavy rocks pursued them. It seemed that the mountain range itself was crumbling. The horses, hurled about as though caught in a storm, were jumping over the rocks, setting their hoofs miraculously on the sharp edges and hovering in space, at a great height.

Soon the mountains were crowned with Indians. The riders then rushed toward the narrow gorge which twisted and turned below them and along which a thin, transparent trickle of water was flowing gently.

The ravines were filled with strange harmonies; the harsh,

discordant sound of the horns was coming from everywhere, and at the end of the gorge a group of men suddenly stood out against the radiant light that divided the two mountains.

At that moment, a huge boulder struck Alvarez's horse; he seemed to hesitate for a second and then fall and roll down the mountainside. Córdova leaped to the ground and began to crawl toward the spot where the dusty mass of horse and rider could be seen.

The Indians started to come down from the summits: they were coming one by one from the crevices and the folds, advancing carefully, stopping every second and watching the bottom of the ravine. When they arrived at the edge of the stream, they spotted the two travelers. Alvarez, stretched out on the ground, was unconscious. Next to him, his companion stood with his arms crossed in despair because of his helplessness and watched the slow and fearful descent of the Indians.

On a small rolling plain, formed by the depressions of the mountain ridges that surround it on its four sides with four broad summits, the old men and the women were assembled awaiting the result of the chase. The Indian women, with their short round skirts of coarse cloth, their cloaks on their chests, their shiny derbies, their uneven tresses falling on their backs, and their bare feet, were silently grouped in a corner, and you could see their fingers performing the dizzying dance of the spindle and the reel.

When the pursuers arrived, they brought the travelers with them, tied to their horses. They advanced to the center of the small plain, and there they threw them to the ground, like two sacks. Then the women approached and looked at them with curiosity, without stopping their spinning and talking softly.

The Indian men took counsel together for a moment. Then a group of them hurried toward the foot of the mountain. They came back with two large pitchers and two large beams. While some dug holes in the ground to get the beams, the others filled small clay jugs with the liquid from the pitchers.

And they drank until the sun started to set on the horizon, and nothing could be heard but the muted conversations of the women and the noise of the liquid falling into the jugs from the raised pitchers.

Pedro and Tomás lifted up the bodies of the two travelers and tied them to the posts. Alvarez, whose spine was broken, uttered a long groan. The two Indians tore off their clothes, throwing each garment one by one far from them. And the women contemplated the white bodies in amazement.

Then the torture began. Pedro Quispe tore out Córdova's tongue and burned his eyes. Tomás covered Alvarez's body with small knife wounds. Then the rest of the Indians came and pulled out their hair and stoned them and stuck splinters in their wounds. A young Indian woman, laughing, poured a large jug of *chicha* over Alvarez's head.

It was getting dark. The two travelers had delivered their souls to the Great Giver of Justice a long time before; and the Indians, tired, by now bored and indifferent, kept on wounding and mangling the bodies.

Then the time came to swear silence. Pedro Quispe drew a cross on the ground, and all the men and women came and kissed the cross. Then, from his neck, he unfastened the rosary, which was always with him, and the Indians swore upon it, and he spat upon the ground and the Indians passed over the moist earth.

By the time the bloody remains disappeared and the last traces of the scene that had just taken place on the rough terrain of the high plateau were erased, night in all its immensity was falling on the mountainous solitude.

— Translated by Margarita Payeras-Cifre

COMMENTARY

This story is one of the very few examples of the application of Modernist techniques to one of the most persistent problems of many Spanish American countries: the exploitation of the Indian. In the twentieth century, many of the Criollista writers between the two World Wars denounced the injustices perpetrated against the Indian, mainly in novels: *Raza de bronce* (1919) by Bolivian Alcides Arguedas, *Huasipungo* (1934) by Ecuadorean Jorge Icaza, *El indio* (1935) by Mexican Gregorio López y Fuentes, and *El mundo es ancho y ajeno* (1941) by Peruvian Ciro Alegría.

Although many of the same abuses that appear in the above novels are present in "Indian Justice," what stands out most about this story is its symphonic composition which actually overshadows the social protest. The protest is further weakened because:

1. All the abuses are presented too quickly in only one page: the theft of the horse, the burning of the hut, the "legal" loss of the land, the forced gift of the sheep and the chickens, and the whipping.
2. Most of the abuses do not actually occur before the reader's eyes.
3. The rationalization of the white men with regard to the horses, to the burning of the hut, and to the food is nothing short of grotesque.
4. The dialogue is so rapid, jumping from theme to theme, that it creates an operatic — and therefore, less serious — effect.

"Indian Justice" is a symphony written for trumpets and drums. Pedro Quispe blows the horn to summon his men. Upon hearing it, the Indian guide flees. Pedro continues to blow his horn and soon the other horns join in to produce a crescendo that resounds on the mountain slopes and in the ravine. At the same time, the intensifying storm of rocks and boulders creates a parallel percussion effect. The use of horns and drums in the central part of the story is so strong that the sounds are heard throughout. A musician would undoubtedly know how to integrate into the symphony the trajectory of the sun, the mythological progenitor of the Indians. The beginning of the story in the early hours of the morning might be gently announced by some woodwind instrument which would gradually be heard more and more as the sun advanced — "the top of the mountain . . . was beginning to shine struck by the first ray of the sun" — and finally becoming a *fortissimo* with the arrival of the sun at its zenith, which probably coincides with the stoning of the travelers. Then, the trumpets and other instruments would gradually grow dimmer with the waning daylight — "and they drank until the sun started to set on the horizon" — blending in with the drums which would also grow muffled until they all faded away totally in the silence of the night — "the night in all its immensity was falling on the mountainous solitude."

The epic tone of the symphony for trumpets and drums is reinforced by the use of adjectives of epic proportions: "vast yard," "heavy pillars," "huge gate," "thick beams," "large pitchers," and "immense night," and the frequent use of the word *cumbre* (summit, peak). The symphony is framed by the initial and final appearance of two leitmotivs: "were drinking," "they drank" and "tied to an iron ring attached to one of the pillars," "tied them to the posts."

Although Jaimes Freyre was mainly a Modernist poet who spent a great part of his life outside his native Bolivia, this story has the same brilliance and victorious Indian rebellion that characterize the Indian novels and short stories of that country in contrast with those of Ecuador and Peru.

Criollismo

Spanish American prose fiction reached maturity between the two World Wars. From 1920 to 1945, the production of short stories and novels of high quality spurted considerably. The themes were almost always strictly national and the term "Criollismo" might well be translated as Nativism if that term did not have its racial connotation. The style also had a strong regional and national flavor.

The primary stimulus for these works came from the authors' quest for self-identification. World War I destroyed the Modernists' illusion that Europe represented culture in contrast with the barbarism of the Americas. The military and economic intervention of the United States in Latin America contributed greatly to arousing the national consciousness of the writers. The new roads and the introduction of the airplane made accessible vast regions that were previously considered more remote than Europe. The 1929 crash and the Great Depression with the subsequent popularity of leftist ideologies converted the novel and the short story, in many cases, into instruments for the denunciation of social inequities. As if local conditions themselves were not sufficiently desperate to engender these works, some of the authors received added inspiration from the social protests launched by Dos Passos in *U.S.A.* and by Steinbeck in *The Grapes of Wrath.* This marked the first clear-cut influence of United States novelists on their Spanish American counterparts.

Although Criollismo, like all the previous isms, prevailed throughout Spanish America, each country had its own particular manifestation of the tendency. Especially noteworthy are

1. The novel and the short story of the Mexican Revolution with their epic style (dramatic and violent but with a poetic touch), the predominance of the anonymous peasant or soldier, and the relatively slight importance given to nature.
2. The proletarian character of Ecuadorean prose with its unrestrained realism, its crude language, and the intemperate use of dialect — but still maintaining a distinct artistic quality.
3. The brevity, the persistence of Costumbrismo, and the combination of literature and painting in some of the short story writers of Central America: Salvadoran Salvador Salazar Arrué (Salarrué) (1899–1975), Costa Ricans Max Jiménez (1900–1947) and Carlos Salazar Herrera (1906), and Panamanian José María Núñez (1894); and

on the other hand anti-imperialism as a dominant theme, especially among the novelists: Guatemalan Miguel Angel Asturias (1899–1974), Nicaraguan Hernán Robleto (1895–1968), and Costa Rican Carlos Luis Fallas (1911–1966).

4. The exuberant and brilliant prose of various Caribbean countries, as exemplified by Colombian José Eustasio Rivera (1888–1928), Venezuelan Rómulo Gallegos (1884–1969), and Dominican Juan Bosch (1909).

5. The importance of the individual human being in Chilean prose fiction and its slow rhythm.

Within Criollismo the novel and the short story were cultivated with equal diligence. Several authors like Rómulo Gallegos and Gregorio López y Fuentes made weak debuts in the short story before attaining greater artistic success in the novel. On the other hand, writers like Horacio Quiroga, Ventura García Calderón, Salarrué, and Juan Bosch either devoted themselves exclusively to the short story, or their short stories clearly surpassed their very few novels.

Although Criollismo had begun to lose its strength as a predominant tendency by 1945, its influence has continued up to the present day, even in such sophisticated writers as Carlos Fuentes (1928) and Mario Vargas Llosa (1936).

Horacio Quiroga

(1878-1937)

Uruguayan. One of the greater figures in the history of the Spanish American short story, he is considered the father of two of the main literary currents of the twentieth century: Criollismo and Cosmopolitanism. His stories reveal an obsession with violent death derived from his own life experiences. His father, stepfather, best friend, wife, and he himself either committed suicide or were the victims of accidental gunshots. He participated in the Bohemian life of the Modernists in Montevideo around 1900 presiding over a literary group with a title reminiscent of the medieval Provençal troubadours: El Consistorio del Gay Saber. He later lived in the tropical province of Misiones, Argentina, which provided him with the material for most of his stories. His best collections are *Cuentos de amor, de locura y de muerte* (1917), *El desierto* (1924), *La gallina degollada y otros cuentos* (1925), *Los desterrados* (1926), and *Más allá* (1935). "The Dead Man" was first published in the Buenos Aires newspaper *La Nación* on June 27, 1920, and later formed part of the volume *Los desterrados*.

THE DEAD MAN

The man and his machete had just finished clearing the fifth lane of the banana grove. They still had two lanes to go, but since these were full of spurges and wild mallows, the task that lay ahead of them was nothing to speak of. The man, therefore, cast a satisfied glance at the cleared out brush and crossed the barbed wire to stretch out for a while on the grass.

But pushing down the barbed wire as his body passed, his left foot slipped on a piece of bark that had fallen from the post, while the machete slipped from his hand. As he fell, the man had the extremely distant feeling that he did not see the machete flat on the ground.

He was already stretched out on the grass, lying on his right side, just as he wanted. His mouth, which had just opened as wide as it could, had also just closed. He lay as he would have wanted to be, with his knees bent and his left hand over his breast. Except that behind his forearm and directly below his belt, the handle and half of the machete's blade protruded from his shirt; but the rest was not visible.

The man attempted to move his head, in vain. Out of the corner of his eye he glanced at the handle of the machete still damp from the sweat of his hand. Mentally, he calculated the extension and trajectory of the machete within his belly, and coldly, mathematically, and inexorably, realized with certainty that he had just reached the end of his existence.

Death. In the course of life we often think that some day, after years, months, weeks and days of preparation, we will reach our turn at the threshold of death. It is the inevitable law, accepted and foreseen, so much so that we are in the habit of allowing ourselves to be pleasantly transported by our imaginations to that moment, supreme among all others, in which we heave our last sigh.

But between the present moment and that dying breath, what dreams, reverses, hopes, and dramas we imagine for ourselves! What things this existence full of vigor still holds in store for us, before it is eliminated from the human stage!

This is the consolation, pleasure, and reason behind our morbid ramblings: death is so far off and we have so many unexpected things to live through still.

Still? . . . Not even two seconds have elapsed: the sun is at exactly the same height; the shadows have not advanced one millimeter. Abruptly, the long-term digressions have just been resolved for the stretched-out man: he is dying.

Dead. He may as well consider himself dead in his comfortable position.

But the man opens his eyes and looks. How much time has gone by? What world cataclysm has he survived? What upheaval in nature is reflected in this horrible event?

He is going to die. Coldly, fatally, and unavoidably, he is going to die.

The man resists—this horror is so unexpected! And he thinks: it's a nightmare; that's what it is! What has changed? Nothing. And he looks: is this not his banana grove? Does he not come here every morning to clear it? Who is as familiar with it as he is? He sees the banana grove perfectly, very thinned out, with its broad leaves exposed to the sun. There they are, very near, frayed by the wind. But now they are not moving. . . . It's the midday calm, why it must be twelve o'clock.

Through the banana trees, up above, the man sees, from the hard ground, the red roof of his house. To the left, he makes out the wild brush and cinnamon trees. He can't see anything more, but he knows very well that the road to the new port is in back of him, and that in the direction of his head, down there at the bottom of the valley, lies the Paraná River, sleeping like a lake. Everything, everything exactly as always; the sun like fire, the atmosphere vibrant and lonely, the banana trees still, the barbed wire fence with its very thick, tall posts which he will soon have to change. . . .

Dead! But is it possible! Isn't this just one of so many days on which he has left his house at dawn, with the machete in his hand? Isn't his horse right there, four meters away, white spot on its forehead, calmly smelling the barbed wire?

But, yes! Someone whistles. . . . He can't see, because his back is turned to the road; yet he hears the horse's hoofs echoing on the little bridge. . . . It's the boy who goes by every morning at eleven-thirty on his way to the new port. And always whistling. . . . From the fence post with its peeling bark which his boots almost touch, to the live fence of brush which separates the banana grove from the road, there are a good fifteen meters. He knows it perfectly well, because he himself measured the distance when he put up the barbed wire fence.

What's going on then? Is this or isn't it a normal midday like so many others in Misiones, in his woods, in his pasture, in the sparsely planted banana grove? Of course! Short grass, anthills, silence, the sun at high noon. Nothing, nothing has changed. Only he is different. For the last two minutes, his person, his living personality has ceased to have anything to do either with the pasture which he himself cleared with a hoe, for five consecutive months, or with the banana grove, the work of his hands alone. Nor with his family. He has been uprooted, brusquely, naturally, by a shiny piece of bark and a machete in the belly. Two minutes: he is dying.

The man, very tired and stretched out on his right side on the grass, still refuses to admit a phenomenon of such transcendence, in the face of the normal and monotonous aspect of everything he sees. He knows well what time it is: eleven-thirty. . . . The boy who comes by every day has just crossed the bridge.

But how could he possibly have slipped! . . . The handle of his machete (he will soon have to replace it; it's almost completely worn out) was grasped perfectly between his left hand and the barbed wire. After ten years in the woods, he knows very well how to handle a bush machete. It's only that he's very tired from this morning's work, and is resting for a while, as usual.

The proof? . . . But he himself planted this grass which now enters the corners of his mouth—he planted it in plugs at one-meter intervals! And this is his banana grove; and this is his horse with the white spot on his forehead, cautiously snorting at the barbs on the wire! He sees it perfectly; he knows that the horse doesn't dare go around the corner of the barbed wire fence because he is lying almost at the foot of the post. He can make it out very well, and he sees the dark beads of sweat that start running from the withers and the rump. The sun beats straight down, and there is absolute calm. Every day, like today, he has seen the same things.

. . . Very weary, but he's only resting. Several minutes must have already gone by. . . . And at a quarter to twelve, from up there, from the red-roofed chalet, his wife and his two children will set out for the banana grove to bring him back for lunch. He always hears the voice of his youngest son before the others, as he tries to free himself from his mother's hand: "Daddy! Daddy!"

Isn't that it? . . . Sure, he hears it! It's already time. He actually hears the voice of his son. . . .

What a nightmare! . . . But it's just another one of so many days, trivial like all the rest, sure! Excessive light, yellowish shadows, still oven-like heat on the skin which makes his motionless horse sweat before the forbidden banana grove.

. . . Very, very, tired, but nothing more. How many times, at noon, like now, going home, had he crossed this field which was a thicket when he got here, and before that had been virgin bush! Then he would return, very tired also, with his machete hanging from his left hand, walking slowly.

In his mind, he can still wander off, if he wants to; he can, if he wishes, abandon his body for an instant and see the trivial everyday landscape from the dam that he constructed: the volcanic gravel with the stiff grass, the banana grove and its red sand, the barbed wire fence which seemed reduced in size on the slope that leans toward the road. And still further on he sees the pasture, the work of his hands alone. And at the foot of a fence post with peeling bark, lying on his right side with his legs gathered up, just like any other day, he can see himself like a heap on the grass exposed to the sun — resting, because he is very tired. . . .

But the horse striped with sweat, and cautiously motionless at the corner of the barbed wire fence, also sees the man on the ground and doesn't dare to go along the edge of the banana grove as it would like to. With the voices already near — "Daddy!" — the horse turns its ears toward the motionless heap for a long, long while: and reassured at last, decides to pass between the post and the stretched out man — who has now rested.

— Translated by Gustavo Pellón

COMMENTARY

Horacio Quiroga is considered one of the initiators of Criollismo in Spanish America. The majority of his stories deal with man's defeat by the barbarous forces of tropical nature, a theme assiduously cultivated by almost all subsequent Criollistas. In addition, Quiroga's stories, which were clearly influenced by Edgar Allen Poe, are characterized by an obsession with death and a highly perfected technique.

The theme of "The Dead Man" is the insignificance of an individual's death in the tropics. The emphasis throughout is on the irony of the absurd manner in which this man dies after having fought successfully against the forces of nature for so many years. The outstanding artistic achievement is the creation of suspense and a feeling of drama even though the story begins with what could have been the climactic moment of the accident. The matter-of-fact, undramatic presentation of the accident creates a strange, eery, uncanny atmosphere which makes this story one of the first examples of Spanish American Magic Realism.

The image of the man pierced through by his own machete and stretched out on the grass becomes unforgettable owing to the frequent repetition of certain key words and phrases: the man, the machete (personified as the man's partner in the initial sentence), the banana grove, the barbed wire, the fence post with its peeling bark, the grass, the horse, the sun at high noon, and variations on the "tired-rest" motif.

Nevertheless, this static picture comes to life through the man's thoughts. Quiroga indicates by his early description of the wound that the man is dying and then proceeds to structure the story on his final thirty minutes of life. Time advances with an incredible slowness established by the precise references: "not even two seconds have elapsed," "the shadows have not advanced one millimeter," "eleven-thirty," "two minutes," "a quarter to twelve," "noon." During those thirty minutes, the man is perplexed by nature's indifference to his plight, and little by little alludes unemphatically to some details of his past life which help round out the picture and also give a little more movement to the story. The actual physical movement of the whistling boy on horseback, the approaching wife and two children, and the leisurely moving horse contrast poignantly with the protagonist's total immobility.

Although this story takes place in the province of Misiones, in exotic northeastern Argentina, it is not one of Quiroga's most typically Criollista stories. The environment of the region near the Paraná River is captured quite effectively, but the appropriate simple language is almost completely free of regionalisms and the main theme of man's precarious and insignificant existence is certainly not restricted to the tropics.

The story's one defect, if it may be called that, is the narrator's philosophizing about death for three short paragraphs. Be that as it may, "The Dead Man" is one of Quiroga's two or three best stories and Quiroga is one of the truly outstanding figures in the history of the Spanish American short story. His well-deserved fame rests on his being one of the pioneers of Criollismo in the second decade of the twentieth century (after starting his literary career as a Modernist) as well as on the intrinsic quality of his works.

Martín Luis Guzmán

(1887-1976)

Mexican. Although born in Chihuahua, he grew up in Mexico City where he studied law. In 1911 he joined the Ateneo de la Juventud among whose members were Antonio Caso, Alfonso Reyes, and José Vasconcelos. After the assassination of Madero, Guzmán joined the revolutionary forces in the North and became Pancho Villa's private secretary. In his masterpiece, *El águila y la serpiente* (1928), he narrates his experiences with Villa, from whom he escaped in 1915 for Spain and later New York. He wrote for a Spanish-language newspaper in that city and several of his articles were published in a book under the title *A orillas del Hudson* (1920). He returned to Mexico in 1920 but four years later was again obliged to take refuge in Spain for political reasons. It was there that the first editions of *El águila y la serpiente* and his political novel *La sombra del caudillo* (1929) appeared. In the *Memorias de Pancho Villa* (1938-1951), Guzmán makes Villa the narrator of his own exploits in his own picturesque speech. Since Guzmán's return to Mexico in 1936, he was active in journalism, founding and directing the magazine *Tiempo* for three decades. In his eighties, he was elected to Congress. "The Festival of the Bullets" is a chapter of *El águila y la serpiente*.

THE FESTIVAL OF THE BULLETS

My interest in Villa and his movement often made me ask myself, while I was in Ciudad Juárez, which exploits would best paint the Division of the North: those supposed to be strictly historical or those rated as legendary; those related exactly as they had been seen, or those in which a touch of poetic fancy brought out their essence more clearly. The latter always seemed to me truer, more worthy of being considered history.

For instance, where could one find a better painting of Rodolfo Fierro—and Fierro and Villa's movements mirrored each other

down to the last detail — than in the account of how he carried
out the terrible orders of his chief after one of the battles, revealing an imagination as cruel as it was creative in death devices.
This vision of him left in my soul the sensation of a reality so
overwhelming that the memory of it lives forever.

That battle, which was successful in every way, had left no less
than five hundred prisoners in Villa's hands. Villa ordered them
divided into two groups: the Orozco volunteers, whom we called
"Reds," in one, and the Federals in the other. And as Villa felt
himself strong enough for grandiose acts, he decided to make an
example of the first group and to act more generously toward the
second. The "Reds" were to be executed before dark; the Federals
were to be given their choice of joining the revolutionary troops
or returning home, after promising not to take up arms against
the Constitutionalist cause.

Fierro, as might have been expected, was put in charge of the
execution, and he displayed in it that efficiency which was already
winning him great favor with Villa, his "chief," as he called him.

The sun was beginning to set. The revolutionary forces, after
breaking camp, were slowly gathering in the little village that had
been the objective of their offensive. The cold, penetrating wind
of the Chihuahuan plains began to blow and the groups of cavalry
and infantry huddled next to the walls of the houses. But Fierro —
whom nothing and nobody ever held back — was not going to flee
from a cool breeze that at most meant frost that night. He rode
along slowly on his short-rumped horse, with the edge of his sarape
against the horse's dark hair dirtied from the dust of the battle.
The wind was hitting him smack in the face, but he neither buried
his chin in his breast nor raised the folds of his sarape around
his face. He carried his head high, his chest thrown out, his feet
firm in the stirrups, and his legs gracefully flexed under the campaign equipment that hung from the saddle straps. The barren
plain and an occasional soldier that passed at a distance were his
only spectators. But he, perhaps unconsciously, reined his horse
to make him show his gaits as though he were on parade. Fierro
was happy; the satisfaction of victory filled his being; and to him
victory was complete only when it meant the utter rout of the
enemy; and in this frame of mind even the buffeting of the wind,

and continuing to ride fifteen consecutive hours in the saddle, produced physical sensations that were exhilarating. The rays of the pale setting sun, a sun prematurely enveloped in incendiary flames, seemed to caress him as they fell.

He reached the corral where the three hundred "Red" condemned prisoners were shut up like a herd of cattle, and he stopped a moment to look at them over the fence rails. In outward appearances those three hundred Huerta supporters could have passed for revolutionaries. They were of the fine Chihuahua breed, tall, lean bodies with strong necks and well-formed shoulders on vigorous supple backs. As Fierro looked over the small captive army and sized up its military value and bravery, a strange pulsation ran through him, a twitching that went from his heart or from his forehead out to the index finger of his right hand. Involuntarily the palm of this hand reached out for the butt of his pistol.

"Here's a battle for you," he thought.

The cavalrymen, bored with their task of guarding the prisoners, paid no attention to him. The only thing that mattered to them was the annoyance of mounting this tiresome guard, all the worse after the excitement of the battle. They had to have their rifles ready on their knees, and when an occasional prisoner left the group, they aimed at him with a determined air, and, if necessary, fired. A wave would then ripple through the vague perimeter of the mass of prisoners, that retracted to avoid the shot. The bullet would either go wide of its mark or bring one of them down.

Fierro rode up to the gate of the corral. He shouted to a soldier, who let down the bars, and went in. Without removing his sarape from his shoulders, he leaped off the horse. His legs were numb with cold and weariness; he stretched them. He arranged his two pistols. Next he began to look slowly over the pens, observing their layout and how they were divided up. He took several steps over to one of the fences without letting go of the reins. He slipped something out of one of the saddle bags into the pockets of his jacket and crossed the corral at a short distance from the prisoners.

Actually, there were three corrals that opened into one another, with gates and a narrow passageway between. From the one where the prisoners were kept, Fierro went into the middle enclosure, slipping through the bars of the gate. He went straight over to the next one. There he stopped. His tall, handsome figure gave off a strange radiance, something superior, awe-inspiring, and yet not out of keeping with the desolation of the corral. His sarape had slipped down until it barely hung from his shoulders; the tassels of the corners dragged on the ground. His gray, broad-brimmed hat turned pink where the slanting rays of the setting sun fell on it. Through the fences the prisoners could see him at a distance, his back turned toward them. His legs formed a herculean compass that glistened: it was the gleam of his leather chaps in the late afternoon light.

About a hundred yards away, outside the corrals, was the officer of the troop in charge of the prisoners. Fierro saw him and signaled him to come closer, and the officer rode over to the point of the fence closest to Fierro. The latter walked toward him. The two began to talk. In the course of the conversation, Fierro pointed out different spots in the enclosure in which he was standing and in the one next to it. Then he described with hand gestures a series of operations, which the officer repeated, as though to understand them better. Fierro insisted two or three times on what seemed to be a very important maneuver, and the officer, now sure about his orders, galloped off toward the prisoners.

Fierro then turned back toward the center of the corral, studying once more the layout of the fence, and other details. That corral was the largest of the three, and the first in line, nearest to the town. On two sides gates opened into the fields; the bars of these, though more worn—from greater use—than those of the farther pens, were of stronger wood. On the other side, there was a gate that opened into the adjoining corral, and on the far side the fence was not of boards, but was an adobe wall, no less than nine feet high. The wall was about sixty yards long, twenty of which formed the back of a shed or stable, with a roof that sloped down from the top of the wall and rested on the one side on the taller end posts of one of the fences that bordered on the open fields and on the other, on a wall, also of adobe, which came out perpendicular from the wall and extended some fifteen yards toward the middle of the corral. Thus, between the shed and the fence of the adjoining corral, there was a space enclosed on two sides by solid walls. In that corner the afternoon wind was piling up rubbish and clanging an iron bucket against the well curb with an irregular rhythm. From the well curb rose two rough forked posts, crossed by a third, from which a pulley and chain hung, which also rattled in the wind. On the very top of one of the forks sat a large still whitish bird, hardly distinguishable from the twisted points of the dry pole.

Fierro was standing about fifty steps from the well. He rested his eyes for a moment on the motionless bird, and as though its presence fitted in perfectly with his thoughts, without a change of attitude or expression, he slowly pulled out his pistol. The long, polished barrel of the gun turned into a pink finger in the fading sunlight. Slowly it rose until it pointed in the direction of the bird. The shot rang out — dull and diminutive in the immensity of the afternoon — and the bird dropped to the ground. Fierro returned his pistol to its holster.

At that moment a soldier jumped over the fence into the yard. It was Fierro's orderly. He had jumped from such a height that it took him several seconds to get to his feet. When he finally did, he walked over to where his master was standing.

Without turning his head Fierro asked him:

"What about them? If they don't come soon, we aren't going to have time."

"I think they're coming."

"Then you hurry up and get over there. Let's see, what pistol have you got?"

"The one you gave me, Chief. The Smith and Wesson."

"Hand it over here and take these boxes of ammunition. How many bullets have you got?"

"About fifteen dozen today, Chief, that I've been able to scrounge up. Some of the other men found lots of them, but I didn't."

"Fifteen dozen? I told you the other day that if you kept on selling ammunition to buy booze, I'd put a bullet through you."

"No, Chief."

"What do you mean: 'No, Chief'?"

"I do get drunk, Chief, but I don't sell the ammunition."

"Well, you watch out, 'cause you know me. And now you move lively so this stunt will come out right. I fire and you load the pistols. And mind what I tell you: if on your account a single one of the Reds gets away, I'll put you to sleep with them."

"Oh, what a chief!"

"You heard what I said."

The orderly spread his blanket on the ground and emptied out the boxes of cartridges that Fierro had just given him. Then he began to take out one by one the bullets in his cartridge belt. He was in such a hurry that it took him longer than it should have. He was so nervous that his fingers seemed all thumbs.

"What a chief!" he kept thinking to himself.

In the meantime, behind the fence of the adjoining corral the soldiers who were guarding the prisoners began to appear. They were on horseback, with their shoulders showing above the top fence rail. There were many others stationed along the two other fences.

Fierro and his orderly were the only ones inside the corral: Fierro with a pistol in his hand, and his sarape fallen at his feet; his orderly squatting and lining up the bullets in rows on his blanket.

The leader of the troop rode up through the gate that opened into the next corral and said:

"I've got the first ten ready. Shall I turn them loose for you?"

"Yes," answered Fierro, "but first explain things to them. As soon as they come through the gate, I'll begin to shoot. Those that reach the wall and get over it are free. If any of them don't want to come through, you shoot them."

The officer went back the same way he came, and Fierro, pistol in hand, stood attentive, his eyes riveted on the narrow space through which the prisoners were going to break out. He stood close enough to the dividing fence so that, as he fired, the bullets would not hit the Reds who were still on the other side. He wanted to keep his promise faithfully. But he was not so close to the fence that the prisoners could not see, the minute they came through the gate, the pistol that was leveled at them twenty paces away. Behind Fierro the setting sun turned the sky a fiery red. The wind kept blowing.

In the corral where the prisoners were herded, the sound of words grew louder, words that the whistling of the wind destroyed, like those used by herders rounding up cattle. It was a hard task to make the three hundred condemned men pass from the last to the middle corral. At the thought of the torture awaiting them, the whole group writhed with the convulsions of a person in the grip of hysteria. The soldiers of the guard were shouting and every minute the rifle shots seemed to gather up the screams as with a whiplash.

Out of the first prisoners that reached the middle corral a group of soldiers separated ten. There were at least twenty-five soldiers. They spurred their horses on to the prisoners to make them move; they pushed the muzzles of their carbines against their bodies.

"Traitors! Dirty bastards! Let's see how you can run and jump. Get a move on, you traitor!"

And in this way they made them advance to the gate where Fierro and his orderly were waiting. Here the resistance of the Reds grew more intense; but the horses' hoofs and the carbine barrels persuaded them to choose the other danger, the danger of Fierro, who was not an inch away, but twenty paces.

As soon as they appeared within his range of vision, Fierro greeted them with a strange phrase, a phrase both cruel and affectionate, containing both irony and hope:

"Come on, boys; I'm the only one shooting, and I'm a bad shot."

The prisoners jumped like goats. The first one tried to throw himself on Fierro, but he had not taken three leaps before he fell, riddled by bullets from the soldiers stationed along the fence. The others ran as fast as they could toward the wall—a mad race that must have seemed to them like a dream. On seeing the well curb, one tried to find refuge there: he was the first one hit by Fierro's bullet. The others fell as they ran, one by one; in less than ten seconds Fierro had fired eight times, and the last of the group dropped just as his fingers were touching the adobe bricks that by a strange whim separated at that moment the zone of life from the zone of death. Some of the bodies still showed signs of life; the soldiers finished them off from their horses.

And then came another group of ten, and then another, and another, and another. Fierro's three pistols—his own two and that of his orderly—alternated with precise rhythm in the homicidal hand. Six shots from each one, six shots fired without stopping to aim and without pause, and then the gun dropped on to the orderly's blanket, where he removed the exploded caps, and re-loaded it. Then, without changing his position, he held out the pistol to Fierro, who took it as he let the other fall. Through the orderly's fingers passed the bullets that seconds later would leave the prisoners stretched lifeless, but he did not raise his eyes to see the men fall. His whole being seemed to concentrate on the pistol in his hand, and on the bullets, with their silver and burnished reflections, spread out on the ground before him. Just two sensa-tions ran through his bones: the cold weight of the bullets that he was putting into the openings of the cylinder, and the contact with the smooth warm surface. Over his head one after another rang out the shots of his "chief," delightfully engrossed in his target practice.

The panic-stricken flight of the prisoners toward the wall of salvation — a fugue of death within a terrifying symphony in which the two themes of the passion to kill and the infinite desire to live struggled with each other — lasted almost two hours.

Not for one moment did Fierro lose his precise aim or his poise. He was firing at moving human targets, targets that jumped and slipped in pools of blood and amidst corpses stretched out in unbelievable postures, but he fired without any emotion except that of hitting or missing. He even calculated the deflection of the bullets caused by the wind, and corrected it with each shot.

Some of the prisoners, crazed by terror, fell to their knees as they came through the gate: the bullets made them keel over. Others danced about grotesquely behind the shelter of the well curb until the bullet cured them of their frenzy or they dropped wounded into the well. But nearly all rushed toward the adobe wall and tried to scale it by climbing over the warm, damp, steam-ing heaps of piled-up bodies. Some managed to dig their nails into the dirt on the top of the wall, but their hands, so actively clutch-ing for life, soon fell lifeless.

A moment arrived in which the mass execution became a noisy tumult, punctuated by the dull snap of the pistol shots, muted by the immense voice of the wind. On one side of the fence could be heard the shouts of those who were trying to flee from death only to die; on the other, those who resisted the pressure of the horsemen and tried to break through the wall that pushed them on toward that terrible gate. And to the shouts of one group and the other were added the voices of the soldiers stationed along the fences. The noise of the shooting, Fierro's marksmanship, and the cries and frantic gestures of the dying men had worked them up to a pitch of great excitement. They greeted with joyful exclamations the somersaults of the falling bodies; they shouted, gesticulated, and laughed uproariously as they fired into the heaps of human flesh in which they noted the slightest evidence of life.

In the last squad of victims there were twelve instead of ten. The twelve piled out of the death pen, falling over one another, each trying to shield himself with the others, as he raced ahead in the horrible race. In order to go forward they had to hop over the piled-up corpses, but that didn't prevent the bullets from hitting the mark. With sinister precision they hit them one by one and left them halfway to the wall, arms and legs outstretched, embracing the mass of their motionless companions. But one of them, the only one left alive, managed to reach the very top of the wall and to clear it. The firing stopped suddenly and the gang of soldiers crowded into the corner of the adjoining corral to see the fugitive.

It was beginning to get dark. It took the soldiers a little while to focus their vision in the twilight. At first they could see nothing. Finally, far off, in the vastness of the semidark plain they managed to make out a moving spot. As it ran, the body bent so far over that it almost seemed to crawl along on the ground.

A soldier took aim. "It's hard to see," he said as he fired.

The shot died away in the evening wind. The moving spot fled on.

Fierro had not moved from his place. With his arm exhausted, he let it hang limp against his side for a long time. Then he became aware of the pain in his forefinger and raised his hand to his face; he could see in the sunlight that his finger had become somewhat swollen. He rubbed it gently between the fingers and the palm of his other hand. And there he stood for quite a while engrossed in the gentle, soft massage. Finally he stooped over and picked up his sarape, which he had taken off at the beginning of the executions. He threw it over his shoulders and started walking to the shelter of the stable. But after a few steps he turned to his orderly:

"As soon as you're finished, bring up the horses."

And he continued on his way.

The orderly was gathering up the exploded caps. In the next corral the soldiers had dismounted and were talking or singing softly. The orderly listened to them silently and without raising his head. Then he rose slowly to his feet. He gathered up the blanket by its four corners and threw it over his shoulder. The empty caps clattered within like a dull rattle or jingle.

It was dark. A few stars glimmered, and on the other side of the fence the tips of the cigarettes were also glimmering. The orderly started to walk heavily and slowly and, half feeling his way, went to the last of the corrals and then returned leading the horses by the bridle — his master's and his own; across one of his shoulders swung the haversack.

He made his way over to the stable. Fierro was sitting on a rock, smoking in the dark. The wind whistled through the cracks in the boards.

"Unsaddle the horse and make up my bed," ordered Fierro. "I'm so tired I can't stand up."

"Here in this corral, chief? Here . . . ?"

"Yes, here. Why not?"

The orderly did as he was ordered. He unsaddled the horse and spread the blankets on the straw, making a kind of pillow out of the haversack and the saddle. Fierro stretched out and in a few minutes was asleep.

The orderly lighted his lantern and bedded the horses for the night. Then he blew out the light, wrapped himself in his blanket, and lay down at his master's feet. But a moment later he got up again, knelt down, and crossed himself. Then he stretched out on the straw again.

Six or seven hours went by. The wind had died down. The silence of the night was bathed in moonlight. Occasionally a horse sneezed nearby. The radiance of the moon gleamed on the dented surface of the bucket that hung by the well and made clear shadows of all the objects in the yard except the mounds of corpses. They rose up, enormous in the stillness of the night, like fantastic hills, with strange and confused outlines.

The silvery blue of the night descended on the corpses like the clearest light. But imperceptibly that light gradually turned into a voice, a voice equally unreal as the night. The voice grew distinct; it was a voice that was barely audible, faint, painful, and dying, but tenuously clear like the shadows cast by the moon. From the center of one of the mounds of corpses the voice seemed to whisper;

"Ow! Ow! . . ."

Then it was silent and the silvery blue of the night became only light again. But the voice was heard a second time:

"Ow! . . . Ow! . . ."

The heaped-up bodies, stiff and cold for hours, lay motionless in the corral. The rays of moonlight penetrated them as though they were an inert mass. But the voice sounded again:

"Ow. . . . Ow. . . . Ow. . . ."

And this last groan reached the spot where Fierro's orderly lay sleeping and brought him out of sleep to the consciousness of hearing. The first thing that came to his mind was the memory of the execution of the three hundred prisoners; the mere thought of it kept him motionless on the straw, his eyes half open and his whole body and soul fixed on the lamenting voice:

"Ow . . . please. . . ."

Fierro tossed on his bed.

"Please . . . water. . . ."

Fierro awoke and listened attentively.

"Please . . . water. . . ."

Fierro stretched out his foot and nudged his orderly.

"Hey, you. Don't you hear? One of those dead men is asking for water."

"Yes, chief."

"You get up and put a bullet through the sniveling son of a bitch. Let's see if he'll let me get some sleep then."

"A bullet through who, chief?"

"The one that's asking for water, you idiot. Don't you understand?"

"Water, please," the voice repeated.

The orderly took his pistol from under the saddle and, clutching it, got up and left the stable in search of the corpses. He was shivering with fear and cold. He felt sick to his soul.

He looked around in the moonlight. Every body he touched was stiff. He hesitated without knowing what to do. Finally he fired in the direction from which the voice seemed to come. The

voice was heard again. The orderly fired a second time. The voice
died away.

The moon sailed along on the endless space of its blue light.
Under the roof of the stable Fierro slept.

— Translated by Seymour Menton

COMMENTARY

  The Mexican Revolution, in which a relatively large
part of the population was directly involved, changed the basic social
structure of the nation. During the 1920s and 1930s, the Mexican
government officially promoted the painting of revolutionary national-
istic murals by Diego Rivera, José Clemente Orozco, and David Alfaro
Siqueiros. Although literati were not subsidized nearly to the same
extent, well over one hundred novels and volumes of short stories related
to the Revolution were written from 1915 through the early 1970s with
most of them appearing between 1928 and 1947. The best way to
appraise this inordinately large number of works is by grouping the
authors according to generations.

  Martín Luis Guzmán (1887) belongs to the first generation of novelists
of the Revolution, which also includes other very well-known figures:
Mariano Azuela (1873-1952), José Vasconcelos (1881-1959), and José
Rubén Romero (1890-1952). Although Azuela was older than the average and Romero younger, they all had the common experience of
growing up under the waning years of the Porfirio Díaz dictatorship.
They all enthusiastically endorsed Francisco Madero's democratic ideals,
but because they were intellectuals and professionals (Azuela was a
doctor, Guzmán and Vasconcelos, lawyers[1]), they soon became disenchanted with the brutality unleashed by the Revolution. The two stylistic
tendencies of this group may be attributed to their geographical origins.
Azuela and Romero, both provincials, use a style that directly reflects
the violence of the Revolution: short sentences, little description, and
much dialogue written in the popular dialect. By contrast, Guzmán and
Vasconcelos, with a more universal culture — both men belonged to the
Ateneo literary-cultural group in Mexico City — write in a much more
polished literary style and resort only infrequently to dialogue. Guzmán
and Vasconcelos view the Revolution through the generals' eyes, while
Azuela and Romero try to capture the point of view of the anonymous
soldier, but without identifying with him.

[1] Romero is a transitional figure between this generation and the second one. Because
he stayed longer in the provinces and came from a less affluent family, he was unable
to pursue a professional career, but he shared this generation's enthusiasm for Madero
and its disillusion with the subsequent brutality.

Although "The Festival of the Bullets" is a chapter from *The Eagle and the Serpent,* which is essentially a book of memoirs, there is no doubt about its being a short story. The narrator himself tells us that what he is going to relate is the thematic concentration, the mathematically logical development of the plot, and the marvelous creation of suspense belies its character as an autobiographical fragment and makes it one of the better examples of the Spanish American short story.

The portrait of Rodolfo Fierro as the most brutal representative of the Villa movement is executed with a carefully preconceived plan. If the first two paragraphs are discounted, the story may be said to begin with the concise and journalistic-like presentation of the immediate historical setting. In the next moment, the narrator transports the reader into the drama with the terse reference to the setting sun. With a measured and precise description, the solitary figure of Fierro defying the wind coming off the desolate plain assumes epic proportions. The vision of the three hundred prisoners enclosed in the corral like cattle also contributes to Fierro's superhuman image. The strange twitch that he feels creates suspense and speeds up the tempo of the story. The tension is maintained during the long description of the preparations by the narrator's alternating the almost mathematically precise and static description of the layout of the corrals with the account of Fierro's very decisive moves. Dialogue is used for the first time to reveal Fierro's diabolical plan. The execution of the prisoners extends over two pages without the reader's interest waning because of the rapidly changing focus on the attitude of the condemned men, Fierro's pistols, the orderly's terror, Fierro's serenity, the noise of the shots, the desperate shouts of the condemned, the happy exclamations of the soldiers, and finally, the escape of one of the "Reds." Fierro's inhuman brutality is made to stand out even more in contrast with the soldier who shoots at but doesn't hit the only prisoner who clears the wall and with the orderly who crosses himself before lying down to sleep and who pretends not to hear Fierro's order to finish off the wounded man begging for water. The ultimate touch on Fierro's portrait is his concern for his swollen finger and the final sentence of the story: "Under the roof of the stable Fierro slept."

The impact of this work depends to a great extent on the totally impersonal quality of the narrator. He never lets slip a word of pity for the prisoners nor a word of censure for Fierro. During the artistic process, it almost seems as though the narrator became infected with Fierro's indifference. He converts human suffering into artistic images: "a wave would then ripple through the vague perimeter of the mass of the prisoners that retracted to avoid the shot"; "the prisoners jumped like goats"; "a fugue of death within a terrifying symphony"; "they rose up, enormous in the stillness of the night, like fantastic hills with strange and confused outlines." Nature also shares Fierro's indifference. The sun, the wind, the moon and the stars are recurring leitmotivs not directly related to the drama.

As a short story, "The Festival of the Bullets" is technically perfect. As a work of the Mexican Revolution, it captures masterfully the bestial and epic cruelty of Rodolfo Fierro. As a Mexican work in general, the lack of compassion for the lower classes, for the underdogs, is surprising and may be attributed to the difficulty experienced by the intellectuals of Guzmán's generation in identifying with the illiterate soldiers. This was not the case with the generation of Mexican writers that followed.

Jorge Ferretis

(1902-1962)

Mexican. From the state of San Luis Potosí, he was a journalist and politician active in the Socialist Party between 1937 and 1947. He represented his state in Congress between 1952 and 1957. For the last seven years of his life, he was the head of the government Bureau of Cinematography. He died in an automobile accident. He published two novels: *Tierra caliente* (1935) and *Cuando engorda el Quijote* (1937); two collections of short novels: *El sur quema* (1937) and *San automóvil* (1939); and two volumes of short stories: *Hombres en tempestad* (1941) and *El coronel que asesinó un palomo* (1952). In 1968 a posthumous collection of short stories appeared under the title *Libertad obligatoria*. All his works reflect his humanitarian socialism and are very representative of the literature of the 1930s. "Men in a Storm" is the title story of the 1941 collection.

MEN IN A STORM

Few trees, large, still. Dark trunks of fluted stone.
The world begins to take shape with the approach of daybreak.
An unseen cow moos, as if the moo was diluted in the shade.
At the foot of one of those solitary trees, there is a form, like a protuberance of the trunk, darker than the color of the bark. But that form is soft, warm. It's Tata José, wrapped in his woolen blanket, squatting next to the trunk. An early riser, one of those old men who get up before the lazy hens.
Before sitting down there, next to the trunk, he had already fed the ox.
In a nearby hut, a light becomes visible through the reed walls. You can picture a woman seated on her heels, on the floor. Diligently she fans the embers until the dried branches which she broke with her hands catch fire.
A moment later, from the same hut, a shivering shadow emerges.

193

It's Tata José's son.

He comes out, wrapped up to his eyes in his blanket, like his father.

He walks up to the old man, and stops, silent, like a piece of wood. The less men speak, the better they understand each other.

However, after several moments, the latecomer says: "Las' night I heard Uncle Jesús."

"Yep," responds the form encrusted in the trunk.

"I heard 'm outside askin' to borrow an ox."

"Yep," repeats the old man's dry voice.

And after a pause, the boy insists: "And dya lend it to 'im?"

"'Course, so as he kin complete the team."

"'n now what'll we use to plow?"

The old man, in an even drier tone, responds almost reproachfully: "Jesús is a lot more behind 'n us. He ain't even got the field ready fer plowin'. And I wasn't about to deny 'm the use of my Josco."

Again they fell silent, like two dark blocks. And on those two blocks, the dawn, with its light, begins to chisel human faces, hardened, silent.

Suddenly the voice of a woman is heard. It's almost as if she was the power to bring statues to life. A sturdy old woman, sticking her head out of the hut's one window, shouts her incantation; she calls them to breakfast.

Breakfast! The two men go sit down near the fire. Oh, those tortillas that puff up, one by one, on the pan! That whiteness which is thinned between the darkened hands of that woman, only to turn golden on that warm earthenware pan. And some strips of dried meat which for a couple of seconds twitch among the red hot coals. And a few gulps of coffee, that coffee, which before being served, may be heard bubbling in the pot. That coffee which warms up people from the inside. Aaah! So nice and hot, that when it is served, a savory mist comes out of the cup, and also provides outside warmth.

Now that it was light outside, the two left the hut. Surely they hadn't eaten their fill; but their stomachs were half-full with the sweetened watered-down coffee, boiled corn, and strips of meat with chile. Enough to fool their guts. And make them hang on (though their stomachs might growl) until past sundown. Their guts! They sure were aware of the price of corn. They sure were aware, by the moderate or abundant way in which the woman served them tortillas.

Tata José and his boy weren't in a hurry, and even less so that day. Of course they couldn't have refused to lend Josco to Uncle Jesús.

Each of them shouldered a hoe and made his way uphill.

Little patches of mist rose from the hills leaving them clear, and spotted with cornfields.

Sun. Noontime. The air was hot. But there, over the northern range, black clouds were beginning to pile up. Tata José, with his small eyes shining amidst his wrinkles, stood silent for a moment, contemplating the thunderheads in the distance.

The son, also looking, remarked: "It's sure rainin' hard up there!"

And they continued hoeing at the clods of dirt.

But behind them, a thunderclap made the air tremble and then vibrate over the fields. If the sky had been made of blue crystal, that enormous thunderbolt would have shattered it. And it would have fallen on the people in bits and pieces.

"Let's go," Tata said, shouldering his hoe. "That storm is goin' to catch us."

But the boy, behind, stopped with a shout, pointing to a hill below where the river twisted: "Look, Tata!"

The two felt as though they were being strangled by the same apprehension. The storm still hadn't arrived, and nevertheless, the river had already risen, catching them by surprise. The men who were working on the other side of the river could no longer ford it. And Uncle Jesús' farmlands were on that side!

The old man and his son trotted downhill. On the banks of the river, the rising waters were beginning to uproot entire banana groves. The waters dug away at the roots of the big trees, bending them over, causing a racket of breaking branches.

Far away, on the other side of the river, you could tell that several men were shouting from a small hilltop. They were waving their arms and shouting themselves hoarse, but the roar of the current drowned out their voices.

The water continued to rise minute by minute. By now, two or three huts had been swept away from the bottomlands.

Women and chickens, pigs and children, were screeching everywhere.

Tata José and his son, running to where the water leveled off, arrived panting opposite Uncle Jesús' land. There, the bottomlands had turned into a large, turbulent lake.

About a kilometer away, they saw Uncle Jesús. The team of unyoked oxen stayed close to him and looked at the flood fearfully. The old man stood immobile, erect, with his long goad in his hand, stuck into the ground next to his feet. The mound where they were standing kept getting smaller and smaller, as if it were melting away. It was even useless to yell.

Enormous drops began to fall on a slant, from the blotchy sky. It was barely starting to rain over there and Josco was going to be carried away by the current! Their ox!

The father and his son began running again. The downpour grew heavier! Running at full speed, they felt as if the clouds were stoning them. The drops were so big and strong that they almost seemed aimed at smashing their eyes. Suddenly it looked as if, among the gushing torrents of lukewarm water, buckets of alcohol or gasoline had been mixed, which would catch fire in the midst of the storm because in the soaked sky noisy flashes of fire appeared. Bursts of laughter from a sky drunk with darkness.

Only after an hour did the downpour abate.

The father and his son, like two desperate goblins, were still walking in the mud of the hillside, peering at the swollen river. Surely the current had dragged away their Josco.

When the sky had grown completely calm, it was almost night. And the two anguished goblins opened their eyes wider in the darkness.

"There ain't nothin', Tata."

"There ain't nothin'," replied the disconsolate old man, his shirt and trousers clinging to his body, drenched in the rain and perspiration.

But suddenly, among pieces of floating garbage and sticks, they made out a form thrashing weakly in the water.

"Could it be Uncle?"

"Jesúuus!" Tata shouted from the shore.

"Unncle!" shouted the boy.

Barely treading water to keep from drowning, the man jerked his head up from the water.

"EEEH!" he replied with a muted cry.

"Where's the ox?" the boy shouted as loud as he could.

"He's coming along," he answered, gathering up strength to make a feeble cry, pointing back with his arm.

And then he was barely able to add: "Wait for 'm at the bend."

Father and son, indeed, noticed a large form farther away. And with their hearts beating wildly, they guessed that it was their ox.

Moved by the same impulse, before thinking about jumping into the water to help Uncle Jesús reach the shore, they started running toward the bend.

The sky was now clear. But the moon was only gradually lighting up the crests of the hills.

And by the dim light of a few stars, the boy threw himself into the current, which swelled up as though it were the ocean.

He flailed away in the darkness until he reached the shadow of the ox. And swimming alongside it, he kept pushing and pushing. He had to get it to the shore before both of them were sucked into a rocky gorge where, in the distance, the floodwaters continued to roar.

Tata José, up to his knees in the water, shouted hoarsely in the darkness to his son and to his ox.

Toward midnight, the moon came out. Toward midnight also, the boy, almost faint, managed to push the ox up against the bank. But the spot was rocky, and the animal, benumbed by so many hours in the water, couldn't get out.

Amidst the shadows, far off, muffled human cries could be heard from time to time.

From the bank, as though he were a large branch, the old man plunged into the water next to the ox, which was so numb that it didn't even bellow. After the splash, the old man could be seen groping until he finally clutched onto the branches of a tree which was still pretty well rooted to the rocky embankment. And in that way, the dark body tightly linked to the branches served as a retaining wall for the animal. That large black floating hulk could have slid slowly away toward the mouth of the river if Tata José hadn't been there, wrapped into a knot, mooring it with his feet.

The son came out drenched and battered, and began to climb the hills. Maybe in the village he would find people who would want to come down to help them.

It was daybreak when the water level began to recede. The boy returned running followed right behind by his mother and by another little man, eleven years old, who more than wanted to help, but who lacked the strength. And with the panting efforts of the four of them, the ox at last was safe, although unable to get up on its feet.

Daybreak found it lying there in the mud, waterlogged with its eyes even sadder than is normal for an ox, and its snout in the ground. It didn't even want to eat. It was useless for the boy to go up and cut fresh grass for it.

It didn't move all morning long, and Tata José stayed to care for it, crouching nearby, distressed and still.

In the early afternoon, the animal, with trembly legs, attempted to get up. And the old man sighed with relief.

They didn't find Uncle Jesús until later in the afternoon, lifeless, far downstream. He had been deposited on the bank as the floodwaters subsided. Surely he must have struggled, swimming hard, until the end.

They found him before he had grown stiff, with his stomach swollen. And they began to shake him.

"He must've swallowed a lot of water," someone said.

And with a round, heavy stone, they began to rub hard on that swelling. Others moved his arms, as if they were working on a pump. Others shouted in his ears, for a long, long time. Later they twisted his head. And in that way, between squeezing and shouting, they brought him back to life. When he started to breathe heavily and half opened one eye, everyone there let out a sacred cry. It was as if each one had worked, in part, that miracle of resurrection.

A few days passed.

In their village there was still no end to the comments about the losses each man had sustained. One, his red pepper field; another, three pigs and a little girl. The one from down below, his banana trees full of bunches. Another, his shack and his pregnant wife.

That one, his black goat. Still another one, his jug without handles, where he kept his loose money.

A few days passed.

One afternoon, they saw Uncle Jesús leaving his hut. It was his first time out since that fateful night.

And his first steps were toward José's hut.

Tata went out to meet him.

It was as if they hadn't seen each other in a long time. On their weather-beaten faces, a strong brotherly joy shone. Their four hands clasped each other in a wonderful greeting.

Then, they both went to sit down in front of the hut, close to the tree.

Uncle Jesús had come to thank him. He was grateful that Tata had lent him the ox.

Tata José, a bit embarrassed, would have preferred not to talk about it.

"I thought you'd be mad," he said without looking him in the face.

"Mad?" Jesús asked, bewildered.

"Well, yeah! 'Cause me and my boy went to save our Josco before you. . . ."

"Well, now!" Uncle Jesús exclaimed. "I'd 've done the same! A human being ain't worth as much as an ox. I'd 've done the same!"

And his face truly did not show the slightest trace of reproach or anger. He was really grateful to the man who had been so generous as to lend him what he treasured so much.

Seated on the ground, Tata and Uncle were quiet for a long time.

The clouds, soaked in sunset, were burning. The horizon was spectacularly on fire, but it didn't impress these two old men, even though they were blinded by the brightness. They were thinking of the bliss of having two oxen. Like Tata José, an old man could die in peace knowing he hadn't wasted his life. He could bequeath that fortune of horns and tails to his son.

In those parts, men hacked each other to death with machetes for the slightest reason. Or the army patrols would execute them on the basis of a piece of gossip. For the most insignificant theft they could be hung. An animal, on the other hand, wasn't sacrificed just like that. One would have to think about it. A cow, even if it had spent a night damaging somebody's cornfield, was captured delicately. Who would bother fighting to take possession of a man? A cow, on the other hand . . .

Uncle Jesús, indifferent to the sky, and sitting on the soft earth, was becoming a sociologist.

And he said: "Ya know what I'd do to make people worth more?"

"What?"

"Well, if I was the boss of Mexico, I would order people killed in slaughterhouses, and their meat to be sold! About five pesos a pound, until we got to like eating one another."

"And why?" asked Tata eyeing him fixedly.

"Well, in that way don't ya figure people wouldn't waste people? I'll bet you've never seen 'm waste a goat anywhere."

"Well, no. . . ."

And the two old men fell silent again. In the distance they looked like two figurines of dried mud, illuminated by the burning of those large black clouds, ignited by the sunset as though they were rags in the sky.

—Translated by Antonia García

COMMENTARY

The authors of the second literary generation of the Mexican Revolution were born between 1895 and 1902. They were teenagers or younger when the Revolution broke out so that their schooling was interrupted at the secondary or primary level. Like the members of the preceding generation, they participated actively in the Revolution but they identified more with the masses of soldiers than with the generals. José Mancisidor (1895-1956), Gregorio López y Fuentes (1897-1966), Rafael F. Muñoz (1899), and Jorge Ferretis (1902-1962) all feel the emotion of the Revolution much more than the intellectuals who followed professional careers during the final years of the Porfirio Díaz dictatorship. Ferretis and his contemporaries describe not only the military action but also the effects of the Revolution, and always from the point of view of the anonymous peasant. Their prose is fast moving and vigorous with discreetly sprinkled poetic images that do not stand out for their originality but rather for the contrast with the very realistic

narrative and dialogue. If these authors did not produce works of sufficient literary sophistication to appeal to the European and American
critics, they did write works that are noteworthy for the deep sincerity
and compassion with which the anonymous, suffering characters are
presented. Their value in the history of Mexican literature is comparable
with that of their American contemporaries, John Steinbeck (1902–1968)
and Erskine Caldwell (1903).

Although "Men in a Storm" has nothing at all to do with the military
action of the Revolution, it is intimately related to the broader concept
of the Revolution as the instrument for the salvation of the Mexican
people. Ferretis tries to create a primitive scene in which the peasant
hardly considers himself as a human being. At the beginning of the
story, the reader gets the impression that he is witnessing the creation
of the world: "the world begins to take shape with the approach of
daybreak"; the man is a "form, like a protuberance of the trunk"; the
son is "like a piece of wood"; and both are "two dark blocks." The image
of the tree-man reappears when they save the ox. The atmosphere of
Genesis is reinforced by the flood and the final image of José and Jesús:
"two figurines of dried mud." The anonymity of the wife and the son as
well as the brotherly loan of the ox also contribute to the creation of
the prehistoric epoch. On the other hand, the precise description of the
food and the hut, and the exclamations and diminutives (in the original
Spanish) give the story a definite Mexican flavor.

Ferretis's style is most appropriate for the theme. He achieves primitive
effects by using very short paragraphs and sentences. In order to capture
the rhythm of the storm, he extends the paragraphs and sentences
through repetition, enumeration, and parallel adjectives. He ends with
a great crescendo produced by the images of raindrops as stones, lightning bolts as alcohol or gasoline fire, and thunderclaps as "burst of
laughter from a sky drunk with darkness." The·very next sentence,
because of its simplicity, restores the primitive atmosphere: "Only after
an hour did the downpour abate." Although the simple "Biblical" style
predominates, there are two other occasions in which the author uses
celestial images which as a whole reinforce the story's structure: "If the
sky had been made of blue crystal, that enormous thunderbolt would
have shattered it. And it would have fallen on the people in bits and
pieces" and the final words of the story: "illuminated by the burning
of those large black clouds, ignited by the sunset as though they were
rags in the sky." The Mexican quality of the scene is intensified with a
judicious use of dialogue in rural dialect. There is good balance between
narrative and dialogue with the latter reserved for the more dramatic
moments.

The authors of the second revolutionary generation are incapable of
maintaining the absolute objectivity of a Martín Luis Guzmán in the
face of the human tragedy that they feel deeply. These writers may be

forgiven the compassion they show for their characters, but Ferretis may be censured for the artistic defect of an occasional phrase that explains what is very obvious: "before thinking about jumping into the water to help Uncle Jesús reach the shore." Uncle Jesús' solution, in the grotesque tradition of Jonathan Swift, also weakens the story, which is partly redeemed by the final paragraph with its evocation of the primitive calm of the initial scene.

José Revueltas

(1914-1975)

Mexican. Although he was from a poor mining-town family in Durango, his brother Silvestre became a famous composer, his brother Fermín, a painter, and his sister Rosaura, a movie actress. Part of his youth was spent in prison because of his Communist Party activities. In *Los muros de agua* (1941) he describes his exile in the penal colony on the Islas Marías. While working as a journalist with the daily newspaper *El Popular,* his novel *El luto humano* (1943) was chosen to represent Mexico in the second Farrar and Rinehart literary contest and still stands as his best novel. The others are *Los días terrenales* (1949), *En algún valle de lágrimas* (1956), *Los motivos de Caín* (1957), *Los errores* (1964), and *El apando* (1969). His two collections of short stories, *Dios en la tierra* (1944) and *Dormir en tierra* (1960), establish him, according to José Agustín, as one of Mexico's three best short-story writers along with Juan Rulfo and Juan José Arreola. In 1961, he broke with the Communist Party after a series of difficulties stemming in part from *Los días terrenales* which presented some of the internal conflicts within the Party. Along with other Marxists, he founded the Liga Leninista Espartaco but dissociated himself from it shortly thereafter. In 1968, he claimed responsibility for the student movement which culminated in the Tlatelolco massacre and was imprisoned for two and one half years. "God on Earth" is the title story of the 1944 volume.

GOD ON EARTH

The town was sealed with hatred and with stones. Completely sealed, as if huge slabs, so large as to lack dimensions, so thick, so God-like, had been placed over doors and windows. An obstinacy, the likes of which had never been witnessed, made of incomprehensible entities, impossible to encompass which came . . . from where? From the Bible, from Genesis, from the Darkness before there was light. Rocks move, the immense stones of the world change places, advancing a millimeter every century. But this was not changing, this hatred was coming from the most remote and most barbaric times. It was God's hatred. God himself was there, crushing life in his grip, clutching at the earth with his thick fingers, his colossal raging fingers of oak. Even an unbeliever can't help but think of God. Because who, if not Him? Who, if not a formless substance, without beginning or end, unmeasurable, can seal doors in such a way? All doors sealed in the name of God. All the madness and stubbornness in the world, in the name of God. The God of hosts; the God of clenched teeth; the strong and terrible God, hostile and deaf, the God of brimstone and frozen blood. And so it was, there and everywhere, because according to an old and maddening curse, He is everywhere: in the sinister silence of the street; in irascible work; in the surprised matrimonial bedroom; in nuptial hatreds; and in churches rising in anathemas above the terror and anguish. God had stored himself up in the hearts of men as only blood can, and emerged in screams, in slow, cautious, and meticulous cruelty. In the North and in the South, inventing points of the compass only to be there, to prevent something there, to deny something with all the forces that man has inherited from the darkest centuries, from the blindest blindness of his history.

Where was this nightmare coming from? How was it born? It seems that men had learned something impossible to learn and that something had turned their heads, like a monstrous ball of fire, where obstinacy was fixed and central, like the thrust of a knife. Refuse. Refuse always, above all things, even if the world should fall apart, even if the Universe should come to a halt and all the planets and stars remain fixed in the air.

The men entered their homes with a delirium of eternity, never to leave again and behind the doors they accumulated impenetrable masses of dry hatred, without saliva, leaving no room for even a pin or a moan.

It was difficult for the soldiers to fight against God, because He was invisible, invisible and present, like a thick layer of solid air or transparent ice or liquid thirst. And look at the soldiers! They have the dark faces of cultivated earth, they are young and have the looks of children unaware of their cruelty. Their authority comes from nowhere. It was loaned to them somewhere along the line and they would rather die, as if they were always only passing through, and felt a bit ashamed about everything. They arrived at the towns only with a certain astonishment, as if they had carried all roads with them to bring them there, in their canvas leggings or in their red scarves, where the crunchy tortillas still lay silent, like dry plants.

The officers raged at the silence, unhinged by the hostile muteness, the stone before them, and then they had to order the sacking of the town, for the towns were sealed with hatred, with slabs of hatred, with petrified seas. Hatred and only hatred, like mountains.

"The *federales!* the *federales!*"

And it was at this cry that the streets of the towns would clad themselves with indifference, with obstinate coldness, and the men would die temporarily, waiting within the hermetic houses or firing their carbines from hidden corners.

The officer would dismount, his face red and with the muzzle of his pistol he would strike the cruel, immovable door.

"We want to eat!"

"We'll pay for everything!"

The reply was a lasting silence, where the years went by, where hands could not even be raised. Then a cry like the baying of a hunted wolf, of a furiously sad beast:

"Long live Christ the King!"

He was a King. Who was he? Where was he? On what frightful roads? The troops could march on for miles and miles without stopping. The soldiers could eat one another. God had walled up the houses and burned the fields so that there would be no rest, no shelter, no spirit, no seed.

The cry was one, unanimous, limitless: "Not even water." Water is tender and full of charm. Water is young and ancient. It is eternally loyal like a distant first woman. The world was made of water and earth and both are joined as if two opposing skies had contracted an imponderable marriage. "Not even water." And everything is born from water. Tears and man's harmonious body, his heart, his sweat. "Not even water." To walk all over the land without rest, in terrible pursuit and not find it, not see it, not hear it, not hear its caressing murmur. To see how the sun plunges down, how it heats the soft inimical dust, how it sucks in all water by the command of God, and of that King without thorns, that furious King, that inspector of hatred who walks the earth sealing all entrances. . . .

When would they come?

They were awaited with anxiety and at the same time with a fear full of wrath. Let them come! Let them enter the town with their big hobnailed boots and their vile olive drab, with their empty canteens, and hungry. Let them enter! No one would make a sign, a gesture. That's what doors were for, to be closed. And the town, full of inhabitants, would seem uninhabited, like a town of the dead, sunk deep in its loneliness.

When and from where would those men in uniform appear, those forsaken men whom God had cursed?

Far away still, on his horse, Lieutenant Medina, was thinking. His soldiers were gray, they looked like grown cactuses on this otherwise barren land. Cactuses that could stand there, without rain, under the rays of the sun. Nevertheless, they had to be thirsty, because when they spat it felt pasty, although they preferred to swallow their saliva as a consolation. It was a thick, ignoble saliva which by now tasted bad, which tasted like a chalk-coated tongue, like a rage, like dirty teeth. Thirst! It is a yearning like that of sex. You feel an inexpressible desire, a rage, with devils casting fire in your stomach and in your ears to make your whole body burn, consume itself and explode. Water then becomes something greater than your wife or your children, something greater than the world, and you would let your hand, your foot or your testicles be cut off, just to submerge in its clarity and breathe its coolness, even if only to die afterward.

Suddenly those men seemed to stop marching, with all enthusiasm gone. But there is always something inhuman and illusory which eternally summons with who knows what words, and allows no interruption. Forward, march! And then the small troop would madly quicken its pace, in its march against God. Against God, who had assumed the form of thirst. God, everywhere! There, amid the cactus, hot with an infernal fire in their guts, so that they would never forget Him, never, never again.

Drums were beating on Medina's forehead and moved down both sides past his temples, to his arms and to the tips of his fingers: "WA-TER, WA-TER, WA-TER. Why repeat that absurd

word? Why did the horses also repeat it with their hoofbeats . . . ?"
He turned to look at his men's faces and noticed only their ashen
lips and their impossible foreheads where one thought was throbbing in the form of a river, a lake, a pitcher, a well: water, water,
water. "If the teacher only keeps his word . . . !"

"Lieutenant . . . ," a sergeant drew near.

But he did not try to continue, and no one, in fact, asked him
to finish, since it was obviously useless to do so.

"Well! What for, really . . . ?" he admitted, breaking into
laughter as if it were funny.

"Lieutenant." What for? No way for them to make a hole in
the ground for water to spring out. No way. "Oh! If that damn
teacher keeps his word . . . !"

"Romero!" shouted the lieutenant.

The sergeant moved quickly and with joy in his eyes, because
you always think your superiors can do extraordinary things, impossible miracles in difficult situations.

". . . do you think the teacher . . . ?"

All of the small troop felt relieved, as if they were seeing the
water right there before them, because they could no longer reason, they could no longer think, there was nothing in their brains
but thirst.

"Yes, Lieutenant, he sent the message saying he'd be there for
sure. . . ."

"For sure!" Damned teacher! Although everything was damned:
the water, the thirst, the distance, the troop, God was damned
and the whole universe.

The teacher would be neither near nor far from the town to
lead them to the water, the good water, to the good water that the
children of God drank.

When would they arrive? When and how? Two opposing enemy
entities, differently constituted, waited there: a mass born of fury,
horrible, lacking eyes and lips, with only an immutable, imperish-
able face where there was nothing but one blow, one thunderclap,
one dark word — "Christ the King" — and one feverish, anxious
man whose heart pounded ceaselessly, terrified, waiting to give
them water, to give them a clear, extraordinary liquid which
would flow down their throats and reach their veins, happy,
trembling, and singing.

The lieutenant rocked his head from side to side noticing how his horse's ears placed a pair of exclamation marks on the dry, hostile landscape. Exclamation marks. Yes, marks of exclamation and astonishment, deep joy, of loud and vital enthusiasm. Because, wasn't that dot . . . that one . . . a man, the teacher . . . ? Wasn't it?

"Romero! Romero! Next to the *huizache* plant . . . Do you make something out . . . ?" Then the cry of the troop could be heard, deafening, impetuous:

"Yippeeee!" and it reechoed in the hills, because that was the water.

A throng that seemed white from a distance was there pressed together. Up close, it was ugly, brutal, obstinate like a curse. "Christ the King!" Once again, it was God whose arms were squeezing the earth like two wrathful pincers. God, alive and angry, wrathful, blind as only He can be, as no one but God can be, who when He descends has only one eye in the middle of his forehead, not to see but to cast lightning bolts and to burn, to punish, to conquer.

On the periphery of the throng, the men who were in the outlying houses still did not know what was going on. Only words, opposing words:

"Yes, yes, yes!"

"No, no, no!"

The poor neighbors! There was no one here anymore, there was only punishment. The Terrible Law that does not forgive even the twentieth generation, not even the hundredth, not even the human race. The Law that does not forgive. The Law that swore vengeance. The Law that swore to grant no rest. The Law that swore to close all doors, wall up the windows, darken the sky and place a cloak of impenetrable purple on the blue lake of aerial water up above. God is here again, to make sinners tremble. God is defending his Church, his great waterless church, his stone church, his age-old church.

In the midst of the white throng, a black dot suddenly appeared, an exhausted, sad, persecuted body. It was the teacher. He was blind with anguish, mad with terror, pale and green in the midst of the throng. He was struck from all sides, without the slightest order or system, according to spontaneous outbursts of hatred.

"Shout, 'Long live Christ the King!'"

The eyes of the teacher were lost in the air as he repeated the war cry, exhausted.

"Long live Christ the King!"

Now, the men on the periphery also knew what was going on. Now you could see their black, hard, animal faces.

"He gave water to the *federales,* the bastard!"

"Water! That transparent liquid from which the world was formed. Water! Nothing less than life itself."

"Traitor! Traitor!"

For those who do not know, the operation, despite everything, is rather simple. Brutally simple. With a machete it can be sharpened very well to a point, to a perfect point. A strong pole should be chosen, one that won't break with the weight of a man, of a "Christian" as the people say. Then it is positioned and you have to pull down on the man's legs, strongly, so it will be well inserted.

From a distance, the teacher looked like a scarecrow on his pole, shaking as if moved by the wind, the wind which blew carrying the deep Cyclopean voice of God, which had passed over the earth.

— Translated by Gustavo Pellón

COMMENTARY

The novelists and short story writers belonging to the third literary generation engendered by the Mexican Revolution were born between 1904 and 1914. Before they reached adolescence, the Revolution, as far as its military campaigns were involved, had ended. Once relative tranquillity was restored, they were able to devote themselves to their studies and they developed as writers under the influence of the experimentation of the 1920s. Agustín Yáñez (1904), Mauricio Magdaleno (1906), and José Revueltas (1914-1975) express, like their predecessors, the epic force and the emotion of the Revolution but they add a new dimension. Because they are somewhat removed from the military action, they are able to place the Revolution in historical perspective with the aid of the new techniques introduced on the international plane, above all, by James Joyce. Actually, this third generation should be classified along with the Cosmopolitanites rather than with the Criollistas, but they are included here in order not to break the thematic unity.

In "God on Earth," a specific but not atypical episode of the religious
Cristeros Rebellion (1926-1929) assumes the proportions of a tragic vision
of the primitive hatred that reigns among mankind in general. Like
Ferretis in "Men in a Storm," Revueltas begins his story with a cosmic
vision. Nevertheless, with more artistic techniques at his disposal, he
goes beyond suggesting a scene from Genesis; he actually creates a Stone
Age scene. He never humanizes his characters. They are carved out of
stone, quite similar to the stonelike Aztecs painted by José Clemente
Orozco.

The plot may be reduced to a struggle between two basic elements:
stone and water. The stone, which is hatred, which is death, which is
God, triumphs over the water that fertilizes the earth with love and
tenderness.

In order to capture the force of this struggle, Revueltas orchestrates
his prose with great skill. His sentences and phrases tend to be brief,
suggestive of epitaphs carved in stone: "The town was sealed with hatred
and with stones." At times sentences are composed of only one to three
words: "Refuse," "Not even water." In order to capture the style of the
Old Testament, Revueltas starts some of his sentences with the word
"and." Rarely are there subordinating conjunctions. This lack of stylistic
interdependence reflects the huge walls that separate the men into two
opposing camps. This same sensation is established in the first paragraph by the use of words like "huge," "immense," "colossal"; by the
repetition of "God," "doors," "sealed," "stones"; by the use of superla-
tives and by the repetition of different forms of the same word: "from
the darkest centuries, from the blindest blindness of his history." Another
type of repetition is the structuring of many sentences on two or three
parallel phrases. Dialogue is almost totally absent. The few words pronounced by the characters, whether they are anonymous or identified
without being individualized, seem to float in the air unanswered in
order to reinforce the very basic image of walls separating men from
one another. The narrator allows himself several rhetorical questions
and exclamations (in series of twos and threes) which have the effect of
underlining man's isolation as well as interrupting the descriptive passages.

Although Revueltas creates his world of hatred with every word, the
drama of the story builds with the gradual movement from the general
to the particular. Only the existence of a "Cyclopean" God could explain
the concentration of all that hatred in the horrible punishment suffered
by the local teacher at the hands of the Cristeros. The narrator gradually
prepares the reader for the climax by alternating scenes between the
two groups, but without clearly labeling them. The reader must participate actively in the story in order to determine whether the narrator
is referring to the federal troops or to the Cristeros. At the same time,
the narrator, despite the fact that his sympathies undoubtedly lie with

the *federales,* uses this technique to project an archetypal vision of man's hatred for his fellow man.

The abrupt change in style of the penultimate paragraph is most significant. The narrator seems to be addressing the reader directly in a very calm, clear, and unapocalyptic tone, almost as though he were teaching a woodworking class. The effect is one of unforgettable horror.

The obsession of Mexican writers with the Revolution continued up through the early 1960s. Whereas the 1920s, 1930s, and 1940s were dominated respectively by the first three generations of writers of the Revolution, the 1950s were dominated by the fourth generation—Juan Rulfo (1918)—and the early 1960s by the fifth generation—Carlos Fuentes (1929). It was not until the mid-1960s that a precocious sixth generation led by José Agustín (1944) and Gustavo Sainz (1940) broke away from the revolutionary theme.

Joaquín Gallegos Lara

(1911–1947)

Ecuadorean. Born in Guayaquil, he was the prime mover of the literary group which included José de la Cuadra, Alfredo Pareja Díez-Canseco, Demetrio Aguilera Malta, and Enrique Gil Gilbert. Although he had no formal schooling, he was very knowledgeable in the classical cultures of Greece and Rome. A journalist, he planned several novels but published only *Las cruces sobre el agua* (1946). His short story production was equally sparse. Besides contributing one third of the stories, including "She Was His Mother!," in the volume *Los que se van* (1930), he published one other story, "La última erranza" (1947) in the Mexican series "Lunes," directed by Juan José Arreola.

SHE WAS HIS MOTHER!

I

He couldn't guess how many yards he had covered. On foot. Plunging through the brush. Leaving shreds of flesh on the deadly gray fangs of the barbed wire.

"Stop, damn niggah!"

"Cut 'm off ovah dere."

"Dat darkie's fastah 'n a deer."

He was panting and in a cold sweat. He heard the footsteps behind him. And the harsh hoofs of the captain's horse resounded on the soft ground of the pasture.

"Now we've really. . . ."

The wind carried off the words. At the edge of the pasture there was a patch of small trees. He might hide there. Although, the resinous bushes were so scrawny and the trumpet-trees so bare!

"Zap. . . . Zap. . . ."

The pistol shots echoed like laughter in his ears. And the detonations of the Winchesters vibrated in his chest: because they were rangers.

Beyond the trees the river could be heard. Some ducklings were quacking.

"Da guy who 'scapes gits ta live. . . ."

Were they playing with him?

"Dey'll git me in da barbed wire. . . ."

The piercing wind howled in his ears.

"Ah'll get through even'f ah leaves half ma hide. . . ."

He slipped his head in between the strands of barbed wire. A barb slit his ear. He held the wires apart, cutting his fingers. The warm blood ran down his sideburns and his temples. The upper wire slipped from his hand, trapping him in the fence. With a single jerk, he pulled his body through leaving a network of deep scratches on his black shoulders and back.

"You'd bettah cross on foot," those behind the man on horseback warned him.

A kick in the butt finally got the black man through the fence. He fell on his face in the grass.

"Ah! Son ov'a bitch. . . ."

This time when the ranger's boot kicked him in the ear, it sounded like the loud clang of a bell. It was in the one that was already cut.

He got up on his knees. The rifle butt hit him squarely in the chest. They kicked him unmercifully.

"Aha, dis'll fix ya. . . ."

But the black man was a fiend. He roared like a lassoed bull. And he grabbed the other man's legs making him fall on his back. He wanted to get up and kick too. He was blind with rage. He crawled on top of the man who had fallen. They struggled noiselessly.

"Aha!"

Now he had him. He had stuck his fingers in his mouth. The other man tried to bite. The Negro stuck his hands further in, forcing the mouth open without feeling the pain from the teeth. And suddenly he yanked. The ranger felt a chill when his cheeks ripped open. They screeched like a piece of calico that women tear when they are sewing.

After pulling away the bloody hands, he heard his voice disappearing. He had no mouth. What laughed was a blackish mass of roots and teeth. He raised his hands to his face picking up the torn shreds of flesh.

"Ah! Ya fuckin' son ov'a bitch. . . ."

From every side the rifle butts and boots poured down on him. The Negro's eyes turned white as his pupils rolled to the corners of their sockets. His thick lips trembled. He tried to talk. On his knees, he looked around at all of them. He remembered that everything had happened because of the drunken, belligerent captain! He covered his face with his arm and fell again.

"Ah! damn ya!"

"He's ruined Rangel. . . ."

"Let's hit 'm hard."

"Damn niggah."

They kept dancing on his corpse.

II

"Hey, ma'am."

An answer came from inside the house. Steps were heard.

"Whad is it? . . . Wacha lookin' fo'?"

"A place ta sleep."

"You rangers?"

"Yeh. What of it?"

"O.K., com'on in."

An oil lamp shone over the head of the old black woman. The light-khaki–colored group in front of the shack looked like a half-opened ear of corn. They were talking among themselves.

"Leave'm ovah dere under da house."

"We should'a buried'm right out dere . . . where he fell."

"We'll bury'm tomorrow. Gwon in. Careful not ta scare de ole woman."

They went up the front steps noisily. The body of the black man, kicked to death, spun around and fell over the edge of the pigpen, under the house.

They stood their rifles up against the wall. The captain sat down on the hammock. The drunkenness that had made him fight

with the black man had already worn off. The others made themselves comfortable, sitting on turned-over vats. On the trunk.
Wherever they could.

"Have ya eaten?"

"Yes ma'am."

"But how 'bout somethin' hot? A cup o' black coffee 'n some
roasted greens?"

"Dat would be nice o' ya."

"Petitaa. . . . Has da fire burned out yet?"

The girl came out from the back room.

"Not yet, Momma."

"Den let's roas' some greens and make some black coffee fo'
dese men."

The girl had made the captain's eyes light up.

"Hey, 'Lightning,' bring da jug o' majorca, and pour some inta
de lady's black coffee, an' in yours too, Miss . . . Miss Petita,
right? I neva thought o' findin' such a beautiful flower heah. . . ."

Petita laughed causing her pink dress to rise with the hills of
her firm breasts as she breathed. And she came and went with a
rhythm in her hips that was driving the ranger mad.

After drinking the black coffee, they gladly would have talked
a while, but the old black woman interrupted:

"Da talkin's very nice . . . but you'll have ta 'scuse me an' my
daughta. . . . We've got ta git up early . . . 'cause maybe my son
who's arrivin' tomorrow from Manabí'll be heah at dawn. . . .
I'll leave ya dat oil lamp."

The dark ocher door, made of old tin-plated bamboo, closed.
Its calfskin hinges creaked. The rangers stared at it with evil intentions. The captain stopped them all with a sweeping look:

"Stay away. . . . Dat fruit's fo' me. And fo' me alone it's 'bout
ta fall ripe from da tree. . . ."

She had winked at him. He turned off the oil lamp. Threads
of yellowish light came through the thin cane of the walls. He
pressed his feverish forehead to the cold cracks.

"She's undressin'. . . ."

He kept looking, stretching his arm behind him to keep the
others away. The old woman in a nightgown walked across to the
window with a gourd in her hand. To empty it outside. Nimbly,

the man stuck his head through the half-closed door. A quick, violent signal: I'm comin'. Wait for me. Petita modestly drew the loose-fitting nightgown across her bosom. She smiled: yes.

The old woman, without noticing anything, got under the red blanket on her cot on the other side of the room and put out her oil lamp.

An hour later the door creaked.

And Petita's cot began to creak.

The old woman was snoring. In the outer room, the rangers were dreaming of their leader's luck.

III

"Ma'am, thank ya very much. We're leavin' now 'cause we got plenty ta do today!"

Petita and the captain smiled at each other behind the old woman's back. Someone said: "Is da girl married or single?"

"She's separated from'r husban'," her mother explained.

"One thing more, Ma'am, so we c'n know who ta thank, what's ya name?"

"Panchita Llorel."

Petita notices the wounded man — the one whose face was ripped apart in yesterday's fight — and asks: "How'd dat happen, Cap'n? I didn' see 'm las' night. . . ."

"He was in a fight day 'fore yestahday. . . ."

"What a monster ta do dat ta him. . . . It must've been wid a knife. . . ."

"No, wid 'is fingers. . . ."

"Jesus Christ! His face's ruined fo' da rest o' his life. . . ."

They went outside. It was light already. The yard was moist from the night dew and shone as if it had rained. Blackbirds were singing on the plum tree fence posts.

The two women started on their chores. Petita's hips hurt: after all, three times! . . .

"Liss'n Petita. . . . Go take a look at de hog. He's been movin' aroun' an' diggin' wid 'is snout all night. . . ."

Petita crawled under the house; her mother heard her scream: "Momma, Momma, dose awful men 've thrown a dead man in wid de hog. . . . Come. . . . Dat's what it's been eatin' de whole night tru. . . . Jesus Christ! Bless'd Saint Jacinto! Come."

"Dose damn rangers! Dey are da plague: dass why I did'n sleep a wink: an' tank God dey didn' try anythin' worse wid you. . . .

She reached the pigpen. Like clucking hens, they walked around not knowing how to take hold of the twisted body with its face stuck in the mud. Its neck eaten away. Its chest. Its ribs showing.

"Oh my, dose damned. . . ! Really, it's jus' like da rangers. . . . An' who could dis poor devil be?"

They were able to pull him up by one arm. His undershirt was full of blood. But his pants, didn't they look familiar? With the edge of her skirt Petita wiped the mud off the black man's stinking face. The body was half resting on the old woman, half on the edge of the pigpen.

Petita's cry was short: "Momma! It's Ranulfo, my brudda. . . ."

The old woman didn't say anything. Her black face — wrinkled like the tough bark of a medlar tree — turned ashen, ashen.

For Petita, the ranger's kisses, those kisses of the dark night, smarted and hurt as though he had slapped her across the face.

— Translated by Judith A. Diez-Herencia

COMMENTARY

In 1930, the publication of *Los que se van* caused a literary scandal in Ecuador which soon had repercussions throughout Spanish America. The stories in this volume were written by three neophytes: Demetrio Aguilera Malta, who was twenty-one years old at the time, Joaquín Gallegos Lara, who was nineteen and Enrique Gil Gilbert, who was eighteen.

Los que se van exemplifies the proletarian spirit that was predominant among the majority of the world's intellectuals between 1929 and 1939. The publication of this book meant the end of taboo themes. The characters are the poorest coastal Indians, mestizos, mulattoes, and blacks whose lives are constantly in danger not only from society's exploiting them but also from the violence of their sexual appetites. The phonetic transcriptions of their dialect are the most extreme that exist in all of Spanish American literature. The crude elements notwithstanding, all three writers display a technical literary skill that has earned them a secure niche in the history of the Spanish American short story.

Of the three authors, Gallegos Lara is the most proletarian. Although at first sight he seems to sacrifice art in favor of social protest, "She Was His Mother!" is impressive precisely because of the artistic form in which the author clothes his cruel theme. Divided into three distinct scenes, the story has a clear structural unity. In addition to the plot and the violent tone, the unity is strengthened by a series of elements that tie the three scenes together. Toward the end of the first scene, the clubbed black soldier recalls that the chase was due to the "drunken, belligerent captain." After the former dies, the scene shifts to the inside of the shack where "the drunkenness that had made him fight with the black man had already worn off." The fact that the author doesn't supply any more details about the cause of the dispute indicates that he is primarily concerned about criticizing the society in general that permits the cruel murder of a human being for an apparently insignificant reason. In the third scene, Petita's ironic horror at the sight of her brother's victim recalls for the reader the desperate fight between Ranulfo and the ranger. The reader shares the surprise of the two women when they identify the corpse, although there is a hint at the ending in the second scene when the woman says that she is expecting her son to arrive the next morning.

The violence of the story is conveyed cleverly through certain techniques. Dialogue, a very rapid dialogue, predominates over the narrative sections; almost all the sentences are very short; and the sound effects provide the appropriate background: "footsteps," "the harsh hoofs of the captain's horse," "the wind," "the pistol shots echoed like laughter," "ducklings were quacking," "they kicked him unmercifully," "he roared," "they screeched," "the door creaked," "the cot began to creak," "the old woman was snoring." In contrast with the abundance of sounds, there are hardly any references to color: a few allusions to black and the dark ocher door. Because of the scarcity of colors, the next to the last paragraph is particularly effective when the woman's wrinkled black face turns "ashen, ashen." The silence of this final scene after so much noise; the change in color after so much darkness; and the extension of the sentence, with the very appropriate simile of the medlar tree, after so many short sentences — all contribute to emphasize the significance of this one moment of human tenderness after so much violence.

Considering the importance of the mother, foreshadowed by the story's title, the final paragraph with its emphasis on the sister's feelings and the renewed insistence on sounds and darkness is somewhat anticlimactic and superfluous.

Demetrio Aguilera Malta

(1909)

Ecuadorean. Born in Guayaquil, he started out as a secondary school teacher and rose through the ranks to the position of undersecretary of Public Education. He is the most prolific of the three Guayaquil writers represented in *Los que se van* (1930). His short stories and his novels *Don Goyo* (1933) and *La isla virgen* (1942) are set in the relatively small area at the mouth of the Guayas River. Other novels of his that take place outside Ecuador suffer from a relatively simplistic social protest: *Canal Zone* (1935), *Madrid* (1939), and *Una cruz en la Sierra Maestra* (1961). In 1964 he began to publish a series of popular historical novels. As of 1979, individual volumes on Simón Bolívar (1964), Francisco de Orellana (1964), and Vasco Núñez de Balboa (1965) have appeared. He is considered his country's best playwright with such works as *Lázaro* (1941), *Dientes blancos* (1955), *El tigre* (1957), *Honorarios* (1957), and *Infierno negro* (1967). He has been visiting professor at Scripps College (1968) and the University of California, Irvine (1970). For the past twenty years, he has lived in Mexico City where he has been active in the Comunidad Latinoamericana de Escritores. His most recent novels, *Siete lunas y siete serpientes* (1970), *El secuestro del general* (1973), and *Requiem para el diablo* (1978), reveal his absorption of many of the experimental techniques popularized by Miguel Angel Asturias and the "Boom" novelists of the 1960s. "The Cholo Who Got His Revenge" was written in 1928 and is one of Aguilera Malta's several cholo[1] stories in *Los que se van*. He was feted in 1978 in Mexico and Ecuador for his fifty years of literary activity; English translations of *Don Goyo* and *Siete lunas y siete serpientes* are in progress; and new critical monographs on his works are soon to be published.

THE CHOLO WHO GOT HIS REVENGE

"I've loved ya like nobody else, dya know dat? Becuz o' you, I became a sailor an' I've traveled all ovah. . . . Becuz

---

[1]In the Ecuadorean highlands, cholo is the equivalent of mestizo but along the coast, cholo means Indian or someone with marked Indian features.

o' you, I almost became a crook an' I even abandoned my poor old mother: becuz o' you who deceived me an' made fun o' me. . . . But I got my revenge: I knew ahead o' time everythin' dat's happened ta ya. Thass why I letcha go wid dat drunkard dat feeds you an' your kids wid blows."

The beach was being covered with foam. Beyond, the sea lashed with rage, and the enormous waves were falling like multicolored fish over the rocks. Andrea was listening to him in silence.

"If it'd been someone else. . . . Ah! . . . he would 'a challenged Andrés ta fight wid machetes and he would 'a killed 'm. . . . But not me. He wuzn' guilty. The only one ta be blamed wuz you, you wuz de one dat fooled me. An' you wuz de only one dat should suffer like I wuz sufferin' . . .

A wave like an immense and transparent stingray fell at their feet interrupting him. The sea was hurling deafening screams. In order to hear Melchiades, she had had to come very close to him. Furthermore, the cold. . . .

"Dya remember how it happened? I do, as if it'd been yesterday. We wuz kids; we'd grown up close togethah. It hadda turn out da way it did. Dya remember? We wuz engaged, we wuz goin' ta get married. . . . All of a sudden dey called me ta work on Don Guayamabe's raft. An' I left 'cuz I wanted money. Ya even cried. I think. A month passed. I wuz workin' aroun' da Guayas River, wid some wood, happy ta be comin' back soon. . . . An den Badulaque tol' me: you'd run away wid Andrés. Nobody knew nuttin' 'boucha. Dya remember?"

It was getting colder. The afternoon, darker. The sea was starting to calm down. The waves fainted softly on the shore. A sloop's sail was coming into sight in the distance.

"I wuz upset an' angry. I would o' liked ta kill'm. But den I saw dat da best thing I could do wuz ta get revenge: I knew Andrés. I knew dat de only things dat was in store fo' ya wid him was beatin's an' misery. So he'd be da best one ta take revenge fo' me. . . . Afterwards? I worked hard, damned hard. I didn't wanna know anythin' else 'boucha. I visited many cities; I met plenty o' women. Only a month ago I tol' myself: go an' see da finished product!"

The sun was hiding behind the greenish-black mangrove trees. Its fantastic beams were dancing over the body of the chola conferring on it bizarre colors. The rocks seemed to be coming alive.

You could say that the sea was a prairie full of multicolored flowers.

"I've found ya changed, dya know dat? You're ugly; you're skinny; ya walk aroun' dirty. Ya ain't worth nuttin' no more. All ya got left ta do is suffer seein' how ya would 'a made out wid me and seein' how you're livin' now, ya know? An' now git goin', cuz your husban' mus' be already waitin' fo' his supper; gwan, move or you'll git a beatin' tonight. . . ."

The sloop's sail was growing larger. A few pelicans were slowly crossing the sky. The sea was calm and quiet and a strange smile was creasing the lips of the cholo who got his revenge.

— *Translated by Judith A. Diez-Herencia*

COMMENTARY

Aguilera Malta also writes about illiterate cholos, primitive sex and violence but this story is radically different from "She Was His Mother!" Of the two characters in this story, only the man speaks. Through his monologue, we learn of the great disillusion suffered by the betrayed man as well as by the mistreated woman. Little by little as the picture is sketched in, suspense grows. In spite of the fact that the title of the story is explained in the first paragraph, the threat of violence is imminent throughout. Consequently, the ending, although totally in keeping with the tone of the whole story, still contains a touch of surprise.

Aguilera Malta raises the artistic level of the cholo life by interpolating the poetic descriptions of the ocean which have more than one function. The rage of the sea reflects the man's emotions as does the subsequent calm. The presence of the sea suggests sex in its most primitive sense and gives more universality to the story. Melchiades and Andrea, because of the sea, are converted from Ecuadorean cholos into *a* man and *a* woman. In addition to the ocean's movements reflecting the man's emotions, the poetic language of the descriptions is in sharp contrast with the man's lower-class dialect. The different shades of light and sound create a series of five paintings that lend themselves beautifully to a symphonic interpretation.

Of the three authors of *Los que se van*, Aguilera Malta is the most artistic. The fact that he is also a playwright helps explain the paradox of the story: its great dramatic force in spite of its lack of action.

Enrique Gil Gilbert

(1912–1973)

Ecuadorean. Born in Guayaquil, he spent most of his life there devoted primarily to his activities in the Communist Party. He taught history at the University of Guayaquil and literature at the Colegio Nacional Vicente Rocafuerte. In addition to the short stories of *Los que se van* (1930), he published two other volumes of short stories, *Yunga* (1933) and *Los relatos de Emmanuel* (1939). His novel *Nuestro pan* (1942) won second prize in the first Farrar and Rinehart literary contest after Ciro Alegría's well-known *Broad and Alien Is the World*. "Da Divil" is from *Los que se van*.

DA DIVIL

"Go to sleep my little baby,
Go to sleep, for God's sake, do
go to sleep my little baby
or the divil 'll come and get you.
Lalalala, lalalala!"

And Leopoldo kept raising his discordant voice while swiftly swinging in the hammock, trying to lull his younger brother to sleep.

"Da Moor!"

They called him that because he was quite grown before he was baptized.

"Da Moor! Jesus, he mus' be evil!"

"An' hasn' de evil bird come ta hoot at 'm yet?"

"Dey say dat wen yousa Moor de evil bird gives birth. . . ."

"No, it pulls out da Moor's little eyes."

"Saint Joseph and Mary
went to Bethlehem
to worship the baby
and Jesus himself.

> Mary washed the diapers
> Saint Joseph hung them up,
> the beautiful diapers
> that the child would wear."

And he kept on rocking. With his body half twisted, one leg higher than the other, with the one most extended serving as a rocking lever. In his mouth a piece of beef: tougher than shoe leather.

Dirtier and more ragged than a beggar, he would make his mother exclaim: "Dere's no life wid dis demon! Why it hasn' been a little wile since I dressed'm an' he awready looks as if it'd been a month ago!"

But he was incorrigible. Mischievous and ill-bred by instinct. Clever; maybe too clever.

His pranks had no rhyme or reason. He committed them because he felt like it.

Now his father and his mother had gone to work where they were clearing the wooded area. He had to cook. Take care of his baby brother. Make him go to sleep, and when he was asleep, go and take lunch to his parents. And then he'd probably get a beating.

No doubt, he knew what was in store for him. But, although the sun "was standing almost straight up," he wasn't concerned about putting the pots on the fire. He would get his beating for sure. But, bah!

What was wrong with playing for a little while? If they hit him, it would hurt for a little and . . . that's all! ... . By just rubbing himself against the ground, against some virgin grass. . . .

And seeing that the baby wasn't falling asleep, he bent down; he bent down until their noses almost touched.

The baby, frightened, started and shook his little hands. He made a face that made him look ugly and he tried to cry.

"Fall asleep!" he ordered.

But the little rascal, instead of falling asleep, began to cry.

"Look, lil' brudda: fall 'sleep cuz I have ta cook!"

And he used all the most convincing reasons that were within reach of his child mentality.

The baby didn't pay any attention to him.

Then he resorted to violent methods.

"So ya don' wanta fall 'sleep? Now you'll see!"

He took him by the small shoulders and shook him.

"If ya don' fall 'sleep, you'll see!"

And he shook him again and again. But the baby screamed and screamed without falling asleep.

"Wah! Wah! Wah!"

"He sounds like a whistle, like doz whistles dey make from a bull's horn and a carob tree's navel."

And the discordant and hardly pleasing music sounded pretty to him.

Hey! How cute the baby boy looked, turning red, contracting his little arms and legs to cry.

"Heh, heh, heh! Look wat he's doin'! Heh, heh, heh!"

If he had breasts like his mother, the baby wouldn't be crying anymore, but. . . . How come he didn't? . . .

. . . And he would be like his father when he was big. . . . He would go. . . .

"Wah! Wah! Wah!"

Damn it, his brother was still crying!

He took him down from the hammock.

"Leopordo!"

"Yeah."

"Haven' ya seen my fine hen?"

"I ain't seen nuttin."

And Chepa walked away muttering:

"He's evil-evil-evil—like da divil himself!"

Silly old woman! Coming here to look for hens when he had to make his brother sleep and then do the cooking. And the sun was already "standing straighter than before."

What a screamer this kid was! He didn't like that music anymore.

And he started to jump around the baby. He jumped, and jumped, and jumped.

And with his eight years of life, he became happier, happier than ever before.

Why he had made the baby shut up, something he could rarely do. . . .

And another thing, the baby was smiling at him. . . . Nobody else laughed with him!

Maybe that's why he was evil.

Evil? And what could that mean? The ones the owl hoots at before they are baptized are evil. . . . And they say it had hooted at him!

But nobody laughed with him.

"Don' go near dat Leopordo." He had heard people telling the other kids. "Don' go near'm, he's evil."

And now his baby brother had smiled at him. And they say that babies are angels!

"Guu! Guu!"

And he jumped again and again around him.

All of a sudden he stopped.

"Ow!"

He cried. He shook his hands. The baby had done the same thing.

"An' where did da machete fall from?"

He looked around from one side to the other.

"But where could it've fallen from? Could it've been Satan?"

And he got scared. Satan must be in the room.

"Oh!"

His eyes opened wide . . . very wide . . . very wide. . . .

So wide that they closed on him because of it. So much cold went into his eyes! And through his eyes, it went into his soul.

The baby on the floor . . . and him seeing: on the little diapers . . . a stain like from pitahaya drink . . . no . . . it was . . . more like mangrove sap . . . and it flowed and flowed . . . so red!

But he didn't cry anymore.

"Lil' brudda'!"

No, he didn't cry anymore. What had happened to him? But where did the machete fall from? Satan!

And he ran out scared. He stopped no sooner had he left the last step. And what if his mother hit him? As they always did. . . !

He went back again. . . . The baby was crying again. . . . Yes! He was crying. . . . But the way he cried! You could barely hear him!

"Oh! How he's stained! And so red! He's so red! He's all smeared!"

He went to undo the messy diapers. He picked them up with the tips of his index finger and thumb: they frightened him so!

The thing that was flowing was like the blood that flowed from his fingers whenever he cut them while making little canoes from balsa wood.

What was flowing was blood.

"How could da machete have fallen?"

Satan was there. . . .

Satan. The devil. Satan.

And he went out again. He didn't *go* out. He found himself there, not knowing how. He ran toward where his father was working.

"It wuzn' me! It wuzn' me."

And he ran.

Everybody saw him go by.

Chepa's children. Meche's. Victoria's. Carmen's. And they all stepped back.

"Da divil!"

And they moved away.

"Dya see how he cries and talks? He's gawn mad! Don' go near'm; de owl hooted at'm!"

But he didn't see them.

Satan . . . his little brother. . . . How did it happen? The devil . . . The evil one. . . . The. . . . The one they called da divil!"

"It wuzn' me! It wuzn' me! I jus' don' know!"

He arrived. He saw them from a distance. If he told them, they would hit him. No: he would tell them. . . .

And he ran to them: "Mom! Daddy!"

"Wa' dya want here? Didn' I leave ya takin' care of da baby?"

And scared, he cried. And he saw:

Satan.

His baby brother.

The machete.

"It wuzn' me. . . . It just fell by itself! Da divil!"

"Wa' happened?"

"In his little belly . . . but it wuzn' me! It jus' fell by itself! Nobody attacked'm! It wuzn' me!"

They realized.

And ran. He, terrified. She, crying and behind him. Leopoldo with a horror that was greater than the happiness he felt when his baby brother smiled at him!

Everybody thought it was quite unusual to see the whole family running like crazy.

Some laughed. Others became frightened. Others remained indifferent.

The boys came close and asked:

"Wa' happened?"

For the first time in their lives, they were talking to da divil.

"It wuzn' me! It was Satan!"

And they drew back from him.

What was he saying!

And everybody went up the steps and they all saw, and nobody believed what he saw. Only him—da divil—scared, so scared that he couldn't talk—a strange thing for him—disheveled, dirty, stinking from sweat, he looked and was convinced that what they were seeing was true.

And his eyes questioningly searched every corner. He thought he was seeing Satan.

The mother cried.

When she took off the diapers, she saw with blurred eyes what she would have never wanted to see. . . .

But who could it have been?

Juan, the father, explained: as usual, he had left the machete among the canes of the roof . . . he, nobody but he, was guilty.

No. They didn't believe him. It had been da divil. They accused him.

Leopoldo, tearfully implored:

"It wuzn' me! It was da divil."

"You are da divil!"

"I am Leopordo!"

"Satan is your dad, not Don Juan."

"Thassa lie," shouted the offended mother.

And old Victoria, witch and healer, argued with her broken voice:

"It ain't been nobody else but Leopordo, cuz he's da divil. An' nobody but him could've done it!"

Leopoldo made his last protest:

"I'm da son of my dad."

Everybody made the sign of the cross.

It had been da divil. It had to be. He had already started. Afterward he would kill more people.

"Somebody's gotta tell da town's Politician!"

They fled from da divil. Then he felt anger toward them. For the first time he hated.

And when all the onlookers had gone and the four of them were left alone, María, the mother, cried. While Juan rubbed one hand against the other and tears flowed down his cheeks.

María saw the dead child. . . . Evil, Leopoldo, evil! He killed his baby brother, evil! But now the Politician would come and take him to jail. . . . Poor boy. How would they treat him? Badly because he was evil. And the rangers were so tough. But he had killed his baby brother! Evil, Leopoldo, evil. . . .

She looked at him. Leopoldo's tearful eyes looked imploringly into hers.

"It wuzn' me, Mom!"

Old Victoria came up the steps grumbling:

"He's evil from birth: he's de one, da divil, nobody but him!"

María embraced her dead son. . . . And how about the other one? Leopoldo? . . . No, it couldn't be!

She ran to embrace him and led him to the corpse. And there she embraced both her sons, the dead one and the live one.

"My baby! Poor boy!"

"The owl hooted at'm. . . ."

The old, rotten machete, partly blood stained, partly rusty, black, partly silvery, by who knows what mystery of light, seemed to laugh.

"Leopoldo is evil, evil."

— Translated by Judith A. Diez-Herencia

COMMENTARY

In this story, as in "She Was His Mother!," the author's presence is hardly felt. The action develops through the dialogue and the thoughts of the characters. The relatively incomplete presentation of the characters and the plot force the reader to participate actively in the creative process. In "Da Divil," the important detail of Leopoldo's age is not revealed until almost the end of the first third of the story, and then in an unemphatic manner. The death of his little brother is particularly impressive because we view it through Leopoldo's eyes and, like him, we are slow to realize exactly what happened.

"Da Divil" surpasses the other stories from *Los que se van* in its greater psychological penetration as well as in its more complex structure. By dividing the story into three scenes, we can better perceive the author's dual purpose of transcribing directly the thoughts and emotions of the eight-year-old protagonist and presenting the force of public opinion. In the first scene, which ends with the baby's death, Leopoldo's inner world predominates as his thoughts alternate with his efforts to make the baby go to sleep. The theme of the neighbors is introduced slightly in Leopoldo's memories and in the unexpected appearance of Chepa. In the second scene, which is comprised of the two mad dashes, the author fuses the two themes quite successfully. The terrified boy flies past as all the neighbors comment. Whereas they step aside to let him go by in the first half of the dash, they pursue him relentlessly when he returns. "And everybody went up the steps, and they all saw and nobody believed what he saw." In the third scene, as in the third act of some Golden Age plays (Calderón de la Barca's *The Mayor of Zalamea*, for example), the theme that was the principal one at the beginning of the work decreases in importance while what was the secondary theme becomes the principal one. In the face of the constant barbs of the neighbors, Leopoldo remains silent. His father's logical explanation of the tragedy is overwhelmed by the neighbors' fanaticism. Even the mother's natural maternal love for Leopoldo wavers under the pressure of the community. At the beginning of the story, Leopoldo remembers how even his mother used to call him "demon." Nevertheless, in the climactic moment, he desperately seeks comfort from her. She responds by hugging him but the story does not end there. The two ensuing anonymous comments have the effect of questioning the strength of the mother's commitment to Leopoldo, without the narrator's saying so. The sentence about the machete's diabolical smile separates the two comments making them stand out more.

In short the delirious terror and the anxiety experienced by this eight-year-old boy is conveyed so skillfully that "Da Divil" has achieved continental recognition in spite of its strong local dialect.

Salvador Salazar Arrué (Salarrué)

(1899-1975)

Salvadoran. Writer, painter, and sculptor, he was born in Sonsonate. His father was a teacher and his mother wrote poetry and translated short stories from the French. Salarrué studied art in El Salvador and the United States. He was a teacher and edited the newspaper *Patria* (1925-1935) and the literary journal *Ámatl* (1939-1940). For several years he was cultural attaché in Washington. His many volumes include stories and novels in the folkloric, the philosophical and the fantastic veins: *El Cristo negro* (1926), *El señor de la burbuja* (1927), *O-Yarkandal* (1929), *Remotando el Uluán* (1932), *Cuentos de barro* (1933), *Eso y más* (1940), *Cuentos de cipotes* (1943), *Trasmallo* (1954), *La espada y otras narraciones* (1960), *Íngrimo* (1970), *Sagitario en Geminis* (1970), *La sed de Slind Bader* (1971), and *Catleya luna* (1974). In his later years, he was cultural advisor in the Ministry of Education. "The Treasure Jug" was published in *Cuentos de barro*.

THE TREASURE JUG

José Pashaca was a body stretched out on a hide; the hide was a hide stretched out in a shack; the shack was a shack stretched out on a hillside.

Petrona Pulunto was the mamma of that mouth: "Son: open your eyes; I awready e'en forgot deir color!"

José Pashaca struggled, and the best he could do was to pull in his leg.

"Watcha want, Mom?"

"Ya gotta get some kind a job, you're awready a grown Indian!"

"Awright! . . ."

The loafer came to life somewhat: from sleeping, he advanced to being sad, yawning.

One day Ulogio Isho came in with a tall tale. It was something like a stone toad that he had found while plowing. The toad had a necklace of beads and three holes: one in the mouth and two in the eyes.

"What an ugly creature," he said as he arrived. He laughed heartily. "It looks just like one-eyed Cande!"

And he left it, so that María Elena's kids could play with it.

But two days later old man Bashuto arrived, and when he saw the toad he said: "These little things were made a long time ago, by our grandparents. You can find'm buried in the fields. It's also possible ta find jugs full o' gold."

José Pashaca deigned to wrinkle the skin between his eyes, where everybody else has a forehead.

"How's dat, Mistah Bashuto?"

Bashuto took hold of the cigar with all the strength of his wrinkles, and took off in a cloud of smoke. Immediately, he told of a thousand discoveries of treasure jugs, all of which "he'd witnessed with these very eyes." When he left, he left without noticing that the seeds of what he had said had dropped on fertile soil.

Since Petrona Pulunto died around that time, José lifted up his mouth and took it for a walk in the neighborhood, with no nutritional results. He ate stolen haws and decided to start looking for treasure jugs. To do it, he placed himself at the tail end of a plow and pushed. Behind the plowshare, his eyes also went plowing. And that was how José Pashaca became the laziest and, at the same time, the most industrious Indian of the whole area. He worked without working — at least without realizing it — and he worked so much, that twilight always found him sweating, with his hand on the plow handle and his eyes on the furrow.

Like a tiny hill louse, he avidly combed away at the black soil, always looking toward the ground so attentively that it seemed as if he was going along sowing his soul among the lumps of earth to make laziness sprout; because it's true, Pashaca knew that he was the most idle Indian in the whole valley. He didn't work. He searched for jugs full of golden coins, that sound "kerplop!" when the plowshare hits them, and they throw up silver and gold, as does the water in the puddle when the sun starts to peer behind Doctor Martínez's place, the plains that extend as far as the horizon.

Just as great as he imagined himself, that's how great his obsession became. Ambition, more than hunger, had made him get up from his hide and had pushed him to the hillsides; where he plowed, he plowed, from the hour when the roosters swallow up the stars with their crowing until the hour when the trogon, hoarse and lugubrious, sitting on the branches of the ceiba, pierces the silence with its harsh screeches.

Pashaca did battle with the hills. The landowner, who was amazed by the miracle that had turned José into the most industrious of farmers, gave him gladly and without measuring wide strips of land, which the Indian treasure dreamer scratched with his eyes which were all set to notify his heart, so that it would fall on the treasure jug, covering it with love and concealment. And Pashaca sowed, because he had to, because the landowner demanded the rent. He also had to harvest, and he had to charge for the abundant grain of his harvest, the product of which he kept putting away indifferently in a hole in his shack, just in case.

None of the farmers felt they had enough guts to work as hard as José. "He's a man of iron," they said. "Since who knows what got into 'im, he decided ta make money. He must have a good treasure by now. . . ."

But José Pashaca hadn't noticed that he really had a treasure. What he looked for unflaggingly was a treasure jug, and since they were said to be buried in the fields, he was sure to find it sooner or later.

He had become not only industrious in his neighbors' eyes, but even generous. Every time he had a day when he couldn't plow because he had no assigned land, he helped the others; he would send them off to rest and he would plow for them. And he did it right: the furrows of his plowshare were always close to each other, wide an' deep, a joy to behold.

"Where'r ya hidin' dumb thing!" the Indian would think without giving up. "An' I'll fin' ya even if ya don't want me ta, even if I have ta kill myself in dese furrows."

And so it was; not the discovery but his death.

One day, at the hour when the sky is greenish and the rivers become white stripes on the plains, José Pashaca realized that there were no more treasure jugs. He got the message as he fell in a feverish faint; he bent over the plow handle; the oxen stopped slowly, as if the plowshare had become entangled in the roots of twilight. They were found black, against the light sky, "turning to see the broken Indian, and breathing heavily the dark air."

José Pashaca fell sick. He didn't want nobody takin' care of 'm. "Since Petrona died, he lived alone in his shack."

One night, with his last ounce of strength, he went out stealthily carrying, in an old pitcher, his treasure. He crouched behind the bushes every time he heard noises, but he kept on digging a hole with his machete. He moaned once in a while, exhausted, but then he would continue his task with determination. He placed the pitcher in the hole, covered it up very well, erased all traces of loose dirt; and, raising his vinelike arms toward the stars, he entwined the following words in a sigh: "Now dere; let'm not say dat der ain't no treasure jugs in da fields anymore! . . ."

— *Translated by Judith A. Diez-Herencia*

COMMENTARY

At first reading, Salarrué's *Cuentos de barro* (Stories of Mud) seem exceedingly regionalistic. They are, but by fusing Regionalism with some avant-garde stylistic traits, Salarrué achieves certain artistic effects that have gained for his stories more than national recognition. He uses dialect not only when his peasant characters talk but also in some of the narrator's own descriptive paragraphs where it is combined with sophisticated similes and metaphors: "Behind the plowshare, his eyes also went plowing"; "sowing his soul . . . to make laziness sprout." Sometimes, the images reveal a sense of humor that is not usually found among the other Criollistas: "José lifted up his mouth and took it for a walk."

"The Treasure Jug," as well as Salarrué's other tall tales, gives the impression that the peasant is a picturesque character who is being ridiculed for his simplicity by the urbane author. This attitude, which was characteristic of the late nineteenth-century Costumbrista authors, is rather exceptional among the Criollistas who tend to identify more with their characters and share their suffering. Nonetheless, "The Treasure Jug" is still a fine little story. The unexpected and tragicomic ending is in keeping with the tone of the whole story established by the style of the very first paragraph and maintained by the contrast between the ingenious narrator and the ingenuous protagonist.

This story stands out above other stories in Salarrué's *Cuentos de barro* because of the delightful way that José Pashaca is portrayed on the first page and his subsequent total transformation.

Víctor Cáceres Lara

(1915)

Honduran. A high school and college teacher and news-paperman, he has also been active in politics serving as congressman, postmaster general, and ambassador to Venezuela. He published two books of national ballads, *Arcilla* and *Romances de la alegría y de la pena*, the best known of which is "Romance del hermano sembrador." The publication of *Humus* in 1952, with "Malaria" as its lead story, established him as the best Honduran short story writer of his generation. In 1970 *Humus* was republished along with fifteen other stories under the title of *Tierra ardiente*. In recent years, he has been president of the Honduran Sociedad de Geografía e Historia and Director of the Instituto Hondureño de Cultura Hispánica.

MALARIA

Night was beginning to cast darkness and anguish in the corners of the dilapidated room where the air entered in strictly rationed quantities and where light, even at the sunniest time of day, never provided full illumination. Outside, as if afraid of being heard, a faucet dripped imperceptibly. The only faucet to quench the thirst of the multitude that inhabited the tenement. A child was begging for bread in a whining tone, and the mother — possibly out of despair — responded to the request with foul language:

"Shut your trap, you bastard, . . . nobody here has eaten!"

She, the sick woman in the dilapidated room, watched how the last light was disappearing; she didn't have electricity and the oil in the cheap lamp was almost used up. She didn't feel a drop of strength in her muscles, or even a warm flow inside her empty veins. A torturing cold was creeping up her emaciated flesh, passing through her waist, formerly as supple and delicate as wild

234

willows, and taking hold of her heart which then seemed to be entwined with sadness, exploding in a silent prayer, tremulous from the intense emotion.

Daylight was slowly ending. In the street you could hear footsteps of people, bent on squandering their lives, on their way to cheap entertainment: the bar, consumer of energy and money; the brothel full of putrid flesh sold at high prices; in short, that whole string of diversions that the poor people in our environment can afford and which, in the long run, far from providing pleasure or enjoyment, cause weariness, sickness, misery, helplessness, death. . . .

Now, in the early evening, while the birds chirped happily outdoors, she could feel herself dying. She felt that the Pale Lady was embracing her and suffocating her slowly, inexorably, completely, while a terrible cold was destroying her bones and making her temples pound madly.

Totally abandoned, nobody arrived with a word, with a crumb of affection, with a glass of milk. She herself had to go out, in the respites between fever chills, to look for a piece of hard tortilla that she would eat, plain because it was impossible for her to buy something to go with it. When she went out, she would beg and she had obtained penny after penny while suffering terrible humiliation.

And she could not explain why she was so abandoned. . . . She had always been good to her fellowman. She had always been charitable and generous. She had always done all she could for her neighbors: she had always loved children, maybe because she herself never had one. But it was possible that they thought she was too thin and yellow. Maybe they heard her cough and thought she had consumption. She knew it was malaria that was killing her. But what could she do to change their minds. In the meantime she had to suffer, to wait for the final moment when her dark sorrows, her fruitless wandering, the terrible bleeding of the soles of her feet on the jagged roads of the world would cease. . . .

Strange shadows were beginning to dance on the ceiling; her temples were beating more strongly and her vision began to fade back into the distant remote past, an almost fuzzy past, without sharp contours, but which when evoked in languid reminiscence, made her hear a voice offering comfort and resignation, and opening a path of light back to the purest and most cherished moments of her life.

She was reliving her childhood days in a remote village where the invigorating fragrance of pines was stored, the music of thrushes in love, the odor of frolicsome calves, the cadence of hurtling streams, the freshness of the fields wet with dew, the purity of the simple country life filled with the devout prayers of the rosary.

In the lush and pure surroundings of the village she saw how her firm breasts took shape and how her flesh vibrated at the first impulses of love, of simple love, without the complexities of civilization but with the rustic sweetness of Longus's[1] idylls. Afterward, her yearning to come to the Coast, suggestive of happiness and promising prospects when dreamt of from afar.

Her illusions sparked brilliant flames in her simple and good mind and her instincts started to burn her dark and firm flesh, with a fire different from that of the tropics' generous sun. She began to delight in looking at herself when, free from the bonds of her dress, the challenging magnificence of her body would emerge in the light and when aroused by the tickling breeze, her breasts, like two fiery cones, would escape the gentle constraints of her blouse.

Then she met the man who ignited her inner fire and turned her in the direction of adventure, with the lure of conquering new horizons. She heard the invitation to come to the Coast as she might have heard one to go to heaven. She liked the man for his strength, his good looks, his wit. Because he offered her what she wanted: love and, besides love, the Northern Coast.

"Up there," he told her, "banana trees grow to be luxuriant, wages are high and soon we will make some real money. You'll help me in what you can and we'll get ahead."

"And what if another woman seduces you and you send me packing?"

"No way, honey, you're the only one I love and we'll be together forever! We'll ride in trains . . . in cars. . . . We'll go to the movies, to parties, everywhere. . . ."

"And are trains pretty?"

---

[1]Longus (A.D. 250), Greek novelist, author of the pastoral *Daphnis and Chloe*.

"Like big black worms that blow smoke through their heads, you know! They carry a mob of people, from place to place, from La Lima to Puerto. A man calls out the names of the stations: Indiana! . . . Mopola! Tibombo! . . . Kele-Kele! . . . It's wonderful! You'll see!"

She craved to leave the town of her elders. To love and to see the world. In her opinion her town was slumbering in a night without dawn, and her beauty was worthless there, as she leaned over the murmuring creek with its rough bed of sharp rocks and pebbles. She wanted to leave the pleasant little town where she spent her childhood and where the virgin countryside and the perfumed earth had deposited in her body fragrances and basic desires. And so she started on her way, at the side of her man, coming down out of the mountains, crossing tumultuous rivers, passing through valleys burnt by a fiery sun to the monotonous concert of the crickets which inserted minute splinters into the desperately monotonous days.

And what a man was her *man*! In the nights of the journey, sleeping under the stars, he fulfilled all her hopes, dreams, and desires. When darkness fell over the fields, when night was at its darkest, when dawn was beginning to paint its red-tinted clouds over the distant eastern sky. . . . She felt the excitement, the fire, the bravery, the indomitable courage of her *man* and felt her whole body tingle with divine palpitations of hope and pride.

They arrived, at last, in La Lima and the search for a job started. Demetrio was always able to find one because, thanks to his clever jokes, he could win the friendship of foremen, timekeepers, and bosses, but he would soon lose it, because in reality he had a bad disposition with a definite bent for vice. Montevista, Omonita, Mopala, Indiana, Tibombo, the fields across the border . . . in short, every banana field that the fruit company had opened was covered in their pilgrimage in search of a living. Sometimes he would work as a weeder, others as a cutter or gatherer of bananas, occasionally spreading insecticide, covered with green from head to toes. Always from dawn to dusk, sweltering under the unbearable heat that made the banana leaves creak from fatigue at noon. At night he would return tired, worn out, speechless from the fatigue that gnawed at his muscles, formerly elastic like those of a wild animal in the jungle.

He fell ill with malaria a few times, and more and more he resorted to whiskey to cure himself. All in vain; the sickness persisted and to stop working meant death from starvation. During that period they were working at Kele-Kele. She was selling food and he had a small contract. One October night the men were fortifying the riverbank by piling up big sandbags. The pounding of the Ulúa River was ferocious. The water was rising above the level of the dike and Demetrio disappeared in the tumultuous current which swelled minute by minute in the storm.

She was left alone and sick. Also sick with malaria. She left the fields with a lump in her throat and went to the port. She went around searching for a job and only in Los Marinos did she find one of which she was never proud and which now, as she recalled it, made her blush in shame. Thousands of men of all different sizes and shapes frolicked in her body. Sick and worn out, with her soul embittered forever, she left the brothel and finally ended up in San Pedro Sula. The malaria wouldn't leave her. Each day the fever attacks grew stronger and now she was lying prostrate on that miserable cot, abandoned by the world, while daylight was ebbing and frightened shadows pirouetted, strangely straddling the beams of the ceiling.

Her eyes that once knew how to love are now two dry wells where only suffering remains; her thin hands no longer hold the promise of caresses or enchanting warmth; her flaccid breasts are almost imperceptible under her humble cotton print blouse; the storm of misery ravaged her, and all that remains for sure is the chilling certainty of death.

Out in the street several children are playing deliriously happy. A couple talks about the ancient and new topic of love. A car breaks the silence with the murderous arrogance of its horn. In the distance, the shrillness of the train whistle is heard, and life goes on because it must. . . .

— Translated by Judith A. Diez-Herencia

COMMENTARY

"Malaria" contains several elements of the classical anti-imperialistic literary work: the protagonist's anonymity; the temptation to get to know the boomtown or zone; the abandonment of the whole-some hometown in search of riches and adventure; the hardships of work in the tropics; the inherent corruption of the people associated with the foreign exploiters; the conversion of the happy country girl into an embittered prostitute; sickness, alcoholism, and death resulting from the violence of nature. Nevertheless, "Malaria" is almost unique among anti-imperialistic works in that the blame for all misfortunes is not cast on the foreign company. Actually, the fruit company is only mentioned once although there is no doubt that the story refers to the United Fruit Company plantations on the northern coast of Honduras. Demetrio loses his job frequently, not because of a hardhearted foreman but because of his own mean character and his "definite bent toward vice." His death was not caused by a lack of quinine but rather by the rainstorm. It is not that the author is trying to defend the fruit company or justify its be-havior but rather that he prefers to focus on the tragic life of the victims: those who let themselves be tempted by the call of the exotic.

Although the theme of anti-imperialism, because of its complexities, lends itself much more to the novel than to the short story, "Malaria" displays a tightly knit structural unity. In the story's present, only a few minutes go by from beginning to end. At the beginning the reader wit-nesses the arrival of night and after completing the section dealing with the woman's memories of her previous life, the narrator tells us that "daylight was ebbing." Of course, light symbolizes life; and night, death. This contrast complements the contrast between the malarial chills and the tropical heat, as well as between the thirst and the shortage of water and the destruction of the rainstorm. Although nature's role in this story makes us think of Romanticism, the indifference of the surrounding world in the final paragraph and the clinical study of the protagonist may be attributed to an anachronistic Naturalism.

Nonetheless, the story has its own intrinsic qualities. Great emphasis is placed on the senses: "she could feel herself dying." Light, representing life, appears in its many variations of sun, fire, electricity, and the lamp. The auditory impressions run the gamut of intensity: "a faucet dripped imperceptibly," "the murmuring creek," "tumultuous rivers," "murderous arrogance of its horn," and "the shrillness of the train whistle." The "putrid flesh," "the invigorating fragrance of pines," and other odors reinforce the sensorial aspect of "Malaria." Although by the standards of the 1950s, '60s, and '70s, this story could hardly be consid-ered one of sophisticated artistry, in comparison with its social protest contemporaries of the 1930s and '40s, its appeal to the senses as well as the variations on the leitmotivs of light and water, added to its rela-tively objective treatment of the anti-imperialistic theme, makes it one of Honduras's most successful stories.

Juan Bosch

(1909)

Dominican. As a political refugee, he traveled through-out Europe and the Americas for twenty-five years, spending much of this time in Cuba. As leader of the Dominican Revolutionary Party (social democrats), he returned to his homeland in 1961 after the assassination of Dictator Trujillo. In 1963 he was elected president but a few months later was ousted by a military coup. When his supporters revolted against the military in 1965, President Lyndon Johnson dispatched the United States Marines "to maintain order." A newly radicalized Bosch lost the presidential election of 1967 to Joaquín Balaguer. His publications include a biography of Hostos, a novel, *La mañosa* (1936), and several volumes of short stories, *Camino real* (1933), *Indios* (1935), *Dos pesos de agua* (1944), *Ocho cuentos* (1947), *La muchacha de la Guaira* (1955), *Cuento de Navidad* (1956), *Más cuentos escritos en el exilio* (1964). "The Woman" was published in *Camino real.*

THE WOMAN

The road is dead. Nobody nor anything will bring it back to life. Long, infinitely long, not even its gray skin betrays any sign of life. The sun killed it; the steel sun, glowing red-hot — a red that turned to white. Later the white steel became transparent, and there it remains, on the road's back.

Many centuries must have passed since its death. Men with pickaxes and shovels dug it up. They sang and dug; there were some, however, who neither sang nor dug. All that took very long. You could tell they came from far away; they sweated and stank. In the afternoon, the white steel would turn red; then a very small bonfire would flare up behind the pupils of the men who were digging up the road.

Death crossed the savannas, and the hills and the winds covered her with dust. Later the dust also died and it came to rest on the gray skin.

240

Along the sides there are thorny bushes. Often the eye grows sick from so much vastness. But the plains are bare. Scrubland in the distance. Perhaps birds of prey crown the cactus. And the cactus are out there, farther off, stuffed into the white steel.

There are huts too, almost all of them low and made of mud. Some are painted white and cannot be seen under the sun. Only the coarse roof stands out, dry, eager to be burned day after day. Gray hairs emanated from those roofs down which water never rolls.

The dead road, totally dead, lies there, dug up, gray. The woman first looked like a black dot, then like a stone that someone might have left on the long mummy. There she lay, without a breeze to stir her rags. The sun did not burn her; only the screams of her child made her feel pain. The child was bronzed, tiny, with his eyes full of light, and he grasped at his mother trying to pull her with his little hands. Soon the road would burn the tiny body, at least the knees, of that naked and screaming child.

The house was nearby, but could not be seen.

As he advanced, what seemed like a stone thrown in the middle of the great dead road grew. It continued to grow, and Quico said to himself: "A calf, no doubt, run over by a car."

He looked around: the plain, the savanna. A distant hill covered with brush, as if that hill were only a little mound of sand piled up by the winds. The bed of a river; the dry jaws of the earth which held water a thousand years ago. The golden plain cracked and split under the heavy transparent·steel. The cactus, crowned with birds of prey.

Now closer, Quico saw that it was a person. He distinctly heard the screams of the child.

Her husband had beaten her. He chased her through the only room of the hut, which was hot like an oven, pulling her by the hair and pounding her head with his fists.

"You slut! You slut! I'm going to kill you like a lousy bitch!"

"But nobody came by, Chepe; nobody came by!" she tried to explain.

"No, eh? Now you're going to see!" And he beat her again.

The child clutched at his father's legs. He saw the woman bleeding through the nose. The blood didn't frighten him, no, it only made him want to cry and scream a lot. Mommy would die for sure if she kept on bleeding.

It was all because the woman didn't sell the goat's milk, as he had ordered her to do. When he returned from the hills, four days later, he didn't find the money. She said the milk had gone sour; the truth was that she had drunk it, preferring not to have a few coins rather than let the child suffer from hunger for so long.

Later he told her to leave with her son: "I'll kill you if you come back to this house!"

The woman lay sprawled on the earth floor, bleeding a lot, hearing nothing. Chepe, in a frenzy, dragged her to the road. And there she lay, half dead, on the back of the great mummy.

Quico had water for two more days of travel, but used almost all of it to sprinkle the woman's forehead. He took her to the hut, by having her lean on his arm, and he considered ripping his striped shirt to wipe off her blood. Chepe came in through the backyard.

"I told you I didn't want to see you here again, damn you!"

It seems that he had not seen the stranger. That white transparent steel had surely turned him into a beast. His hair was bleached stiff and his corneas were red.

Quico shouted at him, but he, half-crazed, once more threatened his victim. He was about to hit her. That was when the fight broke out between the two men.

The child, tiny, so tiny, began to shout again; now he wrapped himself in his mother's skirt.

The fight was like a silent song. They didn't say a word. Only the screams of the child and the violent steps could be heard.

The woman saw how Quico was choking Chepe: his fingers hooked onto her husband's throat. The latter's eyes began to close; his mouth was opening, and the blood was rushing to his face.

She didn't know what happened, but nearby, next to the door there was a rock; a rock like a hunk of lava, rough, almost black, heavy. She felt a brutal force growing within her. She raised it. The blow sounded dull. Quico first let go of the other's throat, bent his knees, then opening his arms wide, he fell backward, without complaining, without a struggle.

The earth of the floor absorbed that blood which was so red, so abundant. Chepe could see the light shimmering on it.

The woman's hands twitched over her face, all her hair loose and her eyes straining to pop out. She ran. She felt weak in all her joints. She wanted to see if someone was coming; but on the big dead road, totally dead, there was only the sun which killed her. In the distance, beyond the plain, the hill of sand which the winds piled up. And the cactus, stuffed into the steel.

— Translated by Gustavo Pellón

COMMENTARY

"The Woman," one of the most anthologized Spanish American short stories, is an audio-visual tropical symphony. If there were any doubt about this interpretation, it would be dispelled by the words of the author himself: "the fight was like a silent song." In this musical composition, the characters are fused with the setting. They are dehumanized while nature and the road assume human traits.

The structure of the composition is based on the crisscrossing of the two main themes: the road starts out as the main theme, is gradually replaced by the woman until it disappears completely during the fight in the hut, but regains its importance in the final paragraph. On the other hand, the woman, invisible at first, appears as a dot, and after playing her dramatic role, disappears in the last two sentences. Although the two themes crisscross, they are identified with each other through the motifs of death, stone, and blood.

The plot is a very important part of the symphony without dominating it excessively. The struggle between the two men is the climactic moment punctuated by the dull blow (drum beat) of the rock. This episode is absorbed into the symphony with the return to the theme of the road. Its gray skin converted into white steel by the red sun creates a blinding image. At the same time, the visual effects are backed up by the sound effects created by the systematic repetition of various motifs, the repetition of words, alliteration, and the brevity of the sentences.

In spite of the dazzling descriptions of the landscape, the reader is deeply impressed by the tragic life of the poor people in the tropics. The anonymous, suffering woman sacrifices herself for her child and accepts the blows of her furious husband maddened by the sun and by the frustration of not being able to earn a living. The woman's defense of her husband comes as a shock because of its being so illogical, but it is understandable within the primitive environment created by the author. It is interesting that a similar situation occurs in two Latin American novels, *El embrujo de Sevilla* by Uruguayan Carlos Reyles and *Historia de arrabal* by Argentinean Manuel Gálvez.

Both the story's musical structure and the importance attached to sound and light bear witness to the author's Modernistic heritage. Like Venezuelan Rómulo Gallegos, Juan Bosch applied the Modernist stylistic innovations to a typically Criollista rural scene of his country. Going one step further in the evolution of literary tendencies, the dazzling imagery of the road is somewhat suggestive of Surrealism.

Manuel Rojas

(1896–1973)

Chilean, although he was born in Buenos Aires. He worked as a laborer on the construction of the Trans-Andean Railway, as a stevedore in Valparaíso, as a prompter for a theatrical company, as a newspaperman, and as a teacher. In 1931 he was appointed Director of Publications at the University of Chile. In 1957 he received the National Prize for Literature. He taught at Middlebury College (1959), at the University of California, Los Angeles (1962), and at the University of Oregon (1963). He is the author of two volumes of short stories, *Hombres del sur* (1926) and *El delincuente* (1929), and seven novels: *Lanchas en la bahía* (1932), *La ciudad de los césares* (1936), *Hijo de ladrón* (1951), *Mejor que el vino* (1958), *Punta de rieles* (1960), *Sombras contra el muro* (1964), and *La oscura vida radiante* (1971). Of the latter, *Hijo de ladrón* is clearly the best and is regarded as one of the first Latin American novels to break out of the relatively simplistic Criollista mold. "The Glass of Milk" was published in the collection entitled *El delincuente*.

THE GLASS OF MILK

Leaning over the starboard rail, the sailor seemed to be waiting for someone. A bundle wrapped in white paper, grease-stained, was in his left hand; his right tended his pipe.

From behind some freight cars, a thin youth appeared; he paused a moment, looked out to sea, and then walked on along the edge of the wharf with his hands in his pockets, distracted or thinking.

When he passed in front of the ship, the sailor called out to him in English:

"I say, look here!"

The youth raised his head, and without stopping, answered in the same language:

"Hello! What?"

"Are you hungry?"

There was a brief silence during which the youth seemed to reflect, and even took one shorter step as if to stop, but then replied, smiling feebly at the sailor:

"No, I'm not hungry. Thanks, sailor."

"Very well."

The sailor took his pipe out of his mouth, spat, and, replacing it, looked away. The youth, ashamed that he had seemed to need charity, walked a little faster, as if afraid he might change his mind.

A moment later, a gaudy tramp with a long, blond beard and blue eyes, dressed in odd rags and oversized, torn shoes, passed before the sailor, who without greeting called to him:

"Are you hungry?"

He had not even finished his question when the tramp, looking with shining eyes at the package the sailor held in his hand, answered hurriedly:

"Yes sir; I'm very much hungry!"

The sailor smiled. The package flew through the air and landed in the eager hands of the hungry fellow. He did not even say "thanks," but sat right down on the ground, opened the still warm bundle, and happily rubbed his hands as he saw what it contained. A port loafer might not speak English well, but he would never forgive himself if he didn't know enough to ask for food from someone who did speak it.

The youth who passed by first had stopped nearby and had seen what happened.

He was hungry too. He had not eaten for exactly three days, three long days. And, more from timidity and shame than from pride, he refused to wait by the gangways at mealtimes, hoping the generosity of the sailors would produce some package of leftovers and bits of meat. He could not do it, he would never be able to do it. And when, as just now, someone did offer him some scraps, the youth refused them heroically, though he felt his hunger increase with the refusal.

He had been wandering for six days around the side streets and docks of that port. An English vessel had left him there after bringing him from Punta Arenas, where he had jumped a previous ship on which he had served as captain's mess boy. He had spent a month there helping an Austrian crabber and then had stowed away on the first ship bound north.

He was discovered the day after sailing and put to work in the boiler room. At the first large port of call, they put him off, and there he had remained, like a bale without a label, without an acquaintance, without a penny, and without a trade.

As long as the ship was in port, the youth managed to eat, but after that. . . . The great city that rose up beyond the back streets with their taverns and cheap inns did not attract him; it seemed like a prison: airless, dark, without the grand sweep of the sea; among its high walls and straight streets people lived and died bewildered by the agonizing hustle-bustle.

The youth was gripped by that terrible fascination of the sea which twists the most peaceful and orderly lives as easily as a strong arm twists a thin metal rod. Although very young, he had already taken several trips along the coast of South Africa on various ships, doing odd jobs and tasks, tasks and odd jobs which were almost useless on land.

After the ship left, the youth walked and walked, hoping to chance upon something that would enable him to live somehow until he could get back to his home grounds; but he found nothing. The port was not very busy, and the few ships that had work would not take him on.

The docks were swarming with confirmed tramps: unemployed sailors, like himself, who had either jumped ship or were fleeing some crime; loafers resigned to idleness, who kept alive, God knows how, by begging or stealing, spending their days as if they were the beads of some grimy rosary, waiting for who knows what extraordinary events, or not expecting anything; people from the strangest and most exotic races and places, including some in whose existence one doesn't believe until a living example is actually seen.

*

The following day, convinced that he could not hold out much longer, the youth decided to resort to any means to get some food.

Walking along, he found himself in front of a ship that had docked the night before and was loading wheat. A line of men, with heavy sacks on their shoulders, shuttled back and forth from the freight cars, across the gangplank to the hatchways of the ship's hold where the stevedores were receiving the cargo.

He watched for a while, until he got up enough courage to speak to the foreman, offering his services. He was accepted, and enthusiastically he took his place in the long line of dock workers.

During the first period of the day he worked well; but later, he began to feel tired and got dizzy; as he swayed while crossing the gangplank, with the heavy load on his shoulder, seeing at his feet the deep opening between the side of the ship and the thick wall of the wharf, at the bottom of which the sea, stained with oil and littered with garbage, lapped quietly.

There was a brief pause at lunch time, and while some of the men went off to the nearby eating places, and others ate what they had brought, he stretched out on the ground to rest, hiding his hunger.

He finished the day's work feeling completely exhausted, covered with sweat, at the end of his rope. While the laborers were leaving, he sat down on some sacks, watching for the foreman, and when the last man had gone, approached him; confused and stuttering, he asked, without explaining what was happening to him, if he could be paid immediately, or if it were possible to get an advance on his earnings.

The foreman answered that it was customary to pay at the end of a job, and that it would still be necessary to work the following day in order to finish loading the ship. One more day! On the other hand, they never paid a cent in advance.

"But," he said, "if you need it, I could lend you about forty cents. . . . That's all I have."

The youth thanked him for his offer with an anguished smile, and left.

Then the youth was seized by acute despair. He was hungry, hungry, hungry! A hunger that doubled him over, like a heavy, broad whiplash. He saw everything through a blue haze, and he walked staggering like a drunk. Nevertheless, he would not have been able to complain or to shout, for his suffering was deep and exhausting; it was not pain but anguish, the end! It seemed to him that he was being pressed down by a great weight.

Suddenly he felt his insides burning, and he stopped. He was bending over, doubling up forcibly like an iron bar, until he thought that he would drop. At that instant, as if a window opened before him, he saw his home, the view from it, the faces of his mother, brothers, and sisters, all that he loved and cherished appeared and disappeared before his eyes shut by fatigue. . . . Then, little by little, the giddiness passed and he began to straighten up, while the burning subsided gradually. Finally, he stood up straight, breathing deeply. One more hour and he would drop unconscious to the ground.

He quickened his step, as if fleeing from another dizzy spell, and, as he walked, he made up his mind to eat anywhere, without paying, even if they shamed him, beat him, sent him to jail, anything; the main thing was to eat, eat, eat. A hundred times he mentally repeated the word: eat, eat, eat, until it lost its meaning, leaving his head feeling hot and empty.

He did not intend to run away; he would simply say to the owner, "Sir, I was hungry, hungry, hungry, and I can't pay. . . . Do what you want."

He managed to get to one of the first streets of the downtown area where he found a milk bar. It was a small, clean and airy place, with marble-top tables. Behind the counter stood a blonde woman in a very white apron.

He chose that place. There were few passersby. He could have eaten at one of the cheap grills near the docks but they were always full of people who gambled and drank.

There was only one customer in the milk bar. He was a little old man with glasses, who sat reading, with his nose stuck in the pages of a newspaper, motionless, as if glued to his chair. On the little table there was a half-empty glass of milk.

He waited for him to leave, walking up and down the sidewalk; feeling the same burning sensation in his stomach returning little by little; and he waited five, ten, up to fifteen minutes. He grew tired, and stood to one side of the door, from where he looked daggers at the old man.

What the devil could he be reading so avidly? He even imagined the old man was his enemy, who knew his intentions and had decided to frustrate them. He felt like entering and saying something insulting that would force the old man to leave, a rude word or phrase that would show him he had no right to sit there reading for an hour for so small a purchase.

Finally, the customer finished what he was reading, or at least, interrupted it. He downed the rest of the milk in one gulp, rose slowly, paid, and walked toward the door. He went out. He was a small stoop-shouldered old man, probably a carpenter or varnisher.

Hardly had he gotten outside, the old man adjusted his glasses, stuck his nose in the newspaper again, and walked away slowly, stopping every ten steps to read more closely.

He waited until the old man was some distance away, and then entered. For a moment he stood by the entrance, hesitant, not knowing where to sit. Finally, he chose a table and walked toward it, but halfway there he changed his mind, walked back, tripped over a chair, and finally installed himself in a corner.

The woman came over, wiped the tabletop with a rag, and in a gentle voice that had a trace of Castilian accent, asked him:

"What will you have?"

Without looking at her, he answered, "A glass of milk."

"Large?"

"Yes, large."

"Is that all?"

"Is there any pastry?"

"No. Vanilla wafers."

"O.K., vanilla wafers."

When the woman turned around, he wiped his hands on his knees, rejoicing, as if he were cold and were about to drink something hot.

The woman returned, and placed before him a large glass of milk, and a small dish full of vanilla wafers; then she went back to her place behind the counter.

His first impulse was to drink the milk in one gulp and then eat the vanilla wafers; but he immediately changed his mind. He felt the woman's eyes watching him with curiosity and attention. He did not dare to look at her; he felt that if he did, she would guess his situation and his shameful intentions, and he would have to get up and leave without touching what he had ordered.

Slowly, he took a vanilla wafer and after drinking the milk, he took a bite; he took a sip of milk, and he felt the burning in his stomach diminishing, going away. But suddenly he became aware of the reality of his desperate situation and he felt something tight and hot well up inside, choking him. He realized that he was about to cry, to sob aloud, and although he knew that the woman was looking at him, he could neither hold back nor undo the burning knot of tears that grew tighter and tighter. He fought it, and as he fought he ate hurriedly, as if frightened, afraid that crying would keep him from eating. When he had finished the milk and the wafers, his eyes clouded and something hot rolled down his nose and into the glass. A terrible sob racked his whole body.

He held his head in his hands, and for a long time he cried, cried from anger, cried from grief, crying as he had never cried before.

He was hunched over crying when he felt a hand caress his tired head, and heard a woman's voice with a soft Castilian accent say to him:

"Cry, son, cry. . . ."

Again his eyes filled with tears and he cried as intensely as before, but this time, not from anguish but from joy; he felt a great refreshing sensation spread inside him, extinguishing the hot feeling that had nearly strangled him. As he cried, it seemed to him that his life and his emotions were cleansed like a glass under a stream of water, recovering the clearness and firmness of former days.

When the crying spell passed, he wiped his eyes and face with his handkerchief, feeling relieved. He raised his head and looked at the woman, but she was no longer looking at him, she was gazing out at the street, at a distant point in space, and her face seemed sad.

On the table before him there was another glass of milk and another dish heaped with vanilla wafers. He ate slowly, without thinking about anything, as if nothing had happened to him, as if he were at home and his mother were that woman who was standing behind the counter.

By the time he finished, it had grown dark, and the place was lit by an electric light. He remained seated for a while, wondering what he would say to the woman when he left, without thinking of anything appropriate.

At last he got up and said simply,

"Thank you very much, ma'am; goodbye."

"Goodbye, son," she answered.

He went outside. The sea breeze cooled his face, still hot from crying. He walked about aimlessly for a while, then went down a street that led to the docks. It was a very beautiful night, and large stars gleamed in the summer sky.

He thought about the blonde woman who had treated him so generously, resolving to repay her, to reward her as she deserved, when he got some money. But these thoughts of gratitude vanished along with the burning sensation in his face, until not one remained, and the recent event faded away and was lost in the recesses of his past life.

Suddenly, he was surprised to catch himself singing something in a low voice. He straightened up happily, striding with assurance and determination.

He came to the edge of the sea, and walked back and forth with a spring in his step; he felt like a new man, as if his inner forces, previously dispersed, had reassembled and united solidly.

Fatigue, like a tingling sensation, climed up his legs, and he sat down on a pile of burlap sacks. He looked at the sea. The lights of the wharf and those of the ships spread over the water in a reddish-gold ripple, trembling softly. He stretched out on his back, looking up at the sky for a long time. He did not feel like thinking, or singing, or talking. He just felt alive, that was all. Then he fell asleep with his face turned toward the sea.

—Based on a translation by Rosalie Torres-Rioseco

COMMENTARY

"The Glass of Milk" differs from the majority of Criollista short stories in its optimistic view of man and life in general. Although the protagonist's hunger is made to stand out by contrasting it with the tramp's opportunism and the little old man's indifference, the understanding and kindness of the woman in the milk bar complements and caps the generosity of the English sailor and the foreman of the stevedores. Once his hunger is overcome, the protagonist falls asleep "with his face turned toward the sea."

The importance of the individual is typically Chilean. The fact that the protagonist is anonymous does not in the least detract from his importance as a human being. In this story, Rojas is not concerned about social protest; he only wants to analyze the feelings and thoughts of a person suffering real hunger. He describes so intensely the various critical moments for the protagonist that the reader identifies with him without knowing much about his background. All that is known is that he's young and slender, he has a mother and brothers and sisters, he worked on a ship, deserted, worked with the Austrian crabber and stowed away. No other physical details are given nor are we told why he left home. What is important is the suffering and the pressure that hunger exerts on shyness and shame.

In addition to stressing the individual's plight, Rojas skillfully creates the port atmosphere: the presence of foreigners (the English sailor, the Austrian crabber, the Spanish woman); the tramps, the stevedores, the diners, the piles of sacks, and the lights of the dock and the ships. Rojas's main goal, unlike that of Mariano Latorre, the titular head of Chilean Criollistas, is not to capture the unique characteristics of a specific geographical region, but rather to present a human drama within a realistic environment.

"The Glass of Milk" gives the impression of a simple, straightforward narrative, without any literary devices. Rojas's stylistic techniques, however, are as significant as the more obvious one of Aguilera Malta or Juan Bosch. The comparison of the youth's hunger to a burning fire gives a richer meaning to the glass of milk, the tears, and the sea. In keeping with the simple plot and the intense emotion, Rojas's style, like that of most Chilean writers, tends to be slow. The long sentences, parallel constructions, and the translation into Spanish (in the original) of the English sailor's words all help establish the slow rhythm. In order to reconcile the emotional intensity with the slow rhythm, Rojas constructs his sentences on a verbal base: "the customer finished what he was reading, or at least interrupted it. He downed the rest of the milk in one gulp, rose slowly, paid, and walked toward the door." The slow rhythm is also felt in the use of the pronoun "those" in the bipartite phrase: "the lights of the wharf and those of the ship."

As for the story's structure, Rojas eschews the common practice of framing his work with a leitmotiv. The unity of the story is based on the single theme of hunger which is liquidated at the end. To a certain extent, the happy ending is anticipated by the false beginning. It seems as though the narrator is trying to fool us by making us believe for over a page that the English sailor is going to be the protagonist. Such a playful technique would be out of keeping with a tragic ending.

The priority given to the individual human being in "The Glass of Milk" (1929) anticipates the end of Criollismo. In Chile, the long years of isolation during the Colonial Period with its pioneer-like conditions, the influence of German and English immigrants, and the relative pre-eminence of urban life have contributed to creating a more anthropo-centric literature than in the majority of the other Spanish American countries. The revolt against Criollismo started in Chile in the late 1920s before that movement received the new stimulus of social protest occasioned by the great depression and the growing awareness of the class struggle. Therefore, it was not until 1945 that the reaction against Criollismo had become widespread throughout Spanish America.

Cosmopolitanism

Although Criollismo dominated Spanish American prose fiction between 1920 and 1945, the Cosmopolitan avant-garde tendency coexisted, albeit in a distinctly minority capacity; but from 1945 on, it won out over Criollismo in almost every Spanish American country.

For the Criollista writer, literature was a means for interpreting the political, economic, and social conditions of his own country. On the other hand, the Cosmopolitan author is much more concerned about psychology, philosophy, and aesthetics, even when he deals with Criollista themes, as in "The Rain" by Arturo Uslar Pietri. In contrast with the Criollista themes, the Cosmopolitanites are more interested in the individual's personal problems, in urban life, and in fantasy. These writers live in large metropolitan centers, they have traveled widely, and they are very conversant with the most advanced international literary movements.

The capital of Spanish American Cosmopolitanism is Buenos Aires and its high priest is clearly Jorge Luis Borges, who was strongly influenced by his years spent in Europe during the post-World War I avant-garde epoch. Although many of his devotees, who belong to different generations and who come from different countries, do not follow Borges's labyrinthine routes, all of them greatly respect his intellectualism and his artistic commitment.

Within the general Cosmopolitanism tendency, there are at least four more clearly defined movements: three that are intimately related to painting: Surrealism, Cubism, and Magic Realism; and Existentialism.

SURREALISM

Based on the work of Freud and his disciples, Surrealism proclaims that reality has a dual character, both exterior and interior, which it tries to capture simultaneously. Thus a certain episode witnessed by a character evokes a whole series of associations and memories. If this character happens to be dreaming, the elements evoked may be intermingled, confused, and distorted in order to achieve greater artistic effects. The most frequent theme of this subconscious world is sexual frustration. Surrealism in Spanish American prose fiction reached its height immediately at the end of World War II as the following novels demonstrate: *El señor Presidente* (1946) by Miguel Angel Asturias; *Al filo del agua* (1947) by Agustín Yáñez; *Manglar* (1947) and *Puerto*

Limón (1950) by Joaquín Gutiérrez; *La ruta de su evasión* (1949) by Yolanda Oreamuno. The foreign authors who exercised the greatest influence were James Joyce and William Faulkner, both of whom also introduced into the novel and the short story some techniques inspired by Cubism.

CUBISM

The influence of Cubism in literature has still not been sufficiently recognized. It was clearly influential in the simultaneous presentation of reality from different angles or points of view. In order to achieve this effect in literature, time is stopped or made eternal. Also attributable to Cubism is the mathematically precise planning with which these works are conceived and developed. Analogies with architecture or chess are hardly exaggerated. Among the best examples of Spanish American Cubism is *El señor Presidente* (which also has Surrealistic traits), inspired in part by Spaniard Valle-Inclán's Cubist novel *Tirano Banderas.*

MAGIC REALISM

Magic Realism, a term invented in 1925 by the German art critic Franz Roh to describe post-Expressionist painting throughout Europe, has been applied very loosely to Latin American literature since 1955. Based on a Jungian world view, Magic Realism may be defined as the unobtrusive, matter-of-fact insertion by the precise, objective artist or author of an unexpected or improbable (but not impossible) element in a predominantly realistic work which creates a strange or eery effect that leaves the viewer or reader disconcerted, bewildered, or delightfully amazed. Inspired by Henri Rousseau and Giorgio de Chirico, the Magic Realist tendency in painting spans a period of over fifty years from 1917 through the 1970s — from the early Joan Miró to the Howard Kanovitz of the 1970s — and includes such artists as the German Franz Radziwill, the Dutch Carel Willink, the French Auguste Herbin, and Americans Charles Sheeler, Edward Hopper, Grant Wood, and Andrew Wyeth. Although examples of Magic Realism in literature may be found in the 1920s, it does not really come into its own until after World War II. In certain stories by Borges, Cortázar, and Truman Capote, and in *One Hundred Years of Solitude* by García Márquez and *Son of Man* by Roa Bastos, everyday, banal occurrences are invested with a magical quality because of the author's apparently objective, precise, low-key approach. The perception of the magic qualities in reality was particularly welcome in the wake of the social and political turmoil that followed World War I and the Existentialist despair that followed World War II.

EXISTENTIALISM

Unlike the preceding tendencies, Existentialism is derived principally from philosophy. The Existentialist writer presents the anguished situation of modern man who feels totally alone and useless in a world mechanized to the point of destroying itself. The traditional values of love and faith are no longer valid. Devoid of all ideals, man only exists. Nothing is important. Cigarette butts and neon lights take the place of the Modernist swan. The plot often has no dramatic denouement. The short stories usually consist of an urban setting—shabby bars predominate—with a noncommunicative dialogue emphasizing the insurmountable walls that exist among individuals. Eduardo Mallea introduced Existentialism into Spanish America in the decade of the 1930s, twenty years before it became fashionable under the threat of an atomic war and the literary influence of Jean-Paul Sartre.

The short stories that follow carry the unmistakable mark of one or various of these tendencies, and encompass two generations of writers: those born between 1899 and 1910: Jorge Luis Borges (1899); Eduardo Mallea (1903); Rogelio Sinán (1904); Arturo Uslar Pietri (1905); Lino Novás Calvo (1905); and María Luisa Bombal (1910); and those born between 1917 and 1921: Augusto Roa Bastos (1917); Juan Rulfo (1918); Juan José Arreola (1918); and Ramón Ferreira (1921).

Jorge Luis Borges

(1899)

Argentinean. The best internationally known of all living Latin American writers, he was born in Buenos Aires and studied in Geneva, Switzerland, and in Cambridge, England. He was active in the post–World War I avant-garde poetry movements, first in Spain and then in Buenos Aires from 1921 on. His three volumes of poetry, *Fervor de Buenos Aires* (1923), *Luna de enfrente* (1925), and *Cuaderno de San Martín* (1929), give special emphasis to the metaphor while volumes of essays like *Inquisiciones* (1925) present some of the metaphysical problems that were to form the core of many of his stories. His first collection of stories, *Historia universal de la infamia*, appeared in 1935, but his reputation stems more from the publication of *El jardín de senderos que se bifurcan* (1941), *Ficciones* (1944), *El aleph* (1949), and *La muerte y la brújula* (1951). During the Perón regime (1945–1955), Borges lost his position at the national library but later regained it after Perón was overthrown. Borges was a visiting professor at the University of Texas in 1961–1962 and at Harvard in 1967–1968. During the 1960s, his works were translated and his international fame grew. His badly impaired vision appeared to put an end to his literary career during most of the 1950s and 1960s but an excellent volume of new poetry, *Elogio de la sombra,* appeared in 1969 and new collections of short stories, *El informe de Brodie* and *El libro de arena,* were published in 1970 and 1975, respectively. "The Garden of Forking Paths" was published as the title story of the 1941 volume.

THE GARDEN OF FORKING PATHS

For Victoria Ocampo

On page 22 of Liddell Hart's *History of World War I* you will read that an attack against the Serre-Montauban line by thirteen British divisions (supported by 1,400 artillery pieces), planned for the 24th of July, 1916, had to be postponed until the morning of the 29th. The torrential rains, Captain Liddell Hart comments, caused this delay, an insignificant one, to be sure.

The following statement, dictated, reread, and signed by Dr. Yu Tsun, former professor of English at the Hochschule at Tsingtao, throws an unsuspected light over the whole affair. The first two pages of the document are missing.

". . . and I hung up the receiver. Immediately afterward, I recognized the voice that had answered in German. It was that of Captain Richard Madden. Madden's presence in Viktor Runeberg's apartment meant the end of our anxieties and—but this seemed, *or should have seemed,* very secondary to me—also the end of our lives. It meant that Runeberg had been arrested or murdered.[1] Before the sun set on that day, I would encounter the same fate. Madden was implacable. Or rather, he was obliged to be so. An Irishman at the service of England, a man accused of laxity and perhaps of treason, how could he fail to seize and be thankful for such a miraculous opportunity: the discovery, capture, maybe even the death of two agents of the German Empire? I went up to my room; absurdly I locked the door and threw myself on my back on the narrow iron cot. Through the window I saw the familiar roofs and the hazy six o'clock sun.

"It seemed incredible to me that that day without premonitions or symbols should be the one of my inexorable death. In spite of my dead father, in spite of having been a child in a symmetrical garden of Hai Feng, was I—now—going to die? Then I reflected that everything happens to a man precisely, precisely *now.* Centuries of centuries and only in the present do things happen; countless men in the air, on the face of the earth and the sea, and all that really is happening is happening to me. . . . The almost intolerable recollection of Madden's horselike face banished these thoughts. In the midst of my hatred and terror (it means nothing to me now to speak of terror, now that I have outwitted Richard Madden, now that my throat yearns for the noose) it occurred to me that that tumultuous and doubtless happy warrior did not

---

[1]A hypothesis both hateful and odd. The Prussian spy Hans Rabener, alias Viktor Runeberg, attacked with drawn automatic the bearer of the warrant for his arrest, Captain Richard Madden. The latter, in self-defense, inflicted the wound which brought about Runeberg's death. (Editor's note.)

suspect that I possessed the Secret. The name of the exact location of the new British artillery park on the River Ancre. A bird streaked across the gray sky and blindly I turned it into an airplane and that airplane into many (against the French sky) annihilating the artillery station with vertical bombs. If only my mouth, before a bullet shattered it, could cry out that secret name so it could be heard in Germany. . . . My human voice was very weak. How might I make it carry to the ear of the Chief? To the ear of that sick and hateful man who knew nothing of Runeberg and me save that we were in Staffordshire and who was waiting in vain for our report in his arid office in Berlin, endlessly examining newspapers. . . . I said out loud: *I must flee.* I sat up noiselessly, in a useless perfection of silence, as if Madden were already lying in wait for me. Something — perhaps the mere vain ostentation of proving my resources were nil — made me look through my pockets. I found what I knew I would find. The American watch, the nickel chain and the square coin, the key ring with the incriminating useless keys to Runeberg's apartment, the notebook, a letter which I resolved to destroy immediately (and which I did not destroy), the false passport, a crown, two shillings and a few pence, the red and blue pencil, the handkerchief, the revolver with one bullet. Absurdly, I took it in my hand and felt its weight in order to fortify my courage. Vaguely I thought that a pistol shot can be heard at a great distance. In ten minutes my plan had been developed. The telephone book listed the name of the only person capable of transmitting the message; he lived in a suburb of Fenton, less than a half hour away by train.

"I am a cowardly man. I say it now, now that I have carried to its conclusion a plan whose perilous nature no one can deny. I know its execution was terrible. I didn't do it for Germany, no. I care nothing for a barbarous country which imposed upon me the abjection of being a spy. Besides, I know of a man from England — a modest man — who for me is no less great than Goethe. I talked with him for scarcely an hour, but during that hour he was Goethe. . . . I did it because I sensed that the Chief somehow looked down upon people of my race — those innumerable ancestors who are merged within me. I wanted to prove to him that a yellow man could save his armies. Besides, I had to flee from

Captain Madden. His hands and his voice could call at my door at any moment. I dressed silently, bade farewell to myself in the mirror, went downstairs, scrutinized the peaceful street, and went out. The station was not far from my home, but I judged it wise to take a cab. I argued that in this way I ran less risk of being recognized; the fact is that in the deserted street I felt visible and vulnerable, infinitely so. I remember that I told the cab driver to stop a little before the main entrance. I got out with a deliberate, almost painful slowness; I was going to the village of Ashgrove but I bought a ticket for a station further on. The train would leave within a very few minutes, at eight-fifty. I hurried; the next one would leave at nine-thirty. There was hardly a soul on the platform. I walked through the coaches; I remember a few farmers, a woman dressed in mourning, a youth enthusiastically engrossed in the *Annals* of Tacitus, and a wounded, happy soldier. At last the train pulled out. A man whom I recognized ran in vain to the end of the platform. It was Captain Richard Madden. Shattered, trembling, I shrank into the far corner of the seat, away from the dreaded window.

"From a state of annihilation, I passed into an almost abject happiness. I told myself that the duel had already begun and that I had won the first encounter by frustrating, even if for forty minutes, even if by a stroke of fate, the attack of my adversary. I argued that this slightest of victories was a sign of an ultimate total victory. I argued that it was not so slight since were it not for that precious difference in time that the train schedule gave me, I would be in prison or dead. I argued (with no less sophistry) that my cowardly happiness proved that I was a man capable of carrying out the adventure successfully. From this weakness I derived strength that never abandoned me. I foresee that man will resign himself each day to more atrocious undertakings; soon there will be no one but warriors and bandits; I give them this advice: *The author of an atrocious undertaking ought to imagine that he has already accomplished it, ought to impose upon himself a future as irrevocable as the past.* Thus I proceeded while my eyes of a man already dead registered the ebbing of that day, which was perhaps my last, and the diffusion of the night. The train ran gently along, amid ash trees. It stopped, almost in the middle

of the fields. No one shouted the name of the station. "Ashgrove?"
I asked a few boys on the platform. "Ashgrove," they replied. I
got off.

"A lamp lit up the platform but the faces of the boys were in
the shadows. One questioned me. 'Are you going to Dr. Stephen
Albert's house?' Without waiting for my answer, another said,
'The house is a long way from here, but you won't get lost if you
take this road to the left and bear to the left at every crossroads.'
I tossed them a coin (my last), descended a few stone steps and
started down the lonely road. It went downhill, slowly. It was of
plain dirt; overhead the branches were intertwined; the moon,
low and round, seemed to accompany me.

"For an instant, I thought that Richard Madden in some way
had penetrated my desperate plan. Very quickly, I understood
that that was impossible. The instructions to turn always to the
left reminded me that such was the common procedure for discovering the central point of certain labyrinths. I have some
understanding of labyrinths: not for nothing am I the great grandson of that Ts'ui Pên who was governor of Yunnan and who renounced worldly power in order to write a novel that might be
even more heavily populated than the *Hung Lu Meng* and to
construct a labyrinth in which all men would become lost. Thirteen
years he dedicated to these heterogeneous tasks, but the hand of
a stranger murdered him—and his novel was incoherent and no
one found the labyrinth. Beneath English trees I meditated on
that lost maze: I imagined it inviolate and perfect on the secret
summit of a mountain; I imagined it erased by rice fields or
beneath the water; I imagined it infinite, no longer composed
of octagonal kiosks and dead-end paths, but of rivers and provinces and kingdoms. . . . I thought of a labyrinth of labyrinths,
of one sinuous spreading labyrinth that would encompass the past
and the future and in some way involve the stars. Absorbed in
these illusory images, I forgot that I was ordained to be pursued.
I felt myself to be, for an indeterminate period of time, an abstract
spectator of the world. The vague, living countryside, the moon,
the remaining hours of the day affected me, as well as the slope
of the road which eliminated any possibility of weariness. The evening was intimate, infinite. The road descended and forked among
the now dimly seen meadows. A high-pitched, almost syllabic

music kept coming and going with the shifting of the wind, muted by leaves and distance. I thought that a man might be an enemy of other men, of the moments of other men, but not of a country: not of fireflies, words, gardens, streams of water, sunsets. Thus I arrived before a high, rusty gate. Between the iron bars I made out a poplar grove and a kind of pavilion. I understood suddenly two things, the first trivial, the second almost unbelievable: the music was coming from the pavilion, and the music was Chinese. For precisely that reason I had completely accepted it without paying it any attention. I do not remember whether there was a bell, a push button, or whether I called by clapping my hands. The sparkling music continued.

"But from the rear of the main house a lantern approached: a lantern that the tree trunks sometimes striped and sometimes blotted out, a paper lantern that had the form of a drum and the color of the moon. A tall man was carrying it. I didn't see his face for the light blinded me. He opened the gate and said slowly, in my own language: 'I see that the pious Hsi P'êng persists in correcting my solitude. You no doubt wish to see the garden?'

"I recognized the name of one of our consuls and I replied, disconcerted, 'The garden?'

"'The garden of forking paths.'

"Something stirred in my memory and I uttered with incomprehensible certainty, 'The garden of my ancestor Ts'ui Pên.'

"'Your ancestor? Your illustrious ancestor? Come in.'

"The damp path zigzagged like those of my childhood. We came to a library of Eastern and Western books. I recognized bound in yellow silk several volumes of the Lost Encyclopedia, which was edited by the Third Emperor of the Luminous Dynasty but which was never printed. The phonograph record was spinning next to a bronze phoenix. I also recall a *famille rose* vase and another, many centuries older, of that shade of blue which our craftsmen copied from the potters of Persia. . . .

"Stephen Albert was observing me with a smile on his face. He was, as I have said, very tall, sharp featured, with gray eyes and gray beard. He looked something like a priest and also a sailor. He told me later that he had been a missionary in Tientsin 'before aspiring to become a Sinologist.'

"We sat down—I on a long, low divan, he with his back to the window and a high circular clock. I calculated that my pursuer, Richard Madden, could not arrive for at least an hour. My irrevocable decision could wait.

"'An astounding fate, that of Ts'ui Pên,' Stephen Albert said. 'Governor of his native province, learned in astronomy, in astrology, and in the tireless interpretation of the canonical books, chess player, famous poet and calligrapher—he abandoned all this in order to compose a book and a maze. He renounced the pleasures of both tyranny and justice, of his oft-frequented bed, of his banquets and even of erudition—and shut himself up for thirteen years in the Pavilion of the Limpid Solitude. When he died, his heirs found nothing save chaotic manuscripts. His family, as you may be aware, wished to consign them to the fire; but his executor—a Taoist or Buddhist monk—insisted on their publication.'

"'We descendants of Ts'ui,' I replied, 'continue to curse that monk. Their publication was senseless. The book is an indeterminate heap of contradictory drafts. I examined it once: in the third chapter the hero dies, in the fourth he is alive. As for the other undertaking of Ts'ui Pên, his labyrinth. . . .'

"'Here is the labyrinth,' he said, indicating a tall lacquered desk.

"'An ivory labyrinth!' I exclaimed. 'A minimal labyrinth.'

"'A labyrinth of symbols,' he corrected me. 'An invisible labyrinth of time. I, a barbarous Englishman, have been entrusted with the revelation of this diaphanous mystery. After more than a hundred years, the details are irretrievable; but it is not difficult to conjecture what happened. Ts'ui Pên must have said once: *I am withdrawing to write a book.* And another time: *I am withdrawing to construct a labyrinth.* Everyone imagined two works; to no one did it occur that the book and the maze were one and the same thing. The Pavilion of the Limpid Solitude stood in the center of a garden that was perhaps intricate; that circumstance could have suggested the idea of a physical labyrinth. Ts'ui Pên died; no one in the vast territories that were his came upon the labyrinth; the confusion of the novel suggested to me that *it* was the maze. Two circumstances gave me the correct solution to the problem. One: the curious legend that Ts'ui Pên had planned to create a labyrinth which would be strictly infinite. The other: a fragment of a letter I discovered.'

"Albert rose. He turned his back on me a few moments; he opened a drawer of the black and gold desk. He turned around holding in his hand a sheet of paper that had once been crimson, but that was now pink and tenuous and cross sectioned. Ts'ui Pên's calligraphy was justly famous. I read, uncomprehendingly and eagerly, these words written with a minute brush by a man of my blood: *I leave to the various futures (not to all) my garden of forking paths.* Without a word, I returned the sheet. Albert continued: 'Before unearthing this letter, I had questioned myself about the ways in which a book can be infinite. I could think of nothing other than a cyclical volume, a circular one. A book whose last page was identical with the first, a book which had the possibility of continuing indefinitely. I remembered too that night which is at the middle of the 1001 Nights when Queen Scheherazade (through a magical oversight of the copyist) begins to relate word for word the story of the 1001 Nights, with the risk of coming once again to the night in which she is telling it, and thus on to infinity. I also imagined a Platonic, hereditary work, transmitted from father to son, in which each new individual would add a chapter or correct with pious care the pages of his elders. These conjectures entertained me; but none seemed to correspond, not even remotely, to the contradictory chapters of Ts'ui Pên. In the midst of this perplexity, I received from Oxford the manuscript you have examined. I focused, naturally, on the sentence: *I leave to the various futures (not to all) my garden of forking paths.* Almost instantly, I understood: *the garden of forking paths* was the chaotic novel; the phrase *the various futures (not to all)* suggested to me the forking in time, not in space. A broad rereading of the work confirmed the theory. In all fictional works, each time a man is confronted with several alternatives, he chooses one and eliminates the others; in the fiction of the almost unfathomable Ts'ui Pên, he chooses—simultaneously—all of them. He *creates*, in this way, diverse futures, diverse times which themselves also proliferate and fork. Here, then, is the explanation of the novel's contradictions. Fang, let us say, has a secret; a stranger calls at his door; Fang resolves to kill him. Naturally, there are several possible outcomes: Fang can kill the intruder, the intruder can kill Fang, they both can be saved, they both can die, etcetera. In the work of Ts'ui Pên, all possible outcomes occur; each one is the point of departure for other forkings. Sometimes, the paths of this labyrinth converge: for example, you arrive at this house, but in one of the possible pasts you are my enemy, in another, my friend. If you will resign yourself to my incurable pronunciation, we shall read a few pages.'

"His face, within the vivid circle of the lamplight, was unquestionably that of an old man, but with something unshakable about it, even immortal. He read with slow precision two versions of the same epic chapter. In the first, an army marches into battle across a desolate mountain; the horror of the rocks and shadows makes the men attach little value to their lives and they gain an easy victory. In the second, the same army marches through a palace where a great party is taking place; the glowing battle seems to them a continuation of the party and they win the victory. I listened with proper veneration to these ancient narratives, perhaps less admirable in themselves than for the fact that they had been thought out by one of my own blood and were being restored to me by a man of a remote empire, in the course of a desperate adventure, on a Western isle. I remember the final words, repeated in each version like a secret commandment: *Thus fought the heroes, tranquil their admirable hearts, violent their swords, resigned to kill and to die.*

"From that moment on, I felt around me and within my dark body an invisible, intangible swarming. Not the swarming of the two divergent, parallel and finally coalescent armies, but a more inaccessible, more intimate agitation that they in some manner prefigured. Stephen Albert continued: 'I don't think that your illustrious ancestor toyed idly with these variations. I don't find it probable that he would sacrifice thirteen years to the never ending execution of an experiment in rhetoric. In your country, the novel is an inferior genre; in those days it was a despicable genre. Ts'ui Pên was a brilliant novelist, but he was also a man of letters who undoubtedly did not consider himself a mere novelist. The testimony of his contemporaries proclaims—and his life fully confirms—his metaphysical and mystical interests. Philosophic controversy usurps a good part of his novel. I know that of all problems, none disturbed him so greatly nor worked upon him so much as the abysmal problem of time. Now then, this is the *only* problem that does not appear in the pages of the *Garden*.

He does not even use the word that signifies *time*. How do you explain this voluntary omission?'

"I proposed several solutions — all inadequate. We discussed them. Finally, Stephen Albert said to me: 'In a riddle whose answer is chess, what is the only prohibited word?'

"I thought a moment and replied, 'The word *chess.*'

"'Precisely,' said Albert. '*The Garden of Forking Paths* is an enormous riddle, or parable, whose theme is time; this secret reason prohibits its being mentioned. To omit a word *always*, to resort to inept metaphors and obvious paraphrases, is perhaps the most emphatic way of stressing it. This is the tortuous method preferred by the oblique Ts'ui Pên in each of the meanderings of his indefatigable novel. I have compared hundreds of manuscripts, I have corrected the errors that the negligence of the copyists has introduced, I have conjectured the plan of this chaos, I have reestablished — I think I have reestablished — the original order, I have translated the entire work: it is clear to me that not once does he employ the word 'time.' The explanation is obvious: *The Garden of Forking Paths* is an incomplete, but not false, image of the universe as Ts'ui Pên conceived it. In contrast to Newton and Schopenhauer, your ancestor did not believe in a uniform, absolute time. He believed in an infinite series of times, in a growing dizzying network of divergent, convergent and parallel times. This web of times that approach one another, fork, break off, or are unaware of each other for centuries, embraces *all* possibilities. We do not exist in the majority of these times; in some you exist, and not I; in others I, and not you; in others, both of us. In the present one, which a favorable fate has granted me, you have arrived at my house; in another, while crossing the garden, you found me dead; in still another, I utter these same words, but I am a mistake, a ghost.'

"'In every one,' I pronounced, not without a tremor in my voice, 'I am grateful to you and revere you for your re-creation of the garden of Ts'ui Pên.'

"'Not in all,' he murmured with a smile. 'Time forks perpetually toward innumerable futures. In one of them I am your enemy.'

"Once again I felt the swarming sensation of which I have spoken. It seemed to me that the humid garden that surrounded the house was infinitely saturated with invisible persons. Those persons were Albert and I, secretive, busy, and multiform in other dimensions of time. I raised my eyes and the tenuous nightmare dissolved. In the yellow and black garden there was only one man; but this man was as strong as a statue, but this man was walking up the path and he was Captain Richard Madden.

"'The future already exists,' I replied, 'but I am your friend. Could I see the letter again?'

"Albert rose. Standing tall, he opened the drawer of the high desk; for a moment he turned his back to me. I had readied the revolver. I fired with extreme caution. Albert fell uncomplainingly, immediately. I swear his death was instantaneous—a lightning stroke.

"The rest is unreal, insignificant. Madden broke in, arrested me. I have been condemned to the gallows. I have won out abominably; I have communicated to Berlin the secret name of the city they must attack. They bombed it yesterday; I read it in the same papers that offered to England the mystery of the learned Sinologist Stephen Albert who was murdered by a stranger, Yu Tsun. The chief had deciphered this mystery. He knew my problem was to indicate (through the uproar of the war) the city called Albert, and that I had found no other means to do so than to kill a man of that name. He does not know (no one can know) my infinite contrition and weariness."

—Based on a translation by Donald A. Yates

COMMENTARY

Borges is not only one of the greatest Spanish American short story writers but one of the most important authors in the world today. In addition to his impact on younger writers in Europe and the United States, he has been responsible for the development of a literature of the fantastic in Spanish America since the early 1950s. Although one of his basic traits is thematic and stylistic variety, "The Garden of Forking Paths" is one of his most representative stories.

Uniquely Borgian is the oxymoron-like combination of the detective story and the philosophical discussions about the labyrinth and literary theory. As in the world of Sherlock Holmes, Fu Man Chu, and their countless successors, Borges challenges his readers to an intellectual duel replete with mystery, murder, escape, pursuit, and the punishment of the criminal. Borges writes, however, for a select public and the intellectual duel is much more complex. Starting out with the detective story framework, he weaves a labyrinth in which he purposely strives to lose his reader. The long discussion of Ts'ui Pên's labyrinth tends to distract the reader's attention from Yu Tsun's mission. Only at the very end of the story does Borges supply the explanation of the trip to Stephen Albert's home. Nevertheless, the digressions are at least as important as the main plot because they contain the basic ideas of Borges's philosophy: the labyrinthine character of the world; the cyclical nature of history; the simultaneity of past, present, and future; the identity of man with his ancestors as well as with every man; the insignificance of the individual. The concept of cyclical history or circular time is reinforced stylistically by "the moon, low and round," "a high circular clock," and "the vivid circle of the lamplight." Furthermore, the protagonist's parenthetical remark toward the beginning of the story "(. . . .now that I have outwitted Richard Madden, now that my throat yearns for the noose)" is the starting point of the circle that closes (like a noose?) in the final paragraph with the equally matter-of-fact statement: "I have been condemned to the gallows."

Like Gide, Unamuno, Pirandello, and many other twentieth-century authors, Borges comments on his own creative process in the course of his story. When Albert speaks of "the meanderings" of Ts'ui Pên's "indefatigable novel," Borges is referring to his own story. In order to complicate the "meanderings," he resorts to his favorite rhetorical device, the oxymoron, and extends it to other aspects of the story. The academic precision of the initial sentence referring to a real book stands in sharp contrast with the footnote referring to a fictitious event. The presence in England of a German spy of Chinese nationality is highly improbable while the coincidence that Stephen Albert should turn out to be a Sinologist is nothing short of Magic Realism. The Magic Realism is reinforced by such improbable phrases as "a youth enthusiastically engrossed in the *Annals* of Tacitus," "a wounded, happy soldier" (even though the soldier could logically be happy for having escaped alive from the war), and "an Irishman at the service of England."

In presenting his philosophical ideas, Borges uses a style that seems more appropriate for the essay than for the short story, a style more typically English than Spanish. Actually, some of his stories are borderline essays but not "The Garden of Forking Paths" in which the expository style is juxtaposed with the detective-story style: "I dressed silently, bade farewell to myself in the mirror, went downstairs, scrutinized the peaceful street, and went out."

Although Borges's importance in the development of the Spanish American short story is undeniable, and although he is Latin America's best-known writer today, he has been criticized, particularly by younger Argentine writers, for turning his back on the social problems besetting his country. They recognize his vast erudition, his ingenuity, and his originality, but they condemn him for being an escapist. The question remains whether a man who has converted the short story form into a vehicle for expressing philosophical ideas about the nature of man and history in all ages deserves to be called an escapist.

María Luisa Bombal

(1910–1980)

Chilean. She was born in Viña del Mar where she attended a French school. At the age of thirteen, after the death of her father, she accompanied her mother and twin sisters to Paris where she continued her studies up through the Sorbonne. She wrote her thesis on the early nineteenth-century short story writer Prosper Mérimée. She returned to Chile in 1931 and performed in different theater groups. Between 1933 and 1941, she lived in Buenos Aires where she worked on the literary journal *Sur,* and published her three short stories, "Las islas nuevas" (1938), "The Tree" (1939), and "María Gricelda" (1946). Her two novels, *La última niebla* (1935) and *La amortajada* (1938), like "The Tree," are among the first literary manifestations of Surrealism in Latin America. For many years she resided in New York but she is now living in Viña del Mar. *La última niebla* and four short stories, including "The Tree," will soon be published in English under the title of *New Islands and Other Discoveries* by Farrar Strauss and Giroux.

THE TREE

The pianist sits down, coughs affectedly, and concentrates for a moment. The cluster of lights illuminating the hall slowly diminishes to a soft, warm glow, as a musical phrase begins to rise in the silence, and to develop, clear, restrained and judiciously capricious.

"Mozart, perhaps," thinks Brígida. As usual, she has forgotten to ask for the program. "Mozart, perhaps, or Scarlatti." She knew so little about music! And it wasn't because she had no ear for it, or interest. As a child it was she who had demanded piano lessons; no one needed to force them on her, as with her sisters. Her sisters, however, played correctly now and read music at sight, while she. . . . She had given up her studies within a year after she began them. The reason for her inconsistency was as simple as

271

it was shameful; she had never succeeded in learning the key of F; never. "I don't understand; my memory is incapable of going beyond the key of G." How indignant her father was! "Oh, how I'd love to give up this job of being a man alone with several daughters to raise! Poor Carmen! She surely must have suffered because of Brígida. This child is retarded."

Brígida was the youngest of six girls, all different in character. When the father finally came to his sixth daughter, he was so perplexed and tired out by the first five that he preferred to simplify matters by declaring her retarded. "I'm not going to struggle any longer, it's useless. Let her be. If she doesn't want to study, let her not study. If she likes to spend time in the kitchen listening to ghost stories, that's up to her. If she likes dolls at sixteen, let her play with them." And Brígida had kept her dolls and remained completely ignorant.

How pleasant it is to be ignorant! Not to know exactly who Mozart was, where he came from, who influenced him, the details of his technique! How nice to just let him lead you by the hand, as now.

And, indeed, Mozart is leading her. He leads her across a bridge suspended over a crystalline stream which runs over a bed of rosy sand. She is dressed in white, with a lace parasol—intricate and fine as a spider web—open over her shoulder.

"You look younger every day, Brígida. I met your husband yesterday, your ex-husband, I mean. His hair is all white."

But she doesn't answer, she doesn't stop, she continues to cross the bridge which Mozart has improvised for her to the garden of her youthful years when she was eighteen: tall fountains in which the water sings; her chestnut braids, which when undone reach her ankles, her golden complexion, her dark eyes opened wide as if questioning; a small mouth with full lips, a sweet smile and the most slender, most graceful body in the world. What was she thinking about as she sat on the edge of the fountain? Nothing. "She is as stupid as she is pretty," they said. But it never mattered to her that she was stupid, or unsought after at dances. One by one, her sisters were asked to marry. No one proposed to her.

Mozart! Now he offers her a staircase of blue marble which she descends, between a double row of icy cold lilies. And now he opens for her a gate of thick iron bars with gilded tips so that she can throw her arms around the neck of Luis, her father's close friend. Ever since she was a very small child, when they all used to abandon her, she would run to Luis. He would pick her up and she would hug him, laughing with little warbling sounds, and shower him with kisses like a downpour of rain, haphazardly, upon his eyes, his forehead and his hair, already gray (had he ever been young?).

"You are a necklace," Luis would say to her. "You are like a necklace of birds."

That is why she married him. Because, with that solemn and taciturn man, she didn't feel guilty of being as she was: silly, playful, and lazy. Yes; now that so many years have passed she understands that she did not marry Luis for love; nevertheless, she doesn't quite understand why, why she went away one day suddenly. . . .

But at this point Mozart takes her nervously by the hand, and dragging her along at a pace which becomes more urgent by the second, compels her to cross the garden in the opposite direction, to recross the bridge at a run, almost in headlong flight. And after having deprived her of the parasol and the transparent skirt, he closes the door of her past with a chord at once gentle and firm, and leaves her in a concert hall, dressed in black, mechanically applauding while the glow of the artificial lights increases.

Once more the half-shadow, and once more the foreboding silence.

And now Beethoven's music begins to stir up the warm waves of his notes under a spring moon. How far the sea has withdrawn! Brígida walks across the beach toward the sea now recoiled in the distance, shimmering and calm, but then, the sea swells, slowly grows, comes to meet her, envelops her, and with gentle waves, gradually pushes her, pushes her from behind until it makes her rest her cheek upon the body of a man. And then it recedes, leaving her forgotten upon Luis's breast.

"You don't have a heart, you don't have a heart," she used to tell Luis. Her husband's heart beat so deep inside him that she could rarely hear it, and then only in an unexpected way. "You are never with me when you are beside me," she protested in the bedroom when he ritually opened the evening papers before going to sleep. "Why did you marry me?"

"Because you have the eyes of a frightened little doe," he answered and kissed her. And she, suddenly happy, proudly welcomed on her shoulder the weight of his gray head. Oh, his shiny, silver hair!

"Luis, you have never told me exactly what color your hair was when you were a boy, and you have never told me either what your mother said when you began to get gray at fifteen. What did she say? Did she laugh? Did she cry? And were you proud or ashamed? And at school, your friends, what did they say? Tell me, Luis, tell me. . . ."

"Tomorrow I'll tell you. I'm sleepy, Brígida. I'm very tired. Turn off the light."

Unconsciously he moved away from her to fall asleep, and she unconsciously, all night long, pursued her husband's shoulder, sought his breath, tried to live beneath his breath, like a plant shut up and thirsty that stretches out its branches in search of a more favorable climate.

In the morning, when the maid opened the blinds, Luis was no longer at her side. He had gotten up stealthily without saying good morning to her for fear that his "necklace of birds" would insist on holding him firmly by the shoulders. "Five minutes, just five minutes. Your office won't disappear because you stay five minutes longer with me, Luis."

Her awakenings. Ah, how sad her awakenings! But—it was strange—scarcely did she step into her dressing room than her sadness vanished, as if by magic.

Waves toss and break in the distance, murmuring like a sea of leaves. Is it Beethoven? No.

It is the tree close to the window of the dressing room. It was enough for her to enter to feel a wonderfully pleasant sensation circulating within her. How hot it always was in the bedroom, in the mornings! And what a harsh light! Here, on the other hand, in the dressing room, even one's eyes felt rested, refreshed. The drab cretonnes, the tree that cast shadows on the walls like rough, cold water, the mirrors that reflected the foliage and receded into an infinite, green forest. How pleasant that room was! It seemed like a world submerged in an aquarium. How that huge rubber tree chattered! All the birds of the neighborhood came to take shelter in it. It was the only tree on that narrow, sloping street which dropped down directly to the river from one corner of the city.

"I'm busy. I can't accompany you. . . . I have a lot to do, I won't make it for lunch. . . . Hello, yes, I'm at the Club. An engagement. Have your dinner and go to bed. . . . No. I don't know. You better not wait for me, Brígida."

"If I only had some girl friends!" she sighed. But everybody was bored with her. If she would only try to be a little less stupid! But how to gain at one stroke so much lost ground? To be intelligent you should begin from childhood, shouldn't you?

Her sisters, however, were taken everywhere by their husbands, but Luis — why shouldn't she confess it to herself? — was ashamed of her, of her ignorance, her timidity, and even her eighteen years. Had he not asked her to say she was at least twenty-one, as if her extreme youth were a secret defect?

And at night, how tired he always was when he went to bed! He never listened to her attentively. He did smile at her, yes, with a smile which she knew was mechanical. He showered her with caresses from which he was absent. Why do you suppose he had married her? To keep up a habit, perhaps to strengthen the old friendly relationship with her father. Perhaps life consisted, for men, of a series of ingrained habits. If one should be broken, probably confusion, failure would result. And then they would begin to wander through the streets of the city, to sit on the benches of the public squares, each day more poorly dressed and more in need of a shave. Luis's life, therefore, consisted of filling every minute of the day with some activity. Why hadn't she understood that before! Her father was right when he declared her retarded.

"I should like to see it snow some time, Luis."

"This summer I'll take you to Europe, and since it is winter there, you will be able to see it snow."

"I know it is winter in Europe when it is summer here. I'm not that ignorant!"

Sometimes, as if to awaken him to the emotion of real love, she would throw herself upon her husband and cover him with kisses, weeping, calling him Luis, Luis, Luis. . . .

"What? What's the matter with you? What do you want?"

"Nothing."

"Why are you calling me that way then?"

"No reason, just to call you. I like to call you." And he would smile, taking kindly to that new game.

Summer arrived, her first summer as a married woman. New duties kept Luis from offering her the promised trip.

"Brígida, the heat is going to be terrible this summer in Buenos Aires. Why don't you go to the ranch with your father?"

"Alone?"

"I would go to see you every weekend."

She had sat down on the bed, ready to insult him. But she sought in vain for cutting words to shout at him. She didn't know anything, anything at all. Not even how to insult.

"What's the matter with you? What are you thinking about, Brígida?"

For the first time Luis had retraced his steps and bent over her, uneasy, letting the time of his arrival at the office pass by.

"I'm sleepy," Brígida had replied childishly, while she hid her face in the pillows.

For the first time he had called her from the Club at lunch time. But she had refused to go to the telephone, furiously wielding that weapon she had found without thinking: silence.

That same evening she ate opposite her husband without raising her eyes, all her nerves taut.

"Are you still angry, Brígida?"

But she did not break the silence.

"You certainly know that I love you, my necklace of birds. But I can't be with you all the time. I'm a very busy man. One reaches my age a slave to a thousand commitments."

". . ."

"Do you want to go out tonight?"

". . ."

"You don't want to? Patience. Tell me, did Roberto call from Montevideo?"

". . ."

"What a pretty dress! Is it new?"

". . ."

"Is it new, Brígida? Answer, answer me."

But she did not break the silence this time either. And a

moment later the unexpected, the astonishing, the absurd happens. Luis gets up from his chair, throws the napkin violently on the table, and leaves the house, slamming doors behind him.

She too had gotten up, stunned, trembling with indignation at such injustice. "And me, and me," she murmured confused; "What about me who for almost a year . . . when for the first time I allow myself one reproach. . . . Oh, I'm leaving, I'm leaving, this very night! I'll never set foot in this house again." And she furiously opened the closets of her dressing room, wildly threw the clothes on the floor.

It was then that someone rapped with his knuckles on the window panes.

She had run, she knew not how or with what unaccustomed courage, to the window. She had opened it. It was the tree, the rubber tree which a great gust of wind was shaking, which was hitting the glass with its branches, which summoned her from outside as if she should see it writhing like an impetuous black flame beneath the fiery sky of that summer evening.

A heavy shower would soon beat against its cold leaves. How delightful! All night long she would be able to hear the rain whipping, trickling through the leaves of the rubber tree as if along the ducts of a thousand imaginary gutters. All night long she would hear the old trunk of the rubber tree creak and groan, telling her of the storm, while she snuggled up very close to Luis, voluntarily shivering between the sheets of the big bed.

Handfuls of pearls that rain buckets upon a silver roof. Chopin. *Études* by Frédéric Chopin.

How many weeks did she wake up suddenly, very early, when she scarcely perceived that her husband, now also stubbornly silent, had slipped out of bed?

The dressing room: the window wide open, an odor of river and pasture floating in that kindly room, and the mirrors veiled by a halo of mist.

Chopin and the rain that slips through the leaves of the rubber tree with the noise of a hidden waterfall that seems to drench even the roses on the cretonnes, become intermingled in her agitated nostalgia.

What does one do in the summertime when it rains so much?

Stay in one's room the whole day feigning convalescence or sadness? Luis had entered timidly one afternoon. He had sat down very stiffly. There was a silence.

"Brígida, then it is true? You no longer love me?"

She had become happy all of a sudden, stupidly. She might have cried out: "No, no; I love you, Luis; I love you," if he had given her time, if he had not added, almost immediately, with his habitual calm:

"In any case, I don't think it is wise for us to separate, Brígida. We have to think it over a great deal."

Her impulses subsided as abruptly as they had arisen. Why become excited uselessly! Luis loved her with tenderness and moderation; if some time he should come to hate her, he would hate her justly and prudently. And that was life. She approached the window, rested her forehead against the icy glass. There was the rubber tree calmly receiving the rain that struck it, softly and steadily. The room stood still in the shadow, orderly and quiet. Everything seemed to come to a stop, eternal and very noble. That was life. And there was a certain greatness in accepting it as it was, mediocre, as something definitive, irremediable. And from the depths of things there seemed to spring forth and rise, a melody of grave, slow words to which she stood listening: "Always." "Never." And thus the hours, the days and the years go by. Always! Never! Life, life!

On regaining her bearings she realized that her husband had slipped out of the room. Always! Never!

And the rain, secretly and constantly, continued to murmur in the music of Chopin.

Summer tore the leaves from its burning calendar. Luminous and blinding pages fell like golden swords, pages of an unwholesome humidity like the breath of the swamps; pages of brief and violent storms, and pages of hot winds, of the winds that bring the "carnation of the air" and hang it in the immense rubber tree.

Children used to play hide-and-seek among the enormous twisted roots that raised the paving stones of the sidewalk, and the tree was filled with laughter and whispering. Then she appeared at the window and clapped her hands; the children dispersed, frightened, without noticing her smile, the smile of a girl who also wanted to take part in the game.

Alone, she would lean for a long time on her elbows at the window watching the trembling of the foliage — some breeze always blew along that street which dropped straight down to the river — and it was like sinking one's gaze in shifting water or in the restless fire of a hearth. One could spend one's idle hours this way, devoid of all thought, in a stupor of well-being.

Scarcely did the room begin to fill with the haze of twilight when she lit the first lamp, and the first lamp shone in the mirrors, multiplied like a firefly wishing to precipitate the coming of night.

And night after night she dozed next to her husband, suffering at intervals. But when her pain increased to the point of wounding her like a knife thrust, when she was beset by too urgent a desire to awaken Luis in order to hit him or caress him, she slipped away on tiptoe to the dressing room and opened the window. The room instantly filled with discreet sounds and presences, with mysterious footfalls, the fluttering of wings, the subtle crackling of vegetation, the soft chirping of a cricket hidden under the bark of the rubber tree submerged in the stars of a hot summer night.

Her fever passed as her bare feet gradually became chilled on the matting. She did not know why it was so easy for her to suffer in that room.

Chopin's melancholy linking one *Étude* after another, linking one melancholy after another, imperturbably.

And autumn came. The dry leaves whirled about for a moment before rolling on the grass of the narrow garden, on the sidewalk of the steep street. The leaves shook loose and fell. . . . The top of the rubber tree remained green, but underneath, the tree turned red, darkened like the worn-out lining of a sumptuous evening cape. And the room now seemed to be submerged in a goblet of dull gold.

Lying on the divan, she patiently waited for suppertime, for Luis's improbable arrival. She had resumed speaking to him, she had become his wife again without enthusiasm and without anger. She no longer loved him. But she no longer suffered. On the contrary, an unexpected feeling of plenitude, of placidity had taken hold of her. Now no one or nothing could hurt her. It may be that true happiness lies in the conviction that happiness has been irremediably lost. Then we begin to move through life without hope or fear, capable of finally enjoying all the small pleasures, which are the most lasting.

A terrible din, then a flash of light that throws her backward, trembling all over.

Is it the intermission? No. It is the rubber tree, she knows it.

They had felled it with a single stroke of the ax. She could not hear the work that began very early in the morning. "The roots were raising the paving stones of the sidewalk and then, naturally, the neighborhood committee. . . ."

Blinded, she has lifted her hands to her eyes. When she recovers her sight, she stands up and looks around her. What is she looking at? The hall suddenly lighted, the people who are dispersing? No. She has remained imprisoned in the web of her past, she cannot leave the dressing room. Her dressing room invaded by a white, terrifying light. It was as if they ripped off the roof; a harsh light came in everywhere, seeped through her pores, burned her with cold. And she saw everything in the light of that cold light; Luis, his wrinkled face, his hands crossed by coarse, discolored veins, and the gaudy colored cretonnes. Frightened, she has run to the window. The window now opens directly on a narrow street, so narrow that her room almost crashes against the front of a dazzling skyscraper. On the ground floor, show windows and more show windows, full of bottles. On the street corner, a row of automobiles lined up in front of a service station painted red. Some boys in shirt sleeves are kicking a ball in the middle of the street.

And all that ugliness had entered her mirrors. Now in her mirrors there were nickel-plated balconies and shabby clotheslines and canary cages.

They had taken away her privacy, her secret; she found herself in the middle of the street, naked beside an old husband who turned his back on her in bed, who had given her no children. She does not understand how until then she had not wanted to have children, how she had come to the idea that she was going to live without children all her life. She does not understand how she could endure for one year Luis's laughter, that over-cheerful laughter, that false laughter of a man who has become skilled in laughter because it is necessary to laugh on certain occasions.

A lie! Her resignation and her serenity were a lie; she wanted love, yes, love; and trips and madness, and love, love. . . .

"But Brígida, why are you going? Why did you stay?" Luis had asked.

Now she would have known how to answer him:

"The tree, Luis, the tree! They have cut down the rubber tree."

—Based on a translation by Rosalie Torres-Rioseco

COMMENTARY

One of the distinguishing characteristics of Chilean prose fiction in general is the greater attention paid to the individual human being, in contrast with the metaphysical preoccupations of Argentine writers and the social concern for the masses in most of the other Spanish American countries. It is not surprising, therefore, that Surrealism, with its special interest in Freud and psychoanalysis, was welcomed as a weapon by young Chileans determined to do battle against the preceding generation of institutionalized and relatively pedestrian Criollistas headed by Marianno Latorre (1886-1955) whose short stories constitute a literary atlas of Chile. María Luisa Bombal's two novels, *La última niebla* (1935) and *La amortajada* (1938), were written a full decade before Surrealism came into its own among Spanish American writers, with the probing into the depths of the female psyche as a favorite theme.

In "The Tree" the protagonist's tragic life is represented symbolically by the tree, the calendar, and the music. The three pieces played at the concert correspond to three stages in Brígida's life. Mozart's frivolous rococo music accompanies the recollections of her carefree childhood and adolescence in a springlike atmosphere which ends with her almost unconscious marriage. Beethoven's romantic music reflects the young wife's unfulfilled passionate desires beginning in the spring and ending with the summer's heat and heavy showers. The melancholy tone of Chopin's *Études* begins with the summer showers and then evokes the sad memories of the autumnal days of the marriage. Brígida's final separation from her husband coincides with the end of the concert marked by the crescendo of applause and the noise of the ax stroke that chops down the rubber tree.

In addition to the music, the water and mirrors—as in many Surrealistic works—help stimulate the memory. With Mozart, water assumes the form of a fountain; with Beethoven, the ocean; and with Chopin, rain and the waterfall. The mirrors are introduced at the same time as the tree, the windowpanes, and the river to which the narrow street slopes sharply. "It seemed like a world submerged in an aquarium"—this nightmarish vision is one of the few occasions in which the narrator ventures boldly into Surrealistic imagery. She is also relatively timid in her use of complex Surrealistic similes and metaphors. There are really only three worthy of note: "icy cold lilies," "necklace of birds," and "a sea of leaves." Nonetheless she does succeed in creating a Surrealistic mood to reflect the protagonist's growing anxiety and frustration.

The point and counterpoint of the personal drama and the concert, the stream of consciousness, the Existentialist note in the strained relations between spouses all call to mind literary influences or parallelisms but they do not explain why the story is so successful. The high quality of "The Tree" depends much more on the great sincerity with which Brígida reviews her tragic story. The nakedness that she feels when the tree is chopped down is the same nakedness that she has revealed to the reader during the whole story.

Ramón Ferreira

(1921)

Cuban. He was born in the province of Lugo in Spain, but at the age of eight, he immigrated to Cuba with his family. When he had to interrupt his studies because of the economic crisis in 1929, he went to Boston and took some courses in photography. Upon returning to Cuba, he won prizes for his early stories. In 1952, he published his first book, *Tiburón y otros cuentos,* which is considered the best and most representative Cuban volume of stories of the 1950s. Later he became interested in the theater, and three of his plays were staged: *Donde está la luz, Un color para este miedo* and *El hombre inmaculado.* In October of 1960, he resigned his position as head of the advertising department of General Electric and left Cuba. After several months in Mexico, he settled in Puerto Rico where he resumed working for General Electric. His story "Sueño sin nombre" won an honorable mention in the 1960-1961 competition of *Life en Español* and was published in the volume *Ceremonia secreta y otros cuentos de la América Latina.* A second volume of stories, *Los malos olores de este mundo,* written between 1952 and 1960, was published in Mexico in 1970. "A Date at Nine" first appeared in the 1952 collection.

A DATE AT NINE

She was standing in front of the mirror again, because it was already five in the afternoon, but she would not appear at the balcony until night fell, when the sun rolled behind the flat rooftops across the street.

She felt the cat around her ankles, and pushed it with her foot, making a friendly sound with her lips to soften the rejection, and then she saw the comb and her hair once again, like yesterday or last year, or always, because for such a long time now, so long that she couldn't remember, she could comb her hair without seeing her face, without feeling that it was she; and this way it was easier to go out on the balcony later and imagine she was someone else. Then the wait would be full of promise, and every man who looked up could desire her.

The thought made her smile, but when she looked for herself in the mirror to see the smile, it had already gone; and now she saw herself, once more as she had those few times, by chance or driven by a secret wish to find someone else in the reflection; but no matter how hard she tried to do so without fixing her eyes on any feature, this time she saw herself in the eyes of the image, and the image in her eyes; and suddenly the idea of appearing at the balcony lost its joy; except she still had time to forget it all if she could think of Daniel, as she always did when beset by fear; and she saw him once again, not the way she had had to see him since he married her sister, and they had gone away, but rather the way it was before, before everything, when they were standing together on the balcony waiting for nightfall and they discovered him for the first time down there, working in the cafe across the street, behind the bar, his eyes seeking their glance.

She would like to have stopped there, to have stopped her recollections at that point and once again live the days of those weeks she had appeared clutching the hope that when Daniel talked to her it would be to tell her that he loved her, because he had seen her on the balcony every sundown waiting for his glances, even though she pretended not to notice as she talked to her sister or laughed or looked elsewhere; but the illusion would not return, although she had kept it in her memory, because she saw Daniel once more strolling in the park and how she and her sister had passed by pretending not to see him, because that was part of the game, until he would take her hand to tell how long he had waited; and how it had been her sister who had taken her hand to tell her to wait for her on the bench, and she had sat down without thinking and had stayed there watching them stroll in the park and laugh, oblivious of how their laughter was hurting her; and how when they passed by her once more without even looking at her, she had gotten up and started to walk home, and how later in bed, with her head under the pillow she had heard the voice of her sister talking with their aunt:

"He loves me, he loves me and he's going to ask permission to visit me."

She heard the words once more, as if they had been hiding behind the mirror waiting for her to recall them, and although the cat came back looking for her leg, she couldn't do anything to chase her, because she felt herself tied to her memory, quiet and erect, searching for street noises, or anything that would take away the laughter which hounded her just like the day when she burst out crying before the two women who looked at her as if for the first time they had discovered she was alive, her aunt's squinting and sharpening the corners of her eyes before wounding her:

"Have you taken a good look at yourself, girl? Who's going to love you with a face like that. . . ?"

Neither her aunt nor her sister saw what happened to her face; but it was that day, that very instant, that she felt the ugliness surge within her for the first time and grow outward until it bathed her, as a cloud moving in front of the sun makes the shadows grow on a hill; and the shadow rose from her feet until it covered her face, leaving her motionless amid the waves, her face feeling like the body feels when it has fever: a piece of something that was alive, only because it was throbbing, like the starfish she had found on the beach, and had stepped on, because she knew it would not shout or grimace with pain, or bleed.

She shook off the memory and the comb went flying over the tiles, but her movement did not banish her surroundings; neither the noises from the street, which entered without brushing against her, nor the pressure of the cat against her leg, which also slipped away without looking at her when she bent over to touch it. It was too early to seek refuge on the balcony, because the sun was still painted on the railing and lit up her face; but when her aunt left for the park that night, she would put out the light and turn the radio on softly, and then she would stand on the balcony and would fall in love with all the men she liked, just like every night, and later, before going to sleep, she would again choose the one she would marry, and she would remember all the faces and would gradually eliminate them one by one until she would fall asleep with only one.

"Why are you standing there like an idiot? . . . the mirror isn't going to fix your face. . . ."

Not thinking about her wasn't enough to erase her from her life, nor could she forget her own face in order to become pretty again;

because her aunt knew that she was ugly, and it was enough to look at her, or to feel her presence through any of the objects that filled the room, in order to remember that she was nothing but that: a face; and once again she thought about a living thing that can be stepped on without its feeling pain, and she was surprised to see how much it hurts when one does not talk or shout or cry. When she leaned on the vanity, she touched the scissors with her hand, and the hard contact aroused her hatred, as if it could only reach her through a defensive object; and she remained still, awaiting the strength which might forever remove the fear of being ugly; if she could lift up her hand and extinguish the secret which glowed in her aunt's eyes. It was as if the words had not come from her, as if her voice was not pronouncing them, and she heard them surprised that they had been there all along without her knowing it, and that they could come out just like that, without thinking:

"You're the one to blame . . . you. You've made me ugly. . . ."

She didn't feel the hand on her face, because the pain in her head when it struck the tiles on the floor came first; and the balcony turned upside down and disappeared before her eyes.

She lay motionless, waiting for the tears, and she opened her eyes to let the tears slide out; but her aunt's face came closer with a new concern in her look, and that stopped the tears, because there was something in her aunt's eyes that made her feel horrified that she might caress her; and it must have been the repugnance that jolted her body that held back her aunt's hand and erased the caress from her eyes, which once again narrowed before disappearing above the tense body. It was at that moment that for the first time she saw her aunt as she really was; at that moment when she had felt the need to defend herself from the intimate gesture that was being extended to her; and now she would not have to wait for her to die, in order to draw near the coffin and look at her without fear; like the day her mother died, when she discovered, seeing her in that state, that she had never really seen her, and that you can live a whole life seeing a face without seeing the person, especially when that person does not want to be seen. Hatred jarred her body taking away her desire to cry; like the day her sister had broken her doll, and her crying had not allowed her desire for another one to return.

From the direction of the sink, she could hear the radio and amidst the noise of the plates, she tried to detect that of the door closing, or of the voice saying "so long," but it had not yet come; the steps fading away from the hall. She entered her bedroom and felt free from shame once again, as if she had never felt it, and she breathed avidly and then went over to the radio and turned it on to a music program that began to fill her loneliness with an intimate anxiety, as if it were all floating in that world of sounds, or as if it were one sound alone, without a body, without hands, without a face; and as she passed in front of the mirror she looked at herself again, because once more she could see herself as if the sun were at her back and she were a glowing silhouette. That is why she could now step out on the balcony and conquer all the men she wanted to.

The bar below was full of people, and even before she could realize that she had sensed it, she noticed that there was a new bartender; and when she saw him with his hands stuck in the sink and his face above the counter, she thought he was going to raise his eyes and discover her. Once more she could feel the onset of the cloud of shame and feel it climbing up her body and she clutched the railing with her hands in order to resist the impulse to cover her face; but it was already too late to defend herself, because his eyes moved up her body and remained fixed on hers.

The bartender's face smiled without showing his teeth, only with his eyes, while continuing to move his hands in the sink and without taking his eyes off the balcony; and she also smiled inwardly, pushing the cloud away from her face, from the neckline down, from around her breasts, encircling her waist and then from her thighs down toward her ankles, until she felt naked in front of him, while he kept caressing her with his eyes.

He made a gesture which she did not understand yet, and then he made it again and she didn't want to understand, and when he did it once more, she thought that it was probably eight o'clock and that she wouldn't see him until nine, and that the park bench by the trolley tracks would be empty and that it would be a good place to wait; while she nodded yes with her head and thought again about the whole hour she would have to wait, after having waited so long without realizing it; and she smiled again because she knew that that would make him smile; and it was as if suddenly

she were at his side and she needed to touch him, because only
that way would she understand why she was alive. When she made
a gesture with her hand, as if to caress him from afar, her aunt's
voice arrived like a knife cutting off the mood, and turning around
she sought her defiantly, in order to show that she wasn't afraid
of her anymore; but she saw only her shape beneath the shadeless
light bulb, deformed and with shadowy hollows below her eyelids.
That made her remember the blue porcelain shade that they were
selling at the Five and Ten, which she hadn't been able to buy
because she needed another nickel; and she kept staring at the
light bulb until it blazed within her eyes, blinding her completely.
Her aunt walked toward the balcony, and she let her go by without moving aside, already imagining her on the railing with her
body leaning out; and she tried to talk so she wouldn't discover
her secret; and she thought of Daniel and her sister, and how
they hadn't written for months; and she also thought about all
the things that can be said about neighbors or the radio or the
weather or the night or the heat; but instead she became totally
expectant, concentrating on what she was going to hear, because
she knew she would say it once more to disarm her, and that she
would always hear it, as long as she could see her eyes, smell her,
as she smelled her now, through the perfumed powder, as if she
were a part of her, from which she could not separate herself,
unless. . . . Her hand clutched her other wrist, trying to stop the
gesture which was growing and which was only waiting for the
thought; but once again it was her aunt's voice that contained
her, following her into the room, and then her body almost next
to her, and suddenly her hand on her shoulder and even her breath
on her neck mangling the words:

"*Don't be silly, no man's going to pay attention to you. It doesn't
matter what you feel . . . that doesn't matter when we're ugly . . .
ugly like you and me.*"

The words didn't touch her because what they said didn't matter, long ago, they had lost their meaning; the meaning was in her
aunt, in her living presence behind her, as if her memory had
fingers and were always touching her, in silence.

"*No man . . . none. Not for us.*"

She kept on talking in the darkness of the room, because she
had turned out the light and was undressing; and the room was

filled with moonlight which came in through the open balcony
door, without her being able to tell when she had stopped seeing
her aunt in order to merely imagine her, slowly, as if her eyes
were taking her out of a forgotten nightmare, of which only the
memory of fear remained, as if it were no more than that: a
memory without a cutting edge: sitting now on the edge of the
bed, in silence, feeling the floor for her slippers, and with her
eyes moist in the moonlight staring at her, waiting in the other
corner of the room for all that she felt to take form so she could
do something: shout or go out on the balcony and hurl herself off
or go down to the bar and ask him to defend her; an act of
rebellion which would tear her loose from her aunt, whom she
felt sticking to her like a spider web wrapped around her naked
body. She was afraid that she would speak again and that the
threat would acquire life, because as long as she remained silent
and went for a stroll and went to sleep, she could not move from
the stool nor cross the room toward the door and open it to the
light of the hall, because that bulb did not have a shade either
and it would spit the light in her face; and she wouldn't be able
to go down the stairs unless she could do it slowly, without fleeing,
letting the light from all the bulbs surround her without feeling
that she had to cover her face with her hands.

Her aunt's breathing began to fill the room, until she stopped
listening to the traffic and didn't even hear the cry of the newspaper boy beneath the balcony; because the breathing speeded up
until it dominated everything; and when the whistle came from
the street like a message without a destination, she didn't hear it,
riveted as she was to the threat that was growing between the
sheets.

She felt a sweet chill as if she had fallen in space knowing that
she would never reach the ground, and when her hands reached
up to her breasts in order to keep the chill there, she again heard
the whistle above the breathing, because she had understood;
and her hands squeezed hard until she felt pain, without being
able to prevent the chill from escaping. She got up trying not to
make a sound, without taking her hands from her breasts, and
when she approached the balcony, without going out into the
night, she leaned her head out groping with her eyes along the
wall across the street until she could make out the sidewalk, and

then she followed it searching for the corner, where the man under the streetlamp waited leaning against a Coca Cola sign. He raised his eyes as if he had felt her presence, and she felt glued to them, unable to retreat into the darkness of the room, because he had already straightened up and had once more made the gesture with his head, and she was unable to say no, or to go inside. He started to walk in the direction of the park, and when he got right across the street, he turned his head to look at her, and she said yes once more because she knew that now nothing could stop her if she could walk across the room and out into the hall. For a while she stood still, waiting for the moon to bounce into the far end of the room and show her the way to the door, and once her back was turned to the street, she again heard the breathing which was attached to the animal lurking between the sheets, stalking her. The beam of light under the door crossed her path like a razor blade's edge waiting for someone's face, and the breathing began to creep up to her, like a living thing that came from every direction, sinking its shadowy fingers into her face and twisting first the lines of her eyes and then those of her mouth, while every part of her softly yielded to the contact, allowing itself to become disfigured without crying out in pain or bleeding.

She walked up to the mirror, and her image trembled in the depths of the mercury, moving toward her, until it became her on both sides, eyes matching eyes, mouth matching mouth, but with only one side weeping. The contact with the mirror burned her face, and her hand resting on the table closed upon the scissors, because the breathing at her back was raking the shadows searching again for her face with its teeth.

The clock struck half-past. She stood up straight and raised her hand placing the scissors between herself and time, because she had just recalled the nights when she used to wake up startled upon hearing the half-hour chime and then lie there trying to guess if it was twelve-thirty or one or one-thirty; only now it was late even if it was only half-past eight, because there in the park he could get up at any minute and leave, looking back before turning the corner, and then never come back, even if she sat down on the bench and waited for half-past twelve or one or one-thirty.

The beam of light was still under the door and the breathing had returned to the bed, menacing there from between the sheets, not attacking, but waiting for her to get close to the door to clutch at her with its fingers, like every time that she came near a light or any object that reflected the memory of her face. With the tip of her foot she pushed a slipper under the bed, and now she realized that she was next to her aunt, who was sleeping, with her breathing throbbing the secret through her open mouth, and her throat swelling like a starfish lying in the sun waiting for the next wave, unaware of the danger of the foot which was rising calculating the violence of the blow before striking, because it knew the starfish would not grimace with pain, or shout or bleed. The hand fell slicing the shadows, and the arms at rest leaped up like the wings of a wounded bird. The body shook curling up in search of a scream, which came up hoarse as far as the throat and was choked off there, returning to the innards in search of new strength to pass beyond the point of the scissors; and then once again, and again, until it wore itself out and slowly yielded, like a drum that falls silent when the hands that beat on its skin stop rubbing it with the fingertips and remain motionless killing the sound.

With the heel of her shoe she kicked the other slipper which slid over the tiles toward the balcony; and that made her think that her aunt would not find them in the morning; and then standing up again, her body began to chill, except for her hands, which seemed to drip fire; and in the room without the breathing she heard her own breath close to her ears, and then, slowly, the street coming back, as if her memories went out in search of it to lose themselves in it, so that she might remain empty and without hatred, as she was before Daniel, and it would be the same as being fifteen again and standing on the balcony with a bow in her hair and her eyes full of a man down there. She started to walk toward the beam of light under the door, free from the fear of being wounded. The door opened and the light lit up the room, but she raised her head up to the light bulb at the end of the hall, and for a moment stood there, defiant, feeling the contact caress her face and slowly erase her ugliness from every part of her, without having to close her eyes or think of blue porcelain shades with which to cover all the light bulbs on earth. She walked unhurriedly until she got under the light and passed over her own shadow toward the other light at the bottom of the stairs; and on she went in search of the man who for years had been waiting for her in the park, while from the forgotten room there came the rhythm of a clock striking nine.

—*Translated by Gustavo Pellón*

COMMENTARY

"A Date at Nine," written around 1950 at the height of the Surrealist influence in Spanish American literature, differs from "The Tree" because of its bolder theme and style. Like so many characters in the works of William Faulkner, Tennessee Williams, and Arthur Miller with which Ferreira undoubtedly became familiar during his prolonged stay in the United States, the protagonist is psychologically abnormal. Sexually frustrated, she takes refuge in a world of fantasy. Her attitude of resignation at the beginning of the story is reminiscent of the protagonist of Tennessee Williams's *Glass Menagerie* but little by little, her *case* becomes more complex. She hates her aunt because the latter does not let her forget her ugliness. Then she realizes that her ugliness and her frustration are reflections of her aunt's. She feels inextricably identified with her aunt—as indicated stylistically by the somewhat confusing use of the pronoun "her"—and only by killing her can she become free.

While the action of "The Tree" occurs almost exclusively in the protagonist's memory, "A Date at Nine" is set in the present, a present clarified by a series of memories: her sister's marriage to Daniel, her mother's death, the broken doll, the blue porcelain lampshade and the half-hour chime marked by the clock. The stimulus for the memories is the mirror, which plays an indispensable role in the story as the constant reminder of the protagonist's ugliness. The latter's psychotic state is reinforced by the abundance of sensorial verbs which highlight her extreme sensitivity: see, feel, hear, smell, and touch. Similarly, the leitmotivs of light and darkness, street noise and the radio, and caresses assume major importance. The typically Surrealistic predilection for water appears in the symbolic use of the starfish and in the protagonist's feeling "bathed" by the first realization of her ugliness.

The knifelike similes and metaphors also reflect the protagonist's state of mental agitation which increases steadily up to the actual murder: "her aunt's squinting and sharpening the corners of her eyes before wounding her," "her aunt's voice arrived like a knife cutting off the wood," and "the beam of light under the door crossed her path like a razor blade's edge waiting for someone's face." At the moment of the murder, the use of the imagery becomes more intensified: the starfish, the wounded bird, and the drum.

After the actual murder, which is transformed into a nightmare by the images trembling in the mirror (a technique also employed in films), the narrator returns us to the world of reality with the mention of the aunt's slippers. When the protagonist thinks that her aunt will not be able to find them in the morning, the reader doubts for a moment that she has really killed her aunt, but her leaving to keep her date with the new bartender dispels that doubt and completes the frame initiated by the memory of her losing Daniel to her sister.

Rogelio Sinán

(1904)

Panamanian. Panama's leading literary figure for many years, Rogelio Sinán was born Bernardo Domínguez Alba on the island of Taboga, off the coast of Panama City. He studied at the Instituto Pedagógico in Santiago, Chile, and at the University of Rome. In 1938, he was named consul of Panama in Calcutta, India, and visited several parts of Asia. Upon returning to Panama, he organized the Department of Fine Arts in 1941 and founded the Biblioteca Selecta which published the works of the new Panamanian short story writers. He spent many years in Mexico in different diplomatic capacities. He has taught drama at the University of Panama. He has written poetry, plays, and a novel, *Plenilunio* (1947), but he is best known for his stories: "Todo un conflicto de sangre" and "A la orilla de las estatuas maduras" (1946), "Dos aventuras en el lejano Oriente" (1947), and "The Red Beret" in *La boina roja y cinco cuentos* (1954, 1961). Fourteen of his stories were published in 1971 by the Editorial Universitaria de Centroamérica under the title *Cuentos de Rogelio Sinán*. In 1977, Sinán was awarded the Ricardo Miró novel prize for *La isla mágica*.

THE RED BERET

"Look, Dr. Paul Ecker, your silence in no way corresponds to the goodwill we have shown in your case. You must understand that justice requires concrete facts. I cannot understand why you persist in maintaining your silence."

Paul Ecker stares into space with his green eyes. He feels hot. He perspires. The isochronic pauses of a large fan send him from time to time a little breeze that plays with the reddish hairs of his beard.

(. . . *There on the small island it wasn't so hot. It was pleasant sitting on the rocks at the edge of the sea . . . Your eyes sinking into the vast waters constantly in motion . . . watching the swift*

*sharks play . . . and feeling the caresses of the wind that sprays
your face with the mist of the waves. . . .)*

"Doctor, we have taken into account not only the well-deserved
prestige which you enjoy as a biologist and doctor but also the
numerous requests for clemency sent by the most famous men, by
universities, academies, museums. . . . Look at this arsenal of letters! . . . From London, Buenos Aires, Stockholm, Paris. . . . This
one from France asks us to recall that two years ago you had the
honor of presiding at the Great World Congress of Ichthyology
which met at the Sorbonne. . . . Do you remember? . . . Well, at
least you are smiling."

*(The Sorbonne! . . . Yes, there he met her . . . She looked like
an innocent schoolgirl, but what an enchantress! What most
seduced him was her short, little navy-blue skirt, and that red
beret slightly tilted over one temple. . . . "I only want your auto-
graph" she told him. "My name is Linda Olsen and I'm studying
at the Sorbonne. I'm interested in the sciences. I would like to
do wonderful things like Madame Curie. . . ." "What state are
you from?" "I'm from Atlanta.")*

Paul Ecker trembles, not knowing whether it is because of the
breeze from the fans or because of a thousand other reasons
which he tries to forget but can't.

The judge continues: "In these letters they implore us to be
merciful. . . . They mention your recent studies on various topics
in ichthyology and, at the same time, as John Hamilton says, the
great importance of your *Monograph on the Erotic Life of Fish*,
in which you relate the color changes that certain species undergo
during the spawning period to the phases of the moon."

*(. . . It was John Hamilton's fault that he met her again in
Pennsylvania. . . . "Don't you remember me? I'm Linda Olsen,
the girl with the red beret! . . . Some memory you have, Dr.
Ecker! Of course, I'm not wearing my red cap nor my blue skirt.
. . . How do I look with glasses? I seem more serious, don't I?
Perhaps that's why you haven't recognized me. . . . I will never
forget our walks in Paris. . . . Remember, in the autumn, how the
leaves were falling? . . . And the evening ride on the barges of
the Seine? And that happy afternoon at the top of the Eiffel
Tower? I have the picture at home, remember it? . . . All right,
Doctor, I don't want to bother you. . . . I must tell you, however,*

*that this meeting hasn't been accidental. . . . I've come to look
for you because in the papers I saw that the Institute of Pisciculture is sending you to study the fish of the Pearl Archipelago,
near Panama. . . . How marvelous! To spend an entire year enjoying the Tropics: the sea, the sun, the air, free and in close contact
with Nature! . . . You have to take me with you! I must be your
assistant. . . . Doctor, I beg you! . . . You see I have reasons for
making this request. . . . I'm desperate now. . . . Tell me if it's
not so. You know I graduated in Paris. . . . Well, that didn't help
at all. I'm still unemployed. . . . Yes, yes I can't deny to you that
I received an offer from John Hamilton! . . . What an insult!
Imagine that! Me, an assistant to a colored man. . . . Oh, sure!
. . . He's as famous as could be. . . . Don't tell me . . . I know
that he is a candidate for the Nobel Prize. . . . Yes, yes. . . . But
even so. . . . You understand, Doctor. . . .")*

The judge breathes uncomfortably. He wipes his bald head
with a damp handkerchief. And, making a great effort to maintain his calm, states: "All these things oblige us to be a little
indulgent . . . but we still need to know the whereabouts of Miss
Olsen. . . . When they found you on the beach at Saboga, you
seemed out of your senses. . . . You were wearing her red beret.
. . . Your clothes, torn to shreds, bore witness to your struggle
with the waves among the reefs. . . . Moreover, your hands and
feet were scraped. . . . The blood from a deeper wound had
stained part of your shirt. . . . As you regained your senses, you
gave us different and almost contradictory details of the mishap,
which encouraged the sailors on the Base to make up and circulate
the strangest versions of the event. . . . Some of them, when they
saw the little boat destroyed, thought that you were with Miss
Olsen when you were surprised by the storm. . . . Others, through
certain unconnected bits of information that you let out, assumed
that you had pushed Miss Olsen into the shark-infested water. . . .
There were those who believed it a suicide due to some kind of
emotional problem. . . ."

*(. . . Why would I murder her? Suicide? Impossible! The causes
and the events were very different; but how can I recount them
without arousing the suspicion that it was all the product of delirium caused by the boatwreck? . . . He could still hear the spine-
tingling laugh of the Haitian woman and he even seemed to hear
Linda Olsen's singing fluttering above the waves like a streamer. . . .)*

"Therefore we decided to hold this preliminary hearing in private. Only absolutely essential people will be present and then only when necessary. We haven't even extended passes to the gentlemen of the press. You understand: it would be a great embarrassment for science. We've been so informed by a cable from the Institute of Pisciculture. . . . Even Washington has sent a message which insists on the discretion that this trial requires, involving a celebrity like yourself. . . . However, we must not deny that certain procedures of routine formality. . . . Oh, only for the sake of appearances. . . . Seeing that, from what your colleagues at the University have confirmed, no indications whatsoever exist that don't bear witness to your innocence. . . . Nevertheless, you must help us. . . . Why do you insist on this absolute silence? I can't exempt you from testifying to the facts . . . the Law demands it, my dear Doctor. . . . Look, in order to help you, I'm going to refresh your memory. . . . One year ago, perhaps a year and a half, you arrived at the Saboga Military Base with good credentials and in the company of your assistant Linda Olsen. . . . You were going to explore the entire coastline of the Archipelago and continue studying, as this note from the Institute says, '. . . the spawning season of certain heteroclitic spawning fish, as well as the ovulation of the parthenogenetic females. . . .' The military commander of the Base offered you his most generous cooperation. . . . He assigned a launch to you and your assistant for your exclusive use as well as two helpers, Joe Ward, a black mechanic, and Ben Parker, a white sailor. . . ."

(. . . *Paul Ecker sees himself at the Saboga Military Base. The commander received him cordially and was delighted with Miss Olsen, who was again sporting her red beret. "You are going to be bored on that barren little island," he said. Surprised, Miss Olsen then asked him: "You mean we're not going to stay here?" And he, moving toward the door, answered: "No, you're not. Come with me to the porch." And, pointing to a nearby little island added: "See that little island with several rocks jutting out of the sea? That's where the laboratory is. Frank Russell began the research, but because he was a military doctor, he left for Asia not too long ago. I, myself, suggested the advantages of bringing a civilian. I assure you that you're going to be very comfortable. On the isle you will find a perfectly equipped cottage. It is kept clean by Yeya, a Haitian who takes care of the chickens*

*and raises a garden. She is a doddering old lady. They call her
'Voodoo'. She speaks a strange dialect, but she understands English. She will see to it that you get everything you need. And if
you still need something, you can send Joe to me. He's a good
boy. He'll live with you and he'll be very useful. There isn't
anything that he doesn't know. He's a cook, mechanic, sailor and
even—surprise!—a great banjo player. Ben Parker is a good helper
and plays the harmonica. He's Joe's partner. They always go
around together. . . .")*

The judge moves his corpulent body provoking a discordant
creaking of weak springs and worn-out parts of the chair.

"I don't know why, but, after a short time, you yourself requested the dismissal of both young men, isn't that so?"

Dr. Ecker trembles slightly. He looks at the judge pleadingly.
And, moving both hands in the air with a gesture of impatience,
he declares: "There are circumstances in which . . . you know,
don't you? . . . This is all so complicated that. . . . In order to
explain the facts and bring out clearly the exact story of what
happened, I would have to accuse persons who are perhaps innocent. . . ."

"If there is proof of that innocence, you won't hurt them at
all . . . and, moreover, I have already told you that we are holding this hearing with the utmost discretion. . . . You can be well
assured that nothing of what is said here will leave this courtroom.
Continue."

"Our first days on the isle were beautiful beyond description.
. . . The house was very comfortable. . . . While the old lady kept
it clean and took care of the cooking, Linda, the two boys, and
I wandered from reef to reef exploring the enchanting coastline.
. . . I couldn't possibly describe the magical feeling that came over
us in that tepid atmosphere of light, color, and the songs of birds.
. . . I, foolish as I was, wasted my time, you might say, getting
excited over the many discoveries of a purely scientific type. Ben
and Joe, the two young men, had to accompany me, lugging my
equipment. That apparently kept them occupied; but, she, in the
plenitude of her explosive adolescence, languished away from
boredom. . . . At times she followed us collecting conches and
snails, but she preferred to roam among the trees. And it was
because she didn't want to stay in the house without us; she felt

a certain distrust for the old lady. . . . Actually it was more a kind of repulsion, disgust, and vague fear. In the afternoons, after finishing work, I used to take long romantic strolls with her.

"I must inform you that I never thought about the possibility of an idyllic love affair. It would have been ridiculous, do you understand? . . . My age and the project on which I was working placed me in a certain position as her tutor. . . . So that for reasons of professional ethics and, above all, because of my constant state of ecstasy, my being distracted and absorbed in my research, such a thing could not. . . ."

Ecker suppresses a grimace that reveals a slight annoyance. The judge realizes that he has struck a raw nerve. Almost unconsciously he presses a buzzer.

"Relax, Doctor."

And, as the orderly enters, he wipes his face while he tells him: "Bring us some cold water."

Dr. Ecker again fixes his eyes on the distant green fields in his memory.

How to make that obese man with the slimy skin understand what the reefs meant to them. . . . How to make him infer that it had a certain Epicurean flavor like that of an ancient ecologue, of a pagan pastoral of a tropical, bucolic symphony? . . .

(. . . *Overcome by the delightful scenery of the little island, blinded by the great solitude that surrounded it amidst the sea and the sky, and obsessed by Linda Olsen's cheerful effusiveness, Paul Ecker awoke into a world he had never imagined; he underwent a kind of magical metamorphosis, and, upon leaving the cocoon which had made him seem severely scientific, he suddenly felt the solar brilliance and the exciting fragrance of the waves. . . . He tried in vain to hide himself in the cells of his rational thoughts by clinging obstinately to science. No matter how much he concentrated on the analysis of certain epiphenomena like that of the eels which change color while in heat, or at the moment of proving that the pituitary glands secrete the hormones . . . he would hear Linda Olsen's voice from above the trees, or from beneath the waves, and he would conjure up a glimpse of her red beret. . . . Paul Ecker recalled several steep rocks in the form of steps among which the sea left small pools where Miss Olsen used to bathe. . . . Once she fell into one that she couldn't get out of because the edges were too slippery. . . . He heard her screams and, thinking about Andromeda attacked by the monster, he rushed to rescue her. . . . He had to take her out naked as she was—damned shyness!—after countless attempts and dangerous slips. . . .*

That night Linda Olsen joked and laughed in the moonlight testing his virility. Finally the moment arrived when his blood suddenly began to boil. . . . He felt himself sinking into a deep abyss. . . . And that night it was Andromeda who devoured Perseus. . . . From then on. . . .)

A greedy fly is caught on the blades of the huge fan.

The fat-cheeked custodian of the law fans himself.

"They say that Linda Olsen was going to have a child, isn't that so?"

"Of course."

"All that as a result of. . . ."

"Of what? . . ."

"Of your love affair. . . ."

"I don't know what you're referring to."

"Well, in short, it has almost been proven. . . ."

"That the child wasn't mine."

"What are you saying, my dear Doctor!"

"I believe I have told you that Miss Olsen roamed from one end of the island to the other, teeming with life, full of youth, dazzled by its magical enchantments. I couldn't stay with her all the time . . . you understand. . . . I was devoted heart and soul to watching over the heteroclite ovulation of the fish in the pools and among the reefs. My rigid habits put a strict wall of austerity between us. . . ."

(. . . On the other side of that wall, everything was a barbaric eclogue, pagan liberty in which he would lustfully leap like a satyr after a nymph in heat. . . .)

"How can you explain then that Linda Olsen? . . ."

"Allow me to tell you. . . . Convinced that I wasn't the type her youthful fancies needed, she, in turn, enticed Ben and Joe with the pretext of accompanying her to look for fruit. . . . I didn't see anything wrong in that. . . . I recognized that it was typical of adolescence. . . . It seemed to me at first that Miss Olsen enjoyed flirting with Ben Parker. . . . That was normal, given her resentment against colored people. . . . In fact, I noted that Ben and Linda would frequently get lost. Nevertheless, I could perceive that after a little while Ben Parker began to avoid her. . . . From then on (very strange indeed!) she used to seek out Joe for her games and outings. . . . It seemed to amuse her because I would hear her laugh heartily. . . . I was also surprised by how spruced up the Negro Joe began to look and by how he would sing plaintive ballads in the moonlight accompanying himself on the banjo. I even remember one of them that undoubtedly had an amorous intent. . . .

> *What a pretty red cap,*
> *little cap of mine,*
> *ocean oh so blue . . .*
> *When I see it I feel like eating*
> *a watermelon*
> *from South Carolina. . . !*

"One afternoon, I remember it very well, I was examining some kind of teguments under the microscope. . . . I was getting drowsy because of the sultry heat, when I heard Miss Olsen shouting. I thought that perhaps a coral snake had bitten her or maybe a tarantula. . . . As I peered out, alarmed, I saw her come running, disheveled, shouting. . . . 'Help! I've been raped! . . .' I noted that the Negro Joe, crazy with panic, ran down, almost flying, toward the bay. . . . I rushed down through the ravine in order to demand an explanation, but he managed to get aboard the launch, whisper to Ben Parker; and they both took off. . . . Without losing a minute, I climbed toward the promontory in order to signal with the semaphore notifying the Base, but surprisingly, incredibly, it was at that moment that Miss Olsen, very meekly, and apparently calmed down, drew near to me and begged me please not to give the alarm. . . . She explained to me that a scandal could hurt her. . . . She preferred that the attack go unpunished. . . . I, who had thought her all full of prejudices, felt the deepest respect for her; I resolved to protect her, help her and even offer her my name, since her attitude meant for me, an indication of full maturity and good sense. . . . From that afternoon on, seeing that she was upset, I decided to distract her and I tried to interest her again in the scientific pursuits she had abandoned, why, I don't know. . . ."

"Excuse me: Ben and Joe didn't return to the island?"

"No, certainly not. . . . When the commander came to investigate. . . ."

"What story did they invent?"

"They had led him to believe that I desired to be alone. Of course, I preferred to confirm their version. . . . And I even told the commander that since it was now time for the spawning season, I prohibited his men from coming near the island because they would frighten the fish and might even interfere with the spawning. . . . When he tried to insist, I assured him that 'Voodoo' was capable by herself of taking care of the house chores. . . . From then on, there were no more distractions and we devoted ourselves completely to the cultures and to the careful observation of the water. . . . The Haitian lived apart from us, and we saw very little of her; above all because she spent her time fishing out at sea. She sailed a fragile sloop that seemed like a nutshell among the waves. . . . It was then that Linda seemed to realize that in her belly. . . ."

"The child! Then it was the Negro's?"

"I can only tell you that it was hers. I was going to recognize it as if it were mine, but things took a different turn."

Dr. Ecker stops to listen. He thinks that he can hear in the distance a mysterious song that seems to surge up from the waves and once again he hears the Haitian's infernal outburst of laughter which constantly pursues him.

The judge insists: "And in short, you weren't sure whether the child was yours or the Negro's. I know for a fact that you and she. . . ."

"Exactly. She and I. . . . You understand. That's what causes my state of mind, my doubts. Above all, because a precedent exists in my life which made me foresee difficulties. I refer to . . . I don't know if I have spoken to you of my first divorce because of a genetic deficiency. . . . My father-in-law, who was rich and obsessed with those idiotic ideas about lineage, wanted at any cost a perfectly healthy grandson, robust, and strong, who would inherit the family name and fortune. A child was born, male, but disfigured, deformed, hideous. . . . Fortunately, he only lasted a few hours. . . . A study was made of my family's clinical history and they found. . . . You know. . . . It's not necessary to dwell upon these things. My father-in-law forced me to yield my place to a stud of unquestionable fecundity. . . . To that initial failure I owe my honors in the scientific field. . . . Aware of the opprobrium of my destiny, I preferred to take refuge in my books and I denied myself the pleasures of a family. Why persist knowing that my children would be born defective? . . . That's why, on the little island, I tried to stay away from Miss Olsen. . . . However, things don't always turn out the way we want them to. Loneliness at times precipitates us into the arms of lust. . . . And so it happened that she was expecting a child that she supposed was mine, one that would be full of life, gorgeous, beautiful. . . . I, unsure of its paternity, was distressed. . . . My anxiety grew as the date of birth approached. . . . It was a dilemma without a possible solution, because if I deluded myself into thinking that it was mine, my thoughts turned to monsters, abnormal human beings, freaks; and if I imagined that it was the child of the Negro, just think! A secret hope comforted me at times, the possibility that, perhaps the beautiful setting of the island could have exercised some beneficial influence upon the gestation of the baby. . . . Only for that reason or perhaps because of my scientific interest, I didn't try to undo what was ordained by Nature. What terrified me most was that Linda might abandon me if she learned about my flaw; therefore, if I had to choose between the two possible births, I preferred that of the Negro. . . . Linda Olsen asked me to take her to the base so that she could be properly attended. I promised her I would, but I was determined to perform the delivery myself on the island, without annoying witnesses. I had decided to anesthetize her so that she wouldn't know the truth until the opportune moment. . . . Such was my impatience that the days and the months seemed longer to me. . . . There were still about seven weeks left when I began to think that maybe my calculations were wrong, since her suffering seemed excessive to me and the bloated stretching of the skin. . . . I forgot to tell you that as the period of pregnancy progressed, Linda fell prey to peculiar whims. . . . She loved to spend hours on end submerged in the sea; and in spite of her almost monstrous, obscene shape, she refused to wear a bathing suit alleging that she couldn't stand it. . . . At meal times,

she would show signs of the most complete lack of appetite. . . .
However, later I would catch her eating oysters and other shellfish
raw. . . . That night, the thunder and lightning had frightened
Linda Olsen. I saw her in a terrified state. She was afraid of dying
on the island. . . . And, now blinded by the fear of death, she
called to the Haitian to help her die in peace. . . . I had realized
that the black Voodoo woman, during my absences, indulged in
occult practices in order to alleviate Linda's pains. . . . The storm
howled under the heavy lashes of the rain. . . . Twisting and
turning, the pregnant girl groaned, tormented by the most atrocious labor pains. . . . I, who was going insane because of the
strain on my nerves, chose (there wasn't any other way out) to precipitate the birth in order to save Linda. Otherwise, I was quite
sure that, even if it was still one month away, her organism couldn't
endure. . . . Driven on by the most heartbreaking and feverish
desperation, I decided to operate. . . . I gave her an injection. . . .
After a short while she entered into a deep sleep. . . . In that state,
it was finally born. I don't want to remember it. . . . It was a
deformed thing, dead, limp. . . . Fearing that Linda Olsen might
realize the truth upon waking up, I ran out into the still stormy
night and hurled the monster into the sea; thus obliterating all
traces or vestiges of its ugliness. Since then my nerves have been
shattered. . . ."

"You mustn't worry. The important thing was to save Linda
Olsen."

"And I did save her, but fearing that if she learned the truth
she might abandon me, I chose to invent the lie of a black baby.
'Where is it?' she shouted at me. 'I want to see it!' Not knowing
how to lie to her, I got myself so tangled up that in her eyes I
turned into a common murderer."

(. . . *Paul Ecker shudders. . . . He opens his eyes unusually
wide as if frightened by a strange vision. He thinks he hears the
Haitian's outburst of laughter again and the mysterious song of
the hurricane. The immense sea spreads out before his eyes, and
he seems to see Linda's head with her pupils fixed as if in a trance,
rising from the waves. Only Ecker hears her voice that says: "I
don't like Negroes. . . . I can't help it. . . . It's something that I've
carried in my blood since I was little. . . . A family defect which*

it's useless to discuss. . . . Nevertheless, I confess that Joe Ward was not in the least responsible for our problem. . . . If anyone is to blame it's me. . . . I lied to you, Paul Ecker, deliberately in a moment of thoughtlessness. . . . That is to say, there wasn't really any lie, but rather a misunderstanding. . . . What is certain is that the setting of the island bewitched me, transformed me, making me see myself as different from the person I used to be. . . . For me, a poor victim of social inhibitions, that was a miracle of freedom. . . . On the island there were no prejudices that might tie me down. . . . I undid my chains and felt completely relaxed wanting to shout, to plunge myself wholly into the delightful setting. . . . Everything on the island seemed to me like a miracle of Nature . . . the colors of the sea; the happy interplay of foam and gulls; the singing of the birds; the splendor of the light; the exuberance of life; the midsummer dry heat; and the penetrating odor of the earth after a storm. . . . Everything spoke of love, everything was a pagan hymn that flooded me like a voluptuous, lascivious whirlpool. . . . My youth was on fire. . . . My young body consumed itself in a dazzling delirium. . . . That's why, enjoying my movements to the fullest, I frolicked barefoot under the rain. . . . I wanted to be a note in the great song of Nature. . . . With what pleasure I longed to make up for the life left behind. . . ! That's why I gave myself without any hesitation to the blond Parker. . . . I did it simply like the songbirds and the birds at sea. . . . Ben, on the other hand, was dazzled only momentarily. . . . He thought about the consequences and, terrified, didn't want to come near me anymore. . . . He shunned me. . . . I, however, desired him without asking for any commitment. . . . I wanted to satisfy my thirst, because it was already too late to curb my impulse. And, determined to overcome his fears, I planned to make him jealous by flirting with Joe. I'm not going to deny that, although I feel repugnance toward Negroes, I didn't mind flirting with Joe. In fact, I enjoyed it. . . . I was delighted by his strutting and the amusing things he would do and say. Radiating youth and strength, he had white teeth and had a charming, infectious laugh. . . . The atmosphere of the island and the salty fragrance of the breeze made me see him as a beautiful black Apollo. . . . I began to realize that I was in danger of giving in because he was already hinting at it. . . . Seeing himself desired, he let himself fall into the devouring trap. . . . One after-noon (Ben Parker was waiting for him in the launch, but Joe preferred to play with me) I was throwing him fruit from a tree when suddenly a bumblebee buzzed near me. . . . Frightened, I tried to climb down from the tree and slipped. . . . Joe, moving closer, caught me in his arms and kissed me on the mouth. . . . I felt a kind of whirlpool was dragging me down. . . . Just at the point of falling, I let loose a scream and fled terrified. . . . When you, Paul, came out, I felt ashamed because I didn't want you to think that I was a silly little girl, so without thinking I shouted hysterically: 'Help! He's raped me!' . . . Poor Joe! Overcome by panic, he ran down the hill and, casting off, headed toward the base accompanied by Ben Parker. . . . Then, they both agreed that they didn't want to return. . . . The Negro said that he had seen ghosts on the island. . . . Undoubtedly what he really foresaw were the gallows and the specter of a lynching. . . . The speed with which you rushed out to defend me and your minute atten-tiveness, apart from your offer of marriage (that I didn't under-stand at first), drew me closer to your life, to your studies. . . . Then, when I realized that I was going to be a mother, I hastily accepted your marriage proposal. . . . That the child was Parker's, there wasn't any doubt; but what did that matter. . . . I knew that you were enchanted. . . . I would marry you, and the baby would have a more suitable father than the blond sailor. . . . When I became sick . . . I remember that that night it was rain-ing terribly hard . . . a thousand bolts of lightning flashed . . . and the thunder and the clamor of the sea terrified me. . . . Then, that was all I knew. . . . when I woke up, it was already dawn. . . . I thought about my daughter. . . . I don't know why I thought it was a girl, with her pretty little face and her little arms that I would kiss. . . . Would she be exactly like Ben? . . . I opened my eyes . . . I found myself alone in the room. . . . I thought: 'Where can Paul Ecker and my little girl be?' I called out. There was no answer. Suddenly I heard your steps. I waited anxiously. You entered. . . . What was the matter with you? I saw you were worried, your clothes were wet, your face was overcast with gloom. 'Poor Paul!' I thought, 'surely he has worn himself out.' You

approached my body with infinite sweetness; you kissed my tem-
ples; you spoke to me of your offer of marriage and you even
told me that now only a short time remained before the trip back
to Philadelphia. . . . I, of course, only insisted on seeing the baby,
but you paid no attention to me. . . . You continued talking, as
though nothing. . . . When, now suspicious, I urged you to show
her to me, I saw you hesitate. First you claimed that you did every-
thing possible to save her. Then, taking pity on me, you told me
that she was a little black girl. . . . That lie made me see the light.
It gave me a clear picture of the crime. . . . I saw at once that
you had killed my little girl because you were jealous of Ben
Parker. You knew very well that it was his. . . . You murdered
my child, my beautiful, lovely little baby! . . . Murderer, mur-
derer! . . .")

The judge impatiently raps the table with a pencil, in order to
get the attention of the accused.

Then, with great patience, he pontificates: "The circumstances
of the wreck and perhaps the blows you received have made the
facts become deeply engraved in your mind. You have exaggerated
them to the point of creating, in your conscience, an annoying
guilt complex. However, what you did that night was normal.
Who is going to accuse you of not preserving a fetus? . . . What I
want to know are the motives that compelled you to set out in a
fragile boat, during the storm, with Linda Olsen. I first thought
that, since you considered yourself incapable of operating on her,
you wanted to take her at any cost, to the base, but there must
have been a different reason, wasn't there?"

(. . . How could he explain to the judge the great truth, if the
closer he drew to it, the less real it seemed to him? And he himself
began to doubt what he had experienced with his own hands, in
which there still lingered the sensation of the miracle. How could
he make him understand without any proof that that extraordinary
marvel wasn't an illusion of his senses? Paul Ecker well knows that
if he declares the truth as he knows it, they will bring in a psychia-
trist to examine him. Nevertheless, that's all he can think of.
That night, while the storm displayed hellish lights and noises,
he, yearning to find out the truth and tired of seeing Linda suffer
so long, resolved to put her to sleep. . . . At that moment, the

*strange mystery emerged. . . . He saw a fine little face, very deli-
cate, pink and such impeccable smooth, little arms. . . . He felt
such joy that he almost neglected the child as it was being born.
. . . And he was all ready to hold the baby in his hands, to feel
it his very own, perfectly healthy, when it jumped, flipped its tail
and bounced on the bed. . . . He stood paralyzed, with ecstatic
hope as if on his next moves, the peace of the world might depend.
. . . What wiggled about in front of him on the sheets was a living
myth: a pink fish like a beautiful barbel, but with a human torso,
with fidgety little arms and with a cherubic little face. . . . That
thing with feminine features had all the appearance of a mermaid.
. . . He had admired them in works of art, in poems. . . . He still
remembered the divine hexameters of the Odyssey; but it never
occurred to him that a daughter of his. . . . Holy Moses! . . . From
what mysterious mating did it originate. . . . He remembered
that, when Ben and Joe left, that is, when Linda regained her
eagerness for research, one morning, with the first light of day,
they were going to bathe among the rocks, when she called to him
signaling from a ledge. . . . The anxiety of her gestures made him
suspect the magnitude of her discovery. . . . He dressed quickly
and, upon reaching the spot where she stood, they were both witnesses, from the rim, of a love scene that was a poem of Nature.
. . . An enormous fish with ostentatious colors was swimming in
the water. . . . The pearl-colored beast [which was a female]
rested on her fins, let her eggs drop toward the sandy bottom and,
after her mission was concluded, withdrew with a smooth rippling
movement. . . . After a little while, the graceful male arrived,
swam prudently over the roe and, accommodating himself for the
ritual ceremony, covered it with his whitish spray. . . . Once he
had satisfied his instinct, he very pompously moved away. . . .
The species was saved. . . . Dazzled by scientific passion, Linda
and he dove into the water in order to observe the ovulation from
close up. . . . Science should never have brought them together
like that. . . . The impression produced by what they had watched,
the warmth of the water, and the stimulating odor of that mixture. . . . Just thinking about it made his nerves twitch. . . . It
was a cry of the blood that they couldn't stifle. . . . It was Nature's
command. . . . And they succumbed surrounded by that gelatin-
ous substance. . . .*

Everything was perfectly clear: the little mermaid with its pinkish skin had oceanic ancestors. . . . It was the mating of fish and human being. . . . However, his passion for science predominated. . . . It was superior to his genetic failure. . . . And, forgetting the trick that destiny was playing on him, he thought about the transcendence of the act itself. . . . Nothing in the world could be more important than that scientific event. His name would fly on the wings of triumph, of fame, of genius. . . . Universities would offer him honors and decorations. . . . And he could even see his name on posters, announcing the glory of Paul Ecker, when he noticed that the baby mermaid was losing its energy, and was jumping less frequently as do fish on the beach. . . . He realized that the sea being its medium, it wouldn't take long for it to die outside of it . . . asphyxiated, in a final life and death struggle. . . . Oh, in that instant, he would have given anything to save it. . . . He picked it up in his arms with the greatest care and quickly ran toward the sea. . . . Already the first daylight was indicating the arrival of dawn and the hurricane had died down. . . . Only a light drizzle continued falling, persistently. . . . He plunged into the water almost up to his waist and submerged the mermaid ritually as though he were performing a baptism. . . . Little by little he observed it revive. And, upon seeing that its tail was now languidly lapping the water, he let it move about in order to see if it could swim. What a crazy notion! . . . He should never have attempted it. . . . The mermaid swished its strong tail, twisted and, although he tried to prevent it, it dove down swiftly. . . . For an instant he still perceived its shimmering in the transparent water and, upon definitely losing it, he was left in a daze. . . . He had let glory slip through his fingers and everything had happened so quickly that even Paul Ecker thought about all that as patches of mist in a dream. . . . How could he explain that mystery to Linda? How could he make her believe what he himself was already consigning to doubt?)

The judge insists: "If everything had happened as you describe it, why did you challenge the storm in that fragile boat with Miss Olsen? Wasn't she willing to resign herself to accepting reality?"

"Actually it seemed that she was resigned, that she thoroughly believed what I told her. . . . I treated her tenderly and had the Haitian come to take care of her. . . . She was still very weak and it was necessary to restore her with tonics and broths. . . . When she began to feel stronger, I accompanied her a few days on her walks, and, since the rains were now letting up, I continued my studies among the reefs. . . . It was then that I noticed the signs of a nervous breakdown in Linda which put me on the alert. . . . Linda was suffering an anguish whose causes I couldn't figure out . . . sea phantoms besieged her in scary nightmares. . . . The world of dreams became, for her, a torture chamber from which she would free herself by waking up with shrieks of terror. . . . She didn't dare fall asleep, because she would see herself encircled by fish-shaped monsters that whirled about in a strange round of laughs, songs, foam and flips of their tails . . . ; a kind of protean carousel with accelerated rhythm in whose vortex she seemed to fall until she would sink into slimy substances of such intense cold that it paralyzed her legs. . . . I had to rub them because they fell asleep on her and she maintained that they were one big piece of ice. . . . The old Haitian diagnosed it as a kind of rheumatism owing to the fact that Linda Olsen would spend hours submerged in the sea, not only for the pleasure of the bath but that she had insisted on her nauseating habit of eating live mollusks. . . . This strange mania which I had previously supposed to be a whim of pregnancy grew so strong that it became intolerable for me. . . . Her great voracity didn't distinguish between seaweed and slugs. . . . I saw her gobble jellyfish to bits with the satisfaction of someone gulping down gelatin molds. . . ."

The judge is unable to repress a look of nausea.

Perplexed, he doesn't know what to say and explains: "As far as I can see, you hit upon a strange psychosis. . . . Fortunately, psychoanalysis. . . ."

"There is no better cure than the sun, the sea, and the fresh air! . . . What was serious was that her conflict was becoming more acute with manifestations of terror. . . ."

"Motivated. . . ."

"By an unknown power. . . . She explained that she felt attracted by an abyss of delightful transparencies. . . . That anticipation of pleasures with possibilities of agony would put her in contradictory fits of repulsion and attraction as occurs with the inexperienced adolescent who, feeling the erotic desire, applies the brakes for fear of guilt feelings. . . . That nebulous idea of her mental disorder acquired at times the seductive form of Tritons which inhibited her by singing obscenities when they weren't reveling with loud, drunken laughter. . . . That's why she was constantly eager to splash in the water among the waves; the feeling was so intense that at times she would get out of bed, sleepwalking and naked, and would half-run half-leap to the beach. . . . These different symptoms indicated to me that she was inevitably going to turn into a siren. . . . I had to catch up with her, wake her up, and return her to her bed. . . . In that state of ecstasy, she talked and discussed with me without realizing what she had done. . . . One night she confessed to me that she was enamored of the sea, and, seduced by it, she was certain that the moment would arrive when she would give herself to it completely. . . . Meditating on that, I came up with the Glaucus Complex which the newspapers have talked so much about. . . . You surely remember that that mythical hero ate certain herbs and he felt himself so attracted to the sea that he couldn't stop his blind impulse. . . . The poor fellow had no alternative but to submit. . . . Submerged in their waves, the Nereids transformed him into a Triton or something like that. . . . I, in my thesis, tried to demonstrate that such a complex occurs very frequently in our times. . . . The strange disease manifests itself in various levels from the brief, delightful ducking to the inevitable suicide, when the drowned person, with his eyes open, finally reposes on a shroud of algae. . . ."

The judge trembles slightly. Unhappy, he asks angrily: "If you knew that her mental disorder could reach such macabre extremes, why were you so neglectful? Why didn't you put a stop to it? . . . I think that the proper thing would have been to take her to the base."

"Not a chance!"

"Why not? Would you please explain yourself?"

"Simply because for me Linda was my only field of research. Oh, you don't know what that means for a scientist. . . . I wanted to draw my conclusions about the new complex, which would have been impossible without the careful study of its evolution up to the point of a cure. . . . And although that may seem to you a selfish reason, it wasn't the only one. . . . If I felt capable of curing Linda Olsen, how was I going to give up? . . . It would have been classified as a failure on my part. To allow other colleagues to work on the case would have seemed to me an absurdity, do you understand? . . . My complex theory would have fallen apart. That was the reason. . . ."

". . . Didn't you have any scruples about endangering a life? . . ."

"No! Not that! I swear to you! Who was more capable than I of taking care of her, above all when in her case, I didn't regard her as an ordinary patient but as something intimately bound to my affections? My passion for science was not that great that I would sacrifice Linda Olsen. Just the opposite. . . . I would have given my life for hers. . . . I wanted to cure her following a fixed plan. . . . What's bad is that we, at times, create symptoms that the patient has never imagined. . . . With all the reason in the world, it has been said that we doctors have invented illnesses. . . . In Linda's case, the Glaucus Complex fascinated me to such an extent that that's all I could talk about. Perhaps it was all counterproductive. . . ."

"What do you mean to insinuate by that?"

"I don't know. . . . Suppositions. . . . Perhaps it was my insistence that made her think that she could change into a mermaid."

"Continue."

"I actually saw in her the appearance of symptoms resembling Glaucus's. . . . For example, I noted that the paralysis of her legs was, to a certain extent, fictitious, seeing that she could move them. . . . But she did imagine them joined as if some invisible force was impending their independent movement. . . . Every once in a while, she would feel them with concern because she had the impression that her skin was acquiring a viscous quality. . . . There wasn't any doubt that the disease was progressing without my having found a way to alleviate it. . . .

"Meditating on the causes that produced her affliction, I remembered that on the night of the birth what most affected her was the explosive noise of the hurricane. The thunder and lightning, the tempestuous roaring of the sea, and the whistling of the wind instilled in her the idea of an ultimate cataclysm in which everything would sink. . . . It wasn't difficult, therefore, to imagine that a similar impression might be beneficial to her. . . . So, I awaited the squall with real excitement. . . . I don't know why it took so long in coming. . . . You well know that on the islands of the Tropics storms are frequent. The good weather lasts only a few weeks. . . . However, to my despair, there couldn't have been any better days than those. . . . I even got to think that the very elements were opposed to my plans. . . . And it really turned out that when I needed the fair weather to study the spawning, the rains fell so fiercely and torrentially that they muddied the water; and when I needed a hurricane, not even the most delicate breeze blew."

"Looking at it objectively, you weren't to blame," says the judge. "From what you've told me, I've been able to infer that Miss Olsen was the victim of destiny. . . . If, as you've probably observed, the facts interest me, it's not because I nourish any doubts about your innocence, but rather to free you from the guilt complex which depresses you. Continue, Doctor."

"Possibly I haven't told you everything in the proper order, but I remember one symptom that heightened my uneasiness. One morning I had gone a little way among the trees with the idea of hunting, when it began to rain and I decided to return. Arriving at the promontory, I realized that it was only a threat, a passing shower, and, absentmindedly, I stood contemplating the impetuous flight of the gulls. Suddenly I saw Linda Olsen, naked, hopping in the direction of the waves. . . . I hurried down to carry her back to her bed again. . . . The Haitian had come out with the same purpose, but when she saw the pirouettes that the sick girl made with every hop, she began to laugh with that brutal laugh characteristic of Negroes. Upon hearing her, Linda Olsen showed immediate signs of displeasure. . . . I thought that the mocking laughter might serve as a stimulus for the patient, feeling herself ridiculous, to stop hopping and to utilize her legs normally. . . . Thinking about this and moreover, affected by the Haitian's hilarity, I began to laugh also; so Yeya and I both besieged Linda with our loud laughter. . . . What I had predicted didn't happen, because without being able to stop herself, Linda lost her calm, and continued hopping furiously; feeling exhausted and now frantic, she threw herself to the ground, screaming, possessed by an attack of hysteria. . . . I ran over to care for her and, as I drew near, I noted that she was suffocating from lack of air. I don't know why I thought that the wisest thing was to carry her to the sea. . . . That's what I did, running, and, upon ducking her, I was amazed at her reaction. . . . Linda began to laugh happily as if nothing had happened and made strange splashing motions with her legs joined together. I no longer doubted that the sea, being the cause, could also be the remedy of her mental disorder. . . . Only by submerging herself in it, could she be saved unless the sea would prevail in that struggle and come to possess her totally. . . . And that's exactly what happened. . . ."

"The laughter of the Haitian didn't have any unpleasant consequences?"

"Yes. Unfortunately that mocking laughter was an ominous sign. As was to be expected, from that day on, Linda couldn't stand to have Voodoo near her. The stridency of that harsh laughter had hurt her sensibility so much that she heard it everywhere: in the roar of the sea, in the murmuring wind, and in the singing of the marine birds. At times she would awake and cover her ears with her hands in order not to hear the laughing and a mysterious song that distressed her although she was unable to describe it. . . . I myself, upon waking up one night in order to take care of her, thought I heard. . . . You understand. . . . By this time I felt exhausted. . . . I remember that after being freed from the heinous nightmare, she confessed to me that she was already feeling very close to her repulsive and total metamorphosis. . . . She had dreamed that she saw herself in the sea already converted into a mermaid and had experienced what it is to have your legs transformed into a tail. . . . 'I don't want that to happen!' she told me. 'Don't leave me!' And she threw herself on my neck crying. . . . The following day, much calmed down, she told me the strangest secret. . . . With a somewhat sly devilish look and a blush she told me that she had seen a strong Triton with long curls and a thick blond beard like mine. . . . On recalling the dream, she began to laugh happily. . . . It seems that the Triton courted her roughly. . . . He shoved her toward the beach without any delicacy whatsoever and there he possessed her snorting and biting ferociously. 'I still feel his bites all over my body,' she said."

The judge, annoyed, fans himself and clears his throat several times.

Ecker continues: "I don't know why I'm telling you all this. . . . It's better to forego the details and get to the awful ending. . . . May I have a drink of water?"

"Of course, Doctor."

Paul Ecker drinks.

"Then. . . ."

"The wind had changed, and the sea, slightly choppy, was a sure sign that the rains were already quite imminent. . . . It seems that the atmosphere, charged with magnetic currents, on those nights had excited Linda Olsen to the point of infuriating her repeatedly. She wanted to go out at any cost. 'I have a date with the sea!' she would shout. . . . I was already tired and I called the Haitian to help me care for her. . . . And that's the way things were when the night of the hurricane occurred. . . . The rain announced itself with a clamorous display of thunder and lightning. The whistling of the wind mixed with the crashing of the waves. . . . Everything led me to believe that a terrible hurricane was approaching. . . . I was observing Linda Olsen to see the effects that the atmospheric noise was having on her. . . . And I could corroborate that my diagnosis was not mistaken because I saw her calm down and I could even detect that she had forgotten the rigidity of her legs. . . . Upon seeing her sleep, I thought that she had passed the crisis, and seeing that the Haitian wanted to leave, I took the chance of letting her go. . . . 'There's no danger,' I told her, 'you can leave.' The Haitian explained to me that she wanted to leave because her launch was crashing against the rocks and she wanted to take it out from among the reefs. When she closed the door, I felt so tired that I stretched out in the hammock and got ready to smoke. . . . I don't think that I had time to light my pipe, because I fell fast asleep. . . .

"A dull thud awoke me with a start. The door was open. The clamoring fury of the hurricane was roaring and the wind was blowing the curtains wildly. I thought at first that perhaps the Haitian hadn't closed the door tightly, but when I looked for Linda, I didn't find her. I searched the house in vain. Suddenly I realized, I saw, the tragedy. I rushed toward the beach in the rain. The night was an inferno of sounds and lights.

"I began to shout: 'Linda Olsen! Linda Olsen!'

"Nobody answered me. . . . The old woman had brought her boat closer to the beach, but the wind and waves prevented her from bringing it out of the surf. . . . It kept on raining heavily and the storm played a concert of howls and thunder in the murky night. . . . I climbed up the rocks and by the light of a lightning bolt, I thought I saw Linda Olsen being carried out to sea by the current. Cupping my hands, I began calling her again. 'Linda Olsen!'

"It seemed to me I could hear her voice in the distance in a kind of distressed shriek.

"I ran to the beach, threw the old woman aside and got into the boat.

"'It's already too late!' she grunted.

"I clutched the oars and made the boat head out to sea. Struggling frantically against the wind and the fury of the waves, I drew closer to the spot in which I thought I had spied her. The light from the lightning allowed me to see her from time to time floating in the current but then I would lose sight of her. But now I realize that perhaps I couldn't have seen her nor could I have heard her heartrending cry. Perhaps it was only an illusion of my senses. In fact, when it seemed to me that I was getting close to her, I saw her further away. There was finally a moment when, with my strength drained, I lost consciousness. I don't remember having hoisted the sail nor if it was the current that dashed the boat to pieces against the rocks of the next island. Nor do I remember the moment when I put the beret on my head. Perhaps it was just when I left the hut. What I can never forget is that, owing to the wild fear that gripped me, or to the noise of the rain, I didn't stop listening for a single instant to the painful shrieking of Miss Olsen and a mysterious song.

". . . How did I get back to the beach? I don't know. Perhaps I walked around lost among the rocks until I collapsed on the sand. What is certain is that upon regaining consciousness, the dawn was already beginning to come up and the storm had subsided, but inside me I continued hearing the far-off echo of the song mixed with the deep resonance of the sea as if my entire soul had been transformed into a gigantic conch shell."

— *Translated by Dennis Seager*

COMMENTARY

In "The Red Beret," Rogelio Sinán utilizes both Surrealist and Cubist techniques in order to present two cases of abnormal psychology within a fantastic plot.

Dr. Paul Ecker, summoned before the judge, explains Linda Olsen's death by alternately speaking and remembering like the typical Surrealist character. Linda's psychological conversion into a mermaid is made to appear plausible by a carefully prepared set of background data. She accompanied Dr. Ecker on his trip to the island in order to study the spawning of the fish. One day, she and Ecker had intercourse in the very waters where they had just observed the spawning and fertilization process of two large handsome fish. When Linda gives birth, Dr. Ecker either kills the baby or lets it escape in the sea. The absolute truth about what happened is never revealed because the same reality is seen simultaneously, in Cubist fasion, from four distinct angles. Ecker tells the judge that he killed the baby because it had been born deformed like his child with his former wife. He told Linda that the child had been born black. She knew that that was impossible because she had never had intercourse with the Negro Joe Ward. Therefore, she thought that Ecker killed the baby because she had been born blonde, the daughter of Ben Parker. Ecker tells himself that Linda gave birth to a mermaid who slipped out of his hands when he took her down to the ocean to save her life. The author presents the four possibilities and, as in the Japanese movie *Rashomon,* the reader has to participate in the creative process choosing the most plausible one . . . or the most artistic one.

Mystery also surrounds Linda's death. When bathing in the ocean, she feels that her legs become paralyzed and she frolics in the waves. Ecker tries to cure her Glaucus Complex but on the night of the hurricane, he falls asleep and she escapes from the house and disappears in the ocean. Ecker looks for her in vain. The enigmatic character of the Haitian woman suggests the possibility that she had bewitched Linda. And Ecker, did he purposely let himself fall asleep?

As in the psychological stories of Rafael Arévalo Martínez, the language of "The Red Beret" is unartistic in the sense that the author does not attempt to create beauty through language. Actually, he needs the pseudoscientific style in order to make this exotic, fantastic, and enigmatic story more credible.

Juan Rulfo

(1918)

Mexican. One of Mexico's most enigmatic literati, he was born in Sayula, Jalisco, and spent his childhood on his grandparents' hacienda. In 1924, his father was killed; his uncle and other relatives were assassinated; his grandfather was hanged by his fingers during the Cristero Revolt. A few years later his mother died. He studied to be an accountant and has worked in the Office of Immigration, the Goodrich Company, and the Papaloapan Commission. He published his first short stories in the Guadalajara magazine *Pan*. His international reputation rests on only two slim but highly regarded volumes: the collection of short stories *El llano en llamas* (1953) and the novel *Pedro Páramo* (1955). For several years, he has been in charge of the publications section of the Instituto Nacional Indigenista and has collaborated in the Centro de Escritores Mexicanos, a writers' workshop that has provided year-long scholarships for some of Mexico's most promising young authors. For more than twenty years readers have been awaiting Rulfo's still unpublished second novel, "La Cordillera."

TELL THEM NOT TO KILL ME![1]

"Tell them not to kill me, Justino! Go on and tell them that. For God's sake! Tell them. Tell them please for God's sake."

"I can't. There's a sergeant there who doesn't want to hear anything about you."

"Make him listen to you. Use your wits and tell him that scaring me has been enough. Tell him please for God's sake."

"But it's not just to scare you. It seems they really mean to kill you. And I don't want to go back there."

"Go on once more. Just once, to see what you can do."

[1]From *The Burning Plain and Other Stories*, trans. George D. Schade, Pan American Paperback Edition (Austin: University of Texas Press, 1971).

"No. I don't feel like going. Because if I do they'll know I'm your son. If I keep bothering them they'll end up knowing who I am and will decide to shoot me too. Better leave things the way they are now."

"Go on, Justino. Tell them to take a little pity on me. Just tell them that."

Justino clenched his teeth and shook his head saying no.

And he kept on shaking his head for some time.

"Tell the sergeant to let you see the colonel. And tell him how old I am — how little I'm worth. What will he get out of killing me? Nothing. After all he must have a soul. Tell him to do it for the blessed salvation of his soul."

Justino got up from the pile of stones which he was sitting on and walked to the gate of the corral. Then he turned around to say, "All right. I'll go. But if they decide to shoot me too, who'll take care of my wife and kids?"

"Providence will take care of them, Justino. You go there now and see what you can do for me. That's what matters."

They'd brought him in at dawn. The morning was well along now and he was still there, tied to a post, waiting. He couldn't keep still. He'd tried to sleep for a while to calm down, but he couldn't. He wasn't hungry either. All he wanted was to live. Now that he knew they were really going to kill him, all he could feel was his great desire to stay alive, like a recently resuscitated man.

Who would've thought that old business that happened so long ago and that was buried the way he thought it was would turn up? That business when he had to kill Don Lupe. Not for nothing either, as the Alimas tried to make out, but because he had his reason. He remembered: Don Lupe Terreros, the owner of the Puerta de Piedra — and besides that, his compadre — was the one he, Juvencio Nava, had to kill, because he'd refused to let him pasture his animals, when he was the owner of the Puerta de Piedra and his compadre too.

At first he didn't do anything because he felt compromised. But later, when the drought[2] came, when he saw how his animals were dying off one by one, plagued by hunger, and how his compadre Lupe continued to refuse to let him use his pastures, that was[3]

---

[2] In the original Schade translation, "drouth."

[3] In the original Schade translation, "then was."

when he began breaking through the fence and driving his herd of skinny animals to the pasture where they could get their fill of grass. And Don Lupe didn't like it and ordered the fence mended, so that he, Juvencio Nava, had to cut open the hole again. So, during the day the hole was stopped up and at night it was opened again, while the stock stayed there right next to the fence, always waiting — his stock that before had lived just smelling the grass without being able to taste it.

And he and Don Lupe argued again and again without coming to any agreement.

Until one day Don Lupe said to him, "Look here, Juvencio, if you let another animal in my pasture, I'll kill it."

And he answered him, "Look here, Don Lupe, it's not my fault that the animals look out for themselves. They're innocent. You'll have to pay for it, if you kill them."

And he killed one of my yearlings.

This happened thirty-five years ago in March because in April I was already up in the mountains, running away from the summons. The ten cows I gave the judge didn't do me any good, or the lien on my house either, to pay for getting me out of jail. Still later they used up what was left to pay so they wouldn't keep after me, but they kept after me just the same. That's why I came to live with my son on this other piece of land of mine which is called Palo de Venado. And my son grew up and got married to my daughter-in-law Ignacia and has had eight children now. So it happened a long time ago and ought to be forgotten by now. But I guess it's not.

I figured then that with about a hundred pesos everything could be fixed up. The dead Don Lupe left just his wife and two little kids still crawling. And his widow died soon afterward too — they say from grief. They took the kids far off to some relatives. So there was nothing to fear from them.

But the rest of the people took the position that I was still summoned to be tried just to scare me so they could keep on robbing me. Every time someone came to the village they told me, "There are some strangers in town, Juvencio."

And I would take off to the mountains, hiding among the madrone thickets and passing the days with nothing to eat but herbs. Sometimes I had to go out at midnight, as though the dogs were after me. It's been that way my whole life. Not just a year or two. My whole life.

And now they've come for him when he no longer expected anyone, confident that people had forgotten all about it, believing that he'd spent at least his last days peacefully. "At least," he thought, "I'll have some peace in my old age. They'll leave me alone."

He'd clung to his hope with all his heart. That's why it was hard for him to imagine that he'd die like this, suddenly, at this time of life, after having fought so much to ward off death, after having spent his best years running from one place to another because of the alarms, now when his body had become all dried up and leathery from the bad days when he had to be in hiding from everybody.

Hadn't he even let his wife go off and leave him? The day when he learned his wife had left him, the idea of going out in search of her didn't even cross his mind. He let her go without trying to find out at all who she went with or where, so he wouldn't have to go down to the village. He let her go as he'd let everything else go, without putting up a fight. All he had left to take care of was his life, and he'd do that, if nothing else. He couldn't let them kill him. He couldn't. Much less now.

But that's why they brought him from there, from Palo de Venado. They didn't need to tie him so he'd follow them. He walked alone, tied by his fear. They realized he couldn't run with his old body, with those skinny legs of his like dry bark, cramped up with the fear of dying. Because that's where he was headed. For death. They told him so.

That's when he knew. He began to feel that stinging in his stomach that always came on suddenly when he saw death nearby, making his eyes big with fear and his mouth swell up with those mouthfuls of sour water he had to swallow unwillingly. And that thing that made his feet heavy while his head felt soft and his heart pounded with all its force against his ribs. No, he couldn't get used to the idea that they were going to kill him.

There must be some hope. Somewhere there must still be some hope left. Maybe they'd made a mistake. Perhaps they were looking for another Juvencio Nava and not him.

He walked along in silence between those men, with his arms

fallen at his sides. The early morning hour was dark, starless. The wind blew slowly, whipping the dry earth back and forth, which was filled with that odor like urine that dusty roads have.

His eyes, that had become squinty with the years, were looking down at the ground, here under his feet, in spite of the darkness. There in the earth was his whole life. Sixty years of living on it, of holding it tight in his hands, of tasting it like one tastes the flavor of meat. For a long time he'd been crumbling it with his eyes, savoring each piece as if it were the last one, almost knowing it would be the last.

Then, as if wanting to say something, he looked at the men who were marching along next to him. He was going to tell them to let him loose, to let him go; "I haven't hurt anybody, boys," he was going to say to them, but he kept silent. "A little further on I'll tell them," he thought. And he just looked at them. He could even imagine they were his friends, but he didn't want to. They weren't. He didn't know who they were. He watched them moving at his side and bending down from time to time to see where the road continued.

He'd seen them for the first time at nightfall, that dusky hour when everything seems scorched. They'd crossed the furrows trodding on the tender corn. And he'd gone down there⁴ to tell them that the corn was beginning to grow. But that didn't stop them.

He'd seen them in time. He'd always had the luck to see everything in time. He could've hidden, gone up in the mountains for a few hours until they left, and then come down again. Already it was time for the rains to have come, but the rains didn't come and the corn was beginning to wither. Soon it'd be all dried up.

So it hadn't even been worthwhile, his going⁵ down and placing himself among those men like in a hole, never to get out again.

And now he continued beside them, holding back how he wanted to tell them to let him go. He didn't see their faces, he only saw their bodies, which swung toward him and then away from him. So when he started talking he didn't know if they'd heard him. He said, "I've never hurt anybody." That's what he said. But nothing changed. Not one of the bodies seemed to pay

⁴In the original Schade translation, "he'd gone down on account of that."
⁵In the original Schade translation, "his coming down."

attention. The faces didn't turn to look at him. They kept right on, as if they were walking in their sleep.

Then he thought that there was nothing else he could say, that he would have to look for hope somewhere else. He let his arms fall again to his sides and went by the first houses of the village, among those four men, darkened by the black color of the night.

"Colonel, here is the man."

They'd stopped in front of the narrow doorway. He stood with his hat in his hand, respectfully, waiting to see someone come out. But only the voice came out, "Which man?"

"From Palo de Venado, Colonel. The one you ordered us to bring in."

"Ask him if he ever lived in Alima," came the voice from inside again.

"Hey, you. Ever lived in Alima?" the sergeant facing him repeated the question.

"Yes. Tell the colonel that's where I'm from. And that I lived there till not long ago."

"Ask him if he knew Guadalupe Terreros."

"He says did you know Guadalupe Terreros?"

"Don Lupe? Yes. Tell him that I knew him. He's dead."

Then the voice inside changed tone: "I know he died," it said. And the voice continued talking, as if it was conversing with someone there on the other side of the reed wall.

"Guadalupe Terreros was my father. When I grew up and looked for him they told me he was dead. It's hard to grow up knowing that the thing we have to hang on to, to[6] take roots from, is dead. That's what happened to us.

"Later on I learned that he was killed by being hacked first with a machete and then an oxgoad stuck in his belly. They told me he lasted more than two days and that when they found him, lying in an arroyo, he was still in agony and begging that his family be taken care of.

"As time goes by you seem to forget this. You try to forget it. What you can't forget is finding out that the one who did it is still alive, feeding his rotten soul with the illusion of eternal life. I couldn't forgive that man, even though I don't know him; but

[6] In the original Schade translation, "to to."

the fact that I know where he is makes me want to finish him off. I can't forgive his still living. He should never have been born."

From here, from outside, all he said was clearly heard. Then he ordered, "Take him and tie him up awhile, so he'll suffer and then shoot him!"

"Look at me, Colonel!" he begged. "I'm not worth anything now. It won't be long before I die all by myself, crippled by old age. Don't kill me!"

"Take him away!" repeated the voice from inside.

"I've already paid, Colonel. I've paid many times over. They took everything away from me. They punished me in many ways. I've spent about forty years hiding like a leper, always with the fear they'd kill me at any moment. I don't deserve to die like this, Colonel. Let the Lord pardon me, at least. Don't kill me! Tell them not to kill me!"

There he was, as if they'd beaten him, waving his hat against the ground. Shouting.

Immediately the voice from inside said, "Tie him up and give him something to drink until he gets drunk so the shots won't hurt him."

Finally, now, he'd been quieted. There he was, slumped down at the foot of the post. His son Justino had come and his son Justino had gone and had returned and now was coming again.

He slung him on top of the burro. He cinched him up tight against the saddle so he wouldn't fall off on the road. He put his head in a sack so it wouldn't give such a bad impression. And then he made the burro giddap, and away they went in a hurry to reach Palo de Venado in time to arrange the wake for the dead man.

"Your daughter-in-law and grandchildren will miss you," he was saying to him. "They'll look at your face and won't believe it's you. They'll think the coyote has been eating on you when they see your face full of holes from all those bullets they shot at you."

— *Translated by George Schade*

COMMENTARY

"Tell Them Not To Kill Me!" seems at first sight to be a belated manifestation of Criollismo. The protagonist is the same tragic peasant as in Jorge Ferretis's "Men in a Storm" and so many other of the so-called stories and novels of the Mexican Revolution. As in Ferretis's story, dialogue is abundant and the language has a distinctly Mexican flavor. Missing, however, are the phonetic transcriptions of the Mexican dialect and the corresponding lexical regionalisms. Actually, this is not a Criollista story. Because of its sophisticated experimental techniques and the greater individualization of the protagonist, it is more properly classified under Cosmopolitanism.

The profusion of simultaneous scenes with a rapidly changing point of view gives the impression of a Cubist painting. The story is structured on alternating dialogues, narrative, and recollections, with four different points of view: Juvencio's, his son's, the colonel's, and the omniscient narrator's. The four dialogues play a key role marking: the beginning (Juvencio and his son Justino) and the ending (Justino and his father's corpse), as well as the motives for both the crime (Juvencio and Don Lupe) and the punishment (the colonel, the soldier, and Juvencio). The dialogues are particularly effective because of the psychological barriers—and a physical one in the case of the colonel—through which the words must pass. The intervention of the omniscient narrator is almost imperceptible because his Hemingway-like pseudopopular style does not differ greatly from that of the characters. The sentences are brief and to the point, the vocabulary is simple, and verbs predominate. Juvencio's and the colonel's recollections, which are essential in reconstructing the plot, are presented through the omniscient narrator as well as directly, without the Surrealistic treatment of the subconscious.

The purpose of the technical experimentation in this story is not so much to challenge the reader to solve a difficult puzzle as it is to emphasize the tragic life of rural Mexico. Juvencio and the other characters are individuals but they could very well be fused into one in order to form the portrait of the long-suffering peasant. Juvencio has been identified with the land for sixty years. Over a question of grazing rights he killed his neighbor and spent thirty-five years in fear of reprisal. When his wife abandoned him, he did not even try to look for her. Nonetheless, his desire to continue living has remained strong, as expressed emotionally in the story's title, words that are directed first to his son and then to the colonel. Justino accompanies his father in his final hours but he hardly dares to intervene. He fears for his own life and thinks of his wife and eight children. His almost indifferent attitude in the face of his father's death contrasts sharply with the attitude of the colonel who felt his father's death more deeply because it occurred when he was a young boy: "It's hard to grow up knowing that the thing we have to hang on to, to take roots from, is dead." The colonel's desire for revenge does not allow him to forgive Juvencio but he cannot completely suppress his human compassion: "Tie him up and give him something to drink until he gets drunk so the shots won't hurt him."

The application of technical experimentation to a national theme is indicative of a closing of the gap between the avant-garde poets of the 1920s and 1930s and their contemporaries, the Criollista novelists and short story writers; and also between the Criollistas and the succeeding generation of Cosmopolitanites. For that reason, Juan Rulfo's volume of short stories *El llano en llamas* (1953) and his novel *Pedro Páramo* (1955)—like Miguel Angel Asturias's *El señor Presidente* (1946) and *Hombres de maíz* (1949) and Alejo Carpentier's *El reino de este mundo* (1949) and *Los pasos perdidos* (1953)—are considered among the earliest of the "new" Latin American prose fiction which was to develop into a "Boom" in the late 1960s.

Arturo Uslar Pietri

(1906)

Venezuelan. He has had a long and distinguished literary, teaching, political, and diplomatic career. Born and raised in Caracas, he belongs to the so-called Generation of 1928 which incorporated European avant-garde techniques into Venezuelan literature. Uslar received his doctorate in political science in 1929 and subsequently served as cultural attaché in Paris (1929) and as secretary of the Venezuelan delegation to the League of Nations (1930-1933). After the fall of Dictator Gómez, he held several cabinet-level positions in the government of General Medina Angarita. When the latter was overthrown in 1945, Uslar went into exile in the United States and remained there during the brief years of the Acción Democrática governments of Rómulo Betancourt and Rómulo Gallegos. He taught Spanish American literature at Columbia University from 1947 to 1950. He had previously taught economics at the Universidad Central in Caracas between 1934 and 1938. In the 1960s Uslar was a senator and an unsuccessful presidential candidate for a conservative party which he himself helped found. In the 1970s he was appointed head of the Venezuelan delegation to UNESCO in Paris.

Over a period of almost fifty years, he has published five volumes of short stories: *Barrabás y otros relatos* (1928), *Red* (1936), *Treinta hombres y sus sombras* (1949), *Pasos y pasajeros* (1966), and *Moscas, árboles y hombres* (1973); four historical novels ranging from the Conquest (*El camino de El Dorado* in 1947) to the Wars of Independence (*Las lanzas coloradas* in 1931) and up to the post-Dictator Gómez period (*Un retrato en la geografía* in 1962 and *Estación de máscaras* in 1964); and several books of literary criticism and essays analyzing some of his country's basic problems. His latest novel, *Oficio de difuntos* (1976), was one of a whole series of novels published in the 1970s on the theme of the Spanish American dictator by García Márquez, Carpentier, Roa Bastos, Aguilera Malta, Avilés Fabila, Ibargüengoitia, and others. "The Rain" was written in 1935 and appeared in the collection *Red* the following year.

THE RAIN

The moonlight filtered through all the cracks in the hut, and the sound of the wind in the cornfield was as compact and fine as rain. In the shadow stabbed by a bright sheet of metal, the old man's hammock was swinging slowly. Rhythmically the knot in the cord squeaked over the wood and there could be heard the short, wheezy breathing of the woman stretched out on the canvas cot in the corner.

The skimming of the light breeze over the dry leaves of the corn and the trees sounded every minute more like rain, bringing a damp echo to the dense, earthy atmosphere.

The sweating and sleepless woman perked up, half-opened her eyes, tried to see by the streaks of lightning, peered a moment, looked at the still sluggish hammock, and cried in a tart voice, "Jesuso!"

She lowered her voice, awaiting an answer, but meanwhile ran on complainingly: "He sleeps like a dog. The good-for-nothing! Lives as if he were dead. . . ."

The sleeping man came to life at the call, stretched, and asked in a tired voice: "What's the matter now, Usebia? What's the fuss? Even at night, you can't let a man rest!"

"Be still, Jesuso, and listen."

"Heh?"

"It's raining, rain-ing, Jesuso; don't you even hear it? Why you've even gone deaf."

With an effort, ill-humored, the old man got up, ran to the door, opened it violently, and received on his face and half-naked body the silvery light of the full moon and the fiery breath of the wind that was rising from the slope of the cornfield, swaying the shadows. All the stars were shining. He held out his hand, without feeling a drop. He let the hand fall, slackened his muscles, and leaned on the doorframe. "See your shower, crazy old woman? You try a man's patience."

The woman kept gazing at the great brightness that came in through the door. A swift drop of sweat tickled her cheek. The steamy heat flooded the hut.

Jesuso closed the door again, walked calmly to the hammock, stretched out, and once more the creaking of the wood could be heard as the hammock rocked. One hand hung to the ground, sliding along the dirt floor.

The earth was as dry as a rough skin, dry to the depths of the roots, already turning into bones; floating over the earth there was a fever of thirst, a panting that tormented every human being.

The clouds dark as the shadow of a tree had gone away, losing themselves behind the last of the highest hills; gone away like sleep, like rest. The day was burning. The night was burning, lit up by fixed, metallic lights. On the hills and stripped valleys, with gaping cracks wide as mouths, people were sluggishly wasting away, obsessed by the glistening mirage of rain, looking for indications, searching for signs. Over the valleys and the hills, in each shack, the same words were being said over and over; "The carrao sang. It's going to rain. . . ."

"It won't rain."

It was a kind of litany of anguish.

"The wind blew from the valley. It's going to rain."

"It won't rain."

They repeated it as if to give each other strength in the never-ending wait. "The cicadas stopped chirping. It's going to rain."

"It won't rain, Jesuso, what's going to happen?"

Jesuso looked at the shadow moving with difficulty on the cot, realized that she meant to increase his suffering with her words, opened his mouth to talk, but drowsiness had already taken hold of his body, he closed his eyes, and felt himself dropping off to sleep.

With the first light of morning, Jesuso went out to the cornfield and began to make his rounds slowly. The glassy leaves crackled under his bare feet. He looked at the long rows of corn on both sides, yellow and parched, the few bare trees, and on top of the hill, an intensely green vertical cactus. From time to time he paused, took in his hand a dried-up beanpod, and crushed it slowly, making the wrinkled, ruined beans jump between his fingers.

As the sun climbed higher, the sensation and the color of dryness increased. Not a cloud could be seen in the flame-blue sky.

Jesuso walked along aimlessly, as he did every day—the planting was already lost—following the paths through the field, partly from unconscious habit, partly to get away from Usebia's bickering.

From the hill, the entire landscape was a single shade of dry yellow extending over narrow valleys and bald hills on whose slopes spots of chalky dust marked the road. There was no movement of life. The wind was still, the light dazzling; the shadows were barely growing smaller. The world seemed ready to catch on fire.

Jesuso was walking slowly, his eyes on the ground, pausing now and then like a trained animal, talking to himself from time to time. "Heaven be praised! What's going to become of poor folk with this drought? This year, not one drop of water, and last year in the rainy season it rained too much, the river rose, flooded the bottomland, and carried off the bridge. . . . There's no sense to it. . . . It rains because it rains . . . and it doesn't rain because it doesn't."

He passed from the monologue to a barren silence, advancing idly, his eyes still on the ground, when without seeing anything, he sensed something unusual up ahead on the path and looked up. It was the body of a child. Thin, small, with his back turned, he was squatting motionless and absorbed, staring at the ground. Jesuso advanced noiselessly, without the child's taking notice, and came up behind him where he could look down and see what he was doing. Running like a snake along the ground was a narrow thread of urine, flattened out and muddy at its end, which was dragging several bits of straw. At that moment, the child was dropping an ant from between his filthy little fingers.

"And the dam breaks . . . and the flood comes . . . bruum . . . bruuum bruuuuuuum . . . and the people run . . . and it carries off the big farm of Uncle Toad . . . and the little farm of Old Lady Grasshopper . . . and all the big trees . . . zaaaas . . . bruuuuuum . . . and now, here's Auntie Ant in the middle of all that water. . . ."

He felt the look, turned abruptly, looked fearfully at the wrinkled face of the old man, and got up, half-angry, half-ashamed.

He was slight, wiry, with long, perfectly shaped hands and feet, narrow of chest, with golden, dirty skin peeping from beneath the rough dark cloth, an intelligent head, eyes never still, a quivering, sharp little nose and a feminine mouth. On his head was an old felt hat, almost human with use, cocked over his ears like a pirate hat, which contributed to the impression of a rodent, of some quick, restless little animal.

Jesuso finished looking him over silently and smiled. "Where did you come from, boy?"

"From over there."

"From where?"

"From over there." He extended his hand vaguely toward the distant fields.

"What have you been doing?"

"Walking." There was in the tone of his reply a kind of firmness and authority that seemed strange to the man.

"What's your name?"

"The one the priest gave me."

Jesuso wrinkled up his face, displeased by the stubborn and evasive attitude. The child seemed to realize it and made up for his words by a confiding and friendly glance.

"Don't be a smart aleck," began the old man, but disarmed by the child's pleasant gesture, he lowered his voice to a more intimate tone. "Why don't you answer?"

"Why do you ask?" he replied with extraordinary candor.

"You're hiding something. Maybe you ran away from home."

"No, sir."

He was asking almost without curiosity, monotonously, as though they were playing a game.

"Or maybe you were naughty."

"No, sir."

"Or maybe they kicked you out, for being a bad boy."

"No, sir."

Jesuso scratched his head and added slyly, "Maybe you got the itching foot — eh, little tramp? — and just took off."

The child did not answer, but began to rock on his heels, with his arms behind his back, clicking his tongue on the roof of his mouth.

"And where are you going now?"

"Nowhere."

"And what are you doing?"

"Just what you see."

"What a filthy mess!"

Old Jesuso found nothing more to say; they remained silent, facing each other without either one daring to look the other in the eye. After a while, annoyed by that silence and stillness he could find no way to break, Jesuso started walking, slowly, like some enormous clumsy animal, almost as if he wished to imitate the gait of a fantastic beast, became aware of what he was doing, and blushed to think it might be to amuse the child.

"Coming?" he asked simply.

The boy tagged behind him without a word. When they arrived at the door of the hut, he found Usebia busy lighting a fire. She was blowing hard upon a little heap of kindling wood and old paper. "Hey, Usebia," he called timidly. "Look what's here."

She grunted without turning to look and went on blowing.

The old man set the child in front of him as though introducing him with his two heavy dark hands on the boy's slight shoulders.

"Now look!"

She turned around and stared bitterly at the group, trying hard to see through eyes tearing from the smoke. "Eh?"

Then a vague sweetness slowly softened her expression. "Aha. Who's this?" The child smiled at her and she smiled at him. "Who are you?"

"You're wasting your breath," said Jesuso. "This little rascal doesn't talk."

She stood there a while watching him, breathing his air, smiling at him, seeming to understand something that escaped Jesuso. Then, very slowly, she went into the corner, rummaged in the bottom of a red cloth bag and fished out a yellow cracker, as polished as a hard old piece of metal. She gave it to the child and while he chewed the tough dough with difficulty, she continued to gaze at them, at the child and the old man in turn, with an air of bewilderment, almost of anguish, as if she were searching painfully for some fine lost thread of memory. "Do you remember Chief, Jesuso? Poor little fellow."

The image of the old faithful dog passed through their memories. The feeling of grief brought them together. "Chi-ef . . ." said the old man as if he were learning to spell it.

The child turned his head and looked at him with pure and candid gaze. Jesuso looked at his wife and they both smiled, shyly and surprised.

And as the day grew full and deep, the light set the image of the boy inside the small and familiar frame of the hut. The color of his skin enriched the brown tone of the trodden-earth floor and in his eyes the cool shade was alive and burning.

Little by little things ceased to be as they had been and arranged themselves around his presence. Already his hand ran easily over the shining wood of the table, his foot found the uneven place in the doorstep, his body molded itself exactly to the hide-covered chair and all his movements fitted gracefully into spaces awaiting them.

Jesuso, half-gay, half-nervous, had gone out again to the field and Usebia busied herself in an effort to escape from the utter loneliness she felt in the presence of the new arrival. She moved the pot around on the fire, went back and forth looking for ingredients for the meal, and once in a while she glanced over her shoulder at the child out of the corner of her eye.

From the spot where she glimpsed him sitting quietly, his hands between his legs, head bent over watching his feet tap the ground, she began to hear soft spontaneous whistling without any recognizable tune.

In a little while she asked, almost impersonally, "Who's the cricket that's chirping?"

She thought she must have spoken very softly, because she received no answer except the whistling, now happier and similar to the sudden bursting into song typical of birds. "Chief," she ventured, almost bashfully—"Chief!"

She enjoyed the child's "Ah!"

"How do you like your name?" she asked. A pause, then she added, "My name is Usebia."

She heard like a smothered echo: "Velita de Sebo."[1]

She smiled, surprised, a little offended. "So you like to give people names?"

"You did it first."

"So I did."

She was going to ask him if he was happy, but the hard crust that her lonely life had imposed on her feelings made expression difficult, almost painful. She became silent again and returned

---

[1] "Little fat candel" in English but similar in sound to Usebia.

to the motions of an imaginary task, resisting the impulse that had made her open and talkative. The child took up his whistling again. The light grew brighter, making the silence more oppressive. She would have liked to talk wildly, say whatever came to her head, or else to run away and be by herself again. She put up with that inner giddiness in silence until it was more than she could bear, and when she found herself speaking, she no longer seemed herself but something that flowed like blood from an open vein.

"You'll see, Chief, how everything's going to change now. I couldn't stand Jesuso any more. . . ."

The vision of the gloomy old man, dried-up and taciturn, appeared between her words. It seemed to her that the boy had said "lechuzo,"[2] and she smiled awkwardly, not knowing whether it was the echo of her own words.

". . . I don't know how I've put up with him all this time. He's always been mean and a liar. Never paid any attention to me. . . ." The whole bitter taste of her harsh life was concentrated in the thought of her man, piling on him all the blame that she could not accept for herself. "He doesn't even know how to work the fields, after all these years at it. Somebody else might have come up a little in the world, but we keep going backward. And now this year, Chief. . . ."

She interrupted herself with a sigh and continued firmly, raising her voice as if she wanted someone farther away to hear: ". . . There's been no rain. The summer has stayed too long burning everything. And not even one drop has fallen. . . ."

The heated voice in the torrid air brought an imperious longing for coolness, an anguished thirst. The glare of the burnt hillside, of the dry leaves, of the cracked earth became another presence in the room, and pushed aside all other grievances. She kept silent awhile, then concluded in a plaintive voice, "Chief, take this can and go down to the brook and fetch some water."

As Jesuso watched Usebia preparing the meal, he felt an inner contentment as if some extraordinary ceremony were about to

---

[2] "Owl" in English but similar in sound to Jesuso.

take place, as if perhaps he had just discovered the religious character of food.

All the usual things had taken on a Sunday air; they seemed more beautiful, they seemed alive for the first time. "Is the meal good, Usebia?"

The answer was as extraordinary as the question. "It's good, old man."

The child was outside, but they felt that he was there with them in some mysterious way. The image of the small, sharp, ferret-like face stimulated in them new associations of ideas. They thought with tenderness about objects which had never before had any importance. Tiny sandals, small wooden horses, little carts made with lime slices for wheels, translucent glass marbles. The silent enjoyment they shared was bringing them together, making them beautiful in each other's eyes. It seemed as though they had just met each other and begun to dream of the years ahead. Even their names were beautiful; it gave them pleasure merely to say them. "Jesuso." "Usebia."

Now time was no longer a desperate waiting, but something light, like a bubbling spring.

When the table was set, the old man rose, pushed open the door, and went to call the child, who was stretched out on the ground, playing with a sort of grasshopper. "Time to eat, Chief!"

The child did not hear him, absorbed in contemplation of the insect, green and fine as the nerve of a leaf. With eyes glued to the ground, he was seeing it grown to his own size, a big animal, monstrous and terrifying. The insect, a *cerbatana*, was hardly moving, turning on its legs in time to the voice of the little boy, which chanted interminably.

> "*Cerbatana*, nice *cerbatana*,
> Tell me how big your cornfield is."

The insect would open and close its long forelegs as if vaguely keeping time to the chant. The singsong continued, accompanying the movement of the *cerbatana*, and each time the child saw in the form of the little insect something new and unexpected, until his imagination no longer recognized it.

"Lunchtime, Chief."

He turned his head and got to his feet with fatigue as if returning from a long journey, and followed the old man into the smoke-
filled hut. Usebia was putting out the food in battered pewter
plates. In the center of the table, the whiteness of the cold wrinkled
corn bread stood out.

Breaking his habit of staying away most of the day roaming
about the sown fields and hillsides, Jesuso came back to the hut
shortly after the meal.

When he returned at the usual time, it was easy for him to go
through the habitual motions, to say the same words, and to find
the exact spot where his presence appeared as a natural fruit of
the hour, but this unusual return was such a tremendous departure from custom that he entered somewhat abashed and realized
how surprised Usebia probably was.

Without looking directly at her, he went to the hammock and
stretched out full-length. He listened to her upbraidings without
surprise.

"Aha! Getting lazier all the time."

He sought an excuse. "And what can I do on that charred hill?"

After a while Usebia's voice replied, now milder and more
pleasant. "What a dry spell! If we could have just one good shower,
good and long. My God!"

"Too hot and the sky's too clear. No sign of rain anywhere."

"But if it rained, we could plant another crop."

"Yes, we could."

"And we could get a better price for it, so many fields have
dried up."

"Indeed we could."

"One single shower would turn the whole lower slope green
again."

"And with the money we could buy the donkey we need so
badly. And something for you to wear, Usebia." The stream of
tenderness spurted forth unexpectedly and with its miracle made
the old couple smile.

"And for you, Jesuso, a good poncho, one that won't let the rain
go through it."

Then both spoke almost in chorus: "And for Chief?"

"We'll take him to town and let him choose what he likes," said Jesuso.

The light entering the door of the hut was becoming dim, diffused, dusky, as if the hour had grown late, and yet it did not seem that so much time had passed since noon. A breeze reached them tinged with dampness, which made the closeness of the dwelling more bearable.

They had spent half the day almost in silence, speaking only at long intervals a few vague and commonplace words which mysteriously and clumsily ushered in a new disposition, a new kind of calm, of peace, of happy weariness.

"It will be dark soon," said Usebia, looking at the ash-gray color which was coming up to the door.

"Soon," nodded the old man absentmindedly; and unexpectedly he added: "What's become of Chief all afternoon? Probably still in the cornfield playing with the bugs he finds. Every beastie he sees, he stops and talks to it as if it were human."

A little later, after having let all the images his words conjured up file slowly through his head, he added: "Guess I'll go look for him."

He rose lazily from the hammock and went to the door. All the yellowness of the dry hill had turned to violet under the light of heavy black clouds which covered the sky. A sharp breeze was stirring up all the burnt crackling leaves. "Look, Usebia," he called.

The old woman came to the threshold asking, "Is Chief there?"

"No. Look at this black, black sky."

"Humph! It's done that before and it didn't rain."

She remained framed in the doorway and he went out in the open, cupped his hands and shouted slowly and deliberately: "Chief! O Chiiieeef!"

His voice was carried off by the breeze, mingled with the sound of the leaves, with the boiling-water sound of a thousand tiny noises that bubbled about the hill.

Jesuso started down the widest footpath of the field. At the first turn he saw Usebia out of the corner of his eye, motionless, embedded in the doorway, then he lost sight of her as he followed the winding path. There was a noise of swift little animals running through the dry, fallen leaves, and the shivering flight of small dark pigeons could be heard above the broad depths of the immense wind that was sweeping by oppressively. The coolness of rain was seeping slowly through light and air. Without realizing it, Jesuso was as though absent from his body, completely involved in other trails more twisted and complicated than those of the cornfield, darker, more mysterious. He was walking mechanically, now fast, now slow; he would stop in one spot, and suddenly he would find himself standing in another. Gradually everything was losing its outline, becoming gray and constantly changing its form, like the substance of water. Every few minutes, Jesuso thought he saw the child's small body squatting among the cornstalks, and he would call quickly, "Chief," but soon the wind and shadow would rub out the picture and form some other, unrecognizable shape. The massive clouds hung lower, increasing the darkness. He was halfway up the hill and already the tall trees seemed columns of smoke dissolving in the gloom. He could no longer trust his eyes, because all forms were fuzzy shadows, but at times he would stop and listen to the confused noises rushing by.

"O . . . Chief!" He was calling in a voice that was still timid, and would stop to listen. He thought he had heard his footsteps, but no, it was a dry branch cracking. "O . . . Chiieef!!"

The air was a boiling sea of murmurs, echoes, creaking, vast and resonant. Clearly he distinguished his voice in the multitude of tiny, scattered noises swept along by the wind.

"*Cerbatana,* nice *cerbatana.* . . ."

That was what he heard, syllables, words of his childish voice and not the echo of a rolling stone, not some distant distorted birdsong, not even his own cry returning faint and thin.

"*Cerbatana,* nice *cerbatana.* . . ."

A cold sharp anguish whipped him on through the vague fog that filled his head, quickening his steps and causing him to plunge forward madly. He poked feverishly among the cornstalks, crouching at times on his hands and knees, stopping continually to listen and hearing nothing but his own loud breathing.

He searched desperately with an ever increasing speed, with uncontainable anxiety, almost as if he himself were the one who was lost and called to.

"O . . . Chiieef!!!! O . . . Chiiieef!!!!"

He had been going in circles panting and shouting, lost, and only now did he become aware that he was going up the hill again. With the darkness, the racing of his blood, and the anguish of the useless search, he no longer recognized in himself the habitual meek old man, but rather a strange animal in the grip of an impulse of nature. He did not see on the hill the familiar contours. They seemed to have swollen in size and become unexpectedly deformed; they were foreign, inhabited by strange movements and sounds. The air was thick and unbreathable, the sweat streamed down his body as he continued to whirl and run goaded on by anguish.

"Chief!!"

Now it was a matter of life or death to find him. To find the small thing that would appear from out of that harsh and tormenting solitude. His own hoarse cry seemed to call him in a thousand different directions, where something that belonged only to the overwhelming night lay waiting for him.

It was agony. It was thirst. A smell of a newly plowed furrow floated now on the level of the ground, an odor of a crushed tender leaf.

No longer recognizable, the child's face was blotted out in the darkness, it had lost its human look; at times he could not recall his features, the tone of his thick voice, nor could he remember his profile.

"Chief!!!" A heavy cool drop burst on his sweating forehead. He lifted his face and another fell on his parted lips, and others on his dirt-covered hands. "Chief!!!" And other cold drops on his chest, greasy with sweat, and others in his troubled eyes causing his vision to blur. "Chief!! Chief!! Chief. . . ." Then the cool freshness caressed his whole skin, made his clothes stick to him, ran down his weary limbs.

A great compact roar rose from all the foliage and drowned his voice. There was a strong smell of roots, of earthworms, of germinating seed — the deafening smell of rain.

He no longer recognized his own voice, absorbed by the round echo of raindrops. His mouth fell silent as if satiated, and he seemed asleep as he walked slowly gripped by the rain, soaked by the rain, rocked by its deep and vast resonance.

He did not know if he would return. Through the clear flecks

of rain, as though through tears, he looked at the dark image of
Usebia, quiet in the light of the doorway.

—*Translated by Seymour Menton*

COMMENTARY

"The Rain" displays the same tropical brilliance and
exuberance as Juan Bosch's Criollista story "The Woman." Nonetheless,
it essentially belongs to the Cosmopolitanite trend. The envelopment of
so traditionally Criollista a theme as a drought in a strange, uncanny,
eery atmosphere places the story squarely within the realm of Magic
Realism. Intense as the description of the drought may be, the author
is less concerned about social protest than he is with converting the
drought into a symbol of a marriage gone dry. The mysterious appearance of the child alleviates the personal drought to such an extent that
when he disappears, Jesuso and Usebia hardly realize that it has begun
to rain. In other words, a phenomenon of nature is gradually displaced
by a human value—exactly the opposite of what occurs in so many
Criollista stories.

The Magic Realism stems from the child as well as from the style of
the whole story. Although there is nothing fantastic or even extraordinary
in the child's behavior, his sudden appearance and disappearance plus
a few other details suggest the possibility of a mirage. In addition to
his symbolic function, Chief appears to extinguish the fire of the drought
with his urine as he recites a children's story: "And the dam breaks . . .
and the flood comes." Later Usebia sends him to fetch water in the brook
startling the reader who has been convinced that there is none. Usebia
identifies Chief with their old long-gone dog, and the use of the words
"image" and "frame" in the following sentence also contributes to his
dehumanization and conversion into a kind of elf: ". . . the light set the
image of the boy inside the small and familiar frame of the hut." The
protagonists themselves at times enter into this world of make-believe.
Usebia says that Jesuso "lives as if he were dead" while she "returned
to the mechanical motions of an imaginary task."

The blend of terms that intensify the drought directly and others
that seemingly alleviate it is extremely clever. The author handles the
drought-reinforcing words so well that he succeeds in creating an image
worthy of comparison with Coleridge's "as idle as a painted ship upon a
painted ocean" from "The Rime of the Ancient Mariner." The contras-
tive ironic effect of the "liquid" words and phrases contributes to both
the intensification of the drought and the eery atmosphere: "a damp
echo," "the steamy heat flooded the hut," "floating over the earth there

was a fever of thirst," "something that flowed like blood from an open vein," "like a bubbling spring."

The abundance of similes, metaphors, and clauses beginning with the words "as if . . ." are more in keeping with the Vanguardista poetry of the early 1920s than they are with the more apparently simple style characteristic of Magic Realism. They are, however, an additional magic touch. Especially original are: "the shadow stabbed by a bright sheet of metal" and "the clouds dark as the shadow of a tree."

Like "Tell Them Not To Kill Me!" "The Rain" is based structurally on a series of fragments. Descriptive paragraphs alternate with the dialogues and the narrative point of view shifts back and forth among the omniscient narrator, Usebia, and Jesuso.

With an experimental technique, Uslar Pietri has thus created an unforgettable picture of a Latin American drought in which the characters are raised to the level of human beings and archetypes in spite of their immediate plight. The author's message is a clear challenge to the Criollista and social protest writers of the 1920s and 1930s: no matter how brutalized man may be by his environment, human values must prevail.

Juan José Arreola

(1918)

Mexican. He was born in the small town of Zapotlán (now Ciudad Guzmán) in the state of Jalisco. He began working at the age of eleven and never finished elementary school. From a delivery boy in the market of Guadalajara, he became a history and literature teacher in Ciudad Guzmán. Because of his early fondness for the theater, he studied in Mexico City with Rodolfo Usigli and Xavier Villaurrutia and also with Louis Jouvet in Paris. With Antonio Alatorre in Guadalajara he founded the magazine *Pan* (1945) where his first short stories appeared. While proofreading for the Fondo de Cultura Económica, he received a scholarship from the Colegio de México that permitted him to finish and publish in 1949 his first book of short stories, *Varia invención.* The first edition of *Confabulario* came out in 1952. The two works together were published in an expanded version in 1955 and 1962. The last edition, called *Confabulario total,* also includes a one-act play, *La hora de todos.* For several years, Arreola edited "Los Presentes," a series of books by young Latin American and Mexican authors. In 1963 he published his first and only novel, *La feria.* In recent years, he has become a popular television personality and has exhibited his paintings. He is an expert chess player and an enthusiastic ping-pong player. "The Switchman" appeared in the 1952 edition of *Confabulario.*

THE SWITCHMAN[1]

The stranger arrived at the deserted station out of breath. His large suitcase, which nobody wanted to carry[2] for him, had really tired him out. He mopped his face with a handkerchief, and with his hand shading his eyes, gazed at the tracks that melted away in the distance. Dejected and thoughtful, he consulted his watch: it was the exact time when the train was supposed to leave.

---

[1] From *Confabulario and Other Inventions,* trans. George D. Schade, Pan American Series (Austin: University of Texas Press, 1964).

[2] In the original Schade translation, "carried."

Somebody, come from heaven knows where, gently tapped him. When he turned around, the stranger found himself before a little old man who looked vaguely like a railroader. In his hand he was carrying a red lantern, but so small it seemed a toy. Smiling, he looked at the stranger, who anxiously asked him: "Excuse me, but has the train already left?"

"Haven't you been in this country very long?"

"I have to leave right away. I must be in T. tomorrow at the latest."

"It's plain you don't know what's going on at all. What you should do right now is go look for lodging at the inn," and he pointed to a strange, ash-colored building that looked more like a jail.

"But I don't want lodging; I want to leave on the train."

"Rent a room immediately if there are any left. In case you can get one, take it by the month. It will be cheaper for you and you will get better attention."

"Are you crazy? I must get to T. by tomorrow."

"Frankly, I ought to leave you to your fate. But just the same, I'll give you some information."

"Please. . . ."

"This country is famous for its railroads, as you know. Up to now it's been impossible to organize them properly, but great progress has been made in publishing timetables and issuing tickets. Railroad guides include and link all the towns in the country; they sell tickets for even the smallest and most remote villages. Now all that is needed is for the trains to follow what the guides indicate and really pass by the stations. The inhabitants of this country hope this will happen; meanwhile, they accept the service's irregularities and their patriotism keeps them from showing any displeasure."

"But is there a train that goes through this city?"

"To say yes would not be accurate. As you can see, the rails exist, though they are in rather bad shape. In some towns they are simply marked on the ground by two chalk lines. Under the present conditions, no train is obliged to pass through here, but nothing keeps that from happening. I've seen lots of trains go by in my life and I've known some travelers who managed to board them. If you wait until the right moment perhaps I myself will have the honor of helping you get on a nice comfortable coach."

"Will that train take me to T.?"

"Why do you insist that it has to be T.? You should be satisfied if you get on it. Once on the train, your life will indeed take on some direction. What difference does it make, whether it's T. or not?"

"But my ticket is all in order to go to T. Logically, I should be taken there, don't you agree?"

"Most people would say you are right. Over at the inn you can talk to people who have taken precautions, acquiring huge quantities of tickets. As a general rule, people with foresight buy passage to all points of the country. There are some who have spent a real fortune on tickets. . . ."

"I thought that to go to T. one ticket was enough. Look at it. . . .[3]"

"The next stretch of the national railways is going to be built with the money of a single person who has just spent his immense capital on round-trip passages for a railroad track that includes extensive tunnels and bridges that the engineers haven't even approved the plans for."

"But is the train that goes through T. still in service?"

"Not just that one. Actually, there are a great many trains in the nation, and travelers can use them relatively often, if they take into account that it's not a formal and definitive service. In other words, nobody expects when he gets aboard a train to be taken where he wants to go."

"Why is that?"

"In its eagerness to serve the citizens, the railway management is forced to take desperate measures. They make trains go through impassable places. These expeditionary trains sometimes take several years on a trip and the passengers' lives suffer important transformations. Deaths are not unusual in such cases, but the management, foreseeing everything, hitches on to those trains a car with a funeral chapel and a cemetery coach. The conductors take pride in depositing the traveler's body, luxuriously embalmed, on the station platform prescribed by his ticket. Occasionally these trains are compelled to run on roadbeds where one of the rails is missing. One whole[4] side of the coaches shudders lamentably as the wheels hit the railroad ties. The first-class passengers—

[3] In the original Schade translation, "look here."
[4] In the original Schade translation, "all one."

another instance of the management's foresight — are seated on the side where there is a rail. But there are other stretches where both rails are missing; there all the passengers suffer equally, until the train is completely wrecked."

"Good Lord!"

"Listen, the village of F. came into being because of one of those accidents. The train found itself in impassable terrain. Smoothed and polished by the sand, the wheels were worn away to their axles. The passengers had spent such a long time together that from the obligatory trivial conversations intimate friendships sprang up. Some of those friendships soon became idylls, and the result is F., a progressive town filled with mischievous children playing with the rusty vestiges of the train."

"For heaven's sake, I'm not one for such adventures!"

"You need to pluck up your courage; perhaps you may even become a hero. You must not think there aren't occasions for the passengers to show their courage and capacity for sacrifice. On one occasion two hundred anonymous passengers wrote one of the most glorious pages in our railroad annals. It happened that on a trial journey the engineer noticed in time that the builders of the line had made a grave omission. A bridge that should have spanned an abyss just wasn't there. Well now, the engineer, instead of backing up, gave the passengers a pep talk and got the necessary cooperation from them to continue forward. Under his forceful direction the train was taken apart piece by piece and carried on the passengers' backs to the other side of the abyss, which held a further surprise: a turbulent river at its bottom. The management was so pleased with the results of this action that it definitely renounced the construction of the bridge, only going so far as to make an attractive discount in the fares of those passengers who dared to take on that additional nuisance."

"But I've got to get to T. tomorrow!"

"All right! I'm glad to see you aren't giving up your project. It's plain that you are a man of conviction. Stay at the inn for the time being and take the first train that comes. At least try to; a thousand people will be there to get in your way. When a train comes in, the travelers, exasperated by an overly long wait, stream tumultuously out of the inn and noisily invade the station. Frequently they cause accidents with their incredible lack of courtesy and prudence. Instead of getting on the train in an orderly fashion, they devote themselves to crushing one another; at least, they keep each other from boarding, and the train goes off leaving them piled up on the station platforms. Exhausted and furious, the travelers curse each other's lack of good breeding and spend a lot of time hitting and insulting each other."

"Don't the police intervene?"

"They tried to organize a police force for each station, but the trains' unpredictable arrivals made such a service useless and very expensive. Besides, the members of the force soon showed their corrupt character, only letting wealthy passengers who gave them everything they had board the trains. Then a special kind of school was established where future travelers receive lessons in etiquette and adequate training so they can spend their lives on the trains. They are taught the correct way to board a train, even though it is moving at great speed. They are also given a kind of armor so the other passengers won't crack their ribs."

"But once on the train, aren't your troubles over?"

"Relatively speaking, yes. But I recommend that you watch the stations very carefully. You might think that you had arrived at T., and it would only be an illusion. In order to regulate life on board the overcrowded coaches, the management has been obliged to take certain expedient measures. There are stations that are for appearance only: they have been built right in the jungle and they bear the name of some important city. But you just need to pay a little attention to see through the deceit. They are like stage sets, and the people on them are stuffed with sawdust. These dummies easily betray the ravages of bad weather, but sometimes they are a perfect image of reality: their faces bear the signs of an infinite weariness."

"Fortunately, T. isn't very far from here."

"But at the moment we don't have any through trains. Nevertheless, it could well happen that you might arrive at T. tomorrow, just as you wish. The management of the railroads, although not very efficient, doesn't exclude the possibility of a nonstop journey. You know, there are people who haven't even realized what is going on. They buy a ticket for T. A train comes, they get on it, and the next day they hear the conductor announce: 'We're at T.' Without making sure, the passengers get off and find themselves indeed in T."

"Could I do something to bring about that result?"

"Of course you could. But it's hard to tell if it will do any good. Try it anyway. Get on the train with the firm idea that you are going to reach T. Don't talk with any of the passengers. They might disillusion you with their travel tales and they might even denounce you."

"What are you saying?"

"Because of the present state of things the trains are full of spies. These spies, mostly volunteers, dedicate their lives to encouraging the company's constructive spirit. Sometimes one doesn't know what one is saying and talks just to be talking. But they immediately see all the meanings in a phrase, however simple it may be. They can twist the most innocent comment around to make it look guilty. If you were to commit the slightest imprudence you would be apprehended without further ado; you would spend the rest of your life in a prison car, if they didn't make you get off at a false station, lost out in the jungle. While you travel, have faith, consume the smallest possible amount of food, and don't step off onto the platform until you see some familiar face at T."

"But I don't know anybody in T."

"In that case, take double precautions. There will be many temptations on the way, I assure you. If you look out the windows, you may fall into the trap of a mirage. The train windows are provided with ingenious devices that create all kinds of illusions in the passengers' minds. You don't have to be weak to fall for them. Certain apparatuses, operated from the engine, make you believe that the train is moving because of the noise and the movements. Nevertheless, the train stands still for whole weeks at a time while the passengers looking through the window panes see captivating landscapes pass by."

"What object is there in that?"

"The management does all this with the wholesome purpose of reducing the passengers' anxiety and, as far as possible, the sensations of moving. The hope is that one day the passengers will capitulate to fate, give themselves into the hands of an omnipotent management, and no longer care to know where they are going or where they have come from."

"And you, have you traveled a lot on trains?"

"Sir, I'm just a switchman. To tell the truth, I'm a retired switchman, and just come here now and then to remember the good old days. I've never traveled and I have no desire to. But the travelers tell me stories. I know that the trains have created many towns besides F., whose origin I told you about. Sometimes the crew on a train receives mysterious orders. They invite the passengers to get off, usually on the pretext that they should admire the beauties of a certain place. They are told about grottoes, falls, or famous ruins: 'Fifteen minutes to admire such and such a grotto,' the conductor amiably calls out. Once the passengers are a certain distance away, the train chugs away at full speed."

"What about the passengers?"

"They wander about disconcertedly from one spot to another for a while, but they end up getting together and establishing a colony. These untimely stops occur in places far from civilization but with adequate resources and sufficient natural riches. Selected lots of young people, and especially an abundant number of women, are abandoned there. Wouldn't you like to end your days in a picturesque unknown spot in the company of a young girl?"

The little old fellow winked, and smiling kindly, continued to gaze roguishly at the traveler. At that moment a faint whistle was heard. The switchman jumped, all upset, and began to make ridiculous, wild signals with his lantern.

"Is it the train?" asked the stranger.

The old man recklessly broke into a run along the track. When he had gone a certain distance he turned around to shout, "You are lucky! Tomorrow you will arrive at your famous station. What did you say its name was?"

"X!" answered the traveler.

At that moment the little old man dissolved in the clear morning. But the red speck of his lantern kept on running and leaping imprudently between the rails to meet the train.

In the distant landscape the train was approaching like a noisy advent.[5]

—Translated by George Schade

---

[5] In the original Schade translation, "was noisily approaching."

COMMENTARY

In "The Switchman," the role of philosophy is more important and the Magic Realism is more magic, verging on the absurd, than in "The Rain." Arreola presents, in this relatively long story for him, his interpretation of the mid-twentieth-century world. The fantastic events narrated by the old switchman constitute Arreola's reply to materialism and Existentialism. He admits sadly that we do not live in the best of all possible worlds and he pokes fun at those people who let themselves be so absorbed by that world that they can never free themselves from its irresistible suction. At the same time, his attitude is more Mexican in that rather than despair, he argues in favor of boarding the train of life without worrying about the route it will follow. Boarding the train in itself is a real feat and should be appreciated as such. Why despair when man is capable of adjusting to any eventuality? In order to cross the abyss, the passengers have to dismantle the train, carry the parts across the abyss, and then reassemble them. The important thing is that the train continue on. Fixed destinations are ridiculous because some passengers are perfectly capable of arriving without realizing it. At the end of the story, the real train approaches and the old switchman disappears, just like Chief in "The Rain," making the reader doubt whether he ever really existed.

Since Magic Realism always has a strong realistic base, Arreola fuses his fantastic symbolism with a satire of the defects of Mexico's railway system. He pokes fun at the trains that do not stick to the timetables, the plans of tunnels and bridges that have not even been approved by the engineers, the better service enjoyed by first-class passengers, the lack of manners of the people at boarding time, police venality, and the sacred custom of getting off and on the train while it is still moving.

In "The Switchman" Arreola combines Mexican reality with fantasy, two discrete elements that are totally separated in the majority of the stories in his collection *Confabulario*. The whole volume must be read in order to appreciate the author's aesthetic purpose. As a representative man of his era, Arreola is an eclectic who attempts to write the history of the modern short story by utilizing the best of all those who have preceded him. The title of his first collection, *Varied Invention* (1949), indicates his intention to put together a panorama of the short story. The inclusion of *Varied Invention* (1949) and *Confabulario* (1952) in a single volume (1955) and its expansion under the title of *Confabulario total* (1962) attests to the interdependence of all the stories. The artistic unit is therefore not exclusively the individual story but the collection.

When his stories were first published, Arreola's cosmopolitan attitude provoked lively debates among Mexican critics. His stories were often contrasted with those of his friend and contemporary Juan Rulfo whose *themes* fit comfortably within the tradition of revolutionary literature.

This was not the first time in Mexican literary history that the relative values of cosmopolitan and nativist literature were debated. Actually this dichotomy is characteristic of much of twentieth-century Mexican press fiction. Although the Revolution has been the constant theme of the majority of writers, there has always been a small group of cosmopolitan heretics. Among the *Ateneístas, Colonialistas,* and *Contemporáneos* may be found such outstanding literary figures as Alfonso Reyes, Artemio de Valle-Arizpe, and Jaime Torres Bodet, whose stories reveal a total escape from the pressing social problems of the twentieth century. Arreola has been identified with this group, but somewhat unjustly. Although it is true that he is related to them through his intellectualism and encyclopedic culture, it is no less true that in "The Switchman" and some other stories he clearly demonstrates a deep concern for the real meaning of the world in which he lives.

Eduardo Mallea

(1903)

Argentinean. He is one of Latin America's most prolific novelists. Born in Bahía Blanca, he was raised in a cultured environment; his father was a doctor, a writer, and a friend of Domingo F. Sarmiento. After studying law for four years, he abandoned it in favor of literature. He made two trips to Europe, in 1928 and 1934, and after 1931 he directed the literary supplement of *La Nación* for many years. Mallea first published two volumes of short stories, *Cuentos para una inglesa desesperada* (1926) and *La ciudad junto al río inmóvil* (1936), but he is better known for his novels: *Fiesta en noviembre* (1938), *La bahía de silencio* (1940), *Todo verdor perecerá* (1941), *Las águilas* (1943), *El retorno* (1946), *El vínculo* (1946), *Los enemigos del alma* (1950), *La torre* (1951), *Chaves* (1954), *Simbad* (1957); and four volumes of short novels or long stories: *Sala de espera* (1954), *Posesión* (1958), and *La razón humana* (1960). With *La barca de hielo* (1967), Mallea demonstrated his capacity to adapt to the novel of the "Boom" without betraying his own basic themes and style. His most recent works are *La penúltima puerta* (1969), *Gabriel Andaral* (1971), *Triste piel del universo* (1971), and *En la creciente oscuridad* (1973). "Conversation" is from *La ciudad junto al río inmóvil*.

CONVERSATION

He did not answer. They went into the bar. He ordered a whisky and water; she a whisky and water. He looked at her; she wore a black velvet cap which was pressed tightly round her small head; her eyes opened, dark, out of a region of blue; she noticed his red tie with its dirty white polka dots and untidy knot. Through the window could be seen the front of a laundry, beside whose door a child was playing; the pavement revealed a gaping mouth through which — an incredible birth — surged the thick trunk of a chestnut tree; the street was very wide.

The waiter came with the bottle and two large glasses and ice; "Cigarettes," he said, "Maspero." The waiter took the order without moving his head, flicked his cloth over the stained surface of the table, and then placed glasses on it.

Nearly all the tables in the saloon were empty; behind an enormous kentia plant the owner was writing in the leaves of a ledger; at a table in the far corner two men were speaking, their heads uncovered, one with a thick, trimmed mustache, the other cleanshaven, repugnant, bald, and yellowish; for a moment, not even the stirring of a fly could be heard in the saloon, but soon the younger of the men in the far corner was heard to speak hurriedly with abrupt pauses; the owner would lift his eyes and look at the speaker as if to listen better to his coarse and irregular manner of speaking, and then would bury himself once more in his figures; it was seven o'clock.

He helped her to some whisky, about two centimeters of it, and then helped her to a bit of ice and water; then he helped himself and immediately took a short, energetic gulp. He lit a cigarette which remained dangling from the corner of his mouth, and he had to half-close his eyes against the smoke in order to look at her; she had her eyes fixed on the child playing by the laundry. The sign over the laundry was painted in silver; and the L, which had been a pretentious baroque capital, now had its two tips broken, and instead of the embellishments, there remained two spots which were much lighter than the homogeneous background of the board on which the many years had gathered their soot. His voice was authoritative, virile, dry.

"You don't wear your white dress any more," he said.

"No," she said.

"It suited you better than this one does," he said.

"It probably did."

"Much better."

"Yes."

"You've become careless. You really have become careless."

She looked at his face, at the two wrinkles which formed themselves pointlike over the angle of the pale strong mouth; she saw the tie, untidily knotted, the stains that covered it diagonally, like splashes.

"Yes," she said.

"Do you want to make yourself some clothes?"

"Later on," she said.

"The eternal 'later on'," he said. "We're not even living anymore. We're not living in the present. Everything is 'later on.'"

She said nothing: the taste of the whisky was pleasant, fresh, and with a barely perceptible bitterness.

The saloon served as a refuge from the evening rush; a man entered, dressed in a white linen suit and dark shirt, with a handkerchief with brown dots peeping out of his jacket pocket; he looked around him and sat near the counter, and the owner lifted his eyes and looked at him; the waiter came and flicked his cloth over the table and listened to the man's order and then repeated it in a loud voice; the man in the far corner who was listening to the one who was talking excitedly turned his slow, heavy eyes toward the customer who had just entered; a sleepy cat was stretched out on the mutilated dark oak balustrade which separated the two sections of the saloon, starting from the window where you could read the sign backward: *Café de la Legalidad.*

She thought: why should it be called *Café de la Legalidad?*; once she had seen, in port, a ship called *Causalidad*; what did *Causalidad* mean?; why had the owner thought of the word *Causalidad?*; what would a dull man of the sea know about causality unless he were a well-educated man who had lost his social position? Perhaps the same word *Causalidad* had had something to do with his personal disaster; or he might have meant to put *Casualidad* —coincidence— that is to say, it might mean the opposite, this word, put there through possible ignorance.

Next door to the laundry the doors were already closed, but the window displayed an orderly accumulation of gray, white, and yellow title pages of books and the heads of photogenic intellectuals and advertisements written in large black letters.

"This is not good whisky," he said.

"Isn't it?" she asked.

"It has a peculiar taste."

She had not noticed any peculiar taste; it was true, however, that she drank whisky very seldom; neither did he drink it often; sometimes, when he came home fatigued, he would have about half a tumbler full before the evening meal; he usually preferred other alcoholic drinks, but hardly ever alone, only with friends, at noon; but those few occasions could not be responsible for the greenish color that spread down from his forehead over the lean bony face to the chin—it was not a sickly color, but neither was it an indication of health; none of the standard remedies had been able to transform this lusterless color which sometimes even approached a livid tone. He asked:

"Why are you looking at me? What's wrong?"

"Nothing," she said.

"For once and for all, shall we be going tomorrow to the Leites'?"

"Yes," she said, "of course, if you want to. Didn't we tell them we would go?"

"That doesn't mean a thing," he said.

"I know it's beside the point, but if we didn't intend going, we should have let them know."

"All right, we'll go."

There was a pause.

"Why do you say we'll go in that manner?" she asked.

"In what manner?"

"You know, with an air of resignation. As if you didn't like going."

"It's not one of my favorite things to do."

There was a pause.

"Yes. You always say that. And yet, when you are there. . . ."

"When I am there, what?" he said.

"When you are there, you seem to like it and to like it in a special way."

"I don't understand," he said.

"Well, you like it in a special way, that's all. For instance, when you talk to Ema, it seems to be a sort of breath of air to you, something refreshing—and you change. . . ."

"Don't be silly."

"You change," she said. "At least, I think you change. Oh, I don't know. Anyhow, don't deny that you wouldn't take a step to see *him.*"

"He's an insignificant, dull man, but I suppose I'm indebted to him," he said.

"Yes. But, I don't know, I still think that a word from Ema uplifts you, does you good."

"Please don't be silly," he said. "She also bores me."

"Why pretend that she bores you? Why say the opposite of what really is?"

"I have no reason for saying the opposite of what really is. You're stubborn. Leites bores me and Ema bores me and all that surrounds them and all that they touch bore me."

"All that surrounds them annoys you," she said. "But there is another thing."

"What other thing?"

"You cannot bear the idea of that grotesque situation — Ema's being united to a man so inferior, so trivial."

"But what you're saying is absurd. What has gotten into your head? Everyone forms his relationships according to his needs. If Ema lives with Leites, it is not through some divine ruling, a law of fate, but simply because she does not see beyond him."

"It's difficult for you to believe that she doesn't see beyond him."

"For God's sake, that's enough. Don't be ridiculous."

There was another pause. The man in the white suit left the bar. . . .

"I'm not ridiculous," she said.

She had meant to add something else, to say something more significant, to throw light on all those cryptic sentences they had been exchanging, but she did not, would not say it; she looked at the letters in the word *Laundry*; the owner of the bar called the waiter and gave him an order in a low voice and the waiter went and spoke to one of the men sitting in the far corner; she swallowed the last drop of the amber whisky.

"In reality, Ema is a woman who is quite contented with her fate," he said.

She did not answer.

"A cold-hearted woman," he said

She did not answer.

"Don't you think so?" he asked.

"Perhaps," she said at last.

"And, you, sometimes it occurs to you to say such absolutely fantastic things."

She did not say anything.

"What do you think might interest me in Ema?" he went on. "What are you thinking?"

"But why return to the same subject?" she said. "It was a passing remark. Simply a passing remark."

They both remained silent; he looked at her, she looked outside at the street which was gradually thickening with shadows, the street where night moved forward by degrees; the pavement once whitish, now gray, would soon be black, black with a certain deep bluish reflection shining on its surface; automobiles passed swiftly by, a bus or two, full; suddenly a strange bell was heard — where was that sound coming from? — the voice of a boy was heard, in the distance, announcing the evening papers, the fifth edition which had just appeared; the man ordered another whisky for himself; she never drank more than one; the waiter turned his back on their table and shouted the order in the stentorian and emphatic voice with which hirelings of a tyrannical master give themselves the pleasure of assuming some authority for themselves; the man knocked on the window and the boy who was running past with his load of papers smelling of fresh ink entered the saloon; the man bought a paper, unfolded it and started to read the headlines; she fixed her attention on two or three photographs on the back page and saw a young woman of the aristocracy who would shortly be married and a manufacturer of British cars who had just arrived in Argentina on a business trip; the cat had gotten up from the balustrade and was playing with one paw in a flower pot, moving the stems of the old and squalid flowers; she asked the man if there was any important news and the man hesitated before answering, and then said:

"The same old thing. The Russians don't get along with the Germans. The Germans don't get along with the French. The French don't get along with the English. Nobody gets along with anybody. It doesn't make any sense. It looks as though everything will go to the devil at one moment or another. Or things might remain as they are: the world steeped in misunderstanding and the planet keeps on spinning."

The man moved the paper aside, filled his glass with a little whisky, and then added an ice cube and then some water.

"It's better not to stir it," he ruminated. "Those who know how to drink say it's better not to stir it."

"Will there be war, do you think?" she asked him.

"Who can say yes, who can say no? Not even those who are involved themselves; not even they themselves. . . ."

"The war would last two weeks, with all those inventions. . . ."

"It was the same with the other one; they said the same about the other one, that it would last two weeks."

"That was different. . . ."

"It was the same. It's always the same. Would a few more grams of blood or a few more thousands of victims deter man? It's like the miser and his money. Nothing satiates the love of money for the sake of money. And so no amount of hate will satiate man's hatred for his fellowman."

"Nobody wants to be massacred," she said. "That is stronger than all the hatreds."

"What?" he exclaimed. "A general blindness obscures everything. In war, the atrocious satisfaction of killing is greater than the fear of dying."

She did not reply; she thought of what he had said and then was about to answer but decided not to say anything; she thought it was not worthwhile. A young woman with gray hair wrapped in a gray smock had stepped out on the opposite sidewalk and with the aid of a long iron rod began pulling down the metal grating of the laundry that fell with a dull clang. The electric lights in the street appeared to be dim and the traffic had thinned somewhat, but people continued to pass at intervals.

"You make me furious every time you broach the subject of Ema," he said.

She did not say anything.

"Women should sometimes be silent," he said, feeling that he must continue.

She did not say anything; the clean-shaven man with the yellowish skin said goodbye to his friend, made his way through the tables, and left the bar; the owner lifted his eyes toward him and then lowered them.

"Do you want to go out somewhere to eat?" he asked bitterly.

"I don't know," she said. "Whatever you like."

When a minute had passed, she said: "If only one could give one's life some purpose."

He remained silent.

They stayed a little longer and then went out; in the temperate night air they roamed those streets of solitude and poverty; between them a mood had established itself, an ominous mood which seemingly conflicted with the mild air; they walked a few blocks, to the central district where the neon signs blazed, and then entered a restaurant.

And here there was laughter, noise, and people talking; the ten-piece orchestra sustained a strange rhythm. They ate in silence; from time to time a question and an answer would cross between them; after the cold turkey, they did not order anything but fruit and coffee; the orchestra continued playing except for short breaks.

When they went out, when the night air and the city received them again, they walked aimlessly as if hypnotized by the blazing neons of the movie theaters. He was distracted, exacerbated, and she was looking at the pink and yellow posters; she would like to have said many things, but what for and so she remained silent.

"Let's go home," he said. "There's really nowhere to go."

"Yes, let's go home," she said. "What else could we do?"

— *Translated by Hugo Manning*

COMMENTARY

In 1936, during the heyday of Criollismo and social protest literature, Argentinean Eduardo Mallea published *La ciudad junto al río inmóvil,* a volume of Existentialist short stories that are related to Criollismo only somewhat artificially through the prologue and epilogue.

"Conversation," even in the ironic meaning of its title, reflects the lack of understanding among human beings. The protagonists, who are identified only by the pronouns "he" and "she," talk to each other without really communicating. When he criticizes her dress, she observes how sloppy he looks, *but without telling him so.* What for? They then proceed to eat in silence in the midst of the typically noisy Buenos Aires restaurant. Ultimately they return home with an apparently simple rhetorical question but one loaded with anxiety: "What else could we do?"

The minor characters, no matter how brief their appearances, reinforce the impression of human loneliness. In the bar, the waiter takes their order without moving his head; the owner writes in his ledger almost hidden behind the giant plant; two men talk silently and "you couldn't even hear the stirring of a fly." Outside, a boy plays alone in front of the laundry that a *young* woman *with gray hair* closes. In the restaurant as well as in the street, in the midst of many people, the protagonists do not feel any less lonely. In order to demonstrate the universality of this affliction, the man reads the newspaper and comments on the lack of international understanding.

Whereas the Naturalist author sought to record details in order to recreate an environment with the greatest possible precision, the Existentialist is much more selective, choosing only a few small key details that reflect the essence of the characters or their situation: the tie with the knot carelessly made and the dirty white polka dots; the stained table tops; the two centimeters of whisky; the dangling cigarette; the broken L of the sign; and a sleepy cat. The tree that emerges from the "gaping mouth" in the sidewalk is much more than a descriptive detail: it symbolizes man's imprisonment (or if the book's prologue and epilogue are taken into account, it symbolizes the birth and growth of the Latin American man in spite of the hostile environment).

Mallea's message is reflected in his style which clearly helps produce a sensation of overwhelming despair. The lack of understanding even extends to words, phrases, and sentences. The repetition of words in a given sentence or in consecutive sentences impedes the development of a smooth rhythm and reinforces the unpleasantness of the situation between the two protagonists. This may be more specifically attributed to the abundant use of the semicolon and the absence of linking words or conjunctions.

Although "Conversation" is a good example of the Existentialist short story, technically it is not typical of Mallea's art. In the majority of his stories, the inner thoughts of the characters are presented more explicitly, there is hardly any dialogue, and the narrator intervenes more actively. Nonetheless, "Conversation" does fit in harmoniously with the other numbered stories of *La ciudad junto al río inmóvil.* By numbering his stories, Mallea underlines the unity of the whole volume. His purpose, like that of Sherwood Anderson in *Winesburg, Ohio* and James Joyce in *Dubliners,* is to capture the spirit of a city through a series of inconsequential personal dramas. Besides the interdependence of all the stories through their Existentialism, Mallea places them within a frame which paradoxically is reminiscent of John Dos Passos' *U.S.A.* The paradox consists of the dynamic optimism of both the prologue, "Diálogo oído en una calle," and the epilogue, "Adiós," which seems to contradict the overwhelmingly pessimistic tone of the stories. Mallea's concept is that lonely and anguish-laden as Argentina and Latin America may be, they are not totally devoid of hope. Quite the contrary, the tortured existence of the characters is associated with the gestation process. In Latin America, people are searching for each other: "there is a great silence on the march."

Lino Novás Calvo

(1905)

Cuban. His 1942 volume *La luna nona y otros cuentos* is considered the most important collection of Cuban stories in the entire prerevolutionary period. Born in a Galician village in Spain, he immigrated to Cuba at the age of seven. As a young man, he worked at many trades including driving a taxi for several years. After a visit to New York in 1926, he became a newspaperman. In 1930, he went to Spain and also visited France and Germany. Subsequently, he covered the Spanish Civil War as a correspondent. After returning to Cuba, he edited the magazine *Bohemia* for many years. He taught French at the Escuela Normal in Havana and translated Aldous Huxley, D. H. Lawrence, and Faulkner. Through his use of experimental techniques, he widely influenced the younger Cuban writers in the 1940s and 1950s. He has published novels: *El negrero* (1933), *Experimento en el barrio chino* (1936); a short novel: *No sé quién soy* (1945); and, above all, short stories: *La luna nona y otros cuentos* (1942), *Un dedo encima* (1943), *Cayo Canas* (1946), and *En los traspatios* (1946). He was one of the first Cuban intellectuals to go into exile after the triumph of the Revolution. He taught Latin American literature for several years at Syracuse University. In *Maneras de contar* (1970), he republished some of his best stories along with nine new antirevolutionary stories. "The Dark Night of Ramón Yendía" was written in 1933 at the time the events described took place, but it was not published until 1942 in the collection *La luna nona y otros cuentos.*

THE DARK NIGHT OF RAMÓN YENDÍA

Ramón Yendía awoke from a troubled sleep aching in every muscle. Worn out, he had slumped down over the wheel while the car was still moving, scraping the curb that separated the street from the vacant lot. On the left side a row of new houses huddled symmetrically together. Some were still unfinished; others were occupied by small businessmen and prosperous working men who had not yet found their place in the community and were therefore not too aggressive. Either by instinct or by chance, Ramón had come here to rest. He had spent four days away from home, sleeping in his taxi in different places. One night he had stayed at the taxi stand right in front of the Parados Bar, and it was there that his troubles had started. He had been afraid, but he had made an effort to control himself and to prove to himself that he could face the situation. He did not want to flee, for he knew in a way that if you fled you were sure to be pursued — unless, of course, you had someone to protect you. Every minute of these four days had been like a death sentence he had seen coming, taking shape like a thick cloud, growing claws. Ramón could not escape, he knew that, but perhaps he might remain, hiding or just waiting. After every earthquake someone is always left to tell the tale. It is a terrifying gamble, but then, life itself is a kind of gamble. Still, on the second night he went out into the outskirts of the city and parked next to a wall; the following night he drove up in front of the house of a revolutionary he knew, though the man probably did not know him. "Maybe he'll want to ride in my cab," he thought. If the man did, then perhaps he might be able to weather the storm unnoticed. Somehow he felt that the storm had to come and that it would pass. His regular customers had already taken off; therefore there was something serious in the wind.

Having had no experience in these struggles, Ramón felt almost as if he had fallen into a maelstrom. He had been driving a cab for three years, and his first daughter was born four years ago — now there were three of them, all girls and not one healthy. His wife did what she could. She left the little one in a cradle tied with ribbons while she went to work in a factory sewing hatbands.

All through these four days he had only been able to slip into their house twice. They still lived on the Calle de Cuarteles in one room. The back door opened on the patio, the front door on the street. Estela had been longing for a little home of their own, even if it was only a shack. They could have gotten one in the new development for a down payment of only one hundred pesos. They would have been able to save the money if their eldest, the boy, had not fallen sick and died in spite of their desperate efforts to save him. Now that Ramón had a good cab, which he rented for three pesos a day, they were beginning to get on their feet again. He also longed for a car of his own, even if it were only a Ford. He had some good regular fares, and he stayed at the wheel up to fifteen hours a day. But then besides his own family, he had to look out for the amazingly fertile Balbina, who had had eight children by three different men. Everything was hard. The cab drank gasoline like water. It was a six-cylinder job, but he did not have the patience to wait his turn in the stand. Now, four days before, he had rented a new car from a different garage. He was a nervous man with big brown eyes, who was quick to catch on. Sometimes, even when there was no actual signal, he could see things coming. The other drivers laughed at him and called him a spiritualist.

On the night of the 6th he put his car away early and did not go back to the garage the next day. On the 8th he went to another garage, the Palanca, and hired a newer car. None of his usual fares was in the street any more. They, too, must have sensed the impending storm. Every day for a year he had been driving them, and when all is said and done, they were all right, at least to him. Their voices were warm and human, and they seemed to believe in what they were doing. They were not gunmen; their mission was to get information and nothing else. And Ramón had helped them out; he had placed himself at their service.

Now, today, the morning of the 12th, his premonitions were more urgent, like something out of a painful dream. Until three o'clock in the morning he had been cruising the streets or waiting outside of dance halls or cabarets. He had not had a bad day; in fact, as far as that goes, there had been nothing unusual about it. Before turning in he had stopped beside a lamppost near the Capitol and counted his take, which amounted to six pesos and change. Just then he felt that he was being stared at hard by a passerby, a young fellow who looked like a college student and who had one hand in his jacket pocket. Ramón decided to go home with the money; he made a detour and stopped a block away from the house. He walked up the side street, crossed the patio, and entered cautiously. He turned on the fine flashlight that one of his regular customers had given him, and played it as though he were a burglar or a policeman instead of a fugitive.

Not that anything as yet implied that he was a fugitive, he just sensed it. He did not dare to switch on the electricity lest he make a target of himself, and he felt his way in. He turned the flashlight on the beds. In one of the cots, two of the girls, the twins, were sleeping naked, cheek to cheek on top of the sheet, with their open hands over their shoulders. In the second cot slept Estela and the baby; the empty one was his. No one awoke. Estela had on a nightgown, and her head was between her hands, which were turned palms up. In spite of all she had gone through, she was still beautiful. She was young; she had a delicate nose, large eyes, heavy hair, a prominent chin, thick, well-formed lips, and a large, sensual mouth. As he stopped for a moment to gaze at her, Ramón could visualize her healthy, slightly protruding row of teeth, her honey-colored eyes, and her lively glance. Then he put the money on the table where his dinner was waiting for him and went out. There was nobody near the automobile. Everything seemed normal except that there were too many cars moving too fast and the lights were on in several houses. That was all—but it was enough!

On his return trip he passed police headquarters. There seemed to be an unusual amount of activity going on inside, and as he went by he thought the two guards on duty moved their guns nervously when they heard his car. He turned into the first street on the right without stopping to think whether it was a one-way street. He stopped at the next corner, in doubt about which way to go; his thoughts had turned back several years, and old scenes flashed before his eyes as if on a movie screen. In those days some sort of revolutionary spirit had taken hold of him; he couldn't say why, for he had never been able to examine his feelings coldly and analytically. Perhaps he had merely caught it from the air, for he did not read much and he did not belong to any group from which he might have absorbed any basic principles or which might have helped him to clarify his own ideas. Twelve years before, he had come with his brothers and sisters from the country. His father had lost his savings when the bank crashed. and had disappeared into the swamps with his head held high and his body as stiff as a corpse. (Nobody had ever seen him since.) He had caught it without warning; it was in the air. The girls had not yet been born, and the little boy was strong and handsome. Ramón did not find business too bad, for he was lucky at picking up steady customers; perhaps it was because he was a good driver; he knew when to speed and when to go slow.

And that's how things were. Almost every day he picked up three or four young fellows, sometimes together and sometimes alone. He had not yet found out who they were; he only knew that they were revolutionaries and they had money to spend. Being a revolutionary was a virtue, for the word recalled the country's struggles for independence, and since childhood he had heard it constantly from people of all classes. It was the national bona fide currency. Therefore it was all right. Things were not so bad at home, and his customers were fond of him, for he seemed to them to be reliable. They would talk to him and gradually he caught their tone, their language, and their enthusiasm. He talked like them at the taxi stand, in the garage—in fact, almost everybody was beginning to talk the same way. There still did not seem to be much danger in it, and a fellow was not afraid to speak his mind and even to pay an occasional brief call late at night. Sometimes he served as a courier, driving his empty car from one place to another. They paid him regularly, and the pay was not bad. After all, Ramón was one of them.

Then the tide turned. Justino, the boy, got sick. Estela was pregnant and irritable. Then came the twins, hard going, and perhaps even doubt. Ramón could get excited and carried away, but he lacked real conviction. He saw that being a revolutionary was not all smooth sailing. One night—a night like this, at the beginning of August, near morning—two men hailed him. He realized at once that something was up. Perhaps they were plain-clothesmen. Others had hailed him in the same way and then, when they were in the car, had said: "Police headquarters." When they reached the station he would discover that he had been charged with cruising, going through a red light, or speeding, or some such thing. Naturally, it was against the law, but the union would bail him out, and sometimes a judge was good-natured enough to let him off without fining him. These two men were not paying passengers, either; they also said: "Police headquarters," but this time, when he got there, he was given different treatment.

He stood it the first time. They took him into a bare room with the cement floor and walls splotched with blood, and they slapped him, punched him, kicked him. There wasn't an insult or foul word that they didn't throw at him; their language besmirched everything he loved; and they threatened that his wife would get hers, too. He took it all. Then, to his surprise, they took him to the front desk, and the lieutenant let him go. He got into his car and somehow managed to drive it to the garage. He did not go home that night, for his lips were cut and he was spitting blood. He could say that he had had a collision; that was the excuse the police told him to give. No, thanks; he was not going to bring home to his wife any more trouble. During those days his best customers were in hiding, and his day's take did not amount to more than two pesos. He slept in the garage that night. Early the next morning he went home and told his wife that he had been out all night with a customer who said he would pay him later. One of the girls was sick; the mother thought she was teething, but he was afraid that it was something else, for she cried all the time and was as thin as a rail.

During the days that followed he did not see any of his old customers, and he had the impression that eyes were watching him from all sides. In the course of those twenty-four hours he got two tickets, and the next day three. The fourth day he was taken back to the police station and beaten again, but this time worse. Then they let him go, but they assigned another cabby he knew to keep an eye on him and put him on the right track. He was a slippery fellow who worked at night, picking up fares in front of hotels and cabarets or waiting in taxi stands. He began his job with kid gloves; then gradually he began to put it into Ramón's head that politicians were out for themselves and looked out for nobody but number one. He told him some stories, and to Ramón the little room he lived in began to appear more and more gloomy and his family more anemic and pitiful. He struggled with himself before he gave in, but the other man's arguments were convincing. He told him that after all it was just a case of one politician fighting another. Didn't "they" have enough money to pay him? They all began in the same way, and they ended up by forgetting the people who had helped them up in the world. No, Ramón was a fool if he didn't switch sides. Naturally, he could continue to drive his regular customers, for he was only asked to follow certain instructions and get certain information.

That was the why and wherefore of it all. He felt himself cornered and he gave in. They would wipe the slate clean and help him out. That was when Estela, trying to get the children back to health, began to dream about owning her own little wooden house, and he about driving his own cab. The doctor said the children needed fresh air and good food. It was always the same old story. Every worker's child needs fresh air and good food, but perhaps his would get it. After all, Ramón was human; unlike some other people, he had warm blood in his veins, and so he yielded for the sake of his family and for his own sake, too. And suppose he hadn't? Could he have let himself go on being arrested and beaten up? Could he have let Estela and the children die? He began to rationalize, for he knew that he was not doing the right thing, and it worried him so that he had to use all his willpower to go through with it. He calmed himself by concentrating on the goals that he had in mind. Perhaps he had done wrong, but his motives were good. Should he have refused and let himself be wiped out?

From then on he hadn't had a peaceful moment. He lost weight, he became more nervous and gloomy, and he had to make a strenuous effort to hide from his wife the drama that was gnawing at him from within. He knew that some of the men he had informed on were in jail and that one had perhaps even been murdered. When he thought about it, his only consolation was that he was poorer than anyone else; all the others, at least, had relatives and friends who could do something for them and would never forget them. But there was nobody to lend him a hand. He could depend only upon himself, himself alone. If the day came when he did not take home his three pesos, his family would not eat; if he did not pay his fee every day, he would lose his car; if he got sick, he would not even be able to get into the hospital. So it was only right and human for him to take care of himself, no matter who had to suffer for it. He was always having to recall these arguments to quiet his conscience, but deep down inside he carried his own accusation, which tortured and pursued him. Every day his spirits sank lower, and he felt that sooner or later something was going to snap. The atmosphere was getting more oppressive; his best customers had disappeared, and he suspected that the others had begun to distrust him. In fact, he was even afraid that he might be assaulted and he began to go about armed, feeling that he was engaged in the struggle. He always kept his Colt within reach; the feel of it had a quieting effect upon his nerves.

Finally he began to feel that he was being deserted by the very men who had got him into this—the other driver and the two or three plainclothesmen. They had enough to do to take care of themselves, and besides he was not much use to them any more. All the revolutionaries' doors were closed to him, and he felt paralyzed, as though he could not go forward or backward. After some months of this tension, he felt that he could not endure it much longer. When he saw the storm gathering, breaking, and spreading, he had a sensation of relief. "Let's get it over with," he said, and he waited.

But soon this feeling of relief, which had been caused by the changed situation, gave way to a new kind of anxiety. He had the impression now that he was surrounded, cut off, blockaded even; he knew that somewhere, sometime, he was being sought for by eyes he might never even have seen, eyes that were perhaps just awaiting a more favorable opportunity that would soon come. Then the situation would be the same as that first time he had been taken to headquarters, only just the opposite; and this time it would take a more violent and decisive form. It would be the end—that's all. If they had found him out—he thought they had—and if the "new ones" won—and he knew they were winning—then there was no way out. There was only one thing to do: lie low and wait—or get the drop on them and defend himself.

Both solutions were bad. Now, while he was trying to make up his mind where to go, he wondered whether there might not be a third possibility. He had imagination, but he had no faith in the images he conjured up. Still, he had to make up his mind one way or other. They wouldn't do anything to Estela; she was not to blame. The worst that could happen would be that she would have to face worse poverty, the children might die, maybe she would, too. . . . But if he saved himself, he would come back for her some day. Could he save himself?

He thought so. He started the car and let it roll slowly, though he did not know exactly where he was going. He thought he would take it to the garage and from there he would get to the country on foot or somehow. In Nuevitas there were still people who would remember him, or at least his father. They might give him some help, hide him, and let him wait. But then it suddenly occurred to him that there was sure to be a general uprising and that to appear in a little town would only be a sure way of attracting more attention, and that town was not revolutionary-minded. He had only a few friends there, as poor as he, whereas here in Havana at least there were plenty of people, plenty of houses. He would move to another garage! And if he could only move into a different house! That was what had been in his mind when he had gone over to that row of houses opposite the vacant lot, where they were building, but then he had suddenly felt utterly exhausted, and had fallen asleep before the automobile had quite stopped.

And now he was waking up on this August morning, when all hell was popping. Ramón realized that there was nothing he could do any more.

Two men with revolvers at their belts were going into one of the seemingly empty houses. At the same time another man appeared at one of the frameless windows, and when the others who were downstairs motioned to him, he rushed down. He, too, was armed. Ramón, who had gotten out of the car, had his head under the hood and was pretending to fix the motor. He did not know any of them, but they might know him. The three men, however, went by briskly and triumphantly up the street. In normal circumstances they would hardly have dared to act like that, for Ramón was sure that they were revolutionaries and that they were going after someone. They were not workers like him; they were well dressed, though at the moment coatless, and they looked well fed. It was their fight, a fight among the upper classes. Why had he been dragged into it, first by one side and then by the other? Still, that's how it was, and now there was no way out. First the old gang had been going to get rid of him, and now the new one was going to finish him off. That was a fact.

Well, perhaps it was, and yet he still had a flicker of hope, though he did not know exactly why. At any rate, he was not going to give up his taxi for a while, and he was not going to put it in the garage. He still had enough money for eight gallons of gas. His first thought was to explore the roads running out of the city, but when he reached the highway he could see that in Aguadulce it was being patrolled. He turned at the first corner and dived back into the heart of the city.

There was excitement everywhere. The whole town was on strike, and the streets were full of people and cars crowded with civilians and soldiers. They were shouting, cheering, leaping about, and brandishing their pistols. Ramón put down the flag of his meter, but it was no use. Four respectable-looking men rushed out of San Joaquín and into his car, ordering him to take them to the Cerro. At Tejas he saw a man struggling to get away from some others who had seized him and who were being egged on by the watching crowd, both men and women. Ramón took advantage of an opening in the mob to try to keep on going, but someone glanced into the car, and a group of men began to follow him, shooting on the run. One of the bullets went through the back window and out through the windshield. Ramón stopped and his passengers jumped out of the car and began to run madly through the side streets, pursued by several youths. Among them there were some who were little more than children—one of them must have been about fifteen—but they were firing large revolvers. Ramón pulled over to the curb, thinking: "Now they are going to come for me," but nobody seemed to pay any attention to him. Some excited bystanders came up to him to ask where he had picked up his passengers, and when he had told them the truth, they ran off toward San Joaquín Street. He even gave them the number of the house the men had come out of, but perhaps they did not live there; most likely they had spent the previous night hiding in one of the stairways. Who could tell what would happen now to the people who lived there? Everybody was openly armed; everybody was looking for someone to shoot at.

Once more Ramón started the car and went back to the same place, saying to himself, almost aloud: "I'll lose myself among them, and they'll think I'm one of them. That should throw them off the track." After all, he had been one of them. But then he wondered whether he could keep his nerve. He looked at himself in the rear view mirror and saw that he was pale and unshaved like a fugitive. At a time like this his face alone would arouse suspicion. But then as he was passing Cuatrocaminos, he saw another group of men running by with guns in their hands; some of them were as bearded and as grimy as he. Doubtless they were men who had been hiding these last months or who had been freed from jail. He might give the same impression; at any rate no one would take him for a person who had been on the payroll of the fallen government. He kept on moving. A few blocks farther along he ran into a mob that was frantically chasing a lone man. He was zigzagging madly down the street, hurling handfuls of bills at his pursuers, who did not stop to pick them up, but stepped on them and kept on following him, shooting as they went. Ramón stopped and waited with interest to see what the outcome would be. Finally the man, who was already wounded and had been leaving a trail of blood behind him, fell on his face a few steps from where Ramón had parked. On seeing that he had fallen, one of his pursuers went over to Ramón with his revolver in his hand and ordered him to give him a can of gasoline. Ramón obeyed, siphoning it from the tank with a tube. Seizing the can, the others sprinkled the wounded man, who was still writhing, while a third set fire to him. Ramón turned his back on the scene.

The streets were full of civilians and soldiers. Ramón started his car again. A few yards farther on, some armed youths piled into it, and kept him driving them around for hours without any apparent objective. Sometimes they would get out, force their way into a house, and come out again. As they passed the garage to which his car belonged, he noticed that it had been broken into. He stopped and asked to have the tank filled. Seeing that the car was full of armed youths, the attendant did as he was asked, and Ramón drove off with his passengers without bothering to pay. An hour later the young men had him stop in front of a small restaurant and invited him to eat with them.

It was past noon. Ramón sat down at the table with the strangers. It surprised him that not one of them had bothered to ask him a single question; apparently they took it for granted that he was one of them, that as an ordinary taxi driver he could be nothing else. While they ate, the young men talked mysteriously and with great excitement. They ate fast and went out into the street, apparently forgetting all about him, for instead of getting into the cab again, they went off down the street and disappeared into the crowd, which was thicker in this zone than anywhere else. They were in the very heart of the city. Ramón got in behind the wheel and sat for a while, wondering what he should do. He felt tired; he had gone so long without eating that his stomach no longer seemed to want food. And yet his fatigue could not outweigh his anxiety. Now he was fully conscious of being in a world to which he did not belong and in which, perhaps, there was no place for him. It would do him no good to seek new friends now; nobody would even recognize a man with whom he had just committed a murder a couple of hours ago unless they had been friends previously. In a few hours those youths he had been driving would not recognize him. Everybody seemed to be looking too high or too low; nobody was staring at eye level. And yet, he thought, there might be an advantage in that, for the people seemed to be possessed of a mysterious, frenzied sense of well-being which would perhaps prevent them from keeping close control of things.

Ramón came out of this daydream to see that a man was staring at him insistently from the opposite sidewalk. The man was watching him with a cold, attentive gaze whose meaning he could not understand, but he was sure that there was something behind it. Making an effort to overcome his nervousness, he got out of the car and as calmly and as naturally as possible pretended to look for something in the motor. He got in again, stepped on the starter without giving it gas, trying to give the impression that there was something wrong with the car (and that was what he was worried about), and then started off with a series of jerks. The man pulled a scrap of paper out of his pocket and jotted down the number of the license. Perhaps he was not sure. Ramón's may have seemed to him one of those faces we do not like, yet cannot recall at the moment exactly where we have seen them before. Otherwise, Ramón was sure, the man would have done something right then and there. He took for granted that his fate had been decided, mentally at least, somewhere, by people he did not know. To escape from the whirlpool seemed completely impossible; he did not even dare think of trying, for the mere attempt would have aroused suspicion. If there was any salvation, it was at the very heart of the maelstrom.

There was no driving down these streets. The whole city had poured into them. Ramón turned into a cross street and stopped when he arrived at the corner of the Prado, for it seemed a place where he would be inconspicuous. To keep people from trying to hire him, he let the air out of a tire and jacked up the wheel. Then he opened his toolbox and began to poke around in the motor. He took off the top and unscrewed the carburetor and a valve. Then he took out the other valves and began to clean them. He noticed that they were full of carbon, and when he got to the carburetor, he saw that it was dirty and almost clogged up. No wonder the car jerked and rattled. The work calmed his nerves a bit. He did not look at anybody or anything except the car, and therefore nobody looked at him. He had taken off his jacket, and in the trunk he discovered an old pair of mechanic's overalls that might almost have been put there on purpose. He put them on and smudged his face with grease. Then, climbing into his seat, he looked at himself in the mirror as he stepped on the starter. He thought it would be hard for anyone to recognize him the way he looked unless they scrutinized him very closely and knew whom they were looking for. Still, some of his features were hard to forget. He had large brown eyes with lids somewhat drawn together at the corners. Above one of his high cheekbones there was a small scar, and the curious line of his lips made him look as though he was on the verge of smiling — a wry smile. "Rabbit-laugh" they called him in the garage. All in all, his features made a strong impression on people. It had never occurred to him that this might be of any importance.

He got out of the car and went on tinkering with it. He took out the battery, cleaned the terminals, and put it back again. By the time he had reassembled everything, it was getting late in the afternoon. Those hours had passed less disagreeably than any other time since the beginning of the strike. The work had quieted his nerves, and the car was running better than ever before. Checking the four tires, Ramón saw that they were new; he had oil and gasoline. Before starting he took the revolver out of the pocket of the front door and examined it; it was a new Colt; with it he had a box of bullets. He took out those in the drum and snapped the trigger six times to make sure it was working right. When he had closed it again, he noticed that two or three boys were watching him enviously. Any one of them would have given his eyeteeth for a gun like it. The revolutionaries seemed to them the luckiest beings in the world. And they would be thinking that Ramón was one.

The car started again. Without knowing how he got there, Ramón soon found himself a block away from his home. He stopped. He felt an irresistible impulse to run in, to pay them a little visit; but at that moment he saw a huge crowd coming down the cross street. They were bearing trophies and shouting cheers and threats. The trophies were scraps of curtains, bedcovers, pictures, a telephone receiver, vases. . . . Ramón did not wait to see any more, but dived into the nearest grocery and turned his back on the crowd. When the people had passed, he raised the hood again and said to one of the children who came over to watch: "Go to Number 12 on that street and tell whoever you see to come over here for a moment." The child charged off, happy to have been noticed, and was back in a couple of minutes to say that there was nobody home. "They must have gone over to Balbina's," Ramón thought. "Estela must have realized"—as much as to say: "Estela knows that I am a dead man and has gone to consult with Balbina about how she's to look after the kids."

Once more he started the automobile. He went aimlessly along the same street as far as the Avenida de las Misiones, and there he turned off toward the sea. But he turned back at once, afraid of straying too far from the downtown area. He felt that as soon as he got to a solitary spot he would be assaulted, and there would be no witness to what happened. But what good were witnesses any more? None at all; but Ramón did not want to die, to be murdered, without someone around to tell the tale. It did not matter if they could not come to his aid; the deed would at least be engraved on their eyes, in their memories, and in a way it would stand as an accusation. Once at his house a crazy relative of his wife's had said: "Murder will out." She could not have been very crazy if she was able to say such deep things.

The sun was setting when he got downtown again. He moved slowly through parks and boulevards crowded with shouting, running people, and officers and soldiers fraternizing in a tremendous sense of triumph. All the cars were in motion; people and vehicles moved around in whirlpools from which strong currents of vengeance emanated. He heard shots high in the air; everybody had bloodthirsty eyes, everybody was hunting something. That was what frightened him most: in everybody's eyes he could see the hunting instinct. The slightest pretext, the slightest justification, would have been enough to unleash the rage he saw in every eye. As night fell, the movements of the crowds seemed to take on a new objective and a definite aim. There were groups that marched in brisk time, cutting like tanks through the others, which were shapeless and yielding. Ramón saw at once that these were like-minded comrades who, in the midst of the excitement and confusion, felt they had a self-assigned mission to accomplish.

These last few days he had often wondered what had become of Servando, the driver who had started him off as a traitor. He had stopped going to the taxi stand; he had left his car, which was his own, in the garage, and Ramón knew nothing about him. Now Ramón was parked in the very stand that used to be Servando's. Cruising about aimlessly, he had stopped there, though he could not have said why or how. He had seldom stopped there in the past. A big wagon appeared along the street where the trolley ran. It was apparently loaded with sacks of sugar; the lone carter was driving a team of old, worn-out mules. As it passed in front of the taxi stand, a group of eight or ten youths came out of a doorway and, going over to the driver, forced him to pull up. They began to throw the sacks on the pavement; after they had unloaded a number of them, three men climbed out from under the rest. The three men leaped to the pavement and shot off in the direction of the Prado. One managed to reach the first group of people and disappear; the second turned down the next street, closely followed by some of the youths, who were firing point-blank at him; Ramón did not have time to see the end. The third dropped right where he was. He had hardly touched the sidewalk, making for the doorway, when he straightened up suddenly, spun about on his heels, and toppled over. Looking out of the car window just as the man turned around, Ramón saw that his face was a mask of terror. It was Servando.

By then it had become completely dark. The people had begun to drift away, and there remained only the few who seemed to be going somewhere. Ramón at a glance could distinguish between the two kinds of people: those who were going somewhere and those who seemed to have no place to go. The latter withdrew early, leaving the streets to the others. "Now there's only them and us left," Ramón thought. Still he lingered for a while in the stand. He was the only one there; now he no longer dared to move away, for the center of the city was all open, while the streets were lined with dark doorways and sinister corners. The die was cast, he thought. Servando had fallen first, and now it was his turn, for his offense was the same. These maddened people were in no mood for explanations: they would not ask what his motives had been; they would only ask whether he was Ramón Yendía. The ghosts of the men he had betrayed would soon rise up to haunt him.

His train of thought was interrupted by the sight of a lone pedestrian who had stopped on the corner and was looking at him suspiciously. Servando's body had already been dragged away, and there was no longer any activity in the place where the car was parked. The pedestrian crossed the street diagonally, passing the car and looking at Ramón out of the corner of his eye as he went by. As he stepped up on the sidewalk, his face was illuminated by the light inside the building, where some factory hands were moving spools of paper. Ramón recognized the face instantly. It was that of one of his earliest (and less important) customers. He had been among the first to disappear when Ramón turned informer. Bad luck, undoubtedly. And now he was the first to turn up again. He would be followed by the others who were still alive. They would surround him. Perhaps they were already waiting for him at the street intersections he would have to cross. They had him cornered, like a runaway slave whose roads of escape have been cut off, and soon they would set the hounds on him.

Which hounds? The one that had stared at him as he passed must have been one of them, he was sure. A few moments later another man — a stranger, this time — passed and also stared hard at him. Ramón realized now that the executioners had arrived and that the execution ground would be that two-block rectangle. In his mind's eye he could see them posted, gun in hand, on the six corners. What were they waiting for?

This thought spurred him to action. He would not stay there. He would not accept death without a fight, huddled behind the wheel. At least he would run, fighting with what strength he had left. Who knows — life is full of surprises and the guy who fights has luck on his side.

Once he had made the decision, he stepped on the starter and took off in second. Thinking only of his driving, he moved down the first block at a good clip. The mounting speed and the hum of the motor brought him a sudden feeling of complete relief. His anguished thinking was over; a sense of action took its place.

The danger, the torment, the foreboding disappeared, leaving only one thing: the determination to run the gauntlet of his enemies and win out. As he approached the intersection where he supposed they would be waiting, he drove with one hand. In the other he held the revolver at the level of the window. But to his surprise no one bothered him, no one was waiting for him. He kept on a little farther along the street with the trolley tracks, and then slowed down. There were few people on the sidewalks, and they seemed to pay no attention to him. No one, not even his probable executioners, would believe that a condemned man could be at liberty and driving an automobile. Still, those men had looked at him meaningfully, and one of them definitely had a score to settle with him. Why hadn't he attacked him right then and there? Perhaps because he was not a killer; very likely he was not made of that kind of stuff. There are men who can't do it, no matter what they feel. There are some who can't even give the order. This man must have gone off with the information, and the other probably had nothing to do with Ramón.

Ramón pulled up beside a lamppost in the park. As he looked up toward an illuminated sign, he happened to see a clock. Time had passed too fast. Absorbed in his own drama, he had not felt it go by, and now it was nine. Now there was no one on the street except those who had something to do. You could see it by the way they acted and walked, but no one paid any special attention to him, though it seemed that everyone was hiding or at least betraying a certain amount of suspicion. Of all the cars that were moving about the city, his was the most conspicuous. He reflected that if it were parked, it would be likely to attract still more attention.

Then began a slow, painful drive. It seemed to Ramón that these were the last two hours of his life, and that very soon, perhaps before daybreak, everything that his eyes could see and his ears could hear would have disappeared, dissolved into eternal nothingness as if nothing had ever existed in the world, as if he himself, Ramón Yendía, had never been born, as if all that he had loved, suffered, and enjoyed had never had any reality. And the scenes of his life began to flash before him in pictures, as on a screen, clear, sharp, and exact, neither hurrying nor lingering. Present reality itself took on a meaning that it had never had; it was the reality of a dream. In it he saw many things at the same time, and still they never ran together or became confused. Past, present, people, things, feelings — everything was sharp, transparent, and definite. And yet all passed in a kind of procession from which no detail was omitted. The streets were fairly empty, and not a traffic policeman was to be seen. As Ramón drove, the car might have been moving on rails or floating in the air. Without knowing why, he went to all the places most closely connected with his life. First he passed the house where he and his two brothers and two sisters had spent their first night in the city, Balbina's home. Then the little factory where Balbina worked, and from there to the house where his elder sister, Lenaida — what could have become of her? — had lived with the Spaniard. After that he drove past the house of the Chinese who had married his sister Zoila, and, forgetting that the city limits might be policed, he reached the outskirts — the little wooden shack where the baby had died. He had met Estela in that neighborhood, first at a dance and then behind the place where they had the cockfights. Where the dance hall had been, there was now a factory; a watchman with a rifle stood at the door. Nobody bothered Ramón as he drove by. In fact, the soldiers who were guarding the exit from the city let him pass, once they had checked to see there was no one else in the car. On his way back, they did not even search it. Once more he passed the familiar places — the theaters, the movies, the nightclubs, the brothels, all those places where he had taken people looking for a good time. It had never occurred to him to think that life really had so many charms. Could it be on account of these charms that men fought and killed one another? And yet they were not satisfied; they always wanted more; they wanted to rise, to stand out above the crowd, to dream, to have power, to command, to be, to rule, to possess. They wanted to rise, trampling on others, just for the sake of rising and not merely in order to enjoy such things as music, women, wine, leisure, flattery, service, fine food, health — health!

This thought suddenly brought him out of his reverie. His car was moving along as though driving itself. There were no obstacles or stops; no one crossed the road; furthermore, he had been driving for five years, and now he could have kept it up all day long through the heaviest, most nerve-racking traffic, without having to think once about what he was doing; he could spend hour after hour musing and dreaming, letting his fancy wander, and still observe all the traffic regulations. Now it was easier. Then, suddenly, he began to concentrate all his thoughts on one thing: his wife and his children. It was for them, after all, that he had done what he had done, that he was where he was now. Where was he? He realized that he was just going by police headquarters, the place where he had been "persuaded" to change sides. Without noticing it, he had passed within a block of his house, and now he was going up Montserrate Street. At the door there was a cluster of soldiers and civilians, and there was evidently a lot going on inside. He braked a little to come to another decision: he still wanted to go home and see whether Estela had come back and how the children were. He would leave the car a short way off; right around the corner, opposite Palacio, was a good place.

Before he reached the corner where he planned to turn, a car sped by, almost scraping his mudguard. A face peered out of the window. It was like a powder flash. The face had appeared only for an instant, and it had been barely visible by the light of a street lamp, but that was more than enough. Ramón tried to go straight ahead and went into second at once, but before he could do so, the other car, which was newer and faster, had cut him off. Ramón then moved it into reverse, made a sharp turn, and took off at full speed in the direction of the sea.

And that's how the chase began. The other car, which was one of the latest models, started after him with the same fury. Two other new, fast cars started at once in support of the first, taking short cuts through different streets, disregarding the one-way arrows. Ramón had recognized that face, but before he had even been able to start off, two bullets had whizzed by his ears. It was strange, but he was not afraid; no one had ever before shot at him from such close range, and yet what he felt was not fear. Nor did he even feel distressed. That meeting had suddenly dissipated the terrible anxiety that had been oppressing him. His bursting brain, which had been pulled in a thousand directions, tortured by a thousand wires, began to work lucidly and with a single purpose. Like the aviator engaged in single combat at an altitude of a thousand feet, he had only one objective: to overcome his enemies, even if it was only by escaping. Before he reached the sea, the first Ford had caught up with him; they had managed to

keep him within range and directly ahead of them. The three or
four occupants at once opened fire with rifles and revolvers, but
none of the bullets hit either the tires or the driver. One of them
just grazed his skull; he had crouched down instinctively. As he
emerged into the avenue, he pulled out the choke, turned the car
rapidly, and gradually gave it all the gas he could. Then he took
his foot off the brake and concentrated completely on the wheel
and the accelerator.

The other car kept tailing him. Seeing the two of them turning
in the distance, another of the pursuers turned in order to head
off Ramón a few blocks farther down on the Paseo del Malecón,
but Ramón turned right instantly and went up the Avenida de las
Misiones. Although he did not have time to think it out, he knew
that he had the advantage on the turns. He had always been outstanding in the races for his skill on sharp curves. He would let
up on the gas entering the curve and then suddenly, coming out
of it, he would give it all he had. Besides, he was a condemned
man, fleeing for his life, and the dangers involved in speeding
were of small consequence. His first pursuer also turned quickly
and fell in behind, determined not to lose sight of him. Then the
race began through the downtown streets. On reaching the Parque
Central, Ramón shot like an arrow into the old city, where the
narrowness of the streets gave him the advantage. Besides, in that
labyrinth which he had covered a thousand times he was able to
maneuver continually and throw the other cars off the track. Of
course, Ramón did not have time to figure all this out. He, the
man who had been so absorbed in thought, had suddenly burst
into action under the guidance of a hidden being within him who
had taken control. Seeing that he was going down Obispo, one of
the other cars tried to take a shortcut through a side street on the
assumption that he would turn to the right. The reasoning was
correct, for two or three blocks farther down, Ramón turned right
on a cross street. Hearing him coming, the other car attempted
to block the way, but Ramón was speeding so fast that the other
went up on the sidewalk and ran head on into a wooden door,
bursting into a brothel. That left him out of the race, at least for
the time being.

The other two continued in hot pursuit without yielding an
inch. Only by turning continually could Ramón manage to keep

out of their line of fire. They saw him for a moment from far off and began shooting, but he had just arrived at an intersection, and he turned quickly. The tires shrieked along the asphalt. Sometimes he took his foot off the accelerator for a moment, at other times he stepped on it hard, heedless of the danger. Even at a distance people realized that it was a race and got out of the way. One man climbed a lamppost like a cat the moment Ramón emerged into the Parque Cristo and—to quote the man—"turned like lightning"—in the direction of Muralla Street. Somehow or other the third pursuing car also foresaw that Ramón would try to come out near the Terminal and sent two or three other cars to cut off that exit. But before Ramón got there, that mysterious being who was now guiding him made him turn about. He went down San Isidro at full speed, turned into the Alameda de Paula, went up Oficios, then along Tacón and came out at the Avenida del Malecón. Now he had another idea, and it was not to avoid the shots of his pursuers in narrow streets. It had suddenly occurred to him that if he got into the open country he could jump out of the car, leave it in motion, and flee through the hills.

But he could not get out into the hills by driving along the wide streets where he would be an easy target, so he turned at once toward the heart of the city, and then, going uptown from there, he started to look for a way out. Now he was being followed by more than two cars, which, however, were still unable to overcome their initial handicap. Their advantage lay in their weapons and numerical superiority, and in the fact that if one ran out of gasoline, the others could still keep on going. Ramón, on the other hand, could not stop to fill his tank; perhaps that was why he made up his mind to flee to the hills.

After weaving in and out of the uptown streets for some minutes, he decided to make a break for it. The moment had come when he would have to go through some wide street for a fairly long stretch. It was a risk he would have to run. His first plan was to go down the Avenida de Carlos Tercero in the direction of Zapata, past the cemetery, and then race down beyond the river. But before actually starting on this route, a strange idea came to him out of nowhere: he would not flee into the country, but would go as far as the hospital, run the car against a lamppost, and then enter the hospital to have his wounds bandaged. If he did not have a wound by then, he would inflict one on himself. Maybe his pursuers would not follow him so far, but would seek him instead among the houses where they found the auto. At the same time he thought that perhaps when day came he would find some way out. He did not know exactly how or what, but in some vague, fuzzy way he still hoped to find it. Naturally, he was not sure whether the hospital was not also in the hands of those who were now his enemies.

Having worked out his plan, he decided to put it into effect at once. In one second he visualized the exact spot where he would crash his car, and the speed that he would have to be going at in order to put it out of commission and yet escape with his life. The thought of the hospital came to him purely by accident. Passing a street corner where he had run over a child years before, he remembered that he had taken him to the hospital; it had been one of the most agonizing moments of his life. While he was waiting for the doctor to operate, he had turned so pale, his face had become so distorted, and his eyes had taken on such a terrified expression that another doctor had taken one look at him and ordered some medicine for him which he did not recognize. After that they had taken him into a room full of strange white machines and examined his heart and asked him a lot of questions. To their surprise, Ramón was not ill, nor had he suffered any attack; his conscience was responsible for the expression on his face. The doctors themselves had asked the mother of the child, who, fortunately, did not die, not to be too hard on Ramón in her accusations. She was a very poor woman, and she did not even lodge a complaint; after that Ramón used to go to see the child when he could and bring him little presents. He had always remembered the doctors' attention as one of the happiest experiences of his life. And now in this moment of supreme peril, when he had put his whole being into this struggle to save himself, he thought about those doctors or others like them as his possible protectors.

So he made a supreme effort to reach the hospital. As he was still in the heart of the uptown section of the city, he would have to cross a wide square before he could reach the place where he hoped to crash the car. Veering continually, cutting sharply, and turning on two wheels, he finally managed to approach his goal, but just as he was about to emerge into the broad avenue, he saw that two cars were drawn up across the street ahead of him. They were probably parked there. Ramón put on the brake as slowly as possible, mounted one of the sidewalks, and made a U-turn. The ones in front began to shoot at him; one of the bullets pierced his left wrist, but he felt very little more pain than if it had been a pinprick. As he turned, he observed that his relentless pursuer was coming toward him like a torpedo and shooting as he came. The bullets hit the car, but none managed to put it out of commission. Ramón gave it all the gas he had and drove straight at the other. For a moment a fatal collision seemed inevitable; the pursuer saw Ramón's car coming toward him and jammed on the brakes just before turning off on the next-to-the-last intersection. Without reducing his speed, Ramón turned into the same street through a hail of bullets. The pursuer lost a few seconds before he could regain full speed, but Ramón had been hit by another bullet, this time right on the temple. It had scraped the skin, like a plowshare turning up the grass cover of the earth. It did not hurt, but the blood forced him to close one eye, which began to smart. And so, blind in one eye, with one wrist perforated, bleeding profusely, he continued the race. He kept up his speed, more determined than ever to reach the hospital. Once more he headed in that direction, but this time by a different route. With the slight advantage that he had gained, he was able to reach the Calle de San Lázaro; turning into it, he pushed the accelerator down to the floorboard and shot off in a straight line.

He was blocked again. From three cars that had been drawn up across one of the last intersections came a hail of bullets, but the shooting had begun too soon, and he had time to turn to the right and get out of the line of fire. But by now the first pursuer had been able to regain the time he had lost, and was almost on top of him.

Ramón was now headed toward the city along the wide Avenida del Maine. He had lost considerable blood, and with it, no doubt, some of the energy and mental alertness that made it possible for him to continue that uneven duel. He began to feel faint; his hand was trembling on the wheel. The car kept on down the middle of the avenue, but no longer as steadily as before. His pursuers noticed what was happening. For a moment he would reduce his

speed as if he was going to stop, and then he would hurtle forward
at full speed. Furthermore, he was no longer traveling at a steady
pace. Sometimes he would veer one way, sometimes the other, as
if his steering gear was twisted. Three more cars caught up with
the first pursuer. The quarry was losing speed. Now they had him!

Still fearing a trick, they did not close in at once. Surely there
was someone else in the car besides the driver. If not, what were
they following him for? One of the men in the first car assured
the others that when the chase had begun he had seen a man
throw himself to the floor of the taxi. Yet no one had answered
their shots; there was only that crazy, desperately fleeing driver.
Then he himself must be guilty; otherwise why expose himself to
such danger? They followed him, no longer shooting, but keeping
their distance. It was obvious that the pursued man was losing
speed and control. Sometimes he appeared to be getting ready
to stop once and for all, but then he would move ahead in a series
of jerks. Now they had him within range not only of their rifles,
but of their pistols too. They gradually crept closer! With what
strength he had left, Ramón once more reached the Avenida de
las Misiones, and then for no apparent reason turned back toward
the city. He kept coming back to the spot where both his home
and police headquarters were located and where the pursuit had
begun. His pursuers guessed that he was trying to make it to headquarters. All they could think of now was not to lose the man who,
they supposed, was in the back seat. In order to make his escape
impossible, the car on the left and the car on the right drew up
almost alongside Ramón, while the one in the middle approached
from behind.

Opposite the Palacio, Ramón's car almost stopped, but then it
moved forward again briefly, as if in the tow of an invisible force.
The others kept their distance, approaching slowly. Once more
Ramón stopped, this time in the very spot from which he had set
out.

The lights were still on in headquarters, and people were going
in and out; the air seemed filled with a distant noise, a noise filtered and deadened through a dense felt wall. The different voices
were merged into a single even, dying murmur. Ramón turned
his eyes toward the building, whose inner lights were bursting

from the windows. His head dropped over his left shoulder, went limp, and sank on his chest. And still there was that smothered, dying noise far away, very far away. . . .

The other three cars stopped side by side in the middle of the street. Several armed men jumped out; others came out of police headquarters and surrounded Ramón's car. One opened the front door, and the driver tumbled out over the running board with his feet still on the pedals. At the same time others threw open the rear doors and searched the inside with their flashlights. They looked at each other in amazement. There was nobody there! Then one of the leaders bent over the driver, who was still lying with his body twisted, his head hanging, and his eyes closed. He flashed the light on him, looked at him slowly; he put out the light and reflected for a moment as though trying to recall something. Then once more he shone the light on the face and once more stopped to think. Everybody around him was silent, awaiting an explanation. The man said: "Does anybody know him?"

Nobody knew him. More men came out of headquarters. The body, still warm, was taken out of the car and carried inside. And in the electric light they were able to distinguish his features clearly. They were not ordinary features. Anybody who had ever known him would have recognized him. But no one recognized him. The first man who had shot at him was called in.

"What did you see in the car?" the policeman on duty asked. "I'm sure I saw a man; he looked out of the window and then he hid. Then I looked at the driver, and he tried to get away at once. That's why I followed him, and when we were out a ways he returned the fire."

They searched the car, but there was no gun. Ramón had not fired; most likely someone in one of the houses had done it. In fact, his revolver had been stolen from the pocket of the door, perhaps in the taxi stand while he was watching one of the men who was staring at him so intently. No one had seen anything else. The only testimony was that of the fellow who thought he had seen a man in the back seat. But why had the driver fled? He was only an ordinary hacker, obviously of no importance at all. They looked at his license, they inquired of the Secret Police and the Justice Department. They could not find his name in any of the

files. Meanwhile the body was there, lying on a table. They had
taken for granted that he was dead, though he was really only in
a state of shock due to loss of blood. But in two hours his body
was rigid and cold. His address was on his license; a policeman
went to his house, woke Estela and asked her some questions,
but got nothing. The terrified, trembling woman could give them
no information. She was living in the greatest poverty; it was
impossible that a government agent could have been so badly
paid.

All who had taken part in the pursuit were now standing perplexed around the body. Why the race, the pursuit, the victim?
No one could throw any light on anything. If there had been a
passenger, he could never have jumped out of the car. There had
been no opportunity, for he had never been traveling slowly
enough, and they had never lost sight of him. As far as the driver
was concerned, they had not been able to get to the bottom of
things even in the garage. Everybody regarded him as a nice guy;
nobody had ever heard that he had any political connections.
(Obviously they did not consider him very important, for the only
person who had known anything about him was his boss, the other
driver, and he had been silenced forever. He had left no written
evidence, for he carried everything in his head.) Finally, near
dawn, there appeared a little old man in uniform who had once
been a policeman and was now a clerk. He shouldered the others
aside and stood staring thoughtfully at the corpse. Then he looked
around while he stroked his long, tobacco-stained mustache.

"Why did you kill this one?" he asked. "He is one of your own
men. I remember him. I don't know who he is or what his name
is, but quite a while ago I saw him brought in here and beaten up.
They said he was a revolutionary. And he must have been one of
the best. They took him in there two or three times, and they beat
him black and blue, but they couldn't get a word out of him.
Then he never came back."

They looked at each other. The old man turned around, once
more shouldered his way through the crowd, and went back to his
work, bowed by the weight of years and experience.

— Translated by Raymond Sayers

COMMENTARY

The final two stories in this section on Cosmopolitanism demonstrate the application of the different aspects of this tendency to very specific local regions.

Ramón Yendía, although identified as a poor taxi driver in Havana during a revolutionary period in the early 1930s, represents the Existentialist man as do the anonymous protagonists of "Conversation." Feeling himself surrounded by death, Ramón lets his imagination run wild and propels himself to his own tragic end. In spite of the melodramatic pursuit, the prevalent tone is ponderous based on Ramón's fear and anguish; on his philosophical thoughts about life which he does not communicate to anyone; on his inability to make contact with his family; and on some stylistic traits: choppy phrasing — several paragraphs begin with very short sentences; the repetition of words in close proximity; and the abundant use of the semicolon. In contrast with the almost exasperating slowness with which the action is prolonged, the climax is lightning-like. The unexpected revelation that Ramón died by mistake completes the Existentialist vision of a purposeless, irrational world.

The influence of Surrealism may be seen in the fragmentary presentation of the past through a series of nightmarish memories. The story begins with the recollections of the past four days. While driving by the police station, Ramón recalls the torture scenes and how he let himself become an informer against his former revolutionary customers. At other moments, he remembers some details of his two families. Although his memories help the reader understand the present situation, they do not play as important a role as in the more exclusively Surrealist stories like "The Tree" and "A Nine O'Clock Date."

On the other hand, a very basic element of this story is the Cubist combination of a very precise, slowly moving time with eternal time. The whole action transpires in one day and one night. Therefore, the title's meaning extends beyond its chronological sense. Ramón's "dark night" refers to his life of agony. It almost resembles a scene from Dante's "Inferno": time seems to have stopped and Ramón continues driving in his futile effort to escape. It's almost as though he were living outside of chronological time like the protagonist of "Tell Them Not To Kill Me!" Like Rulfo, Novás Calvo uses the changing point of view, but only once, in the climax of the story.

The juxtaposition of Surrealist and Cubist elements with the exaggerated details and the precise names of Havana's streets envelops the whole story in a dreamlike, or nightmarelike aura, typical of Magic Realism. There are no magic figures as in "The Rain" and "The Switchman" but the pursuit is narrated with such minute precision that it takes on an unreal quality.

The combination in this story of the different Cosmopolitan tendencies and a very Cuban theme represents the genre's readiness to pass on to its next stage.

Augusto Roa Bastos

(1917)

Paraguayan. He began working early in life as a journalist. During World War II, he traveled as a correspondent through many
countries of Europe and Africa. He was exiled from Paraguay in 1947
and has lived in Buenos Aires since then. He started his literary career
as a poet but it is as a novelist and short story writer that he has achieved
a well-earned international reputation. In *El trueno entre las hojas*
(1953), his first collection of short stories, he utilized various themes
and stylistic devices that he later combined masterfully in one of the
best of the new Latin American novels, *Hijo de hombre* (1960). He wrote
the scripts for several controversial Argentine films. In 1966, he published
El baldío, a collection of short stories written between 1955 and 1961.
Los pies sobre el agua (1968) includes a few unpublished short stories
together with some that had already been published and two passages
from *Hijo de hombre.* His latest work is *Yo el supremo* (1974), a very
thoroughly documented and complex biographical novel of Dictator
Francia. "The Prisoner" was published in *El trueno entre las hojas.*

THE PRISONER

The shots answered one another intermittently in
the cold wintry night. They formed a wavering and indecisive line
around the hut. Between long anxious pauses, they advanced and
retreated along the edge of the forest and the marshes adjacent
to the riverbank, like the mesh of a net which cautiously but implacably closes. The echo of the shots went bouncing through thin
acoustic layers in the air which broke as they gave way. From the
duration of the echo, it was possible to calculate the diameter of
the dragnet. Taking the hut as the center, it was perhaps about
four or five kilometers long. But that square league of terrain,
tracked and scouted in every direction, was practically without
boundaries. The same thing was happening everywhere.

The popular uprising refused to die out completely. Unaware that it had already been cheated of its triumph, it stubbornly continued to raise hopes, with its threadbare guerrillas, in the swamps, in the thickets, in the razed villages.

It was when it ended, more than during the fighting itself, that hatred wrote its most heinous pages. The factional struggle degenerated into a brutal orgy of vengeance. The fate of whole families was sealed by the color of the partisan badge worn by the father or the brothers. The tragic storm devastated everything it could. It was the cyclical blood rite. The carnivorous aboriginal deities had once more revealed their fiery eyes through the foliage; in them men were reflected like the shadows of an old primeval dream. And the green stone jaws were grinding up those fleeing shadows. A cry in the night, the screech of an owl impossible to locate, the hiss of a snake in the tall grass erected walls which the fugitives did not dare to cross. They were boxed into a sinister funnel, trapped between the automatic rifles and the Mausers at their backs and the waves of hallucinatory terror that stalked their flight. Some chose to face the government patrols, and end it, once and for all.

The burned-out hut in the middle of the thicket was an appropriate setting for the things that were happening. It was a mournful and, at the same time, a peaceful sight — a scene whose effectiveness resided in its innocence ripped to shreds. Violence itself had not finished its work. It had not been able to erase certain small details in which the memory of another time still survived. The burned poles pointed squarely to the sky amid the crumbling adobe walls. The moon burnished the four charred stumps with a hue of milky whiteness. But this was not the most important thing. On a window ledge at the rear of the hut, for example, a tiny flowerpot still persisted: a rusty little tin can from which there emerged the stem of a carnation singed by the flames. There it persisted in spite of everything, like a forgotten memory, oblivious to change, surrounded by the eternal shining of the moon, like the eye of a blind child that has witnessed a crime without seeing it.

The hut lay at a strategic point. It commanded the only exit from the marshy zone, where the searching was taking place and where it was assumed that the last rebel guerrilla group of that region was hiding. The hut was something like the center of operations for the government patrol.

The weapons and the crates of ammunition were piled up in what had been the hut's only room. Amid the weapons and the crates of ammunition was an old splintered bench. A soldier, with his cap over his eyes, was sleeping on it. By the feeble flickering of the fire which, despite the officer's strict orders, the soldiers had kindled to protect themselves from the cold, one could see the worn edges of the bench, made smooth by years and years of rural weariness and sweat. Elsewhere, a piece of the wall shadowed a nearly intact small stone step with a black bottle dripping with tallow and a half-burned candle stuck in its neck. Behind the hut, leaning against the trunk of a sour orange tree, a small iron plough, with its ploughshare shining opaquely, seemed to await the early morning pull of the yoke on its splinter bar, and on its plough handles, the wrinkled and soft fists which now would probably be rotting in who knows what forsaken fold of the earth. These traces brought back the memory of life. The soldiers meant nothing, nor did the automatic weapons, the bullets, the violence. The only things that mattered were these scraps of a vanished tenderness.

Through them, one could see the invisible, feel in their hidden story the pulse of what is permanent. Between shots, which in turn seemed to echo other shots farther off, the hut propped itself up on its small relics. The rusty little tin can with the singed carnation was linked to someone's hands, someone's eyes. And those hands and those eyes had not completely faded away. They were there, they persisted as part of the undying aura that emanated from the hut, the aura of the life that had dwelt in it. The old shiny bench, the useless plough against the orange tree, the black bottle with its bit of candle and the tallow drippings stood out with a more intense and natural pathos than the total picture of the half-destroyed hut. One of the charred stumps with part of a beam still attached to it continued to smoke slightly. The thin column of smoke rose, disintegrating into bluish, cotton-like locks which the currents of wind fought over. It was like the breathing of the hard wood which would go on smouldering for many days yet. The heart of the *timbó* tree is as resistant to fire as it is to the ax and to time. But it was smoking too, and would end up as a somewhat pink ash.

On the earth floor of the hut, the other three soldiers of the squad warmed themselves by the feeble fire and fought off sleep with an incoherent chatter pierced by yawns and unrestrainable nodding. They had not slept for three nights now. The officer in charge of the detachment had kept his men in constant action since the moment of arrival.

A distant whistle coming from the thicket startled them. It was the password agreed upon. They grasped their rifles. Two of them quickly put out the fire with the butts of their weapons, and the other awoke the one who was sleeping on the bench, shaking him energetically:

"Get up . . . Saldívar! Epac-pue . . . Óuma jhina,"[1] Lieutenant . . . gonna settle things with you, kangüeaky[2] recruit. . . ."

The soldier stood up rubbing his eyes, as the rest rushed to man their supposed stations in the chilly night air.

One of the sentries answered the special whistle which was repeated, this time nearer. They heard approaching footsteps. A moment later, the patrol appeared. They could make out the officer walking ahead among the coconut palms because of his boots, his cap and his leather windbreaker. His short thick silhouette advanced under the moonlight which a film of cirrus clouds was beginning to dim. Three of the five soldiers who came behind were dragging the body of a man. Probably another hostage, Saldívar thought, like the old peasant the night before whom the officer had tortured in order to tear from him certain information about the rebels' hideout. The old man died unable to say anything. It was terrible. Suddenly, while they were beating him, the old man, his teeth firmly shut, began to sing quietly, with his teeth clenched, something like an unrecognizable polka, lively and mournful at the same time. It seemed that he had gone mad. Remembering this, Saldívar shuddered.

The manhunt gave no sign yet of coming to an end. Peralta was irritated, obsessed by this phantom redoubt which lay encysted

---

[1]"Hey, wake up! Come on!" in Guaraní. Many Paraguayans are bilingual in Spanish and Guaraní.
[2]"Tenderfoot" in Guaraní.

somewhere in the marshes and which continued to elude his grasp.

Lieutenant Peralta was a hard man, and one obsessed — an appropriate trait for the clean-up operation that was being carried out. Formerly an officer in the military police during the Chaco War, he was in retirement from the service when the revolt broke out. Being neither timid nor lazy, Peralta reenlisted. His name was in no way mentioned during the fighting, but it began to make the rounds when the need arose for an expert and relentless man to track down the rebels. That is why he found himself in this spot of rebel resistance. He wanted to put an end to it as soon as possible, in order to return to the capital and enjoy his share of the victory celebration.

Evidently, Peralta had found a track during his scouting forays, and was preparing to unleash the final blow. Amid the almost total numbness of his senses, Saldívar vaguely heard Peralta's voice giving out orders. He also vaguely saw his comrades load two heavy machine guns and leave in the direction indicated by Peralta. He heard something about the guerrillas being trapped on a small wooded island in a marsh. He vaguely heard Peralta saying to him: "Saldívar, you'll remain here alone. We're gonna corner those outlaws in the marsh. I'm leaving you in charge of the prisoner and the supplies."

Saldívar made a painful effort to understand. He finally managed to understand only after the others had already left. The night had grown very dark. The wind wailed harshly through the coconut palms that completely surrounded the hut. On the earth floor lay the motionless body of the man. Maybe he was asleep, or dead. It was all the same to Saldívar. His mind moved among a variety of widely differing scenes, each one increasingly incoherent. Sleep was gradually anesthetizing his will. It was like a sticky rubber sheath around his limbs. He wanted only to sleep. But in a very confused way, he knew he should not sleep. On his neck, he felt a bubble of air. His tongue had become pasty; he felt that it was slowly swelling in his mouth and that at a given moment, it would cut off his breathing. He tried to walk around the prisoner, but his feet refused to obey him. He tottered like a drunk. He tried to think about something definite and concrete, but his jumbled memories slowly circled around weblike in confusion gliding through his head, formless and weightless. In one or two flashes of lucidity, Saldívar thought about his mother and his brother. They were like painful grooves in his soft and spongy dullness. Sleep no longer seemed to reside within him, it was something outside him, an element of nature which nuzzled against him from the night, from time, from violence, from the weariness of things, and forced him to bow lower, and lower. . . .

The boy's body trembled less from the cold than from that sleep which was doubling him over in painful exhaustion. But he still remained standing. The earth was calling him. The motionless body of the man on the earth floor called to him with its silent and comfortable example, but the boy resisted, his pulse trembling like a young bird on a thin branch.

At eighteen, Hugo Saldívar was one of the many draftees from Asunción who had been snatched into military service at the outbreak of the civil war. The bitter chain of chance events which had forced him to undergo countless absurd experiences had brought him here, absurdly, to serve in the detachment of headhunters led by Peralta in the marshes of the south, near the Paraná.

He was the only boy in the group, truly a misfit among those men from varied rural backgrounds who were yoked to the execution of a sinister task which fed on itself like a cancer. Hugo Saldívar thought several times about deserting, about running away. But in the end he decided that it was useless. Violence overwhelmed him, it was everywhere. He was but a squalid bud, a drooping leaf nourished on books and school, on the rotting tree which was collapsing.

His brother Víctor had in fact fought resolutely. But he was strong and vigorous, and had his deep ideas about brotherhood among men and the effort that was necessary to attain it. He felt his brother's words on his skin, but he would have wished them engraved in his heart: "We must all unite, Hugo, to overthrow all this which no longer has anything to offer, and erect in its place a social structure in which we may all live without feeling like enemies, where the desire to live as friends will be the natural goal of everyone. . . ."

Víctor had fought in the Chaco War and had brought back with him that turbulent and also methodical urgency to do something for his fellowmen. His older brother's transformation was a marvelous phenomenon for the ten-year-old child, who now, eight years later, was already an old man. Víctor had returned from the immense bonfire ignited by the petroleum in the Chaco with a deep scar on his forehead. But beneath the bullet's reddish furrow, he harbored an intelligent and generous conviction. And he had built himself a world in which, more than clouded memories and resentment, there was ample faith and precise hopes for the things which could be attained.

It would truly be beautiful to live for such a world as Víctor's, the boy often thought, moved but feeling distant from himself. Later, he saw and understood many things. Víctor's words were slowly penetrating from his skin to his heart. When they met again, everything would be different. But that was still very far off.

He did not even know where Víctor might be now. Nevertheless, he had the vague impression that his brother had gone south to the tea plantations, to organize a revolt among the farm laborers. What if Víctor were with those last guerrillas whom Peralta was pursuing through the marshes? This wild thought had occurred to him many times, but he tried to cast it off in horror. No, his brother had to live, he had to live. . . . He needed him.

The compelling pressure of sleep continued to nuzzle against his skin, against his bones. It wrapped itself around him like a viscous, relentless boa, slowly choking him. He was going to sleep, but there was the prisoner. He might escape and then Peralta would be implacable with the negligent sentry. He had already shown this on other occasions.

Moving clumsily in his heavy rubber sheath, Saldívar poked around in the darkness searching for a piece of wire or rope to tie the prisoner. He might be a corpse, but perhaps he was pretending to be dead in order to escape in a moment of carelessness. His hands groped at every corner of the burned hovel in vain. Finally, he found a piece of vine—too dry and too short. It was no good. Then in a last, desperate flash of lucidity, Hugo Saldívar remembered that in front of the hut there was a deep hole, perhaps dug for a new post to support a roof which would never be raised. A man standing upright would fit in the hole up to his chest. Surrounding the hole was a pile of dirt which had been dug out. Hugo Saldívar leaned the Mauser against the remains of a wall, and began to drag the prisoner toward the hole. With an almost superhuman effort, he managed to put him into the black hole, which turned out to be like a pipe made to order. The prisoner stood upright in the hole. Only his head and his shoulders stuck out. Saldívar pushed the dirt from the mound with his hands and his boots, until he had somehow filled in all the open spaces around the man. The prisoner did not resist at any moment. Apparently, he accepted the sentry's act with absolute indifference. Hugo Saldívar barely noticed this. The effort expended revived him artificially for a little while. He even had enough energy to get his rifle and pack down the earth with the butt. Then, he dropped like a rock on the bench, as the hammering of the machine guns increased on the marshy plain.

Lieutenant Peralta returned with his men about noon. The mission was completed. A brutal smile illuminated his face, which was dark like that of a bird of prey. The soldiers prodded two or three bloody prisoners. They shoved them forward with curses, obscene insults, and rifle butts. They were more farm laborers from the upper Paraná. Only their bodies had been conquered. A glimmer of absurd happiness floated in their eyes. But that glimmer was already floating beyond death. They were only physically lingering a while longer on the impassive and thirsty earth.

Peralta called loudly:

"Saldívar!"

The prisoners blinked with a remnant of painful surprise.

Peralta called again furiously:

"Saldívar!"

No one answered. Then he glanced at the prisoner's head sticking out of the hole. It looked like a bust carved of moss-covered wood, a bust left behind long long ago. A line of ants was climbing the abandoned face to the forehead, like a dark ribbon from which the sun drew no glare. On the bust's forehead, there was a deep scar like a pale half moon.

The prisoners' eyes were fixed on the strange sculpture. Behind the greenish mask, crawling with ants, they recognized the comrade who had been captured the night before. They thought that Peralta's cry, calling the dead man by his real last name, was a supreme shout of triumph by the soldier tightly stuffed in the leather windbreaker.

Hugo Saldívar's rifle lay on the floor of the hut—the only clue of his desperate flight. Inside his narrow head Peralta was turning over fierce punishments for the deserter. He could not guess that Hugo Saldívar had fled at dawn like a madman, haunted by the bloody copper face of his brother, whom he himself had buried like a tree trunk in the hole.

The ants crawled up and down the face of Víctor Saldívar, the dead guerrilla.

The next day, Peralta's men found the corpse of Hugo Saldívar floating on the muddy waters of the marsh. His hair had gone completely gray, and all semblance of human expression had fled from his face.

—Translated by Gustavo Pellón

COMMENTARY

Friend of Miguel Angel Asturias and contemporary of Juan Rulfo and René Marqués, Roa Bastos utilizes Cosmopolitanite techniques to capture both the tragic reality of Paraguay as well as the basic relations among human beings.

Although this story is based on a single episode of a frustrated rebellion, the author uses it to present his world view. The key to the understanding of Roa's Paraguayan world is his concept of time which, in spite of its similarity to that of Borges and other Cosmopolitanites, has a special meaning within the Paraguayan context. The wars that have devastated the entire nation from 1865 on lead the author to eliminate progressive chronological time. Everything is repeated and the past is confused with the present, and at times, even with the future: "it was the cyclical blood rite"; "the carnivorous aboriginal deities"; "when they met again, everything would be different." The memory of the tortured old peasant who died after losing his mind presages Hugo Saldívar's own death.

Just as the past is not distinguished from the present, death is not distinguished from life. Similarly, reality and fantasy are blended. The geometric precision (a Cubist trait) in the description of the first paragraph takes on a fantastic air with the phrase "was practically without boundaries." The men's sleepiness transforms everything into a world of shadows and fantasy. Three times in one paragraph the word "vaguely" is used to reflect Hugo's somnolent state.

Within this world which is both brutally realistic and incredibly fantastic — in the vein of Magic Realism — the element of chance with all its absurdities predominates. Among these absurdities, the greatest one for Roa is that man should be condemned to kill his own brother, as a heritage of the biblical tragedy of Cain and Abel. In this story, the personal tragedy of the Saldívar brothers is a microcosm of what has happened, what is happening, and what will happen in the whole nation. Peralta is totally capable of relentlessly pursuing Víctor Saldívar and his fellow revolutionaries even though they all fought side by side against the Bolivians in the Chaco War.

Cain and Abel, reality and fantasy, life and death, present and past form part of the dualistic world of Paraguay with its origins in the co-existence of the two languages, Spanish and Guaraní, and the cultures they represent. There is also a stylistic echo of Paraguayan dualism, the predilection for series of two parallel or opposing words or phrases: "wavering and indecisive"; "advanced and retreated"; "cautiously, implacably"; the "mournful" and "peaceful" hut; "old" and "splintered" bench; "deserting"; "running away."

In order to emphasize the sleepy and fantastic atmosphere, the author uses respectively a very slow rhythm based on detailed descriptions and repetition of words and phrases; and a select group of Surrealistic similes and metaphors: "the green stone jaws were grinding up those fleeing shadows"; "the moon burnished the four charred stumps with a hue of milky whiteness"; "the eternal shining of the moon, like the eye of a blind child that has witnessed a crime without seeing it"; "it was like a sticky rubber sheath around his limbs."

Although Roa Bastos reveals in this story that he is a very talented writer with ample thematic material, he is really a better novelist than a short story writer. "The Prisoner" as well as the other stories in the collection *El trueno entre las hojas* constitute Roa's apprenticeship in preparation for his masterpiece, the novel *Hijo de hombre*. "The Prisoner" is superior to the other stories in the collection because of its structural unity, its creation of the Paraguayan atmosphere, and its transcendence, but the ending is a little weak. The realism of Peralta's brusque return and the excessive explanation of Víctor Saldívar's identity and Hugo's death do not jibe completely with the air of fantasy and the slow rhythm that the author has carefully created through the major part of the story.

Neorealism

In the early 1960s, it seemed as though Cosmopolitanism was being replaced by a Neorealist tendency adopted by authors born around 1930. Many of them started out by displaying their mastery of the technical innovations of the previous generation, but they soon convinced themselves of the need for a less "escapist" and more socially committed literature. Although they began writing in the period of the Cold War with the anxieties caused by a possible future atomic holocaust, these younger authors did not accept Existentialism as the final answer. The establishment of the new nations of Asia and Africa and the Cuban Revolution with its repercussions felt all over Latin America aroused their enthusiasm and social conscience.

For their themes, the Neorealists avoided the fantastic of some of the Cosmopolitanites as well as the ruralism of the Criollistas. Their characters are almost exclusively the poor — often children and adolescents — who live in the filthy slums of the big cities. There is no protest against nature or against human exploiters. Realizing the complexity of the social problems, these authors do not offer easy solutions. Influenced by Hemingway, their stories take place on only one plane, the present. There is a minimum of historical, geographical, social, and individual background. The emphasis is on a single episode by means of which the reader may create for himself all the background he wishes. The style is succinct in contrast with both the epic descriptions of the Criollistas and the experimentation of the Cosmopolitanites.

Although the Neorealist tendency was overwhelmed by the novelistic boom of the 1960s, it did play an important albeit short role in the development of the Spanish American short story. In contrast with the previous tendencies and movements, Neorealism rejected the exalted tone of Romanticism, the caricature aspect of Realism, the clinical studies and detailed description of Naturalism, the exotic themes and the *préciosité* of Modernism, the epic tone of Criollismo, and the hermetic character of Cosmopolitanism. The Neorealists were aware of their predecessors' contributions, they absorbed them, and with their professional attitude toward their craft, they too left their mark on the genre.

Pedro Juan Soto

(1928)

Puerto Rican. Among his colleagues of the so-called Generation of 1940, he is considered the best interpreter of the psychological traumas caused by the culture shock suffered by Puerto Ricans in New York City and even on their own island. Soto went to New York with the idea of becoming a doctor but abandoned his studies in favor of writing. He contributed to newspapers and magazines in New York City and Puerto Rico. Drafted into the army in 1950, he participated in the Korean War. After being discharged, he enrolled in Teachers' College of Columbia University where he received an M.A. in English. Unable to find a suitable position in New York, he returned to Puerto Rico in 1954 where he worked for over ten years in the publications department of the Office of Community Education. In addition to his volume of short stories *Spiks* (1957), the source of "Champs," he has published four novels: *Usmaíl* (1959), *Ardiente suelo, fría estación* (1961), *El francotirador* (1969), about the Cuban Revolution, and *Temporada de duendes* (1970); and two dramas: *El huésped* (1955) and *Las máscaras* (1958). In the 1970s, he taught and lectured in several American and Spanish universities.

CHAMPS

The cue made one more sweep over the green felt, hit the cue ball, and smacked it against the fifteen ball. The plump, yellowish hands remained still until the ball went clop into the pocket, and then they raised the cue until it was diagonally in front of his acned and fatuous face: his vaselined little curl fell neatly over his forehead, his cigarette was tucked jauntily behind an ear, his glance was oblique and mocking, and the fuzz on his upper lip had been accentuated with a pencil.

"Quiubo, man. Wha's up?" asked a shrill voice. "That was sure a champeen shot, eh?"

He started to laugh. His squat, pudgy body became a gaily trembling blob inside his tight jeans and sweaty T-shirt.

He contemplated Gavilán—his eyes once alive now no longer so, his three-day beard trying to conceal the ill humor on his face and not succeeding, the long-ashed cigarette gripped between lips behind which swam curses—and enjoyed the feat he had perpetrated. He had beaten him two games in a row. Of course, Gavilán had been in jail for six months, but that did not matter now. What mattered was that Gavilán had lost two games to him, and these victories placed him in a privileged position. They put him above the others, above the best players of the barrio, above those who had thrown the inferiority of his sixteen years, his childishness, in his face. No one now could deprive him of his place in Harlem. He was *el nuevo*, the successor to Gavilán and other respected individuals. He was equal. . . . No. Superior, because of his youth: he had more time and greater opportunity to surpass all their deeds.

He felt like going out in the street and shouting: "I won two games in a row off Gavilán! Now say somethin', go ahead an say somethin'!" But he didn't. He merely chalked his cue and told himself it wouldn't be worth it. It was sunny outside, but it was Saturday and the neighbors would be at the market at this hour of the morning. His audience would be snot-nosed kids and indifferent grandmothers. Anyhow, some humility was good in champions.

He picked up the quarter Gavilán had thrown down on the felt and exchanged a self-satisfied smile with the scorekeeper and the three spectators.

"Take wha's yours!" he said to the scorekeeper, wishing that one of the spectators would move to the other tables and spread the news, comment that he—Puruco, that fat kid, the one with the pimply face and the funny voice—had made the great Gavilán look ridiculous. But apparently the three were waiting for more proof.

He put away his fifteen cents and said to Gavilán, who was wiping the sweat from his face: "Wanna play another?"

"Sure," said Gavilán, picking another cue from the rack and chalking it meticulously.

The scorekeeper took down the triangle and set up for the next game.

Puruco broke, starting immediately to whistle and stroll elastically around the table, almost on the tips of his sneakers.

Gavilán approached the cue ball with his characteristic slowness and aimed at it, but he did not shoot. He simply raised his bushy head, his body leaning over the cue and the cloth, and said: "Lissen, quit whistlin'."

"Okay, man," said Puruco, and swung his cue until he heard Gavilán's cue stroke and the balls rolled and cracked once again. Not one was pocketed.

"Ay bendito," laughed Puruco. "Man, I got this guy licked."

He shot at the one ball, made it and left the two ball lined up with the left pocket. The two ball also went in. He could not keep from smiling at all corners of the pool hall. He seemed to invite the spiders, the flies, the various numbers runners among the crowd at the other tables to witness this.

He studied the position of each ball carefully. He wanted to win this game too, to take advantage of his recent reading of Willie Hoppe's book and all those months of practice taunted by his rivals. Last year he was no more than a little pisser; now real life was beginning, a champ's life. With Gavilán beaten, he would defeat Mamerto and Bimbo. . . . "Make way for Puruco!" the connoisseurs would say. And he would impress the owners of the pool halls, he'd get good connections. He'd be bodyguard for some, intimate friends of others. He'd have cigarettes and beer for free. And women, not stupid girls who were always afraid and who wouldn't go further than some squeezing at the movies. From there to fame: the neighborhood macho, the man with a hand in everything — numbers, dope, the chick from Riverside Drive slumming in the barrio, the rumble between this gang and that to settle things "like men."

With a grunt he miscued the three ball and swore. Gavilán was behind him when he turned around.

"Careful — doncha gimme that evil eye," he said bristling.

And Gavilán: "Aw, cuddid out."

"Naw, don' gimme that, man. Jus' 'cause yer losin'."

Gavilán didn't answer. He aimed at the cue ball through the

smoke which was wrinkling his features, and shot, pocketing two balls on opposite sides.

"See that?" said Puruco, and he crossed his fingers to ward off evil.

"Shut yer mouth!"

Gavilán tried to ricochet the five ball, but he missed. Puruco studied the position of the ball and decided on the further but better lined-up pocket. As he was aiming, he realized he would have to uncross his fingers. He looked at Gavilán suspiciously and crossed his legs to shoot. He missed.

When he looked up, Gavilán was smiling and sucking his sick upper gums, to spit out the bloody pus. Puruco no longer doubted that he was the victim of an evil spell.

"Don' fool aroun', man. Play clean."

Gavilán looked at him surprised, stepping on his cigarette casually.

"Wassa matter with you?"

"Naw," said Puruco, "don' go on with that *bilongo,* that evil eye."

"Jeezus," laughed Gavilán. "He believes in witches!"

He brought the cue behind his waist, feinted once, and pocketed the ball easily. He pocketed the next one. And the next. Puruco got nervous. Either Gavilán was recovering his skill or that *bilongo* was pushing his cue. He had to step it up, or Gavilán would win this game.

He chalked his cue, knocked on wood three times, and waited his turn. Gavilán missed his fifth shot. Then Puruco gauged the distance. He dropped the eight ball in. He did a combination to pocket the eleven with the nine ball. Then he got the nine ball in. He cannoned the twelve ball into the pocket and then missed on the ten ball. Gavilán also missed it. Finally Puruco managed to make it, but for the thirteen ball he almost ripped the felt. He added up to himself. Only eight points missing now, so he felt he could relax.

He moved the cigarette from his ear to his lips. As he was lighting it with his back to the table so that the fan would not blow out the match, he saw the scorekeeper's sly smile. He turned quickly and caught Gavilán in the act: his feet were off the ground and his body rested on the edge of the table to make the shot easier. Before he could speak, Gavilán had pocketed the ball.

"Lissen, man!"

"Watsa matter?" Gavilán said calmly, eyeing the next shot.

"Don' gimme that, kid! You ain' gonna win like that!"

Gavilán raised an eyebrow to look at him and sucked in his cheeks, biting the inside of his mouth.

"Wha's botherin you?" he said.

"No, not like that." Puruco opened his arms, almost hitting the scorekeeper with his cue. He threw down his cigarette violently and said to the spectators: "You saw' im, dinchya?"

"Saw what?" asked Gavilán, deadpan.

"That dirty move," shrilled Puruco: "You think I'm a fool?"

"Aw Jeezus Christ," laughed Gavilán. "Don' ask me 'cause I might just tell you!"

Puruco struck the table edge with his cue.

"You gotta play clean with me. It ain' enough you make magic first, but then you gotta cheat too."

"Who cheated?" said Gavilán. He left his cue on the table and approached Puruco, smiling. "You tellin' me I cheat?"

"No," said Puruco, his tone changing, sounding more like a child, his body wobbly. "But you shouldn' play like that, man. They seen you."

Gavilán turned around to the others.

"Did I cheat?"

Only the scorekeeper shook his head. The others said nothing, just looked away.

"But you was on top uh the table, man!" said Puruco.

Gavilán grabbed the front of his T-shirt almost casually, baring Puruco's pudgy back as he pulled him forward.

"Nobody calls me a cheat!"

At all the other tables the games stopped. The others watched from a distance. Nothing but the hum of the fan and the flies could be heard, and the shouts of the kids in the street.

"You think a pile uh shit like you can call me a cheat?" said Gavilán, pushing into Puruco's chest with the fist that gripped his shirt. "I let you win two games so you could have somethin' to brag about, and you think yer king or somethin'. Geddoudahere, you miserable . . . ," he said between his teeth. "When you grow up I'll see you."

The shove pushed Puruco against the plaster wall, crashing him flat on his back. The crash shattered the silence. Someone laughed, snickering. Someone said, "Wadda boaster!"

"An geddoudahere fore I kick yer ass," said Gavilán.

"Okay, man," stammered Puruco, letting the cue drop.

He walked out without daring to raise his eyes, hearing again the cue strokes on the tables, the little laughs. In the street he felt like crying but he didn't. That was sissy stuff. The blow he had received had not hurt him; what hurt was the other: "When you grow up I'll see you." He *was* a man. If they beat him, if they killed him, let 'em do it forgetting that he was sixteen. He was already a man. He could make trouble, lots of trouble, and he could also survive it.

He crossed the street furiously kicking a beer can, his hands in his pockets pinching the body nailed to the cross of adolescence.

He had let him win two games, said Gavilán. Liar. He knew that from now on he would lose all of them to him, the new champ. That's why the witchcraft, the cheating, the blow. Ah, but those three guys would spread the news of Gavilán's fall. Then Mamerto and Bimbo. No one could stop him now. The neighborhood, the whole world, would be his.

When the barrel hoop got caught between his legs, he kicked it to one side and slapped the kid who came to pick it up.

"Wachout, man, I'll split yer eye."

And he went on walking, ignoring the mother who cursed him as she ran toward her crying child. He breathed deeply, his lips closed tight. As he moved along he saw streamers fall and cheers rain from the deserted and closed windows.

He was a champ, walking along ready for trouble.

— *Based on a translation by Victoria Ortiz in* Spiks, *New York: Monthly Review Press, 1973*

COMMENTARY

By concentrating on a very specific episode, Soto captures the flavor of Puerto Rican life in New York City as well as the psychology of any sixteen-year-old boy. At first, the somewhat technical vocabulary and the hybrid Spanish used in the dialogue might not appeal to the uninitiated reader but little by little, the universal character of the story predominates. From the very first page, the boastful attitude of the protagonist and the fact that Gavilán had recently spent six months in jail create a tension that continues to grow until the climax. As the story progresses, Puruco becomes more and more real as the narrative point of view gradually changes to him from the objective omniscient narrator of the first paragraph. In the last seven paragraphs, Puruco's name is deliberately omitted so that the reader may feel closer to him. It is obvious by this time that all the third-person singular verbs and pronouns refer to Puruco. Puruco's final attitude—his venting his anger on the child with the hoop and his vision of streamers—nail down the universalization process.

"Champs" is an integral part of the collection entitled *Spiks,* whose purpose is more sociological than aesthetic. In "Champs," the following details, presented unemphatically, suggest the whole life style of the young Puerto Ricans in Harlem who frequent the pool parlors: the vaselined little curl, the cigarette behind the ear, the beer, the women, the superstitions, the numbers game, the drugs and the gang fights. The other seven stories in the collection and the six "miniatures" (short short stories) with which they alternate present other aspects of the same situation. The title *Spiks* indicates the author's protest against the racial prejudice and other difficulties that these new immigrants encounter. It's important to bear in mind that Soto and his Latin American contemporaries belong to the same generation as the American "beatniks" and the British "angry young men," who are less interested in artistic experimentation than the Cosmopolitanites. Of the seven stories and six miniatures, only "The Innocent" could be called experimental. In all the others, the very intense social consciousness of the New Realism predominates.

Enrique Congrains Martín

(1932)

Peruvian. A contemporary of Mario Vargas Llosa, his short stories of the 1950s along with those of his colleagues have been completely overshadowed by Vargas Llosa's successful novels of the 1960s and 1970s. Congrains was born and raised in Lima. As a youngster, he worked at several odd jobs including soap manufacturing. At the age of sixteen, he began submitting his stories to the Sunday literary page of *La Crónica*. In 1953, he founded the Círculo de Novelistas Peruanos for the purpose of publishing the works of young unknown writers. His own short stories appeared in the volumes entitled *Lima, hora cero* (1954), *Anselmo Amancio* (1955), and *Kikuyo* (1955). His last literary work was a novel: *No una, sino muchas muertes* (1957). He has since then devoted himself to writing pedagogical texts and resides in Venezuela. "The Boy from 'Next to Heaven'" is one of the four slum stories of *Lima, hora cero*.

THE BOY FROM NEXT TO HEAVEN

For some unknown reason, Esteban had come to the exact spot, to precisely the only spot. . . . But would it not be, rather, that "it" had come toward him? He lowered his eyes and looked again. Yes, there it was, still there, the orange-colored bill, near his feet, near his very life.

Why, why him?

His mother had shrugged her shoulders when he had asked her permission to explore the city, but later she had warned him to beware of the cars and the people. He had come down from the hill and, after walking a short distance, had spied "it" near the path that ran parallel to the road.

Hesitating, he bent down in disbelief and took it in his hands. Ten, ten, ten, it was a ten sol bill, a bill that contained many pesetas, countless reales. How many reales, how many medios exactly? Esteban's knowledge did not cover such complexities. But it was enough for him to know that it was an orange-colored piece of paper that read "ten" on both sides.

He continued along the path, heading in the direction of the buildings that could be seen beyond the houses that covered the other hill. Esteban would walk a few yards, stop and take the bill out of his pocket just to check its continued existence. Had the bill come toward him—he asked himself—or was it he who had gone toward the bill?

He crossed the road and came upon a vacant lot strewn with garbage, debris, and dung; he reached a street and there he caught a glimpse of the famous market, the wholesale market he had heard so much about. Was this Lima, Lima, Lima? . . . The word sounded empty. He remembered: his uncle had told him that Lima was a large city, so large that in it there lived a million people.

The beast with a million heads? A few days ago, before the trip, Esteban had dreamt of this: a beast with a million heads. And now he, with every step, was penetrating the beast . . .

He stopped, looked, and meditated: the city, the market, the three- and four-story buildings, the cars, the endless number of people—some like him, others not like him—and the orange-colored bill, still quietly in the pocket of his pants. The bill had the "ten" on both sides. In that respect, it resembled Esteban. He too wore the "ten" on his face and in his mind. His "ten years" made him feel secure and confident, but only to a certain extent. In the past, when he started to have an idea of things, his goal, his horizon had been fixed at the age of ten. And now? No, unfortunately not. Ten years was not everything. Esteban still felt incomplete. Perhaps when he would be twelve; perhaps fifteen. Perhaps this very instant, with the help of the orange-colored bill.

He walked around, prying deeper into the beast, until he felt he had become a part of it. A million heads, and, now, one more. People moved about, rushing, some went one way, some another, and he, Esteban, with the orange-colored bill, always remained in the center at the very navel.

Some boys his age were playing on the sidewalk. Esteban stopped a few yards from them and watched the game of marbles; two were playing and the rest formed a circle around them. Well, he had walked a few blocks and at last he had found people like him, people who did not constantly move about. It seemed, apparently, that even in the city there were human beings.

For how long did he watch them? Fifteen minutes? Half an hour? One hour, perhaps two? All the boys had left, all except one. Esteban kept looking at him, while his hand inside his pocket was caressing the bill.

"Hi, there!"

"Hi . . . ," answered Esteban nearly whispering.

The boy was more or less his age and was wearing pants and a shirt of the same color, something that must have been khaki a long time ago, but now belonged to that category of vague and indefinable colors.

"Are you from around here?" he asked Esteban.

"Yeh, uh . . . ," he became confused and did not know how to explain that he lived on the hill and that he was exploring the beast with a million heads.

"From where, huh?" he came closer and was in front of Esteban. He was taller and his restless eyes were examining Esteban from head to foot. "From where, huh?" he asked again.

"From there, from the hill," and Esteban pointed in the direction from which he had come.

"San Cosme?"

Esteban shook his head.

"From El Agustino?"

"That's right, from there!" he cried out smiling. That was the name and now he remembered it. For months now, since he had found out his uncle's intention to come and settle in Lima, he had been finding out things about the city. That is how he knew that Lima was very big, perhaps too big; that there was a place called Callao where ships from other countries arrived; that there were very pretty places, huge stores, very long streets. . . . Lima! His uncle had left two months before them for the purpose of getting a house. A house. "Where will it be?" he had asked his mother. She did not know either. Days went by and after many weeks the letter arrived ordering them to leave for Lima. Lima! . . . The hill of El Agustino, Esteban? But he did not call it that. The place had another name. The hut his uncle had built stood in the district of Next to Heaven. And Esteban was the only one who knew it.

"I don't have a home . . . ," the boy said after a while. He threw a marble to the floor and cried out: "Gosh, I don't have one!"

"Where do you live then?" Esteban got up enough courage to ask.

The boy picked up the marble, rubbed it in his hand, and then answered:

"In the marketplace; I look after the fruit, I sleep from time to time. . . ." Friendly and smiling, he put a hand on Esteban's shoulder and asked him: "What's your name?"

"Esteban. . . ."

"Mine is Pedro," he threw the marble in the air and caught it in the palm of his hand. "I'll play you, O.K., Esteban?"

The marbles rolled on the ground pursuing one another. Minutes went by, men and women passed by them, cars passed along the street, and the minutes kept on passing. The game was over, Esteban's ability was nothing compared to Pedro's. The marbles went back in his pocket and their feet back on the gray concrete of the sidewalk. Where to now? They started to walk together. Esteban felt much better in the company of Pedro than being alone.

They walked around. More and more buildings. More and more people. More and more cars in the streets. And the orange-colored bill remained in his pocket. Esteban remembered.

"Look what I found!" he had it between his fingers and the wind made it waver gently.

"Gosh!" Pedro exclaimed and took it, inspecting it in detail. "Ten soles, gosh! Where did you find it?"

"By the road, near the hill," Esteban explained.

Pedro returned the bill and thought for a while. Then he asked:

"What are you thinking of doing with it, Esteban?"

"I don't know, keep it, I guess. . . ," and he smiled timidly.

"Gosh, if I had ten soles, I'd go into business with it. Believe me, I would!"

"How?"

Pedro made a vague gesture that could mean many things at the same time. His gesture could be interpreted as meaning a total lack of interest in the matter—business, that is—or a great number of possibilities and prospects. Esteban did not understand.

"What type of business?"

"Any type!" he kicked an orange peel, which rolled from the sidewalk to the street; almost immediately a bus passed and crushed it against the pavement. "There are plenty of businesses, believe me, there are. And in about two days each of us could have another ten soles in our pockets."

"Another ten soles?" Esteban asked, amazed.

"But, of course; of course! . . ." He examined Esteban again and asked: "Are you from Lima?"

Esteban blushed. No, he had not grown up at the foot of the gray walls, nor had he played on the rough and indifferent pavement. Nothing like it in his ten years, except for today.

"No, I'm not from here, I'm from Tarma; I arrived yesterday. . . ."

"Ah!" Pedro exclaimed, observing him furtively. "From Tarma, are you?"

"Yeh, from Tarma. . . ."

They had left the marketplace behind and were now alongside the main road. Half a kilometer away rose El Agustino hill, the district of Next to Heaven, according to Esteban. Before the trip, in Tarma, he had asked himself: "Shall we go and live in Miraflores, in Callao, in San Isidro, in Chorrillos; in which of these districts will my uncle's house be?" They had taken the bus and after several hours of a dull and tiring ride, they had arrived in Lima. Miraflores? La Victoria? San Isidro? Callao? Where, Esteban, where? His uncle had mentioned the place and it was the first time that Esteban had heard its name. "It must be some new district," he thought. They had taken a taxi and crossed street after street. All different, but, curiously enough, all similar too. The taxi had left them at the foot of a hill. There were houses at the bottom of the hill, houses in the middle of the hill, houses on top of the hill.

They had climbed, and once they got to the top, next to the hut his uncle had built, Esteban contemplated the beast with a million heads. The "thing" stretched out covering the ground with houses, streets, roofs, buildings, farther than his eyes could see. Then Esteban had raised his eyes and had felt himself so high above everything—or perhaps so far below—that he had thought that he was in the district of Next to Heaven.

"Listen, would you like to go into business with me?" Pedro had stopped and was looking at him, expecting an answer.

"Me? . . ." he asked, hesitating. "What type of business? Would I have another bill tomorrow?"

"Naturally, of course!" he replied with assurance.

Esteban's hand caressed the bill and he thought that he might have another bill, and another, and many more. Many more bills, certainly. Then his "ten years" would be that goal he had always dreamt about.

"What type of business, huh?" asked Esteban.

Pedro smiled and explained:

"There are many businesses. . . . We could buy newspapers and sell them around Lima; we could buy magazines, comics . . . ," he paused and spat violently. Then he said, becoming excited: "Look, we'll buy ten soles worth of magazines and sell them right now, this afternoon, and we'll get fifteen soles, I promise you."

"Fifteen soles?"

"Of course, fifteen soles! Two fifty for you and two fifty for me! What do you think, huh?"

They agreed to meet at the foot of the hill in an hour; they agreed that Esteban would say nothing to his mother or to his uncle; they agreed that they would sell magazines and that from Esteban's ten soles many things would develop.

Esteban had eaten lunch in a hurry and asked his mother to let him go down to the city again. His uncle didn't have lunch with them, since where he worked he was given a free lunch, absolutely free, as he had emphasized when he explained his working conditions to them. Esteban walked down the winding path, jumped over the stream and stopped at the edge of the main road, at exactly the same spot where, in the morning, he had found the ten sol bill. After a little while Pedro appeared and they started to walk together, entering into the beast with a million heads.

"You'll see how easy it is to sell magazines, Esteban. We'll put them anywhere, the people will see them and, presto, they'll buy them for their children. And if we want to, we'll start shouting the names of the magazines in the street, and that way the people will come faster. . . . You'll see how easy it is to make money. . . ."

"Is the place very far?" Esteban asked, on seeing that the streets seemed to go on forever. How far away Tarma was now, how far away was everything which, until a few days ago, had been familiar to him.

"No, not much more. Now we're near the trolley and we can bum a ride downtown."

"How much is the trolley?"

"Nothing!" and he laughed heartily. We just take it and tell the driver to let us go as far as the Plaza San Martín.

More and more blocks. And the cars, some old, some incredibly new and shiny, passed swiftly heading for God knows where.

"Where do all these people in the cars go?"

Pedro smiled and looked at Esteban. But, where were they really going? Pedro couldn't find a satisfactory answer and he just shook his head. More and more blocks. At last the street came to an end and they came to a kind of park.

"Run!" Pedro shouted at him suddenly. The trolley was starting to move. They ran, they leaped across the street and jumped on to the lower step.

Once aboard, they looked at each other smiling. Esteban began to lose his fear and came to the conclusion that he was still the center of everything. The beast with a million heads was not so frightening as he had dreamt, and he did not mind staying there always, here or there, in the very center, in the very navel of the beast. It seemed that the trolley had stopped for good this time, after several stops. Everybody had left his seat and Pedro was pushing him.

"Come on, what are you waiting for?"

"It's here?"

"Of course, come on."

"They got off and once again they started to move about on the beast's concrete skin. Esteban saw more people and saw them going—God knows where—faster than before. Why didn't they walk calmly, gently, with ease, like the people in Tarma?

"Later we'll come back and we'll sell the magazines right around here."

"All right," Esteban agreed. The place did not matter at all, he told himself, what mattered was to sell the magazines, and that the ten soles should multiply. That's what mattered.

"You don't have a father either?" Pedro asked him, as they turned toward a street along which the trolley tracks passed.

"No, I don't. . . . ," and he lowered his head sadly. A moment later, Esteban asked: "And you?"

"Me neither, no father or mother," Pedro shrugged his shoulders and walked faster. Then he inquired casually: "And the man you call 'uncle'?"

"Oh . . . he lives with my mother; he's come to Lima to work as a driver. . . ." he stopped talking, but then said: "My father died when I was little. . . ."

"Oh. . . . And your 'uncle,' how does he treat you?"

"O.K.; he leaves me alone."

"Ah!"

They had arrived at the place. Behind a gate, you could see a rather large patio, doors, windows, and two signs advertising wholesale magazines.

"Come on, let's go in," Pedro ordered him.

They were inside. There magazines from the ground up to the roof, and some boys like them; two women and a man were deciding on which magazines to buy. Pedro went to one of the shelves and started accumulating magazines under his arm. He counted them and examined them again.

"Pay."

Esteban hesitated for a second. To let go of the orange-colored bill was more unpleasant than he had imagined. It was good having it in his pocket and being able to caress it as often as he liked.

"Pay," Pedro repeated, showing the magazines to a fat salesman.

"It's exactly ten soles?"

He clung to the bill desperately, but finally pulled it from his pocket. Pedro took it rapidly and handed it over to the man.

"Come on," he said, pulling him.

They set themselves up in the Plaza San Martín and placed the ten magazines in a line on one of the walls that surrounds the park. "Magazines, magazines, magazines, Mr.; magazines, Miss, magazines, magazines." Every time one of the magazines disappeared with a customer, Esteban sighed with relief. There were six magazines left and soon, if things continued this way, there would be none left.

"What do you think, huh?" Pedro asked, smiling with pride.

"It's good, good. . . ." and he felt enormously thankful to his friend and partner.

"Magazines, magazines; don't you want a comic, Mr.?"

The man stopped and looked at the magazines.

"How much?"

"Only one sol fifty. . . ."

The man held two magazines. "Which one, which one will he take?" At last he made up his mind.

"Here you are."

And the coins fell, clinking, into Pedro's pocket. Esteban did nothing but observe; he was thinking and reaching his own conclusions: one thing was to dream, there in Tarma, about a beast with a million heads, and another was to be in Lima, in the very center of the Universe, absorbing and savoring life with satisfaction. He was the capitalist partner and the business was going stupendously. "Magazines, magazines," the technical partner was shouting, and one more magazine disappeared into impatient hands. "Hurry up with the change!" the customer shouted. And everybody walked quickly, rapidly. Where are they going, that they are in such a hurry?" Esteban thought.

Well, well, the beast was a kind, friendly beast, although somewhat hard to understand. This did not matter; surely, with time, he would get used to it. It was a wonderful beast that was allowing the ten sol bill to multiply. Now there were only two magazines left on the wall. Only two and eight scattered around unknown and ignored corners of the beast. "Magazines, magazines, comics at one sol fifty, comics. . . ." Now there was only one magazine left and Pedro announced that it was four-thirty.

"Good God, I'm starving, I haven't had lunch! . . ." he then exclaimed.

"You haven't had lunch?"

"No, I haven't. . . ." He observed possible customers among the passersby and suggested: "Could you go and buy me a roll or a piece of cake?"

"All right," Esteban agreed immediately.

Pedro took a sol out of his pocket and explained:

"This is from the two fifty of my profits, O.K.?"

"Sure, I understand."

"Do you see that movie theater?" Pedro asked, pointing to the one on the corner. Esteban nodded. All right, you take that street and halfway up the block there's a small shop run by some Japanese. Go and buy me a ham sandwich or bring me a banana and some cookies, anything, O.K., Esteban?"

"Sure."

He took the sol, crossed the street, passing between two parked cars and walked up the street that Pedro had pointed out to him. Yes, there was the shop. He went in.

"Give me a ham sandwich," he asked the girl who waited on him.

She took a roll out of the window, wrapped it in a piece of paper and gave it to him. Esteban put the coin on the counter.

"It's one sol twenty," the girl told him.

"One sol twenty! . . ." he returned the roll and hesitated for a second. Then he made up his mind: "Give me a sol's worth of cookies then."

He had the bag of cookies in his hand and was walking slowly. He passed the movie theater and stopped to look at the attractive advertisements. He took his time looking and then continued walking. Would Pedro have sold the last magazine by now?

Later, he would return to Next to Heaven happy, absolutely happy. He thought about this, hurried, waited for some cars to pass and crossed the street. Twenty or thirty yards from where Pedro had stood. Or had he made a mistake? Because Pedro was no longer there or anywhere. He came to the exact spot and nothing, neither Pedro nor the magazine, nor the fifteen soles, nor. . . . How had he managed to get lost or so mixed up? But wasn't it here where they had been selling the magazines? Was it or wasn't it? He looked around. Yes, in the park behind him the chocolate wrapper was still there. The paper was yellow with red and black letters, and he had noticed it when they had set up more than two hours ago. Then, he hadn't made a mistake? And Pedro, and the fifteen soles, and the magazine?

Well, there was no need to get scared, he thought. Surely he had taken too long and Pedro was looking for him. That had to be it. The minutes passed by. No, Pedro had not gone to look for him: otherwise he would be back by now. Perhaps he had gone with a customer to get some change. More and more minutes passed by. No, Pedro had not gone to look for change: in that case he would be back already. Then? . . .

"Mr., do you have the time?" he asked a young man who was passing by.

"Yes, five o'clock sharp."

Esteban looked down, his gaze sinking into the skin of the beast, and he preferred not to think. He understood that, if he did, he would end up crying and that could not be. He was already ten years old, and ten years were not eight or nine. They were ten!

"Do you have the time, Miss?"

"Yes" she smiled and said in a pretty voice: "Ten after six," and she continued on in a hurry.

And Pedro, and the fifteen soles, and the magazine? . . . Where were they, in which part of the beast with a million heads were they? . . . Unfortunately he did not know and the only possibility left was to wait and to keep on waiting. . . .

"Do you have the time, Mr.?"

"A quarter to seven."

"Thanks. . . ."

Then? . . . Then, Pedro was not going to return? . . . Neither Pedro, nor the fifteen soles, nor the magazine were going to return? . . . Scores of neon signs had turned on; neon signs that were flickering on and off; and more and more people walking on the skin of the beast. And the people were walking faster now. Quickly, quickly, hurry up, faster still, more, more, one must hurry up, hurry up more. . . . And Esteban remained there motionless, leaning against the wall, with the bag of cookies in his hand and his hopes in Pedro's pocket. . . . Motionless, exercising self-control in order not to end up in a complete flood of tears.

Then, Pedro had tricked him? . . . Pedro, his friend, had stolen his orange-colored bill? . . . Or couldn't it be, rather, that the beast with a million heads was the cause of everything? . . . And, do you think for one moment that Pedro wasn't an integral part of the beast? . . .

Yes and no. But nothing mattered any more. He left the wall, bit into a cookie, and sadly went to take the trolley.

—Translated by Margarita Payeras-Cifre

COMMENTARY

In the 1950s a new generation of Peruvian short story writers seems to have concentrated on one theme alone: life in the rapidly expanding slums of Lima. "La sequía" by José Bonilla Amado (1927), "El muñeco" by Carlos E. Zavaleta (1928), "Los gallinazos sin plumas" by Julio Ramón Ribeyro (1929), "El niño de junto al cielo" by Enrique Congrains Martín (1932), and "Arreglo de cuentas" by Mario Vargas Llosa (1936) all deal with the cruel world in which the poor children of a large city are raised. Sociologically, these stories reflect the flight from the countryside and the chaotic growth of the large population centers throughout the world. The authors, however, who are professional literati — some have received Ph.D.s in literature — never forget that they are artists and they know how to capture the personal dramas that stem from the sociological problems. Whereas these writers dominated the 1950s with their short stories, from the mid-1960s on, they seem to have been overwhelmed by the success of the Latin American novel in general and by that of their colleague Mario Vargas Llosa in particular.

Although the combination of fantasy and reality in "The Boy from 'Next to Heaven'" is somewhat suggestive of Magic Realism, there is never any doubt about the reality of the plot or the existence of the two characters. Actually, the occasional touches of fantasy help reinforce the realism of the child protagonist's view of the world. Likewise, a time that is simultaneously rapidly moving and immobile as in Esteban's contemplation of the game of marbles and his waiting for Pedro's return is not derived from Cubist experimentation but rather from a child's unawareness of the passage of time.

From the very beginning, the narrator uses rhetorical questions and repetition to capture a child's manner of speaking and to make it appear that Esteban himself is the indirect narrator. The insistence on the image of the city as the beast with a million heads in contrast with the name of the district, "Next to Heaven," is made less to produce an artistic effect than to capture the spirit of children's literature. The moment in which Esteban becomes aware of Pedro's betrayal coincides with the dizzyingly rapid movement of the beast that wants to swallow him up. The impassive resistance of the child might indicate the unyielding force of the stoic Indian, except that in this story the author does not stress Esteban's Indian background. Above all, he is a child for whom life is a series of incomprehensible chance occurrences. The finding of the ten sol bill, which he associates with his own ten years, is as fortuitous as the revelation of the find to Pedro. That's precisely one of the good points of the story. Pedro becomes Esteban's friend without any premeditated malice. Only after Esteban impulsively tells Pedro of the find does the latter begin to plan the theft. Esteban's incredulity in the face of his first betrayal by a peer gradually turns into painful certainty. The biting into the cookie is a reaction as bitter, as resigned . . . and as universal as Peruco's revenge in "Champs" against the world's irrational injustice.

Decade of the Boom: 1960–1970, and Beyond

The great prestige attained by the Spanish American short story in the 1950s has helped it survive in the 1960s and 1970s in spite of the fierce competition from the new novel of the so-called Boom. Although no new writers of the quality of Borges, Onetti, Cortázar, Arreola, and Rulfo have emerged in recent years, the continued production of the first three authors and the truly astounding number of new anthologies and critical studies have contributed to a widespread diffusion of the short story among an increasingly larger reading public.

In addition to the continuous efforts of the Fondo de Cultura Económica in Mexico and the intensified program of the Editorial Sudamericana in Buenos Aires, the Spanish American short story—and Spanish American literature in general—has greatly profited from the establishment of several new publishing houses: in Mexico, Joaquín Mortiz, Era, and Siglo XXI; in Montevideo, Alfa and Arca; in Caracas, Monte Avila; in Cuba, the Casa de las Américas with its annual contests, its journal, and its editions of both Cuban and Spanish American authors. In Spain, Seix Barral in Barcelona and Alianza Editorial in Madrid have contributed very significantly to the current worldwide vogue of Spanish American literature. Key roles have also been played by certain journals like *Imagen* (1967–) in Caracas and the Paris-based *Mundo Nuevo* (1966-1968) directed by Emir Rodríguez Monegal.

The great increase in the number of readers reflects, in part, the tremendous growth of the capital cities with the corresponding increase in student enrollment in the universities and a consequent proliferation of other cultural activities. At the same time, the Spanish American consumers of the Generation of 1954 no longer snobbishly reject national products simply because they are national. This reaction against the traditional deprecation of the national culture is reinforced by the lively interest of European and American intellectuals aroused by both the intrinsic value of the new literary works and the international repercussions of the Cuban Revolution.

The Generation of 1954, according to the generational theory of José Juan Arrom, is comprised of the authors born between 1924 and 1954 who dominate the period between 1954 and 1984. Therefore, the same events indicated as decisive in the formation of the Puerto Rican and

Peruvian Neorealists of the preceding chapter continue to be valid throughout the nineteen-sixties and early seventies. The need to become socially involved sprang from the Vietnam War and the student protests that broke out in 1968 in Mexico, France, Japan, the United States and in so many other countries. This revolutionary spirit with its reaction against the hallowed values of the rationalistic bourgeois world was reflected not only in literature but also in films and popular music. Thus the barriers between literary genres and also between the different media of artistic expression were eliminated.

There is no doubt that starting precisely in 1960 the novel recovers its traditional hegemony over the short story. From the publication of *Hijo de hombre* by Augusto Roa Bastos, through the astounding year of 1967 (June: publication and immediate success of *Cien años de soledad* by Gabriel García Márquez; August: the Hollywood-Academy-Award atmosphere surrounding Vargas Llosa in Caracas for his prize-winning *La case verde*; October: the bestowing of the Nobel Prize on Miguel Angel Asturias) and through the 1970s, all the important authors have preferred the novel in order to capture their panoramic visions of a reality that transcends national borders. Although Roa Bastos, García Márquez, Carlos Fuentes, José Donoso, Cabrera Infante, and Julio Cortázar published volumes of short stories during these years, only those of Cortázar surpass his novels even though some critics might argue for the superiority of his *Rayuela*.

Just as Borges dominated the decade of the fifties with his fantastic and philosophical short stories, Julio Cortázar prevailed as the undisputed master in the sixties with a more personal and at times a more socially conscious type of Magic Realism. At the end of the decade of the fifties, it appeared that Neorealism would replace Borgian Cosmopolitanism. With the vantage point of an additional decade, it is apparent that Neorealism was quite short-lived and was overwhelmed by the exuberant experimentation of the "Boom." Precisely in the two countries, Peru and Puerto Rico, where Neorealism demonstrated the greatest vigor, short story production has declined notably. Of the truly Neorealistic short stories of the 1960s, two by the Chilean Fernando Alegría (1918)—"A veces, peleaba con su sombra" and "Los simpatizantes"—are particularly outstanding. It should be pointed out, however, that in his other stories, Alegría does not limit himself to the linear development of a single episode in the present; he prefers to compete with the younger writers of the "Boom" in their constant search for structural stylistic innovations.

Actually, if there is one single trait that characterizes the majority of the short stories written between 1960 and the present, it is formal experimentation, whether it be in the allegorical simplicity of the mini-stories, in the chronological complexity of the psychoanalytical stories, or in the ambiguities of Magic Realism. Rather than a reaction against Borges, these stories are different modifications. In Argentina, Borges, after apparently abandoning the short story for poetry, published *El informe de Brodie* in 1970 and *El libro de arena* in 1975 which are restatements, albeit in simpler terms, of his previous works. Borges's colleague Adolfo Bioy Casares (1914) continued to follow the tradition of the fantastic story with his volume *El gran serafín* (1967). Other authors followed the Borgian interpretation of history ("Historia del guerrero y la cautiva"), although they may have been inspired more directly by Juan José Arreola ("Teoría de Dulcinea," "El discípulo") and Alejo Carpentier ("Semejante a la noche"), in treating historical events and characters as if they were contemporaneous: Guatemalan Augusto Monterroso (1921), Colombians Pedro Gómez Valderrama (1923), and Alvaro Mutis (1923), and Ecuadorean Vladimiro Rivas Iturralde (1944).

From Borges, passing through Arreola, also comes the fondness for the stories of the absurd which are sometimes compressed into mini- or micro-stories by Argentineans Cortázar, Enrique Anderson Imbert (1910), and Marco Denevi (1922); Cuban Virgilio Piñera (1912); Guatemalan Monterroso; Salvadoran Alvaro Menéndez Leal (1931); Honduran Oscar Acosta (1933); and Mexican René Avilés Fabila (1940).

In the short stories of the youngest writers of this last group, one notes a greater sociopolitical concern, absent from the work of Borges. Although it is totally unjust to call him an escapist, Borges did prefer the metaphysical themes of universal man to the immediate problems of his fellow Argentineans. Nevertheless, one of his very best stories, "El sur," is undoubtedly one of the finest examples of Magic Realism. This tendency, although its antecedents go back to Uslar Pietri, Arreola, Novás Calvo, and Roa Bastos, did not reach its height until the sixties when a whole group of short story writers led by Cortázar stands out: Uruguayans Juan Carlos Onetti (1909) and the Mario Benedetti of *La muerte y otras sorpreses* (1968); Chilean Jorge Edwards (1931); Colombians Gabriel García Márquez (1928) and Oscar Collazos (1942); Venezuelans Salvador Garmendia (1928) and Adriano González León (1931); Mexicans Carlos Fuentes (1929) and Juan Tovar (1941).

In opposition to the prevailing Magic Realist tendency, the late 1960s and early 1970s witnessed a reaction by the revolutionary youth, inspired in part by Cortázar's *Rayuela*. Heirs of the beatnik movement initiated literarily by Jack Kerouac (1922–1969), the Mexican *onderos* Gerardo de la Torre (1938), José Agustín (1944), Juan Ortuño Mora (1944), and Manuel Farill Guzmán (1945); the Colombian J. Mario Arbeláez (1939); the Chilean Antonio Skármeta (1940), and others reject the magic element in order to capture the sensation of the moment. Voracious readers of Cortázar and Fuentes, of Gunther Grass and Malcolm Lowry, of J. D. Salinger and Truman Capote, these young writers employ a consciously anti-rhetorical tone to comment on the creative process; they do not confine themselves within the limits of the traditional genres; they make language itself the protagonist of the work; and they do not hesitate to express openly their revolutionary ideology following the example of rock music.

By the mid 1970s, the revolutionary fervor seems to have subsided and most of these promising young writers have failed to show further artistic development. It may not be purely coincidental that the next generation (according to Arrom's generational theory) will not inaugurate its new vision of reality with its new aesthetics until 1984, the same year chosen by George Orwell for his novel about the dehumanizing consequences of a government based on technocracy.

Julio Cortázar

(1914)

Argentinean. His international reputation was enhanced by the American translation of his experimental novel *Hopscotch* and by Antonioni's film *Blow-up*, inspired by one of his most complex short stories. Cortázar was born in Belgium but grew up in the outskirts of Buenos Aires. He taught for five years in various high schools before moving to the University of Cuyo in Mendoza where he offered courses in French literature. He resigned in protest against the Perón regime, moved to Buenos Aires, and in 1951 left Argentina for Paris where he has worked as a translator for UNESCO. Although he has published some poetry, he is best known for his fiction. His first volume of short stories, *Bestiario*, appeared in 1951 and a few other stories were published in 1956 in Mexico in the "Los presentes" series directed by Juan José Arreola. These were later republished together with other stories under the title *Final de juego* (1956). It was not until 1959 with the publication of "El perseguidor" in *Las armas secretas* that Cortázar became recognized as an outstanding writer. Since then he has published four novels: *Los premios* (1960), *Rayuela* (1963), *62 Modelo para armar* (1968), and *Libro de Manuel* (1973); four more volumes of short stories: *Historias de cronopios y de famas* (1962), *Todos los fuegos el fuego* (1966), *Octaedro* (1974), and *Alguien que anda por ahí* (1977); two potpourris: *La vuelta al día en ochenta mundos* (1967) and *Ultimo round* (1969); and one experimental comic book version of the 1975 Bertrand Russell Tribunal in Brussels, *Fantasmas contra los vampiros multinacionales*. Since the mid-1960s, Cortázar has become increasingly more committed to Latin American revolutionary causes. "Meeting" was first published in the May 1964 issue of the *Revista de la Universidad de México* but did not circulate widely until it appeared in the author's collection *Todos los fuegos el fuego.*

MEETING

> I recalled a Jack London story in which the hero . . .
> leans calmly against a tree and prepares to die in a dig-
> nified manner.
>
> —Ernesto "Che" Guevara, in *Episodes of the Revolutionary
> War,* 1963 (originally from *La sierra y el llano* [Havana,
> 1961]).

Things couldn't be worse, but at least we were no
longer in the damn yacht, rolling in vomit and high seas and wet
crackers and machine guns and drivel, filthy dirty, soothing ourselves
when we could with the little tobacco that remained dry because
Luis (whose name wasn't Luis, but we had sworn not to remember
our names until that day arrived) had had the good sense to put it
into a tin box that we would open more carefully than if it had been
full of scorpions. But not even tobacco or slugs of rum in that
goddam yacht, swaying five days like a drunken turtle, facing a
northerly wind that whipped it mercilessly, waves coming and
going, the buckets scraping the skin off our hands, me with an
infernal asthma attack and almost everybody seasick, doubling
over to vomit as if they were going to split in half. Even Luis, the
second night, a green bile that dampened his spirits, between that
and the northerly that kept us from seeing the Cabo Cruz Light,
a disaster which nobody had expected; and to call that a landing
expedition was enough to keep you vomiting but out of pure
sadness. Oh well, anything to be able to leave the yacht behind,
anything, even though it would be what was waiting for us on
land—but we knew what was waiting for us and that's why it
didn't matter so much—the weather that clears up at precisely
the wrong time and wham the reconnaissance plane, what can
you do, ford the swamp or whatever it is, with the water up to
your ribs, seeking the cover of the dirty grasslands and mangroves,
and me like an idiot with my adrenalin spray to keep me going,
with Roberto carrying my Springfield to help me make it through
the swamp (if it was a swamp, because the thought had already
occurred to many of us that we might have gone off course and
that instead of land we had blundered into some muddy shoal in
the sea, twenty miles from the island . . .); and everything the

same, badly planned and hopelessly executed, in a continuous confusion of acts and notions, a mixture of inexplicable joy and of anger at the hard time the planes were giving us and at what was waiting for us on the highway if we ever got there, if we were in a swamp on the coast and not going around in circles like duped clowns in a circus of mud and of total failure for the amusement of the baboon in his Palace.

Now nobody remembers how long it lasted, we measured the time by the clearings in the grasslands, the pieces of land where they could gun us down in a dive, the scream I heard on my left, faraway, and that I think was Roque's (I can give him, his poor skeleton among the lianas and toads, his own name). Because of all the plans, only the final goal remained, to reach the Sierra and meet up with Luis if he also managed to get there; the rest had been torn to shreds by the northerly, the makeshift landing, the marshes. But let's be fair: something did happen on schedule, the attack of the enemy planes. It had been expected and provoked; it didn't fail. And that's why, even though Roque's cry still made my face ache, my malignant way of understanding the world helped me to laugh, cautiously (and I choked even more, and Roberto carried the Springfield so that I could inhale adrenalin with my nose almost in the water, swallowing more mud than anything else), because if the planes were there it meant we couldn't have gotten the wrong beach, we had gone off a few miles at the most, but the highway would be beyond the grasslands, and then the open field and to the north the first hills. The fact that the enemy affirmed the excellence of our landing had its comic side.

It lasted God knows how long, and afterward it was night, and there were six of us under some thin trees, for the first time on almost dry land, chewing damp tobacco and some miserable crackers. From Luis, Pablo, Lucas, no news; scattered, probably dead, in any case as lost and wet as we were. But I liked feeling how, with the end of that amphibian march, my ideas began to organize, and how death, more probably than ever, would no longer be a chance bullet in the middle of a swamp but a dryly dialectic operation, perfectly orchestrated by the parts in play. The army must have been controlling the highway, surrounding the marshes, waiting for us to come out in twos and threes, exhausted by the mud and varmints and hunger. Now I could see it all clearly, again I had the cardinal points in my pocket, it made me laugh to feel so alive and so awake on the verge of the epilogue. Nothing seemed funnier to me than to get Roberto mad by reciting some of old Pancho's verses in his ear, which he found abominable. "If only we could get rid of the mud," the Lieutenant complained. "Or smoke for real" (someone, more to the left, I no longer know who, someone we lost at dawn). Organization of the death agony: sentries, sleeping by turns, chewing tobacco, sucking crackers swollen like sponges. Nobody mentioned Luis, the fear that they had killed him was the only real enemy, because its confirmation would nullify us more than the pursuit, the lack of weapons, or our blistered feet. I know that I slept while Roberto kept watch, but before that, I was thinking that all we had done in those days was too reckless for us to suddenly admit the possibility that they had killed Luis. In some way, the recklessness would have to continue until the end, which would perhaps be victory, and in that absurd game which had reached the scandalous proportions of letting the enemy know that we were landing, the possibility of losing Luis did not enter. I believe I also thought that if we triumphed, if we managed to meet up again with Luis, only then would the game really begin, the atonement for so much necessary and unbridled and dangerous romanticism. Before falling asleep I had a sort of vision: Luis beside a tree, surrounded by all of us, slowly raised his hand to his face and took it off as if it were a mask. With his face in his hand he approached his brother Pablo, myself, the Lieutenant, Roque, asking us with a gesture to accept it, to put it on. But they all refused one by one, and I also refused, smiling myself to tears, and then Luis put his face on again and I saw in him an infinite weariness as he shrugged his shoulders and took a cigarette out of the pocket of his shirt. Professionally speaking, a hallucination from light sleep and fever, easily interpreted. But if they had really killed Luis during the landing, who would go up to the Sierra now with his face? We would all try to get up there, but none with Luis's face. "The Diadochi," I thought, already half-asleep. "But it all went to pot with the Diadochi, everybody knows that."

Although this story happened a while back, pieces and moments remain so clearly etched in my memory that they can be told only in present tense, like being flat on our backs again in the grass, beside the tree that shelters us from the open sky. It's the third night, but at the dawn of that day we crossed the highway in spite of the jeeps and the machine guns. Now we've got to wait for another dawn because they've killed our guide and we're lost, we'll have to find some peasant who can take us to where we can buy something to eat, and when I say buy it almost makes me laugh and I choke again, but in that as in the rest nobody would think of disobeying Luis, and we've got to pay for the food and explain to the people who we are and why we're doing what we're doing. Roberto's expression in the abandoned hut on the hill, leaving five pesos under a plate in exchange for the little we found and which tasted like heaven, like the food in the Ritz if people really do eat well there. I have so much fever my asthma is going away, well, every cloud has its silver lining, but again I think of Roberto's expression leaving the five pesos in the empty hut', and it makes me laugh so hard that I choke again and curse myself. We should sleep now, Tinti stands guard, the boys rest against each other, I have gone a little further away because I have the impression that I bother them with my cough and wheeze, and besides I do something I shouldn't, which is that two or three times a night I make a screen of leaves and put my face underneath and slowly light the cigar to reconcile myself with life a little.

In substance the only good thing all day has been not getting any news about Luis, the rest is a disaster, out of eighty they've killed fifty or sixty of us; Javier was among the first to fall, the Peruvian lost an eye and lay dying for three hours without my being able to do anything, not even finish him off when the others weren't looking. The whole day we feared that some runner (three had gotten through with incredible risk, under the very noses of the enemy) would bring us the news of Luis's death. In the end it's better to know nothing, to imagine him alive, to be able to keep waiting. Coldly I weigh the possibilities and conclude that they've killed him, we all know how he is, how the damn fool is capable of going out into the open with a pistol in his hand, and the devil may care. No, López must have taken care of him, nobody can fool him the way he does sometimes, almost treating him like a kid, convincing him that he has to do the opposite of what he feels like doing in that moment. But, if López. . . . No use worrying myself to death, we have no basis for any conjecture, and besides this calm is strange, this easy life flat on our backs as if everything were just fine, as if our mission had been accomplished (I almost thought: "had been consummated," which would have been stupid) as planned. It could be the fever or the fatigue, it could be the fact that they're going to exterminate us all like toads before the sun comes out. But now it's worth taking advantage of this absurd moment of rest, letting myself look at the stretch of the tree branches against the clearer sky, with some stars, following with half-closed eyes that casual design of the branches and leaves, those rhythms that meet, ride upon each other, and separate, and sometimes gently change when a whiff of boiling air passes over the treetops, coming from the swamps. I think of my son but he's far away, thousands of miles away, in a country where they still sleep in bed, and his image seems unreal to me, it tapers, and disappears among the leaves of the tree, and instead it does me so much good to remember a Mozart theme that has always been with me, the first movement of *The Hunt* quartet, the evocation of the hallali, the death flourish, in the gentle voice of the violins, that transposing of a savage rite to a clear introspective joy. I think it, I repeat it, I hum it in my memory, and at the same time feel how the melody and the sketch of the treetop against the sky draw near, become friends, feel each other out a few times until the sketch is suddenly organized into the visible presence of the melody, a rhythm coming from a lower branch, almost at the level of my head, rises to a certain height and then opens like a fan of stems, while the second violin is that thinner branch placing itself next to the other, to fuse its leaves into a point situated to the right, toward the end of the phrase, letting it end so that the eye moves down the trunk and can, if it wishes, repeat the melody. And all that is also our rebellion, it is what we are doing, even though Mozart and the tree cannot know, we, too, in our way, have wanted to transpose a clumsy war into an order that gives it meaning, justifies it, and finally carries it to a victory that might be like the restoration of a melody after so many years of raucous hunting horns, it might be that final allegro which follows the adagio like an encounter with light. What a kick Luis would get out of knowing that in this moment I am comparing him to Mozart, seeing him put this recklessness to order little by little, raising it to its primal reason which annihilates with its evidence and its excess all prudent temporal reasons. But what a bitter, what a desperate task to be a musician of men, to plot, despite mud and bullets and discouragement, that song we believed impossible, the song that will make friends with the treetop, with the earth returned to its sons! Yes, it is fever. And how Luis would laugh, although he, too, likes Mozart, I am sure.

And so in the end I'll fall asleep, but before that I shall manage to wonder if some day we will know how to pass from the movement where the hunter's hallali still sounds, to the conquered fullness of the adagio and from there to the final allegro which I hum with a thread of voice, if we will be capable of reaching the reconciliation with all that has remained alive in front of us. We would have to be like Luis, no longer follow him but be like him, leave hate and vengeance irrepealably behind, look at the enemy as Luis looks at him, with a relentless magnanimity which has so often revived in my memory (but how can I say this to anyone?) an image of a Pantocrator, a judge who begins by being the accused and the witness and who does not judge, who simply separates the lands from the waters so that finally, someday, a nation of men is born on a trembling dawn, on the banks of a cleaner time.

But what an adagio! Why, with the first light, they were on us from all sides, and we had to forget about continuing northeast and head into a poorly known area, wasting the last ammunition while the Lieutenant along with a comrade held a hill and from there stopped them short for a while, giving Roberto and myself time to carry Tinti wounded in his thigh, and find another more sheltered spot higher up to hold up in until nightfall. They never attacked at night although they had flares and electrical equipment; a kind of terror of feeling less protected by numbers and their wasting of weapons would come over them; but until night we had almost a whole day to get through, and we were only five against those courageous boys who harassed us to be in good standing with the baboon, not counting the planes that dived into the clearings in the woods from time to time and spoiled a quantity of palm trees with their bursts of fire.

A half-hour later the Lieutenant ceased fire and joined us; we had made little headway. As nobody even thought of abandoning Tinti—we knew only too well the fate of prisoners—we figured that there, on that slope and in those thickets, we would burn the last cartridges. It was funny to learn that instead the regulars were attacking a hill quite off to the east, deceived by an aeronautical error, and so we headed uphill on a hellish path, reaching two hours later an almost bald hill where a comrade had the good eye to find a cave covered by tall grass, and we sat down breathing hard after calculating a possible retreat directly north, toward the Sierra where maybe Luis had already arrived.

While I tended unconscious Tinti, the Lieutenant told me that a little before the regulars' attack at daybreak he had heard the fire of automatic rifles and pistols toward the west. It could be Pablo with his boys, or maybe even Luis. We had the reasonable conviction that the survivors were divided into three groups, and perhaps Pablo's wasn't so far off. The Lieutenant asked me if it wouldn't be worthwhile sending a runner at nightfall.

"If you're asking me it's because you're offering to go," I told him. We had laid Tinti down on a bed of dry grass, in the coolest part of the cave, and we rested and smoked. The other comrades stood guard outside.

"Can you imagine that, Kid?" the Lieutenant said to me, looking amused. "I get a kick out of these little excursions."

We went on like that for a while, joking with Tinti, who was getting delirious, and when the Lieutenant was about to go, in came Roberto with a mountaineer and a side of roast kid goat. We couldn't believe it, we ate like one who eats a ghost. Even Tinti nibbled on a piece which he would vomit two hours later along with his life. The mountaineer brought us news of Luis's death; we didn't stop eating for that, but it was a lot of salt for so little meat. He had not seen him, but his eldest son, who also had stuck to us with an old hunting rifle, formed part of the group that had helped Luis and five comrades ford a river under machine-gun fire, and he was sure that Luis had been wounded almost before coming out of the water and before he could reach the first bushes. The mountaineers had climbed through the woods they knew better than anybody, and with them two men from Luis's group, who would arrive by night with more than enough weapons and some ammunition.

The Lieutenant lit another cigar and went out to organize the camp and get to know the new men better; I stayed beside Tinti, who was sinking slowly, almost painlessly. That is to say Luis had died, the kid goat was fingerlickin' good, that night there would be nine or ten of us, and we would have ammunition to continue fighting. Some news! It was like a kind of cold madness which on the one hand reinforced the present with men and food, but all that to erase the future in one blow, the very reason for this recklessness which had just come to an end with a piece of news and a taste of roast kid goat. In the darkness of the cave, making my cigar last, I felt in that moment I could not allow myself the luxury of accepting Luis's death, I could handle it only as one more datum within the campaign plan, because if Pablo had died, too, I was the leader by Luis's will, and the Lieutenant and all the comrades knew that, and the only thing to do was to take command and reach the Sierra and keep going as if nothing had happened. I believe I closed my eyes, and the memory of my vision was again the vision itself, and for a second it seemed that Luis separated himself from his face and offered it to me, and I defended my face with my two hands saying: "No, no, please no, Luis," and when I opened my eyes the Lieutenant was back looking at Tinti, who was breathing heavily, and I heard him say that two boys from the woods had just joined us, nothing but good news, ammunition and fried sweet potatoes, a medicine chest, the regulars lost in the east hills, fabulous spring water fifty yards away. But he didn't look me in the eyes, he chewed his cigar and seemed to wait for me to say something, for me to be the first to mention Luis again.

Afterward there's a sort of confused gap, Tinti lost his blood and we him, the mountaineers offered to bury him, I remained resting in the cave although it smelled of vomit and cold sweat, and curiously I got to thinking about my best friend of former times, of before that break in my life that had torn me from my country and thrust me thousands of miles away, to Luis, to the landing on the island, to the cave. Calculating the time difference I imagined that at that moment Wednesday, he would be walking into his office, hanging his hat on the hook, glancing over the mail. It wasn't a hallucination, it was enough just to think of those years in which we had lived so close to each other in the city, sharing politics, women, and books, meeting daily in the hospital; every one of his gestures was so familiar to me, and those gestures were not only his but embraced my whole world then, myself, my wife, my father, my newspaper with its inflated editorials, my midday coffee with the doctors on duty, my readings and my movies and my ideals. I wondered what my friend would be thinking about all that, of Luis or of me, and it was as if I saw the answer written on his face (but that was the fever, I would have to take quinine), a self-satisfied face, filled out by the good life and good editions and the efficiency of the accredited surgeon's knife. It wasn't even necessary for him to open his mouth to tell me I think your revolution is nothing but. . . . It wasn't necessary but it had to be that way, those people could not accept a change that uncovered the real reasons for their easy and timetabled mercy, their regulated and metered charity, their good nature among equals, their drawing room liberalism but what do you mean our daughter's going to marry that mulatto, huh, their Catholicism with its annual dividend and ephemeris in the bannered squares, their tapioca literature, their folklore in numbered copies and maté with a silver sipper, their gatherings of genuflecting chancellors, their stupid inevitable short- or long-term death agony (quinine, quinine, and again asthma). I felt pity at imagining him defending like an idiot precisely the false values that would be the end of him or at best his sons; defending the feudal right to property and unlimited wealth, he who had only his doctor's office and a nice house, defending the principles of the Church when his wife's bourgeois Catholicism had served only to make him look for comfort in universities and censored publications, and defending out of fear, out of a horror of change, out of skepticism and mistrust which were the only living gods in his poor lost country. And that's what I was thinking when the Lieutenant rushed in shouting that Luis was alive, that they had just made a connection with the north, that Luis was more alive than a son of a bitch, he had reached the top of the Sierra with fifty peasants and all the weapons they had gotten off a battalion of regulars cornered in a ravine, and we hugged each other like idiots and said those things that afterward, for a long time, bring you anger and shame and perfume, because that and eating roast goat and pushing on were the only things that made sense, that counted, and grew while we didn't dare look each other in the eye and lit cigars on the firebrand, with our eyes staring at the firebrand and drying the tears the smoke drew from us with its known tear-producing properties.

There's not much left to tell now. At daybreak one of our mountaineers took the Lieutenant and Roberto to where Pablo and his three comrades were, and the Lieutenant lifted Pablo in his arms because his feet were mangled from the swamps. Now we were twenty, I remember Pablo hugging me in his quick and expedient way, and saying to me without taking his cigarette out of his mouth: "If Luis is alive, we can still win," and I bandaging his feet, which was beautiful, and the boys pulling his leg because it looked like he was showing off new white shoes and telling him that his brother would scold him for that inappropriate luxury. "Let him scold me," Pablo joked smoking like crazy. "To scold someone you have to be alive, pal, and you've heard he's alive, haven't you, more alive than an alligator, and we're going up there right now, boy you've put some bandages on me, there's luxury for you. . . ." But it couldn't last, with the sun came the lead from above and below, at some point a bullet grazed me on the ear that, had it been two inches more accurate, you, son, who may be reading all this, would be left without knowing what your old man was up to. With the blood and the pain and the fright, things went stereoscopic on me, each image clear-cut, in bas-relief, in colors that must have been my desire to live and besides there was nothing wrong with me, a handkerchief firmly tied and keep moving; but two mountaineers stayed behind, and Pablo's adjutant with a .45 bullet hole in his face. In those moments silly things get fixed forever in your mind; I remember a fat guy, from Pablo's group, too, I think, who in the worst of the battle tried to hide behind a stalk of sugar cane, kneeling in profile behind the cane, and I especially remember that someone began shouting that we had to surrender, and then a voice that answered him between two bursts of a Thompson gun, the Lieutenant's voice, a roar above the shooting, a: "No, fuck it, nobody surrenders here!"

until the shortest of the mountaineers, so quiet and shy up until then, let me know that there was a path 100 yards from there, twisting upward and to the left, and I shouted it to the Lieutenant and I took the lead with the mountaineers following me and shooting like all hell broke loose, in the thick of a baptism of fire and savoring the pleasure of seeing them at it, and finally we all joined at the ceiba tree where the path began and the little mountaineer climbed with us behind him, me with an asthma that didn't even let me walk and the back of my neck more bloody than a pig with his head chopped off, but also sure that we would escape that day, I don't know why, but it was as evident as a theorem that that very night we would meet up with Luis.

You can never figure out how you leave your pursuers behind. Little by little the fire tapers off, then the familiar cursing and "Cowards, they split instead of fighting," then suddenly it's silence, the trees are again living and friendly things, the bumps in the terrain, the wounded that must be tended, the canteen of water with a little rum that runs from mouth to mouth, the sighs, someone complains, the moment of rest and the cigar, keep moving, climb climb although my lungs were coming out of my ears, and Pablo saying to me hey, you made them forty-two and my size is forty-three, pal, and the laughter, the top of the hill, the hut where a peasant had a little yuca with sauce and very cool water, and Roberto, persistent and finicky, taking out his four pesos to pay the expense and everybody, beginning with the peasant, laughing themselves sick, and midday inviting that siesta we had to refuse as if we were letting a pretty girl get away, looking at her legs till the last.

At nightfall the path got steeper and more difficult, but we licked our chops thinking of the position Luis had chosen to wait for us, not even a deerbuck could get up there. "It'll be like being in a church," Pablo said at my side, "we even have a harmonium," and he looked at me jokingly while I panted a kind of passacaglia which only he thought funny. I don't remember those hours very clearly, it was getting dark when we reached the first sentry and passed one after the other, letting them know who we were and answering for the mountaineers as well, until finally stepping into the clearing between the trees where Luis was leaning on a tree trunk, wearing, naturally, his cap with its perennial eyeshade and the cigar in his mouth. It was as hard as hell to stay behind, letting Pablo run and hug his brother, and then waiting for the Lieutenant and the others to also embrace him, and then I put the medicine chest and the Springfield down and with my hands in my pockets walked over and stood looking at him, knowing what he was going to say, the same old joke:

"Still using those silly eyeglasses," Luis said.

"And you those spectacles," I answered, and we doubled over with laughter, and his jaw against my face made my bullet hurt like hell, but it was a pain I would have liked to have felt forever.

"So you made it, Che," Luis said.

Naturally, he said "Che" very badly.

"What d'ya think?" I answered him, equally badly. And we doubled over like idiots, and almost everybody laughed without knowing why. They brought water and the news, we made the usual circle around Luis, and only then did we realize how thin he'd grown and how his eyes shined behind the damn spectacles.

Further below they were fighting again, but the camp was momentarily safe from danger. We would tend the wounded, bathe in the spring, sleep, above all sleep, even Pablo who wanted so much to speak with his brother. But as asthma is my mistress and has taught me to take advantage of the night, I sat with Luis against the trunk of a tree, smoking and looking at the sketches of the leaves against the sky and we talked from time to time about what had happened to us since the landing, but above all we talked about the future, about what was going to begin that day when we'd have to move from the rifle to the office with telephones, from the mountains to the city, and I remembered the hunting horns and I was about to tell Luis what I had thought that night, just to make him laugh. In the end I didn't tell him, but I felt that we were passing into the adagio of the quartet, into a precarious plenitude a few hours old which nevertheless was a certainty, a sign that we wouldn't forget. How many hunting horns still waited, how many of us would leave our bones like Roque, like Tinti, like the Peruvian. But it was enough to look at the treetop to feel that they will again put its chaos to order, imposed on it the sketch of the adagio that would some day pass into the final allegro and accede to a reality worthy of that name. And while Luis was bringing me up to date on international news and on what was happening in the capital and provinces, I saw how the leaves and branches were bending little by little to my desire, they were my melody, Luis's melody whose talk was miles apart from my fantasies, and then I saw a star inscribed in the center of the sketch, and it was a little star and very blue, and though I don't know anything about astronomy and wouldn't be able to say whether it was a star or a planet, I did feel sure that it was neither Mars nor Mercury, it shined too much in the center of the adagio, too much in the center of Luis's words to be mistaken for Mars or Mercury.

—Translated by Suzanne Jill Levine

COMMENTARY

Although the historical theme of "Meeting" is unique among Cortázar's short stories, it does reflect his increasing political commitment from the mid-1960s to the present, as seen in *La vuelta al día en ochenta mundos* (1967), *Ultimo round* (1969), *Libro de Manuel* (1973), and *Fantasmas contra los vampiros multinacionales* (1975). At the same time, the story's Magic Realism, its musical structure, and the significance of the double are typical of many of Cortázar's stories.

What is so impressive about "Meeting" is Cortázar's ability to single out the most absurd elements of perhaps the most dramatic episode of the Cuban Revolution—the landing from the *Granma* and the ascent to the Sierra Maestra—in order to mythify the rebel leaders. At the end of the story, the Argentine narrator, who is obviously Che Guevara, sees "a star inscribed in the center of the sketch," which represents the apotheosis of Luis, who is obviously Fidel Castro. The implicit comparison of Fidel Castro with Jesus, which is almost a commonplace in the Cuban novels of the Revolution, is reinforced by the contrast with the "diabolical" Argentine narrator: "infernal asthma attack," "my malignant way of understanding the world," "everything went to pot [to the devil] with the Diadochi," "hellish path," "the darkness of the cave." The religious symbolism is saved from degenerating into trite propaganda by the atmosphere of Magic Realism with which Cortázar effectively envelops his characters. In spite of the historical details of the landing, the fact that the narrator is a feverish asthmatic intellectual who recognizes the absurdity of his own situation—"Me like an idiot with my adrenalin spray"—transforms reality into fantasy. The absurd nature of the landing is further underlined by the use of circus imagery. The landing launch reels and staggers "like a drunken turtle," while the invaders wander around in the marshes "like duped clowns in a circus of mud and total failure for the amusement of the baboon in his Palace." The use of Mozart's quartet *The Hunt* to symbolize the Revolution in its three movements: charge (*hallali*), rest (*adagio*), and victory (*allegro finale*) adds still another touch of fantasy.

The fusion of reality and fantasy is also reflected in the ultimate encounter on top of the mountain. The humor of the following dialogue (lost in translation), in which the Jesus-like Cuban leader and the demonic Argentine doctor imitate each other's national dialects, not only makes the religious exaltation more acceptable but also reinforces Cortázar's concept, derived from Borges, that one man is the double of the other, that each man is both hero and coward, capable of both good and evil.

"So you made it, Che," said Luis. Naturally he said "Che" very badly.
"What d'ya think?" I answered him, equally badly. And we doubled over like idiots, and almost everybody laughed without knowing why.

By his conscious choice of the Cuban leader as his double, the narrator rejects his other double, the Argentine friend who chose to remain in Argentina and who absurdly continues to defend the false values of the decadent bourgeois society of his poor lost country, "out of fear, out of a horror of change, out of skepticism and mistrust, which were the only living gods in his poor lost country."

Although the narrator's vision of Argentine life occupies only about one twentieth of the story, its importance is underscored by its role in the mythification process. The fact that the vision appears to the narrator in the darkness of the cave after he has received the false news of Luis's death identifies the episode with the archetypal descent into the underworld, as in Don Quixote's descent into the cave of Montesinos. Endowed with a greater and truer knowledge of the world, the demonic hero sallies forth and begins his ascent to the summit. At the same time, by restricting the vision of Argentina to the confines of the cave, Cortázar makes his point without violating one of the short story's principal canons, concentration.

Humberto Arenal

(1926)

Cuban. Born in Havana, he went to the United States in 1948 and did not return until shortly after the triumph of the Revolution. He was a theater director and contributed to the principal literary journals in the early 1960s. He is the author of the first novel of the Cuban Revolution, *El sol a plomo* (1959); of an Existentialist denationalized novel, *Los animales sagrados* (1967); and of two small collections of short stories, *La vuelta en redondo* (1962) and *El tiempo ha descendido* (1964). "Mr. Charles" is from the latter.

MR. CHARLES

"Ah, those were better days," said the man, "weren't they, Miss Clarita? Everything was different then. As Mr. Charles's sister used to say. . . . What was it? . . . Huh, Miss Clarita?"

"What. . . ?"

"What Mr. Charles's sister used to say . . . the thing about opu. . . . Opu what?"

The woman was stretched out on the bed with her eyes closed, barely listening to what the man was saying. Her lids trembled imperceptibly. She opened them a bit: "Such opulence, such wealth!" she said and shut her eyes. With one hand she made sure that her bathrobe was wrapped around her and with the other she looked for a handkerchief. Then she continued listening to the music coming from the radio at her side.

"You know what I say, huh, Miss Clarita? The late Mr. Charles, may he rest in peace, knew how to live. What suits he wore! One hundred percent linen, yes sir, one hundred percent linen. Do you remember "The Merry Widow," Miss Esperanza Iris? She was a real lady, a princess she was, Miss Esperanza, wasn't she, Miss Clarita?"

"Not all that much," said the woman, opening her eyes for a moment. She closed them again and continued listening to the music. She also heard the neighbor's cat purring down the hall. She had come to recognize all the sounds of the house.

For several years now, Jacinto had been coming to see her every Sunday morning always saying the same things. At first she had enjoyed his company, now she found him a burden. He would leave after a while. He had been Charles's chauffeur for twenty or thirty years; up to his death.

"I hardly go out. I come to see you. And I go to the cemetery to take flowers to my mother — may she rest in peace — and to Mr. Charles, and that's it. What else is there to do?"

He was silent for a moment. The woman heard the cat enter the room; it always lay beneath the table and waited for the food which she gave it every day.

"Do you remember when Caruso sang in Havana?"

The woman nodded.

"I still remember. I can see it all so clearly. You wore that red dress which Mr. Charles liked so much. They say by then Caruso had lost something. What do you think, Miss Clarita?"

He has asked me that so many times, I've lost count. She answered that Caruso was then still in his prime.

"Envy, that's all it is . . . people were envious of him. There was a Spanish gardener over at Mr. Charles's house who used to say Lázaro was a better singer than Caruso. You knew them both; you were on the stage! What do you think, Miss Clarita?" Most of the questions, she didn't answer, that way he left sooner.

"Huh, Miss Clarita?"

The woman got up. She looked at herself in the mirror. She had gotten fat and her gray hair showed through the dye. She hardly ever looked at herself, nowadays. She didn't remember her birthdays either. Previously she had lived on memories, dates, moments from the past. Now she cared more about the present, what little of it she had left.

"You were in Mexico several times, right, Miss Clarita?"

"Eight times," she said, picking up the cat from under the table.

"And you worked there, didn't you, Miss Clarita?"

He knew she did, but he always asked again. He knew the details of her life better than she did. He had photograph albums and

souvenirs from her whole stage career, which Charles had kept.
When Charles died, he had managed to get them out of the house
without his wife's knowledge.

"Yes, I worked there."

"With Miss Esperanza Iris?"

"Yes, with Iris."

"Oh, how lucky you were. I've always thought so. You are one
lucky woman, a very lucky woman."

She thought of saying, "What do you know, Jacinto."

At one time she too had thought she was a very lucky woman.
She looked at the man for a moment. He was observing Charles's
photograph which was on top of the wardrobe. Then she stroked
the cat's back as it slowly ate what she had served it. The cat
looked at her and licked its face.

"When you and Mr. Charles went away to Paris and Madrid
and all those faraway places in Europe, I took you to the docks.
I remember it perfectly. You looked like a queen there in the
Packard, and Mr. Charles, who was what you call a gentleman,
a real gentleman, was wearing white flannel pants and a blue
jacket. Everybody knew the two of you. Miss Eusebia, Mr. Charles's
sister, used to say that he looked like the Prince of Wales. I still
have the postcard at home that the two of you sent me from Paris.
I keep everything. . . . I was thinking just the other day. . . ."

In Paris, Charles promised me that when we returned, he would
get divorced and we would get married immediately. Afterward,
he never mentioned it again, until I reminded him about it six
months after our return from Europe.

"I know, I know I promised you, but you'll have to wait now.
Things are not going well at home. You'll have to wait," he said
then.

He also explained to her that his daughter Alicia was going to
be fifteen soon and he wanted to avoid upsetting her now. She
would have to wait a bit. I had never thought of having a child
with him, but after that, I tried to convince him that a child
would keep me company, but Charles wouldn't hear of it.

"You were wearing a broad pink hat and carrying a mother-
of-pearl lorgnette. Everybody knew the two of you."

"That was a long time ago, Jacinto."

"Not for me," he looked at her for the first time. "Sometimes I think that not even a minute has gone by." He brought his hand to his forehead and started to look out the nearby window, through which he could see the ocean. "My sister Eloísa says that I suffer a lot because of that, but I think she's the one who suffers. I always have my memories. She says I should forget all those things, that they hurt me, but I don't want anyone to take them away from me. Sometimes I close my eyes and I see everything so clearly. Sometimes I hear Mr. Charles's voice, as if he were standing beside me. Remember how he used to laugh, Miss Clarita? I remember all his conversations, and the things he used to say to me. He used to say to me, 'Jacinto, you're a very special Negro; you're a different Negro; you're almost white. . . .' He was so nice. . . . He used to say that to me, Miss Clarita. I remember everything."

The woman took a dress from the wardrobe and went into the bathroom.

In the old days, this man was part of a pattern, and she had never noticed him, never analyzed him, never judged him. He was an inevitable, efficient part of a scheme of things which made her life easy. Now, he seemed to be a different man.

She came out of the bathroom and went to the mirror. While she powdered her face, the man kept looking out the window.

"I started working for Mr. Charles during the government of General Menocal," he said without turning around, "during the famous fights between the Conservatives and the Liberals. A lot of water has gone under the bridge since then, yes sir. In those days, I used to play ball in the old Almendares. I once hit a home run off the great Adolfo Luque."

He paused and smiled. Then he turned around and sat down again on the chair.

"I remember it as if it were only yesterday. There was a stuck-up young Negro who was playing first base and he told me they had spoken to him about a chauffeur's job, and would I want it. I think he used to drive an old jalopy fifty-fifty with a cousin of his at the marketplace. And in addition to that, he was dying to play in the big leagues and all that stuff. He used to say Luque was going to take him up North, and do this, that, and the other thing for him."

The woman was combing her hair and looked at him in the mirror. Now she seemed more interested.

"You can imagine, at the time I was practically starving. At home we had twelve mouths to feed and practically the only money that came in was what my sister Eulalia made—she was a seamstress and worked for Bernabeu, the designer—and what my mother made, which wasn't much, the poor woman, taking in laundry. Then, this young Negro friend of mine. Genovevo, Genovevo was his name, it's been on the tip of my tongue for a while now. Genovevo took me to see Mr. Charles."

The woman had finished getting ready and picked up a purse that was on the bed.

"Jacinto, I have to go out to do some shopping, you must excuse me, but. . . ."

"I'll go with you, Miss Clarita, I'll be happy to go with you, of course I will."

She looked at him very seriously for a moment, as if she were going to say something important to him and finally said: "All right."

They went out into the hall.

"Mr. Charles received me in his office on the Manzana de Gómez, and I gave him the little piece of paper that Genovevo had given me, and he read it in his usual serious manner. And I immediately said to myself that I liked that man. And he finished reading the piece of paper and. . . ."

They passed in front of an open door and a very fat woman dressed in white, who was sitting on a rocking chair fanning herself slowly looked at them and said: "Hey, Neighbor, where are you going so dressed up?"

"To do some shopping," she replied.

. . . and then he told me to start work on Monday. It was a Saturday; a Saturday or a Friday, I don't quite recall. . . ."

"Say, Fefa, I gave your cat a bit of hash and rice that I had left over from lunch."

"Thanks, Neighbor. And how are you getting along with your rheumatism?"

"Better, much better. I think I'll go to San Diego with a friend of mine to take the sulphur baths there and see if I can't get rid of it for good. I had a lot of pain for a few days, but now I'm better." She started to walk away. "See you later, Fefa, see you later."

"Goodbye, Neighbor, get well. If you see Julito, send him over, I want to order something from the grocery store."

The man had stepped away from her a little and was observing her with a smile. He lowered his head and said: "I was telling you, it was a Saturday or Friday, when I met Mr. Charles. . . ."

"It was a Saturday, Jacinto; you've already told me that many times."

The man seemed not to hear her.

"He took ten pesos from his wallet and told me to buy myself a white shirt and a black tie and a cap and to be at his house on Monday morning at eight o'clock. That's how I started with Mr. Charles. I'll never forget it." The woman walked ahead, without listening, barely acknowledging his presence. He had put on his cap which up until now he had held in his hands and was trying to catch up with her.

The day I told Charles I was pregnant, he didn't say anything for a while and then said: "Look Darling, it's out of the question. I know a doctor who can do the curettage for you. He's a friend whom I've known all my life and a good doctor. He lives nearby on the Calle San Lázaro. I'll take you there this very week. Don't worry about anything."

I asked him twice to let me have the child, I tried to explain to him that I had nothing, to let me at least keep the child.

"Don't be silly, Darling," he said, "you know it's impossible. You've got me, and you have your career. You don't need anything else. We have to take care of this right away. It's a simple matter."

She went to her room to cry and he knocked on the door several times and she didn't answer, and finally he left. The next day he came and told her that he had arranged everything with his friend the doctor and that they would go to see him the next day, in the afternoon.

At first I felt a little nervous in his presence. He was a man who inspired so much respect. I used to see him with the lawyers and with all those wealthy people from the sugar mills and I used to see how they treated him, with such respect. Mr. Charles was a man of few words, but when he spoke he inspired great respect. Everybody listened to him.

She was looking at some fruit and the vendor came over.

"How are you, Ma'am, how's your rheumatism?" he asked.

"A little better, thanks. How much are these mammees?"

"Those are twenty-five, the others are forty. I also have some beautiful zapotes here," he bent down and pulled out a basket from beneath the cart. "They're as sweet as honey, Ma'am."

"The day we buried my poor mother," said Jacinto, "Mr. Charles called me and told me not to worry about anything, that he would take care of all the expenses. Not counting the money which he had lent me for medicine which he later refused to accept. And the wreath that he sent. It was the nicest of them all, Miss Clarita. The nicest."

She took one of the mammees and gave it to the vendor and began to feel the zapotes.

"He always gave me very good advice. Thanks to him I never got too involved with that widow I was going with. One day I told him about it and he listened to the whole story. Then he said, 'Look, Jacinto, why get mixed up with a widow with children? Find yourself a girl who's young like you, if you want to get married, and don't make life difficult for yourself. Besides, you're all right the way you are. Don't make life difficult for yourself.' That's what Mr. Charles said to me. He was a very good man, wasn't he, Miss Clarita?"

We were on the deck of the Santa Rosa. *A friend of Charles, who was a theatrical agent had gotten me a good contract to work in Colombia. Charles liked for me to sing. I think it stimulated him, it used to put him in touch with a world that had always fascinated him. Once he told me that his great wish had been to be an actor. We had planned the trip for several months. Charles had some business to do in Colombia and used it as an excuse to come with me. Whenever I worked outside Havana, he liked to accompany me, to see who worked with me, to read the music I was going to sing, and even to approve the costumes I was going to wear. He used to say that he couldn't leave me on my own because I lacked the shrewdness and the common sense to deal with these people whom he said were very immoral and very clever. I used to love watching the dawn come up. We used to get up very early and go to the prow of the ship to see the sunrise. We did it almost every day. Charles would take me by the arm and we would stand*

*there almost without talking. Those were moments of great pleas-
ure that I'll never forget. One morning while we were standing
there, Charles saw a married couple who were friends of his and
his wife walking on deck. They didn't see us, but as a measure of
precaution, Charles never again allowed himself to be seen in
public with me. He always used to say: "The most important
thing in life is to keep up appearances."*

Fefa had lived next door to Clarita for twenty years. They were
not really friends, but they had always respected each other, and
shared a mutual affection. Fefa was a widow. Her husband had
worked for forty years as a bookkeeper. They had never had any
children. One morning she woke up to find him dead beside her.
Now she only spoke of him once a month, when she went to the
cemetery. She always called him, "poor Faustino." Fefa had a cat
and a canary to whom she spoke all day long. She insisted that
they understood everything she said to them. At times Clarita
thought this was more than just an idiosyncrasy, as the neighbors
maintained.

Fefa was worried about Clarita. Lately she had found her very
pale and heard her walking around her room all night long and
she no longer heard her sing as before, when she was always singing tunes from zarzuelas and operettas. She, who had always kept
herself looking so young, all of a sudden had aged perceptibly.
Her face had hardened. She had been wanting to tell her all these
things for some time now, but Clarita was such a hermetic and
strong woman that she feared a rude reply.

Fefa was thinking about all these things and brushing her long
graying hair, as she did every Sunday, when Clarita came by with
Jacinto.

"Say, Neighbor," she said to her, "I've been thinking about a
medicine which poor Faustino used to take for his rheumatism
and which I'm sure would do you good."

Clarita stopped for a moment and Jacinto smiled at the woman.

"I've been taking some pills and I think if I take the baths at
San Diego, it will go away."

"I'm going to look for that little jar which I know I've kept
somewhere, so you can try them, Neighbor. Maybe they'll help
you."

She said all right and continued walking to her room.

While she was peeling the potatoes and then when she went behind the screen to put her bathrobe on again, Jacinto said: "Sometimes I get to thinking. . . . I don't know. . . . Do you believe in the hereafter, Miss Clarita?"

She shrugged her shoulders to indicate that she did not know.

"I never used to believe in those things because I thought it was a matter of witchcraft and that stuff is more for the ignorant, but a very intelligent friend of mine gave me some books by that scientist Alan Kardec and then, some time ago, I met Sister Blanca Rosa, a medium who lives out by Mantilla, and I've really had some very good proof. Do you know that I've talked with my mother, may she rest in peace?"

She looked at him for a moment and then said no.

"You see, I never talk about these things with anyone, but I've always thought of you as part of my family, and please forgive my boldness, but I tell you that I've talked to my mother. It's been a great comfort for me. Do you know something, Miss Clarita, I think you should go to see her."

"Me, what for?"

"Well, it seems to me that it would do you good to see if you can communicate with Mr. Charles. . . . It would be a great comfort. Don't you think so?"

She was taking off her bathrobe behind the screen and for a moment she paused, thinking what to reply.

"I don't believe in those things, Jacinto."

"You should have faith in something, Miss Clarita, faith saves."

She didn't answer him. When she came out, Jacinto kept looking at her and didn't say anything. He seemed upset. She went to the bed and stretched herself out on it very properly.

"Jacinto," she said to him, and he looked at her attentively, "next Sunday, I won't be here, so don't come. I'm going to take the baths at San Diego."

"Then I'll come by the following Sunday, Miss Clarita."

"No, the following Sunday I still won't be back. You'd better phone me."

Jacinto kept looking at the floor and blinking, as he always did when he was nervous.

"All right, Miss Clarita; I'll call you. All right," he got up, "I think I'd better be going now. My sister always yells at me if I'm not there for lunch."

She smiled.

"Well, so long, Miss Clarita. I hope you feel better soon. So long."

"Goodbye, Jacinto."

She saw him leave and then closed her eyes. She heard Fefa slowly rocking on her rocking chair, the motor of the water tank, a distant radio, a dripping faucet, the bubbling of the water in which the potatoes were cooking, the breeze blowing the curtains on the window. She opened her eyes for a moment and looked at the portrait of Charles. Then she closed them again immediately.

— Translated by Gustavo Pellón

COMMENTARY

Since 1959 one of the goals of the Cuban Revolution has been to make Cuba the cultural leader of Latin America. Although that ambitious goal has not been fulfilled, there is no question about the Revolution's having fomented literary activity in Cuba to a far greater extent than ever before. With regard to the short story, about one hundred individual collections have been published since 1959 plus over a dozen anthologies. The latter have been published not only in Havana but in Madrid, Buenos Aires, Montevideo, Santiago (Chile), Lima, Guayaquil, Caracas, Mexico City, and Baltimore. The authors of these short stories are usually divided into four distinct literary generations. Of those identified with the *Revista de Avance* in the late 1920s, novelist Alejo Carpentier (1904) is clearly the most famous. In the following generation, the two most outstanding authors are, unlike Carpentier, primarily short story writers: Virgilio Piñera (1912), in the fantastic, absurdist vein, and the Criollista Onelio Jorge Cardoso (1914). Those authors who were born between 1923 and 1935 and made their literary debuts in the decade of the 1950s are the first generation of revolutionary writers. Many of them resided for significant periods of time in the United States and their almost obsessive theme is the exorcism of the past. By portraying a bleak picture of prerevolutionary Cuba inhabited by Existentialist anguish-laden characters, they indirectly justified the rapid transformation of Cuba into a socialist state. At the same time they avoided writing about contemporary problems in what has been called a self-imposed censorship between 1961 and 1965. The most important of these short story writers are Calvert Casey (1923-1969), Humberto Arenal (1926), Guillermo Cabrera Infante (1929), and Antonio Benítez Rojo (1931). The youngest Cuban literary generation is comprised of writers born in the early 1940s who for the most part have reacted against the unbridled experimentation of the Latin American, including Cuban, "Boom" novels and have concentrated on specific dramatic moments of the Revolution in a Hemingway-like hyper-realistic style: Jesús Díaz Rodríguez (1941), Eduardo Heras León (1941), and Norberto Fuentes Cobas (1943).

In "Mr. Charles," Humberto Arenal presents a negative vision of pre-revolutionary Cuba through the experiences of the two protagonists and their relationships with Mr. Charles. Although the mention of General Menocal, opera singer Enrico Caruso, and baseball pitcher Adolfo Luque identify the time period of the memories as around World War I, the absence of any specific time references for the story's present creates the vague impression of a period extending from the early 1930s to the late 1950s. Mr. Charles, by his name, his opulence, his trips abroad, his contacts with lawyers and sugar mill owners, symbolizes the wealthy, xenophile Cubans who exploited their compatriots, the latter blinded by their passion for music (Clarita) and baseball (Jacinto). That world belongs to the past: Mr. Charles is dead; Clarita suffers from rheumatism and loneliness; Jacinto survives on his memories alone. To indicate that Clarita is not a special case, the author presents her neighbor Fefa as leading an equally tragic existence. Widowed and without any children, she spends the whole day rocking and talking to her cat and her canary.

The dramatic tension of the story is based on the counterpoint between Jacinto's idealized memories and those of the disenchanted Clarita. While Clarita is completely aware of Charles's true character (she never refers to him as Mr. Charles), she prefers not to disillusion the Negro chauffeur who still maintains his slave mentality. In fact, the author seems to portray Jacinto as being psychologically castrated by framing the story with Miss Clarita stretched out on her bed without Jacinto's becoming the least bit aroused. It is also significant that Mr. Charles discouraged Jacinto from continuing his relationship with the widow.

The Existentialist loneliness of the characters in the present is emphasized, as in Mallea's "Conversation," by the lack of true dialogue. Jacinto talks to Miss Clarita but she hardly listens to him. With a very simple style (short sentences, slow rhythm, unemphatic tone, absence of images, and the frequent use of "the man," "the woman," "he," "she"), Arenal succeeds in painting a world totally devoid of illusions. The characters only exist.

Even the "happy" ending, from Miss Clarita's point of view, is illusory. Although she summons up enough energy to rid herself of the obsequious Jacinto—his "so long" is contrasted with her "goodbye"—her existence does not show any promise of improving. She continues to lie in bed, alone and listening to the different noises that represent the insignificance of human life.

Alvaro Menéndez Leal

(1931)

Salvadoran. He prefaced his first important book of short stories, *Cuentos breves y maravillosos* (1962), with an apocryphal letter of introduction from Jorge Luis Borges. After being expelled from the national military academy and exiled for his political ideas, he studied and practiced journalism in Mexico. Upon returning to his country, he studied and then taught sociology at the Universidad de El Salvador (1961-1966). His book on urban sociology, *Ciudad, casa de todos,* was published in 1968 but he is best known for his stories and his plays, the most famous of which, *Luz negra* (1967), has been translated and performed in the United States and several European countrie.. A group of one-act plays, *El circo y otras piezas falsas,* was published in El Salvador (1966) and Spain (1969). His most recent collections of stories, with some overlapping, are *Una cuerda de nylon y oro* (1969), *Revolución en el país que edificó un castillo de hadas* (1971), *Hacer el amor en el refugio atómico* (1972), and *La ilustre familia androide* (1972). Since 1970, he has taught a variety of university courses on Latin American literature and civilization in Konstanz, West Germany; Irvine, California; St. Etienne, France; and Algiers. "'Fire and Ice'" was written in 1965, with the title in English, and was published in *Una cuerda de nylon y oro.*

"FIRE AND ICE"

Fire and Ice . . . Fire and Ice . . . Is that the title? . . . Yes . . . ; that's it: Fire and Ice . . . I don't know why, but just now, something became important that never was important before; not at school, whent he professor insisted that we memorize Frost's poem:

> Some say the world will end in fire,
> Some say in ice . . .
> From what I've tasted of desire
> I hold with those who favor fire.

I never memorized it - at least then I couldn't repeat more than two or three lines -- but now, I believe that I remember it perfectly --- but why is it important? ---- I don't know ----- it never was - for all the professor's insistence - it never was important for me to know it - to memorize it - except while at school - and now it's not important that I remember it - why should it be - it's no more - no more important than that little boy who right now lies crushed against the pilot's cabin - it's no more important - why should it be - I see part of his face smashed - blood by his nose - blood by his ears - blood by his mouth - blood by holes and cracks that one doesn't normally have - wounds - those cracks are wounds - why should it be important now - in a moment there won't be a drop of blood - everything everything will be burned - and I can't feel sorry for him - although he was a good little boy - through the whole flight he sat quietly in his seat - without bothering anybody - without going to the bathroom - without asking for anything - in spite of being besieged by the stewardess - in spite of the fuss the old ladies made over him - without bothering anybody - without importance - he stayed quiet - fascinated with the flight through the clouds - with the slight vibration of the airplane - with the wonder of a little boy riding in a jet - without bothering anybody - not even when the plane - after breaking its wing on that peak - crashed on its belly - and / the / whole / length / of / the / floor / o-p-e-n-e-d / the / wide / terrible / gap / between the two rows of seats - from the first-class ones to . . . . - the terrible gap from the cabin to the tail - and now blood is oozing - blood is oozing from it - and I worried that the boy would disappear swallowed up by the voracity of the floor - the open floor - mother earth's sex - but it couldn't happen that way because nothing was leaving the plane - it was only coming in - dirt was coming in - stones were coming in - dirt and stones and pieces of trees - pines - yes - pines - larch trees - spruce trees - fir trees - I don't know - and dirt - conifers - and dirt was coming in - and snow - a lot of snow - and dirt and stones and snow

But if it had to perish twice

it's not important / why shout it be / and less now that the fire is reaching the body of that lady in the blue suit / the lady with the extravagant hat / it covers her suit / engulfs it / scorches the

flower pot on her head / her hair crackles a little / it crackles only
a little / because everything is so sudden / and the fire burns her
/ and the lady who had the blue suit doesn't scream / she's burning
like a Buddhist monk / but she doesn't scream / she doesn't scream
/ nobody screams / and I ask myself why doesn't anybody scream
/ and I tell myself that nobody screams because perhaps everybody
has died / (because) (perhaps) (we) (all) (have) (died) and I don't
believe it because some women are looking for their shoes / after
receiving the blow on my head / I did bang my head / the Argentinean sitting across from me in the other row of seats looks disconcerted tries to find an explanation it's not important but the
accident caught him asleep the Argentinean looks opening wide
one eye / only one / only ( ) one / because his other one has
popped out / he opens wide one eye ₒne one One / from the socket
of the other a cascade of blood begins to spurt / a cascade of blood
and nerves / he doesn't know that he is already minus ₒne eye / he
thinks that he looks with two / I crossed myself / it's not important
but I had crossed myself before . . . / before settling down in my
seat / and he looked at me with his two eyes / not with only one /
with two / he looks at me with one eye out dangling by some whitish fibers while I find a more comfortable position in my seat / he
looks at me with one eye he looked at me with two / and the
Argentinean also found a more comfortable position in his seat /
and the blood spreads on his cheek / the other eye he closes with
the look of / it's not important / why should it be / satisfied with
finding an explanation for his disturbed sleep / and he can't close
the other one because it hangs so low / several kilometers from his
will / but it's not important because in a little while he will burn
also / and I will burn just like the little boy burned / like the lady
with the ridiculous hat burned / like the other people have already
burned / inside the plane everything is fire / sonorous and swift
fire that goes that comes devouring people things / luggage hair /
shoes / faces / a fire that laughs as it walks over the skin over the
clothes soaked with fuel / we are all soaked with fuel / somehow
the fuel lines must have broken / the tanks / the reserve tanks /
and then each one of us is like the wick of a lighter / it's not important / but as soon as the spark strikes / whoosh! / someone is
ablaze o)n)e i)s a)b)l)a)z)e//// flame from head to toe / like that
newlywed couple who are burning over there / s.o.m.e s.e.a.t.s

farther up / one is ablaze / that's the way I will burn in a little while / a pyre / in a second / in less time than that / one doesn't know in how much time everything seems to go more slowly / the blood of the Argentinean moves slowly / it bubbles slowly from the hole / the eyeball that dangles kilometers away from his will / his eye / deflated / but the blood seems like it's frozen in mid air / in time / it never reaches the bottom of his cheek / and I can see clearly when the blood does flow / it creeps along like a snake / wiggling like a 〜〜〜〜 worm / like a hot fat worm / and fast / yes / fast / no / slowly / it's not important / when the fire reaches the Argentinean his blood will toast on his skin / it will be stopped forever in its tracks / because the only thing that moves fast is the fire / the pure flame that fills more than half of everything / the live flame that is approaching me with its hot fingers / moving its pseudopodia on the floor and the ceiling / crawling over things and people / it's the only thing that's quick / the only desirable thing / the only thing that animates the inside of the plane / it's not important / the flames have shifted enough to allow me to see what has burned up front / what it has left in its path / the twisted metal / the burned / bodies / after its caress / the bodies burned to a crisp / shrunken / nobody would be able to recognize them if some day they should find this lonely place / the rescue teams / no news / find the pieces of the plane / the dangling eye / and that makes me feel superior / I still know who they were who they are / I know who was who is that charred piece of flesh / that little pile was is the little boy who didn't bother anybody during the flight / the big chunk / smoky and stinking / was is the bride / the nearby piece was is her husband / the white wedding dress / a simple wedding / I know that over there was is a lady dressed in blue / a-lady-with-the-ridiculous-hat / that-shrunken-and-battered-flesh-was-is-hers / and-I-know-that-that-blood-that-has-moved-a-few-milli-meters / that-barely-reaches / despite-the-cataract-that-it-is / -mid-cheek- / -I-know-and-only-I-that-it-is-the-blood-of-an-Argentinean- / -nobody-else-will-be-able-to-say-the-same-thing-in-a-little-while- / nor will I be able to repeat it because the fire is jealous / outside-by contrast-everything is dirty and broken up around the plane-knocked awry the smooth hills that are seen a few meters further on / knocked awry this world of silence and loneliness / this-Christmas-card-that-natu. . . in which nature takes its pleasure every day-in-these-latitudes-the fire crackles -Frost crackles-

> But if it had to perish twice,
> I think that I know enough of hate
> To say that for destruction ice
> Is also great
> And would suffice.

-I didn't get to enjoy the frozen landscape / the flight was so short so short / I didn't get to enjoy any of the frozen landscape / my ears hurt a lot / my brain was ready to burst / in this condition, one doesn't enjoy the landscape / can't enjoy the landscape / I didn't have time to get used to the altitude / it's not important but between Santiago and Buenos Aires all that the plane does is climb / is climb like something possessed (suddenly) (it) (collides) (with) (something) nobody knows what happens -- a sudden thump -- deep -- nobody knows what happens but (suddenly) (the) (plane) (collides) (with) (something) a - wing - c/o/m/e/s - o - f - f = . (-__/ . . . . through the huge hole in the floor comes snow and dirt and snow and rocks and rocks trees no they are pieces of bodies arms torsos legs arms hands shoulders and Santiago is down there and Buenos Aires up there from Cerrillos to Ezeiza all that the plane does is climb climb . . . a few days in the city taught me that the Cordillera was at the end of the longest street-precisely-the-longest-street . . . you could ski only a few kilometers from downtown . . . there here the Cordillera with its eternal snow . . . the Cordillera came in through the porthole . . . through the window of my room . . . fifth floor of the Hotel Bonaparte . . . through the window of my room . . . the snow came in every morning . . . on O'Higgins Avenue . . . the sun struck constantly on the snow-covered peaks . . . the snow comes in through the huge hole . . . and I knew that this could happen / when I boarded the plane I was afraid of something / actually I always feared something / now I was more afraid / more afraid / more certainly afraid / perhaps it's not important / but I was more certainly afraid / I had a ticket / on another airline / things are so bad in Argentina / I changed the ticket to this company / a new model jet / the safest - the safest plane -- the most tested --- but things are so bad that an Argentine company is a risk - but it was - all told - a recent model jet - I didn't enjoy the view because a jet that leaves Santiago for Buenos Aires all it does is climb / climb / climb like something possessed / we leave the Cordillera below - small - toylike - and suddenly - the Cordillera comes in through the huge hole my ears hurt so much climb so much climb the stewardess tells me to swallow saliva I crunch chewing gum in desperation the plane is climbing there isn't time to see the snow (not until now) (but I can look at it in peace because my ears don't hurt anymore) ((nothing hurts me)) (not even that bone that perforated the skin of my left arm) (not the perforated skin) (nor does the blood that floods my throat hurt either) (not the bone nor the skin of my left arm which now (so shamelessly (with the bone (so exposed (there (it's not all white (and I enjoy it (enjoy that peaceful snow (peaceful (that Christmas card . . . I don't care about the bloody and mutilated corpses that dirty the landscape; nor the hunks of metal, nor the scraps of luggage. I don't care about those smashed jet engines; so much the better, they won't climb anymore, won't roar anymore, won't torment anyone else . . . Nor those tangled wires and electrical connections. . . I don't care about anything; only the clean snow that is below . . . the soft little mounds of picture postcard . . . . And the fire / the Argentinean at my side catches on fire just now / the blood still spurts out in bubbles / a thick vein like a water pipe / the Argentinean ignites like tinder / and doesn't say anything / nobody says anything / when we fall nobody shouts / when the airplane breaks and bursts into flame nobody says anything / the Argentinean breaks and bursts into flame now / the fire dries the blood and makes it sticky / the fire put an end to its course / it didn't even get to his chin / no and nevertheless / I thought that it would get farther down / creep from the burst eye and fall in a little thread / fall like a menacing cataract over the chest of his neighbor who is now burning / and his other eye, open, burns / the eyelashes are burning / the little hairs make little curls before catching on fire / and the burned body smells / smells like when cattle are abandoned to fire / cremation oven / their ashes will be scattered to the wind / over the Ganges / you are dust / cremation oven six million Jews / and now / the-fire-comes-to-me / it-touches-my-arm / the one with the bone poking out / it-starts-its-march / downward upward / it-burns-my-skin / sears-it / I-feel-it-being-scorched / it must smell bad / and doesn't hurt (anymore) (fire soothes) (when we have all burned) (when we'll all be only unrecognizable pieces) (blackened torsos) (when silence returns and penetrates the snow through its cracks) (all of us burnt to a cinder) (there won't be any more fire) (it's certain that there won't be any more fire) (the cold will freeze the member that hasn't been burned) (the snow will crystallize the drop of blood that hasn't turned to dust) (ashes) (but that won't be important we'll be extinguished charcoal we won't feel cold) (although) (the) (fire) (doesn't) (burn) (it's a lie that fire burns) (now-it's-in-my-groin) (I-feel-it-reach-my-hips) pass-by-my-thighs / climb / still climb / stop for a longer moment at my shoes / I-feel-it-climb-up-my-chest / it's now climbing / up / my / neck / it-covers- / it's-covering / my-face / my eyebrows are burning (I don't see the snow) (don't see anything) and yes / it's-sufficient / the fire is sufficient / and it's a friend . . . it's a friend.

—Translated by Dennis Seager

COMMENTARY

Since the performance in the 1950s of the plays of Samuel Beckett (1906) and Eugene Ionesco (1912), the term "theater of the absurd" has been widely used and has become universally accepted. In Spanish America, there are now a sufficient number of short story writers who share the same philosophical and artistic vision to justify the term "short story of the absurd." Although the most prominent devotees of this tendency do not belong to Arrom's Generation of 1954— Julio Cortázar (1914), Juan José Arreola (1918), Virgilio Piñera (1912), and Augusto Monterroso (1921)—their Absurdist works were published in both the 1950s and the 1960s: Cortázar's *Historias de cronopios y de famas* (1962); Arreola's *Confabulario* (1952) and *Confabulario total (1941–1961)* (1962); Piñera's *Cuentos fríos* (1956) and *Cuentos* (1964); Monterroso's *Obras completas y otros cuentos* (1960) and *La oreja negra y demás fábulas* (1970). Menéndez Leal (1931) shares with his Neorealistic contemporaries the concept of a politically and socially committed art but his world vision coincides with that of the master Absurdists. His signature Menén Desleal is more than a game of shifting syllables; it points to the imperceptible differences between loyalty and disloyalty (cf. Jorge Luis Borges's story "Tema del traidor y del héroe"), between good and evil in a world where traditional values are no longer accepted. In his two-sentence mini-short story "The Rainmaker" — "In a certain town there was a man who could make it rain whenever he wanted. One day, while drunk, he unleashed a storm and drowned." — the reader's first reaction is to laugh but a few moments of thought reveal the author's intent to portray the current suicide of the human race, as in Arreola's "Topos."

Whereas on a realistic level of interpretation, "Fire and Ice" is the story of a plane crash in the Andes, on a deeper level it symbolizes the destruction of our technological society for having committed the deadly capital sin of considering itself superior to God: "climb / climb / climb like something possessed [by the devil]/ we leave the Cordillera below - small - toylike." This interpretation reflects both the meaning of "Fire and Ice" and Robert Frost's philosophy in general.

In order to mislead the unsuspecting reader, the Absurdist author uses a very simple language and an undramatic tone in his descriptions of the most horrible incidents: the little boy crushed and bleeding, the lady with the extravagant hat burning, the Argentinean with one eye ripped out. Moreover, the repetition of the phrase "it's not important" with all its variants is precisely the Absurdist way of underlining the story's importance.

This contradiction is one of the many in the story that contribute to the transformation of reality into fantasy. The passengers die charred . . . in the midst of the snow ("Fire and Ice"). The narrator cannot feel pity for the crushed boy. Nobody shouts. The narrator's death must be instantaneous and yet there is time for him to evoke memories of his schooldays and the time spent in Santiago and the rhythm actually becomes slow in spots. Other elements that contribute to the air of fantasy are: the rapid alternation of present and past tenses; the grotesqueness of the eye that "hangs so low/ several kilometers form his will"; the humorous coincidence that all the women lost their shoes; the punctuation tricks in the tradition of E. E. Cummings. The use of parentheses toward the end of the story suggests visually the passengers' death: the corpses enclosed in their coffins; the typographical game with "one, one, One" eye intensifies the Argentinean's condition; the parentheses and the slashes suggest the movement of the flames; the periods between the letters of "s.o.m.e s.e.a.t.s" represent the orderly but cold and impersonal isolation of human beings; the wavy line before the word "worm" suggests how that creature crawls; the wing's breaking off is captured by the dashes at different levels and the slash.

In spite of its Absurdist traits, this story differs from many of its kind because of its realistic base. According to the author, in 1959 he himself survived the crash of a commercial jet in Paraguay.

José Agustín

(1944)

Mexican. One of the more prolific of the youngest generation of Mexican writers, José Agustín was born in Guadalajara. The publication of his first two novels, *La tumba* (1964) and *De perfil* (1966), was instrumental in creating a whole new sub-genre, the novel of adolescence. He was awarded a scholarship for 1966-1967 at the Centro Mexicano de Escritores, Mexico's most important writers' workshop. Traditional boundary lines between literary genres are violated in *Inventando que sueño* (1968) and *Abolición de la propiedad* (1969). His latest novel, *Se está haciendo tarde* (1973), is relatively conventional. He has published an autobiography (1966), a book of essays on rock music, *La nueva música clásica* (1968), and he writes songs and film scripts. More recently he published a play *Círculo vicioso* (1974) and a volume of short stories entitled *La mirada en el centro* (1977). In 1978, he was a visiting professor at the University of Denver and the University of California, Irvine. "What's Cool" is part of *Inventando que sueño*.

WHAT'S COOL

When I begin to play I forget everything. So there I was beating, double beating, rolling, counterpointing or consorting with the piano and the bass and I could hardly make out the table with my friends, the gloomy and the timid and the funny ones, who were seated in the darkness of the room.

Guillermo Cabrera Infante, *Three Trapped Tigers*

Show me the way to the next whiskey bar. And don't ask why. Show me the way to the next whiskey bar. I tell you we must die.

Bertolt Brecht and Kurt Weill according to
The Doors

Requelle seated, leaning her head forward to hear better.

A table close to the orchestra, but very.

Requelle turned to the drummer and directed, with skillful fingers, the movements of the drumsticks.

Her badness, this girl is
as they say: gone, but Oliveira, the drummer, very stupid, as one
would never expect a drummer to be, was wrong.

Mistaken, she would say.

Requelle was sober, *very* sober, perhaps
only to antagonize the boys who invited her to the Prado Floresta.
They danced and laughed and drank enjoying A Night Out Night-
clubhopping and Cool Things Like That.

What's cool, nobody said.

But let's forget them and Nobody: Requelle is the one who
matters; and the drummer, since she was directing him.

A question: beloved, dear Requelle,
can you affirm that you are doing what you
should; that is to say, your friends are
going to get mad.

Requelle looked with moist eyes at the oft-beaten drumskin and
although you may not believe it — in fact, you surely won't — she
rose from her chair — of course — and went up to the drummer,
and said:

I'd like to dance with you.

He looked at her perhaps annoyed,
no, rather, indifferently, without seeing her; what I mean is that
he looked at her as if to say:

but prettygirl, can't you see I'm playing.

Requelle, seeing his look, assumed that Oliveira wanted to add:

bad music, O.K., but since I'm playing it, the least I can do is
get into it.

Requelle pretended to ignore the silent reply
(In Spanish, you should say "reply
silent," there is no reason to change
the order of the facs even though they
don't change the outcome).

She simply
stayed next to Drummer, without knowing that his name was Oliveira; perhaps had she known she would never have stayed there,
like a good girl.

The case is that Drummer never seemed to notice the presence
of the girl, Requelle, radiant in her evening gown with hardly any

makeup on just like a girl who isn't sure she's pretty and distrusts Halftheworld.

Requelle would have been surprised had she guessed that Oliveira Drummer thought:

what an attractive girl, that's another one I lose because of the drums

(because of being a damn dummy,

Character would say).

When, a little sweaty, but not overly so, Oliveira finished playing, Requelle without hesitation, decided to repeat, repeated:

I'd like to dance with you;

she didn't say:

good-looking,

but her look seemed to say it.

Oliveira was extremely surprised, he had always considered himself the Abdominable Snowman Ofetcetera. He looked at Requelle as if she hadn't been standing there, next to him for almost an hour.

(rather, owl-er considering the noise of the drums).

Without saying a word (Requelle already considered him quasi-mute, all right, semimute, then) he left the drums, took Requelle's hand,

pretty girl, he thought,

and without further ado he escorted her to the dance floor.

They were quasi alone: by then a *worse* orchestra was playing and which of those cute guys would get up to dance to that quasi-music.

Oliveira Drummer and Linda Requelle did; and furthermore, without hesitation, in spite of the barely veiled, in fact, obvious jeers of the requellian acquaintances from the table:

you've already noticed Requelle

always hunting for strongemotions

strong is your scent

pretty R look who you wound up with.

R paid no attention to the shoutwarnings and danced with Oliveira.

Les jump, someone shouted from the orchestra baton and the rhythm, poorly synchronized, disguised itself as Afrocuban: at this point Requelle and Oliveira noticed that they were alone on the dance floor and decided to put on a show, to play a Swedish-Film-Sequence; that is:

Oliveira took her gently and drew in the trembling, fragrant body, which in spite of the aforesaid adjectives, presented no resistance.

Then the ahas followed|

awright, we'll tell Mommy on you|

you little babe (in the woods)|

Requelle, like a good little babe (in the woods), paid no attention; she merely rested her head on the Oliveric shoulder and suddenly decided to say:

I would like to read your fingers.

And she said it, that is to say, she said:

I would like your fingers to read.

Oliveira or Drummer or Quasimute to R, moved his cheek away and looked at the young girl with deep, touched, and knowing eyes as he said:

I suspect I don't understand you.

Yes, insisted Capital R, I would like to read your fingers.

My palmo, I mean, my palm, you mean.

Nope, Quasi, I *know* how to read palms; in your case I would like to read your fingers.

Try, you sinner, thought Oliveira,

but he only said:

try.

Here, impossible, *my* dearest.

I wonder, insisted Oliveira, why.

You can wonder all you want, Requelle charged, and then said: with her eyes, because she really hadn't said anything:

because here there are some idiots escorting me, gorgeous, and I wouldn't be able to get on the right wavelength.

And although it may appear inconceivable, Oliveira — only-a-drummer — understood; maybe because he had seen Les Cousins

(without the Joint Declaration)[1]

---

[1] An allusion to Agustín's novel *De perfil*, in which two of the characters called The Cousins sign a Joint Declaration.

and he supposed
that in circumstances such as these it was de rigueur to know how
to read eyes. He did know how and said:

my love, I have to play again.

I, Requelle affirmed most seriously, would abandon everything
considering what I have on hand.

Faux pas, because Oliveira tried to find out what she had on
hand and squeezed her: like this:

he squeezed her.

Wow, thought Bold Girl, but she didn't protest in order to
appear more worldly.

You are victorious, Milady, my dumb drumming be damned.

They separated.

(or separated from each other, to be more explicit):
Olivista ran to the street with the pre-Olympian ruse of buying
cigarettes and innocent Requelle went to her table, took her jacket
(very sailor-like, very cool), said:

chao bourgeformists

to her startled friends and left in search of Irresponsible Drummer.
Naturally she found him, just like you find the way to ask:

Oh, Requelle, my child, what
are you doing with this man, why
are you so interested in this dude.

Requelle smiled when she saw Oliveira waiting for her: a smile
that responded affirmatively to the previous question without
guessing that dude could, and probably does mean, the same as:

cool, mod, groovy,

trip, kick, far out, et cetera,

in this slang, so expressive and now
how literary.

The problem that troubled our friend Olivista was:
where should I take this beautiful chick.

He opted, as a good drummer, for the worst; he said to her
(or said, why the to her):

Say, good-looking, how about going to a small hotel.

To the total surprise of Oliconoli she said yes and even added:

I always wanted to see a shack-up hotel, let's go to the *shackiest*.

Oliveira, more than hesitating, stammered

Thou sayest it.

Oliveira, a Christian!
He tried to look for a taxi, with his nerves gnawing at him
(a phrase exclusively for the
pleasure of traditional readers),

                                                                but no taxi
came to his aid.

Good gosh, Oliverista said to himself. At that moment he couldn't remember any cheap hotel around there. He then said, very stupidly:

let's go walking along Vértiz, who knows maybe we'll find what we're looking for, and then all alone we'll enjoy what we crave today, whatcha say, baby, if you want we'll do it.

Sonova, murmured Expressiverequelle.

Hotel Joutel, groaned Oliveira not knowing what to say.
He only muttered:

do you study or work.

do You study or work, she echoechoed.

Okay, what's your name, little girl.

Little girl, my foot, answered Requelle, I'm a big girl now and good-legged too, otherwise, you wouldn't propose a 500 pesos[2] a day hotel.

Agreedy, Oliveira conceded, but what's your appellation?

I don't peel *anything*.

By what name are you known.

Requelle.

Request?

No: Requelle, old man.

Old are the hills.

And bushes still grow on them; sighed Requelle.

You've got me bushed, Oliwhat joked half-heartedly.

What amoebas? said Req Ingenious.

Bad start for Greatlove, adds the Author, but he can't help it.

Requelle and Oliveira walking several blocks without saying a word.

And the fingers, Olidigtator finally asked.

What, Heroine deemed opportune to inquire.

I said, when are you going to read my fingers.

[2]$40.00.

Oh that, in the hotel.

Hohoho, brayed Oliclaus energetically until he saw:

Hope Hotel,

and Olivitas thought he read momentarily:

she picked you up in the Floresta and you left your orchestra, proceed don't be a dope and keep up your hope.

Hope, Hope.

What's your name! howled Drummer.

Requelle, I already told you.

Yes, you already told me, the musician sighed,

as he paid the eighteen pesos[3] for the hotel, surprised because Requelle didn't even attempt to hide herself, but only asked:

what time isn't it,

and Interpellant answered:

It's not three; it's twelve, Requita.

Oh, Requita answered with a frown, annoyed and justifiably so:

it was the first time anyone called her Requita.

Sixteen, announced the hotel clerk.

Didn't you say eighteen.

No, sixteen.

Then I gave you two pesos too much.

Hah hah. Sixteen is your room number, sir.

He said sir begrudgingly, or at least that's the way Drummeringo preferred to consider it.

Second floor to the left.

To the gauch, Requelle set herself up for the pun,

and of course: the answer: you're an Argentinean.

No, I'm Argentonian, a gorilla from the Pink House.[4]

Laughing fervently, to herself.

Oliveira, in spite of his name, took off his jacket and his tie, but Requita didn't seem impressed. The young musician then sighed and sat down on the bed, next to Little Girl.

[3]$1.50.

[4]The conservative and reactionary Argentine military who have been ruling the country on and off from the Presidential Palace, the Pink House, for the past twenty odd years are often referred to by their enemies as gorillas.

Let's see your fingers.

So fast, he kidded.

Don't be smart, that's why I brought you here, Beat.

With another sigh—more like a cry and forgive the rhyme—Oliveira extended his fingers.

One two three four five. You have five, she intelligented, smiling.

Really.

Five years of good luck await you.

Oliveira counted his fingers too, discovered there were five and thought:

good grief, this girl is intelligent;

but he did say it.

Forget the chatter, Requelle specified.

Pretty good English, where did you learn it.

And Requelle fell into Trap recounting:

oldie, I spent *siglos* which literally means centuries at the Mexican-U.S. Institute for Cultural Relations, Hamburgo near the corner of Génova good movies on Mondays.

Sexual Relations, Oliveto almost said, but he held back and preferred:

is that all my fingers suggest to you.

To Requelle, clever girl, the allusion seemed idiotic and said:

No, no, music man; much more much more: your fingers indicate that you have a sewer for a mouth and that you're the irrefutable proof of Darwin's theories as they were analyzed by One-Eyed Reyes[5] at the Colegio de México and you should look at your self in a mirror so that you can kick yourself and it would be good for you to dig a hole and in, uf, ter yourself and you would do well to prete, tee, hee, end to shut up and if you would shut up really and truly and honest to God and to everyone else: et cetera.

I don't understand, he defended himself.

Of course, charged Requelle Sarcastic, you ought to work in one of these hotels.

God, I'm in the wrong profession.

---

[5]Reference to Alfonso Reyes, one of Mexico's and Latin America's greatest essayists (1889-1959). Since his name means "kings," this is also an irreverent reference to the one-eyed kings in a deck of playing cards.

Thou sayest it.
                    Requelle a Christian!
By this time — as you may well imagine although surely it won't
be easy — Requelle didn't consider Oliveira either mute or even
deftly mute, so she asked, sure that she would obtain a docile
reply:
and your name.
Oliveira, still.
Oliveira Still, hey, gee whiz, your name has a certain pedigree,
tu t'appelles Oliveira Still Salazar Cocker.
Yes, Requelle Belle, he said with gallantry, and guessed:
I bet you're a dirty intellectuelle.
Of course, she said, can't you see I only spout nonsense.
That's it exactly; I mean, that's exactly what I was thinking;
well gimme five, Requilla, I'm also an intellectual, a music man
of the new wave and all that jazz.
Intellectumoron, Olivista; you exaggerate saying stupid things.
That's right, but I can't help it: I'm a quore matto intellectual;
but tell me, Rebelle, who were those spruced up elmbeciles who
were accompanying you.
They were friends of mine and from Las Lomas,[6] but they're
not intellectuballs.
Nor do they have any, mused Oliveira Crude.
                                        And although it
may appear incredible, Girl understood.
                                    And she even liked it, she
thought:
How thrilling, I'm in a hotel with a guy who's clever and
                                            even

                                                  c

                                                ru

                                                    de.

Olilubric, to tell the truth, was looking gluttonously at Requelle's
thighs. But he didn't know what to do.
Ha, ha, alliterates Unscrupulous Author.
Oliveira opted for oldtrick.
I'm going to take a shower, he announced.
You're going to *what*.

[6]One of Mexico City's most elegant districts near upper Chapultepec Park.

It's just that I'm so sweaty from beating the drums, he said boastfully, and Requelle agreed like a nice little inexperienced girl.

Without a further word, Oliveira forced a leer and put himself in the bathroom,
in spite of the problems that the
reflexive causes us, because we could
just as well have said: he entered
the bathroom.

The thing and la chose is that he did get there and Requelle heard him undress, really:

she heard the sound of the clothes falling to the ground.

And the only thing that occurred to her to do was to stand up too, and almost involuntarily, she fixed the bed:
and she not only spread out the bedspread

she also unmade the
bed so she could make it up again,

with the utmost care.

Sonova, quel stupid am I, she thought while hearing the flow of the shower. But on the other hand she was annoyed because the room wasn't quite as *dirty* as she hoped it would be.

(The italics indicate emphasis; it's not a
mere whim, you idiots.)

It even has a shower, she thought ill at ease.

But she heard:

hey, beautiful why doncha join me for a chat.

Papapapapá,
roared an imagin-
ary machine gun,
with which the
cynical use of puns
is justified.

Requelle didn't try to think at all and entered the bathroom
(at last!: that is to say: at last
she entered the bathroom)
to contemplate a plus que dirty curtain and see through it a naked body under the shower who wasn't singing cmon baby light my fire.

Hélas, thought she pedantically, not all of us can be perfect.

She sat down on the pan trying not to go cross-eyed as she tried to make out the naked body of, oh God, Man in the shower.

(Private joke dedicated to John Toovad.[7] N. of the translator.)

He smiled, and without knowing why, asked:

why are you an easy woman, Rebelle.

By heredity, she discoursed, it happens that all the damsels in my genealogical trunk have been the *worst*. Did you notice, I said trunk instead of tree, may the Attorney General's office forgive me; that's how far my perversion goes.

And how, as Jacqueline Kennedy would say; added Oliveira Clean.

And do you know what the height of my perversion is, she ventured.

Er no, the answer.

Ollie, the height of my perversion is coming to a one peso flop house|

Eighteen pesos.

Okay, eighteen; being here next to a naked man, behind a curtain, granted, and not doing niente, rien, nichts, not even getting drunk. How does that grab you.

Oliveira was so surprised by her logic that he thought and even said:

I love this gal.

He said, textually:

Requelle, I love you.

Don't be crude; besides I'm not in the mood, I just finished explaining it to you.

I love you.

Okay, you talk and I'll listen.

No, I love you.

You don't love me.

Yes, yes I love you, after something like this I can't help but love you. Leave this room, get out of the hotel, I can't attack you; file, scram, beat it.

[7]Reference to Juan Tovar (1941), contemporary Mexican novelist. In changing his name to Toovad, the author makes it the equivalent of "too bad" since the v and b are pronounced the same in Spanish.

You're crazy, Olejo; what I'm thinking is that if you're desweated we can return to the Floresta.

You're delirious, Requita, can't you see I escaped.

You should say I fled.

Can't you see I fled.

I can't see that you fled.

Okay, darlita, then we can go somewhere else.

To your apartment, frinstance, Salazar.

Don't be hasty, loveofmylife, better yet to your chez.

My *whole* family is at my place: seven brothers and my parents. seven!

Seven brothers. . . !

Yep, my pops is against the pill; but explain: what's wrong with your apartment.

Oh well my mother is in my apartment, my aunt Irene and my two cousins Renata and Tompiata; they're twins.

Incester, she accused.

You lie like a cossack, you'll soon get to meet my ugly cousins, they're the most effective antidote for incest: I would like to introduce them to some Mexicay writers.

Well where are we going.

We can go to another hotel,

Oliveira joked.

Perfect, I really would like to get to know sinfulplaces, Requelle affirmed without hesitation.

Drummer dressed, not allowing her to peek at his naked body: not out of decency, but because he would have had a hard time holding in his belly all the time.

A skillful and necessary observation:

Requelle, measure the consequences
of your acts with which you are infringing
upon our best and most solid traditions.

The two walking down Vértiz, crossing Obrero Mundial, the Viaduct,

or the Viadick, as he said
so that she could answer oh
how crude you are,

and Avenida Central.

Do you know what, started Drummer, we're in the regenerated Buenos Aires district; I see a hotel over there.

Over there I see a hotel.

O.K.; over there I see a hotel. Do you want to go.

You bet, Requelle replied emphatically; but I'm paying, otherwise you're going to spend a fortune.

Don't worry, love, I just got paid.

Any old way, I'm paying, let's be fair.

Let's be: after all, your habitat is Las Lomas, Oliveira pronounced smiling.

The truth is that he was wrong and found that out in room eleven of the Buen Paso Hotel.[8]

Requelle explained:

                    the only wealth in her family is in the names
of its members.

You're sitting pretty, he inserted but Prettygirl didn't understand.

Whatever, Oliever.

But what do you mean you're not rich, that does alarm me, Oliveira asked after she confessed that

the story about the seven brothers was not a lie and that, oh my, their names were

Euclevio, strong soul,

Simbrosio, heart of stone,

Everio, poet athlete,

Leoporino, black but noble,

Ruto, good body,

Ano, pass me the salt,

Hermenegasto, the impressive,

and

elle

Requelle.

Ma belle, he insisted, really loving her.

He told her so.

I love you, he said.

She started to get aroused perhaps because the room had cost fourteen pesos.

Give me your hand, she asked.

                              Sincerely concerned.

He extended it.

---

[8]Literally "good step" or "good passage" but there is also the clear implication of "passing through quickly" or hotel for transients.

And Requelle began to study the lines, hills, canals, and she found out

(premonition):

this man will die of leukemia, oh God, he lives in Xochimilco, poor darling, and he fights every night for a taxi to take him home without overcharging him.

As if reading her thoughts Olivín said:

do you know why I know a few cheap hotels, mylove, well because I live far away, but not far out, and I often prefer to stay here rather than fight for a taxi to take me home.

Premonition déjà ronde.

Requelle looked at him, with tearful eyes; she was no longer aroused but confirmed that she loved him,

I can grow to love him in any case, she assured herself.

In the Nuevoleto Hotel.

Why do you say that your family is only rich in names.

Well because my daddy played the dirty trick on us of continuing to live after he went broke, you know, if he had died just a little bit earlier the fam would have inherited close to a million.

But don't you love your family, Oliveira screamed.

But of course I do, she screamedback, there are so many brothers plus mother and father that if I didn't love them I would go crazy trying to decide whom I hated the most.

Requellian transition:

look, music man, what counts is that I do love them, because if I didn't I would be an intellectual girl with fine traumas and all the rest; but tell me, do you love your mother and your cousins and your aunts.

Dolly-in by trackless Smith-Corona 250, manual, until framing in bcu the face — immersed in interest — of Heroine.

My aunt no, my cousins so-so and mommy oodles.

You see how right I was in talking about incest

Ah gee, because I've fornicated four hundred and twelve times with mein Mutter you want to accuse me of incest: I won't take that from anyone; well, from you I will because I love you.

No, no, no, my little baby cut the clowning and explain:

how did you ever become a drummer if you really love your fammy.

Well because I like it, what the heck.

What the heck,

Huh?

Huh.

Your God, what a clown you are, mylovotomy, it even seems that your name is Requelle la Belle.

If you call me la Belle again I'll bite your ankle, I'm ugly, ugly, ugly though no one will believe me.

Don't be silly, Rejillie, you are prillie; besides, they're words that go well together.

Requelle threw herself on Oliveira's leg with explosive speed (speedily as well as explosively)

and she bit his ankle.

Drummer screamed but then covered his mouth, feeling the urge to laugh and make love while experiencing pain at the same time, since Pretty continued biting his ankle furiously.

Hey, Requelle.

Mmmmm, she replied, biting him.

Baby, don't overdo it, I swear I'm bleeding.

Mmmhmmm, she affirmed, without stopping.

Look, he observed restraining himself from screaming from pain; it hurts me a lot, would it be a real bother for you to stop biting me.

Requelle stopped biting him;

I'm tired anyway, was all she said.

And they both studied carefully the marks of the Requaillian trail.

Requelita, if you had bitten my finger you would have cut it off.

She laughed but suddenly fell silent when

someone

knocked

at the

door.

Neither he nor she ventured a word, they only looked at one another, frightened.

Hey, what's going on in there, why are you screaming.

It's nothing it's nothing, Oliveira said feeling like a perfect idiot.

All right, can't you do what you have to quietly.

What we have to, what a bastard.

The footsteps indicated that the guy was leaving, as Our Heroes intelligently discovered.

What a pig, Requelle labeled him, annoyed.

and what lack of objectivity, he said

and then added without a transition:

Look, Reja, why do you get mad when I tell you you're pretty.

Because I'm ugly, so there.

I swear you're not, angelmine, you're foxy.

If you insist I'll bite you again, I'm Ugly, Requelle the Ugly; Requelle the Ugly; I dare you, say it, coward.

You're Requelle the Ugly.

But anyway you love me: I dare you to say it, you mentally retarded son of Colonel Cárdenas.[9]

Butt, fannyway, I adore you.

Oh, you whore me.

I adore you and I esteem you, he screamed.

I gore you and I steam you, she corrected.

I core you and I ream you, I floor you and I beam you, I bore you and I cream you, you want more, here goes.

Shut up or I'll slug you, yes or no; Requelle warned.

Certo, said the Cellist.

Hey, man, your staff and the grass are hanging out.

And this reply permitted

Oliveira to explain:

he *adores* drums, he understands that you can't do much with a *terrible* orchestra like the one he plays in and which has the gall to call itself Sol Iver and his Drippling Rhythm.

A better name might be and his Drooling Rism, Oliveira declared. You know who's the best, spaced-out girl, he added, well none other than Mustache Starr and also this kid Carlitos Watts and Keith Moon; I swear, I'd like to play in that kinda cool group.

Oh, so you're a rock 'n roll pig, she charged, what do you have against Mahler.

Nothing, Rävel, if you like him: what you like is law für mich.

For dich.

Yesch.

---

[9] An irreverent reference to *General* Lázaro Cárdenas, Mexico's most universally revered president (1934-40) since the Revolution.

Uch.

Night not too cold.

They walked down Vértiz and with little hesitation they got into
(they penetrated, why not)
the district whose streets are named after doctors.

Docs, Oliveira Stout screamed, how much are a hundred ben-
nies, but

Requelle:

serious.

At the Hotel Morgasm.

She decided to bathe, not to be left out.

Don't peek because I'll kick you, Drummeringo.

Her qualms were understandable because there was no curtain
by the shower.

Shower.

Oliveira decided that he really loved her since he resisted the
temptation of peeking to catch a glimpse of the thin but well-
proportioned figure of his Requelle.

Oh, holy calf, she is *my* Re-
quelle; I've known so many women and I wind up with a Requelle
Trèsbelle; that's life, my children and readers too.

At this moment Oliveira ad-
dresses the readers:

listen, readers, realize that this is *my* Requelle; not yours, don't
think that because my love wasn't born in the accustomed manner
that I love her less. By now I'm crazy about her; I mean, I adore
her. This is the first time that this has happened to me, oh, and it
doesn't matter to me that this Requelle has been transited, paved,
applauded, or received ovations previously. Although now that I
think about it. . . . If you'll excuse me, I'm going to ask her.

Oliveira warily approached the bathroom door.

Requelle. Requita.

There was no answer.

Oliveira cleared his throat and was able to stammer:

Requelle, answer me; or don't tell me you already went down
the drain.

I won't answer you, she said, because you want to come in the
bathroom and screw me; go not beyond that door, Satan; don't
you dare enter or it will rain hot sauce.

Requelle, pardon me but hot sauce doesn't rain.

Olito, this is a colloquial expression by which some people understand that blood will flow in quantities sufficient to donate.

Yes, and that's a cliché.

Bah, between a cliché and a colloquialism there lies an abyss and I'll stand on the edge.

That's a metaphor and a bad one.

No, that's a warning that I'm going to whack you over die Mutter if you dare enter.

No my life, my Blue Skies, My Blue Heaven, I only wanted to ask, I ask; by how many men have you been wooed,

to which of them have you cooed,

how far were you pursued and what do you feel for this poor dude.

I don't feel, I only regret that you're such an idiot that you rhyme your questions about these *things.*

Requelle Blush.

Oliveira explained that they were of interest to him and to his surprise she didn't answer.

Drummer then considered that for the first time he found himself in the presence of a woman of the world, with a turbulent-past.

Requelle entered the room with her hair wet but perfectly dressed, even with stockings and a pocketbook hanging from her arm.

Arm.

Look, Requeja, you're a woman of the world.

Yep, she acted, I've towhored the principal bordellos of Dorient, but without walking the streets: accompanied by the most famous magnates, Gusy Díaz[10] freignstance.

That, Requi, I Believe.

Your ankle doesn't hurt you now.

And how, as Monsignor's daughter said.

Actually, his ankle burned him and was swollen.

She led Oliveira to the bathroom and made him raise his foot to the wash basin in order to massage the ankle with warm water.

---

[10] Allusion to President Gustavo Díaz Ordaz (1964-1970), who was considered responsible for the 1968 student massacre at Tlatelolco.

My death, Requeshima monamour, he shouted; wouldn't it be easier that I put my foot in the shower.

In spite of your terrible construction, you're right, Olitight.

What's wrong with my instruction, are you looking for a fight.

And as punishment for such an elementary play on words, Requelle left his foot in the wash basin.

> Exterior. Gloomy streets with lovers incognito from the Workers district. Night. (Interior. Taxi. Night.) [Or back Projection.]

The radiotaxi arrived in five minutes. Requelle, her hair wet, got in slowly as, courteously, Oliveira opened the door for her.

Chauffeur with a plaid cap, the head of a plastic child encased in a plastic knob at the end of the stick shift, seventeen engraved cards of virgins with babyjesuses and without the latter, visit the shrine of Guadalupe when you come to the Olympics, Protect me patron saint of drivers, Soup me, Lupie; decals of the America, America team, ra ra ra, chevrolet 1949.

Where to, kids.

> Oliveira Wary.

You know, my dear sir, we're a bit disoriented, we would like to locate an establishment where we might be able to rest a few hours.

Well I'll be, hey man, this crap about hotels; the truth is that it really bugs me.

But why sir.

> Requelle Giggles.

Well, 'cause you know that's no fuckin' part of my job; I mean, tell me where to, and I'll go with pleasure, but for me to tell you turns my stomach especially since you're with such a tender young thing.

Man, you must know some place.

Well yeah, but now, like it's not right. Just imagine.

I'm imagining Requelle said automatically.

And besides, then you get into lots of fights, people act real lowdown and even want you to enter one of these motels like the ones around here with garage in this Workers district and well my job is only to drive around in the street, not to go into private property, what the hell.

Excuse us, sir, but we really do *not* want you to enter *any* hotel, we only want you to leave us at the door.

Well I'll be, hey man, like it's not right.

Look sir, we'll be more than happy to give you a tip for your information.

Now that's a horse of a different color, my dear squire, but just don't forget it. A man's gotta earn a living at night and there's damn few fares. Sometimes you don't get a single one in the whole shift.

Of course.

Now let's see, I'm going to take you to a hotel of a buddy of mine and the truth is that it is a very decent place and the lady won't feel a bit uncomfortable, in fact, she'll even like it. There's hot water and clean towels.

> Requelle holding back her
> laughter.

Your radio won't work, Mr., pried Requelle.

No, missie, you see it went on the blink a year ago and sometimes it works, but it only gets the government program.

It must be a radio assembled in Mexico.

Well, who knows, but it sure is a pain to turn on the radio and hear the same things over and over again, sure they're good things, because they talk about the nation and the family and then they give you some heart-felt poems and stuff like that, but then you kinda get bored.

Well, the government program doesn't bore *me*, Requelle remarked.

No, no, me neither, it's a good thing, what happens is that one hears all that talk that the government is the best and what progress and stability and the communist menace everywhere, and because don't tell me it's not true that a guy gets fed up with all that talk. In the newspapers and on the radio and on TV and even in the toilets, pardon me, miss, they say the same thing. Sometimes, I get the feeling that it can't be all that true if they have to repeat it so much.

Well, it seems to me they *are* right in repeating it, Requelle said, it's necessary for all Mexicans to realize that we live in a perfect country.

Right on, Missie, there's only one Mexico. That's why even the

Virgin Mary said that she would be better off here, even the song says so.

Oliveira Serious and Adult.

It is truly unusual to find a taxi driver like you, sir, I congratulate you.

Thanks, Mr., I do the best I can. Excuse me, but I'd like to ask a question, if you and the little lady won't get offended, but it's because I don't want my conscience to bother me later.

The car stopped in front of a sinister looking hotel.

Sure, speak up, sir.

But I'm kind of ashamed to.

Don't worry. My girlfriend is very understanding.

Well, O.K., missie make like you don't hear, but I'm dying to know if you, I mean, how can I put it, well if this isn't going to be the first time for the little lady.

Oh no, not at all, sir, I swear it. On my word of honor. I would never do such a thing.

Phew, well you don't know what a relief that is for me; you sure have taken a load off my mind. It'd be a crime to take such a decent young girl like missie knowing she's gonna bounce the mattress for the first time. You know, I have daughters of my own.

I understand perfectly, sir, you need not say another word. I also have sisters. Besides, my girlfriend and I will soon be married.

Oh, that's wonderful, sir. Really, get married, because it's so easy to carry on and fool around as if our dear God didn't exist, you've gotta do things right. O.K., here we are, at my buddy's hotel, if you want I can introduce you so he'll treat you first class.

No thanks, sir. Don't bother. How much do I owe you.

Well, that's up to you. Whatever you wish.

No, no, you tell me how much.

Gee, sir, you're a good guy and you understand. Whatever you want.

Well, O.K., here's ten pesos.

What, ten pesos, buddy.

Ten pesos is about right, I think. We only came about ten blocks.

Yeah, but you said you'd give me a good send-off, besides I brought you to a hotel and not just any old dive. My friend's hotel.

How much do you want then.

What do you mean how much do I want, don't try to screw me, man, cross my palm with a fifty. You're goin' to have royal fuck with that broad in just a few minutes and all you give me is ten pesos. That takes nerve.

Look here, fifty pesos really seems excessive to me.

Ah so it's excessive now, so that's the tune you're playing. That's why I like to work with gringos, in the hotels, they don't pout like babies and they're not afraid to give out with the dough. Christ, and I thought you were a respectable person; shit, you're even well dressed.

Look I really can't give you fifty pesos.

Ha, what a miserable pauper, why did you call a taxi, you should've hoofed it. Give me your stinkin' ten pesos and go to hell.

Listen don't insult me. Show respect, you're in the presence of a lady.

A lady, ha ha, don't make me laugh. She's no more a lady than your mother.

Look you bastard, get out so I can bust your ass.

Cool it, kid; give me the ten spot and drop dead.

Here take it and drop dead.

Drop dead.

Oliveira and Requelle got out of the taxi. The driver took off at full speed, shouting obscenities at the top of his lungs,
to   the   absolute   joy   of   our   Heroes.
                                        Ninth Cloud Hotel,
anything you want just holler. Room number thirty-two, third floor, view of the street. Two more pesos.

In the window, hugging, Requelle and Oliveira saw how a horribly battered car managed to get into the garage of a house. At that moment, spontaneously, they both imitated the whistle of a traffic cop and sirens, and closed the curtains, laughing uncontrollably.

                                        Laughing untiringly.

But Olivinho continued to worry because she didn't answer his t r a n s c e n d e n t a l   q u e s t i o n s; that is to say, she acted dumb, went off on a tangent, eluded the moment of truth, to paraphrase Jaime Torres.[11]

---

[11]Jaime Torres Bodet (1902-1974) Mexican poet, Minister of Education from 1943 to 1946 and from 1958 to 1964, and director of UNESCO from 1948 to 1952.

And
Oliveira wound up asking himself (asking himself?) seeing the
questions being superimposed on Requelle's smiling
   (How about this abundance of
gerunds)
and somewhat tired face (face!)
                                   (on se peut voir sans aucune
                                   hésitation l'absence de con-
                                   sonances; reader's note)
   don't tell me I'm a Mexican macho, what do I care about her
turbulent past if I really likr.
   He decided to smile when a sob distorted Requelle's face.
   Why are you crying, Requelle.
   I'm not crying, stupid, I only sobbed.
   Why are you sobbing, Requelle.
   Because it feels good.
   Oh, seriously . . .
   Sergiously?
   Sergio Cannabab, don't tell me you know him.
   Yes, Oli, I can't *stand* him, he's into drugs and I'm beginning
to think that you too are into some vice.
   What kind of vice: explain yourself my pretty princess: grass,
weed, potpoppy, speed, Mary-jane or windowpane; are you refer-
ring to dark heavy shades or what kind of vice: uppers, downers,
sunshine, snow or purple haze, because really, none of that adds
up to vice.
   Vice, vice, whatever, all you musicians are into vices and most
of all the rock musicians.
   Requina, I only get loaded from time to day, but I latch on to
the vibes when I'm sober, like right now; but I'm not an addict,
and even if I were, that wouldn't be a reason to cry, only an idiot
would cry, like that Sergio Frothel.
   What Sergio Brothel. Don't mention people I don't know, it's
not polite; and besides only an idiot would *not* cry.
   That's it, but since you're intelligent and bright, you only sob;
and for your exclusive information it is my melancholy duty to
add that you look pretty sobbing.
   I don't see myself as pretty, Oliveira, I already told you that.
   Don't be a clown, Requarlie, for a joke it's gone too far, darlie.

Your family in Xochimilco eats barley.
My family from where.
Xochimilco, don't they live in Xochimilco.
Of course not, we live in the district of Sinantel.
Where's that.
By the Von Tlalpan Causeway, I mean to the left of it.
That's the road to Xochimilco!
Sure, why not, but it's also the road to Ixtapalapa, my queen,
and also, to Acapulco passing through Cuernavaca, Taxco, and
Anexas el Chico.

Oliveira, you have leukemia, you're going to die; I know, you
can't fool me.

Don't be silly. All I have is a cool; in your parley, my jewel,
I'm as healthy as a Harley.

The rhyme is divine but you don't convince me; you're going
to die.

All right; if you insist, let it be tonight and in your arms, as
that jerk Yevtushenko said; come, let's go to bed.

I'm not in the mood, really.

What difference does it make.

                              Apparently convinced, Raquelle
lay down; tensebody as you can imagine.
but he didn't try anything; well:
he fondled one breast naturally and rested on the requellian stomach, and she was able to relax seeing that Oliveira was staying
calm.

She only mumbled, this time sincerely:
I feel as if I were listening to Mozart.
Don't fart, he said, let me sleep.

                              And he fell asleep, to the com-
plete bewilderment of Requelle. First it was very nice to feel him
lying on her stomach, but later she found it very uncomfortable;
                              now I feel like a Mary
                              McCarthy character,
but she could only sigh and say, thinking he was asleep:
Oliveira Salazar, I'm talking to you so I won't feel so uncomfortable, let me tell you, I study theater with all the clichés which
that implies; I'm going to be an actress, I am an actress,
                              I'm Requelle Theactress:
I study at the University, I didn't go to Nancy and I don't regret

it too much. When I live with you I'm going to continue working even if you don't like it, leer leer Oliveer Steer, my dear; I guess you won't like it because you're already showing your opposition by snoring.

The truth is that Oliveira was snoring but he wasn't sleeping ————————————on the contrary, he was thinking:

so, an actress, how nice, you've strutted around in mi*ll*ions of orgies for sure, that environment is one of the worst, very freaky.

Sure he was kidding, but then again Oliveira
wasn't
so
sure
that
he
was
kidding.

Deep down in my mother, I'm a middleclass prude at heart.

Requelle's stomach was numb and she was already resigned to the abdominal sacrifice when, without any sign of sleepiness, Oliveira got up and said almost with anxiety:

Requeya, Reyuela, Rayuela, daughter of Cortázar; besides being a master on the drums I can play rickenbaker guitar, piano, electric bass, organ, moog synthesizer, I can work the wa-wa, the vibrator, assorted percussions, distortion booster et fuzztone: I know how to elicit distantecho for my platters in the feedback and I almost do all right on the clavichord, I mean, I would really love to play the clavichord well and master the electric viola and the melodica; and I also compose, my belle, my wedding, my bed; I'm going to compose tender songs for you which will cause a sensation.

Oh how cool, she said, I had never inspired anything.

And you still haven't inspired anything, my beauty, I mean; my ugly, I said that I'm *going to* compose them, not that I have already done it.

Hey, wait, are you trying to tell me that I didn't inspire you when you were playing at the Floresta.

Of course not.

In the street, dawn's early light.

I'm hungry, Requelle announced.

Walking in search of a res-
taurant.
A policeman appeared magically and barked:
why are you bothering the young lady.
I'm not bothering the strung lady.
He's not bothering me.
You're not bothering her, the policeman affirmed before leaving.
Requelle and Oliveira laughed even when they were eating some
chicken soup with the inevitable chicken *sopes*[12] on the side.
What time does the courthouse open, Oliveira asked.
I think, about nine, she responded
with solemnity.
Ah, then it gives us time to go to another small hotel.
Honeymoon Hotel.
The hotel clerk looked at Oliveira with a frown.
Now we're in for it, at last, Requelle knew intuitively.
Are you two married.
Of course, Oliveira replied not too convincingly.
Requelle took hold of his arm and rested her head on the oli-
veric shoulder while adding:
We are.
And your luggage.
We don't have any, we'll pay in advance.
Yes, sir, but this is a decent hotel, sir.
Oh well we thought it was a hotel for transients.
Well it isn't, sir; and didn't you tell me youweremarried.
And we are, my estimated, but we feel like coming to a hotel,
is that against the law.
And you don't think that I'm going to believe you.
No, nor do we want you to.
Well, rooms here cost forty pesos, Clerk boasted.
Well, I'll be, you'd think it was the Fucklton, see you later.
Listen no, Oli, I'm very tired: I'll pay.
It looks to me like you're performing extortion on the lady.
It looks to me like you're an ass.
Look, sir, no one insults me, damn it, wait and see; if I don't
talk to the police.
Not before I bust your face.

---

[12] A small thick tortilla pinched up at the sides and filled.

You and who else.

Me by my lonesome.

Olifierce, please don't get into a fight.

I'm not going to fight, I'm only going to clobber this clod, just like the song by the Castrato Brothers goes, on the RCA Victor record.

Oh boy, big macho.

No sir, a macho *never* but I will clobber you.

You don't say.

Yes I do say.

Don't work me up or I'll really call the cops.

Let's go, Oliveira.

Like hell we'll go.

Well, are you or aren't you going to take the room.

At forty pesos, no way.

All right then, Let's make it twenty.

Now, you're singing another song, let's have the key.

The room turned out to be more run down than the others.

> She collapsed on the bed but the squeaks made her jump immediately.

She blushed.

Don't be a clown, Requelle.

Gee, you're something else.

Gee, I'm something else.

> Convenient pause.

Ooh, am I sleepy, she ventured.

Me too, let's go to sleep, come on.

No I mean, I'm not sleepy anymore.

> Oliveric look of controlled exasperation.

Come on.

But then who's going to wake us up.

I'll wake up myself, don't worry.

Oliveira began to take off his shoes.

You're going to get undressed.

Of course, he replied.

And me.

Get undressed too, or don't try to tell me that in Las Lomas they sleep with their clothes on.

No.

There you are.

Oliveira had already taken off his pants and thrown them in a corner.

They'll get wrinkled, Oli.

>   Lack of concern plus sleep-
>   iness.

Who cares.

He took off his shirt.

You're so skinny, you should vitaminate yourself.

To hell with vitaminants and that's a serious piece of advice I offer you.

He got under the covers.

>   Tilt up for a better shot of
>   requellian blush.

Aren't you going to sleep.

But I'm not tired, Olipeep.

Well, I am; see you the day after tomorrow.

He gave her a kiss on the cheek and closed his eyes.

Requelle thought:

I really am sleepy.

>   Dying of shame.

Girl took off her clothes, folded them with care, got into bed and tried to sleep....

>   Oliveira moved and Requelle jumped.

Oliveira, wake up, your feet are so cold.

You sure are something, Requi, I was already falling asleep. Besides which, it wasn't my foot but my hand.

Yes, I know. I want to leave.

>   Pounding on the door.

Who is it, Drummer snarled.

The police.

Go to hell, Oliveira yelled.

Open the door or we'll open it, we have a master key.

Requelle was trying to get dressed at full speed.

Go to the devil, we haven't done anything.

To hell you haven't, isn't there a minor in there.

Are you a minor, Oliveira asked Requelle.

No, she answered.

No, Drummer yelled at the door.

Yes, there is. Open up or we'll open it.

O.K., go ahead and open it.

> They opened the door. A guy dressed in civilian clothes and Clerk.

Requelle had finished dressing.

You see, we opened it.

I see you opened it.

Well, what's your name, the plainclothesman asked Requelle, but it was Oliveira who answered:

her name is the one and only true Lupita Tovar.

Miss Tovar, are you a virgin, I mean, are you a minor.

You are, Oliveira slipped in without getting out of bed.

Stop clowning around or I'll haul you off to jail.

You're not hauling me anywhere, and even less to jail because my neighborhood would miss me. By the way, who are you.

The police.

Man, what sleazy uniforms they gave you, you should complain.

I'm the secret police, you clown.

You're the secret police.

Yes sir.

Just think, I do believe you, I can tell because your mustache's full of cream.

Oliveira stopped talking and Requelle took a seat on the bed.

(Notice the absence of the more trite and incorrect: she sat down.)

> Our Requelle suddenly calm.

She even yawned.

The detective: also silent, perplexed;

let him be pot-bellied too, adds a friend of Author.

Oliveira looked at them a moment and then found himself a more comfortable spot in bed, he closed his eyes.

Hey, don't go to sleep.

I didn't go to sleep, sir, I only closed my eyes; how can I sleep if you don't leave.

See how tough he is, whined Clerk.

What time is it, asked Drummer.

Eight-thirty, they replied.

Wow, it's late; we have to go to the courthouse, my love, Oliveira said as if the intruders were not there: he rose and began to dress.

> (Notice how the absence of;
> he rose up; editor's note.)

Miss Tovar, the agent said, you're a minor.

If you say so, sir. I'm twelve years old and no one's dependent, and don't talk to me so rough or my brother will beat you up.

Oh yeah, send him over to me.

I'm her brother, Oliveira specified.

> Agent scandalized.

What do you mean her brother, don't tell me nothing like that or you'll make it worse for yourself.

Don't tell me anything like that, corrected Oliveira,
making all grammar teachers sigh
with relief.

He put on his jacket and put his tie in his pocket.

O.K., let's go, he said to Requelle.

Where are you going, don't try to get out of it, you little punks.

Oliveira glanced at the plainclothesman with the look of a man with connections.

All right, let's stop playing games. What's your name.

Victor Villela, answered the plainclothesman.

Don't forget his name, sis.

I won't, brud.

> They walked out slowly, without anyone's trying to stop them. When they got to the street, they both began to run desperately. When they reached the corner, they stopped.

No one was following them.

Why are we running, asked Requelle Lingenua.

> The ingenuous prankster.

Because, he answered.

What do you mean because.

Yes, we have to get in shape for the olympics, little girl: mens putrida in corpore sano.

They arrived at the courthouse just as it was opening and they had to wait for the judge for a half hour.

At last he arrived, old man, how did you get around the retirement law. Oliveira affirmed:

my little gal here is a good twenty-five years old with   crop of four abortions on her cu*rri*culum; me, I'm twenty-eight, yeh, sure, twenty-eight years old; the truth, the honest-to-God truth, Mr. Judge is that we've been living together, you know, shackin' up and we even have a child, a little boy and the fact of the matter is that we would like to legalize this ignominious situation in order to relieve our rather conservative neighbors with a five hundred peso bill.

And your papers, asked the judge.

I already told you, my lordship, there's only one: it says five hundred on it.

The judge gave a boy-these-modern-kids smile and explained:

Look, in the Capital you're not going to be able to get married just like that, as if you didn't know, you can get away with things like that in the state of Hidalgo or in Morelos. Here, no way.

No way, Drummer conceded, at least we tried.

Outside the sun was getting stronger and stronger and Requelle took off her coat.

Fuh, she said, I'll have to ask my mother's permission and all that crap.

Are you or aren't you a minor, Oliveira asked.

Of course I am.

Sheeet, he agreed.

Walking slowly.
Under the sun.

Servants with bundles of bread were looking at Requelle's evening gown.

Requelle, ma belle, sont des mots qui vont très bien ensemble, Oliveira sang.

Don't call me that, you dirty rat: I swear by the very virginity of your cousins Renata and Tompiata that I'm going to bite you again.

Hey, lay off, my ankle is still swollen.

There, you see.

Apartment for rent one room fully equipped.

Let's see it, Requelle proposed.

Old building.

It is as old as the pyramids, but it's still standing, he ventured.

It's awful, Requelle affirmed, but so what.

The janitor took them to the owner of the building, she has the information you see.

Friendly woman. With little dog.

Oliveira paused to play with the canine.

We would like to see the apartment for rent, Ma'am, Requelle said, sa belle;

   meet my husband, Dr. Filiberto Rodríguez Ramírez; Filiberto, my love, leave the cute little dog alone and greet the lady.

Good day, Madam, declaimed Oliveira Obedient, Dr. Domínguez Martínez at your service and at your feet if they don't bark at you, as Dr. Vargas[13] would say.

Oh what a lovely couple you make, and so young, so tender.

         Exchanging looks.

You flatter us, Ma'am. Doesn't she, Honey, Oliveira commented.

She sure does, Sugar.

Come, you're going to love the apartment, it has lots of good light, just imagine.

We can *imag*ine, Requelle responded automatically.

To Angélica María.[14]

       —*Translated by Antonia García*

COMMENTARY

    Reacting against the perfectly polished stories of the "sacred monsters"[15] of the short story establishment, Revueltas, Rulfo, and Arreola, José Agustín erupted onto the literary scene of the mid and late 1960s with an apparently chaotic style. Representing the rebellious youth who rejected the values of everyone over thirty, Agustín breaks with the traditional notion of the short story's formal perfection, a

---

[13] According to the author, this is a reference to Gabriel Vargas, "Mexico's most extraordinary comedian."

[14] Famous contemporary Mexican TV and movie star.

[15] José Agustín, "Los monstruos sagrados del cuento mexicano," *Deslinde*, 2-3 (Sept.-Dec. 1968; Jan.-April 1969), 31-35.

tradition which has its roots in Poe and Quiroga and which in Mexico culminates in Rulfo and Arreola.

Neither Criollista nor Absurdist, neither Existentialist nor Magic Realist, "What's Cool" captures the dynamic, anarchic, and emotional world of the revolutionary youth of the sixties. With the literary inspiration coming from Argentinean Julio Cortázar, Cuban Guillermo Cabrera Infante, and Mexican Carlos Fuentes, this story displays a world vision that is both authentically Mexican and international in its linguistic, literary, musical, political, and social aspects. The epigraph from Cabrera Infante's novel with its tongue-twisting title of *Three Trapped Tigers* indicates the primordial importance of language. The dialogue is not only sprinkled with English, French, German, Italian, and Portuguese words but the characters speak a kind of new international language with bilingual puns and jokes about syntax. The multiple variations of the names Oliveira and Requelle add to the linguistic virtuosity and constitute a leitmotiv that strengthens the unity of this apparently chaotic symphony.

Nevertheless, in spite of all the emphasis on the linguistic games and in spite of the levity, there is a genuine human aspect to the story. Just as the "new classical music" includes the two branches of the hard rock of the Rolling Stones and the folk rock of Bob Dylan, "What's Cool" presents beneath its superficial, playful exterior the almost mythical voyage of the couple in love in search of lasting happiness. In spite of all the apparent sexual freedom, Requelle and Oliveira never consummate their union before reaching the judge's chambers. Even though the judge cannot marry them without the necessary papers, they now consider themselves married and instead of looking for still another motel for transients, they rent an apartment under the bourgeois name of Dr. Rodríguez Ramírez or Domínguez Martínez. The author is obviously poking fun at the very Mexican manner of speech of the landlady, but the linguistic communication that exists between "Honey" and "Sugar," an echo of the "sis" and "brud" of the previous motel, is a far cry from the lack of communication between the anguish-laden married couples in Existentialist stories and novels.

Rather than trying to conceal his literary precursors, Agustín displays them ostentatiously. His protagonist Oliveira has exactly the same name as the hero of *Rayuela*, whose title lends itself to playful similarities with Requelle. While Cortázar's characters are very fond of the saxophone in keeping with the contemplative and philosophical tone of the Argentinean's novels and short stories, Agustín's character Oliveira is a drummer, who captures with his staccato the violence of the late 1960s.

The second of the two epigraphs identifies its author Brecht as one of the forerunners of the youthful revolutionaries because of his irreverent attitude toward both society and traditional literary forms. Like Brecht, Agustín interrupts in different ways the dialogues of his characters to prevent the reader from identifying emotionally with them. He does this by a series of stage directions indented from the right rather than from the left margin.

These idealistic teenagers reject, on the one hand, the idea that love between human beings is impossible and on the other, the inevitability of unjust governments. They are, therefore, equally prepared to protest against the "gorillas" residing in Argentina's presidential palace and the secret police and the government's hour-long radio program in Mexico.

José Agustín initiated the *onda* movement in Mexico in 1964 with the publication of his novel *La tumba*. Although as a novelist, his leadership of the movement is disputed by Gustavo Sainz, as a short story writer Agustín is the one who has best succeeded in capturing the flavor of the *onda*, the new wave, what's in, what's mod, or what's cool. In doing so, he has opened new perspectives for the evolution of the genre.

BIBLIOGRAPHY

ANTHOLOGIES OF THE SPANISH AMERICAN
SHORT STORY[1]

SPANISH AMERICA

Anderson Imbert, Enrique, and Lawrence B. Kiddle. *Veinte cuentos hispanoamericanos del siglo XX.* New York: Appleton-Century-Crofts, 1956.

Donoso Pareja, Miguel. *Prosa joven de América Hispana.* Mexico City: Sep-Setentas, 1972. 2 vols.

Flores, Angel. *Historia y antología del cuento y la novela en Hispanoamérica.* New York: Las Américas Publishing Co., 1959.

Jofre Barroso, Haydée M., and María Angélica Bosco. *Antología del joven relato latinoamericano.* Buenos Aires: Fabril, 1972.

Latcham, Ricardo. *Antología del cuento hispanoamericano contemporáneo (1910-1956).* Santiago de Chile: Zig-Zag, 1958.

Manzor, Antonio R. *Antología del cuento hispanoamericano.* Santiago de Chile: Zig-Zag, 1940.

Quijano, Aníbal. *Los mejores cuentos americanos.* Lima: Mejía Baca, n.d.

Sanz y Díaz, José. *Antología de cuentistas hispanoamericanos.* Madrid: Aguilar, 1946.

CENTRAL AMERICA

Lindo, Hugo. *Antología del cuento moderno centroamericano.* San Salvador: Universidad Autónoma de El Salvador, 1949.

Primer Festival del Libro Centroamericano. *Panorama del cuento centroamericano.* Lima: Editorial Latinoamericana, 1959.

Ramírez, Sergio. *Antología del cuento centroamericano.* San José: E.D.U.C.A., 1973. 2 vols.

ARGENTINA

Mastrángelo, Carlos. *25 cuentos argentinos magistrales: historia y evolución comentada del cuento argentino.* Buenos Aires: Editorial Plus Ultra, 1975.

Mazzei, Angel. *Treinta cuentos argentinos (1880-1940).* Buenos Aires: Editorial Guadalupe, 1968.

Pagés Larraya, Antonio. *Cuentos de nuestra tierra.* Buenos Aires: Editorial Raigal, 1953.

_____. *20 ficciones argentinas.* Buenos Aires: EUDEBA, 1963.

_____. *20 relatos argentinos, 1838-1887.* Buenos Aires: Editorial Universitaria, 1961.

Sorrentino, Fernando. *35 cuentos breves argentinos, siglo XX.* Buenos Aires: Editorial Plus Ultra, 1974.

_____. *40 cuentos breves argentinos, siglo XX.* Buenos Aires: Editorial Plus Ultra, 1977.

Yahni, Roberto. *70 años de narrativa argentina 1900/1970.* Madrid: Alianza Editorial, 1970.

[1]For a more complete bibliography, see: Bernice D. Matlowsky, *Antologías del cuento americano. Guía bibliográfica* (Washington, D.C.: Unión Panamericana, 1950).

BOLIVIA

Gumucio, Mariano Baptiste. *Narradores bolivianos.* Caracas: Monte Avila, 1969.
Rodrigo, Saturnino. *Antología de cuentistas bolivianos contemporáneos.* Buenos Aires: Editorial Sopena, 1942.

CHILE

Atenea. *El cuento chileno.* Santiago: Editorial Nascimento, 1948.
Instituto de Literatura Chilena. *Antología del cuento chileno.* Santiago: Editorial Universitaria, 1963.
Lafourcade, Enrique. *Antología del cuento chileno.* Barcelona: Ediciones Acervo, 1969. 3 vols.

COLOMBIA

Arbeláez, Fernando. *Nuevos narradores colombianos.* Caracas: Monte Avila, 1968.
Pachón Padilla, Eduardo. *Antología del cuento colombiano.* Bogotá: Ministerio de Educación Nacional, 1959.
Primer Festival del Libro Colombiano. *Los mejores cuentos colombianos.* Lima: Editora Latinoamericana, 1959, Vol. I, selection by Andrés Holguín; Vol. II, selection by Daniel Arango.

COSTA RICA

Bolaños, Elizabeth Portuguez de. *El cuento en Costa Rica.* San José: Librería e Imprenta Atenea, 1964.
Chase, Alfonso. *Narrativa contemporánea de Costa Rica.* San José: Ministerio de Cultura, 1975. 2 vols.
Menton, Seymour. *El cuento costarricense: estudio, antología y bibliografía.* Mexico City: Studium, 1964.

CUBA

Bueno, Salvador. *Antología del cuento en Cuba (1902-1952).* Havana: Ministerio de Educación, 1953.
Caballero Bonald, José Manuel. *Narrativa cubana de la revolución.* Madrid: Alianza Editorial, 1968.
Fornet, Ambrosio. *Antología del cuento cubano contemporáneo.* Mexico City: Ediciones Era, 1967.
Oviedo, José Miguel. *Antología del cuento cubano.* Lima: Ediciones Paradiso, 1968.

DOMINICAN REPUBLIC

Cartagena, Aída. *Narradores dominicanos.* Caracas: Editorial Monte Avila, 1969.
Nolasco, Sócrates. *El cuento en Santo Domingo.* Santo Domingo: Librería Dominicana, 1957. 2 vols.

ECUADOR

Carrión, Benjamín. *El nuevo relato ecuatoriano.* 2d rev. ed. Quito: Casa de la Cultura Ecuatoriana, 1958.

EL SALVADOR

Barba Salinas, Manuel. *Antología del cuento salvadoreño (1880–1955)*. San Salvador: Ministerio de Cultura, 1959.

GUATEMALA

Lamb, Ruth. *Antología del cuento guatemalteco*. Mexico City: Studium, 1959.

HONDURAS

Acosta, Oscar, and Roberto Sosa. *Antología del cuento hondureño*. Tegucigalpa: Universidad Nacional Autónoma de Honduras, 1968.

MEXICO

Carballo, Emmanuel. *Cuentistas mexicanos modernos (1949–1956)*. Mexico City: Ediciones Libro-Mex., 1956. 2 vols.
_____. *El cuento mexicano del siglo XX*. Mexico City: Empresas Editoriales, 1964.
_____. *Narrativa mexicana de hoy*. Madrid: Alianza Editorial, 1969.
Glantz, Margo. *Onda y escritura en México: jóvenes de 20 a 33*. Mexico City: Siglo XXI, 1971.
Leal, Luis. *Antología del cuento mexicano*. Mexico City: Studium, 1957.
Mancisidor, José. *Cuentos mexicanos de autores contemporáneos*. Mexico City: Editorial Nueva España, 1946.
_____. *Cuentos mexicanos del siglo XIX*. Mexico City: Editorial Nueva España, 1947.

PANAMA

Cabezas, Berta María. *Cuentos panameños*. Bogotá: Instituto Colombiano de Cultura, 1972. 2 vols.
Jaramillo Levi, Enrique. *Antología crítica de joven narrativa panameña*. Mexico City: FEM, 1971.
Miró, Rodrigo. *El cuento en Panamá: estudio, selección, bibliografía*. Panama City: Imprenta de la Academia, 1950.

PARAGUAY

Pérez Maricevich, Francisco. *Breve antología del cuento paraguayo*. Asunción: Ediciones Comuneros, 1969.

PERU

Escobar, Alberto. *La narración en el Perú: estudio preliminar, antología y notas (1956)*. 2d. ed. Lima: Editorial Juan Mejía Baca, 1960.
Núñez, Estuardo. *Los mejores cuentos peruanos*. Vol. II. Lima: Patronato del Libro Peruano, 1956.
Oquendo, Abelardo. *Narrativa peruana 1950/1970*. Madrid: Alianza Editorial, 1973.
Oviedo, José Miguel. *Narradores peruanos*. Caracas: Monte Avila, 1968.
Suárez Miraval, Manuel. *Los mejores cuentos peruanos*. Vol. I. Lima: Patronato del Libro Peruano, 1956.

PUERTO RICO

Cooke, Paul L. *Antología de cuentos puertorriqueños.* Godfrey, III.: Monticello College, 1956.

Marqués, René. *Cuentos puertorriqueños de hoy.* Mexico City: Club del Libro de Puerto Rico, 1959.

Meléndez, Concha. *El arte del cuento en Puerto Rico.* New York: Las Américas, 1961.

————. *El cuento: antología de autores puertorriqueños.* San Juan: Ediciones del Estado Libre Asociado de Puerto Rico, 1957.

URUGUAY

Cotelo, Rubén. *Narradores uruguayos.* Caracas: Monte Avila, 1969.

García Serafín, J. *Panorama del cuento nativista del Uruguay.* Montevideo: Editorial Claridad, 1943.

Lasplaces, Alberto. *Antología del cuento uruguayo.* Montevideo: C. García y Cía., 1943. 2 vols.

Visca, Arturo Sergio. *Antología del cuento uruguayo contemporáneo.* Montevideo: Universidad de la República, 1962.

VENEZUELA

Di Prisco, Rafael. *Narrativa venezolana contemporánea.* Madrid: Alianza Editorial, 1971

Meneses, Guillermo. *Antología del cuento venezolano.* Caracas: Ministerio de Educación, 1955.

Uslar Pietri, Arturo, and Julián Padrón. *Antología del cuento moderno venezolano (1895-1935).* Caracas: Escuela Técnica Industrial, 1940. 2 vols.

OTHER WORKS CONSULTED

SPANISH AMERICA

Anderson Imbert, Enrique. *Historia de la literatura hispanoamericana.* 3d ed. Mexico City: Fondo de Cultura Económica, 1961. 2 vols.

Carvalho, Joaquim de Montezuma de. *Panorama das literaturas das Américas.* Angola: Edição do Município de Nova Lisboa. Vol. I, 1958; Vol. II, 1958; Vol. III, 1959; Vol. IV, 1965.

Henríquez Ureña, Max. *Breve historia del modernismo.* 2d ed. Mexico City: Fondo de Cultura Económica. 1961.

Hespelt, E. Herman, et al. *An Outline History of Spanish American Literature.* 2d ed., New York: F.S. Crofts, 1944; 3d ed., Appleton-Century-Crofts, 1965.

Leal, Luis. *Historia del cuento hispanoamericano.* Mexico City: Studium, 1966.

ANTILLES

Olivera, Otto. *Breve historia de la literatura antillana.* Mexico City: Studium, 1957.

ARGENTINA

Lichtblau, Myron I. *The Argentine Novel in the Nineteenth Century.* New York: Hispanic Institute, 1959.

Soto, Luis Emilio. "El cuento," in Rafael Alberto Arrieta, *Historia de la literatura argentina*. Vol. IV. Buenos Aires: Peuser, 1959. Pp. 285-450.

CHILE

Poblete Varas, Hernán. "El cuento en Chile," *Journal of Inter-American Studies*, IV. 4 (Oct., 1962), 463-501.
Torres Rioseco, Arturo. *Breve historia de la literatura chilena*. Mexico City: Studium, 1956.

COLOMBIA

Curcio Altamar, Antonio. *Evolución de la novela en Colombia*. Bogotá: Instituto Caro y Cuervo, 1957.
Sanín Cano, Baldomero. *Letras colombianas*. Mexico City: Fondo de Cultura Económica, 1944.

COSTA RICA

Bonilla, Abelardo. *Historia y antología de la literatura costarricense*. San José: Trejos. Vol. I, 1957; Vol. II, 1961.

CUBA

Menton, Seymour. *Prose Fiction of the Cuban Revolution*. Austin: University of Texas Press, 1975. Pp. 165-214, 234-246.
Portuondo, José Antonio. "Lino Novás Calvo y el cuento hispanoamericano," *Cuadernos Americanos*, VI, 5 (Sept.-Oct., 1947), 245-263.

ECUADOR

Rojas, Angel F. *La novela ecuatoriana*. Mexico City: Fondo de Cultura Económica, 1948.

EL SALVADOR

Toruño, Juan Felipe. *Desarrollo literario de El Salvador*. San Salvador: Ministerio de Cultura, 1958.

GUATEMALA

López Valdizón, José María. "Panorama del cuento guatemalteco contemporáneo," *La Gaceta* (Mexico City: Fondo de Cultura Económica), VI, 79 (March, 1961), 4.
Orantes, Alfonso. "El cuento en Centroamérica," *Cultura* (San Salvador), 32 (April-May-June, 1964), 42-50; 33 (July-Sept., 1964), 40-49; refers almost exclusively to Guatemala and El Salvador.

MEXICO

González Peña, Carlos. *Historia de la literatura mexicana*. 6th ed. Mexico City: Porrúa, 1859.
Leal, Luis. *Breve historia del cuento mexicano*. Mexico City: Studium, 1956.
Martínez, José Luis. *Literatura mexicana (siglo XX)*. Mexico City: Robredo, 1950. 2 vols.

PARAGUAY

Rodríguez-Alcalá, *Historia de la literatura paraguaya*. Mexico City: Studium, 1970.

PERU

Aldrich, Earl M., Jr. *The Modern Short Story in Peru.* Madison: University of Wisconsin Press, 1966.

Núñez, Estuardo. "El cuento peruano contemporáneo," *Revista Nacional de Cultura* (Caracas), XXIV (1962), 68-90.

URUGUAY

Benedetti, Mario. *Literatura uruguaya siglo XX.* Montevideo: Alfa, 1963.

Englekirk, John E., and Margaret M. Ramos. *La narrativa uruguaya: estudio crítico bibliográfico.* Berkeley: University of California Press, 1967.

VENEZUELA

Fabbiani Ruiz, José. *Cuentos y cuentistas.* Caracas: Librería Cruz del Sur, 1951.

Rivera Silvestrini, José. *El cuento moderno venezolano.* Río Piedras, Puerto Rico: Colección Prometeo, 1967.

Uslar Pietri, Arturo. "El cuento venezolano," *Letras y hombres de Venezuela,* in *Obras selectas.* Madrid: Ediciones Edime, 1956. Pp. 1065-1072.